S0-AIH-075

Handbook of BASIC for the IBM PC

Limits of Liability and
Disclaimer of Warranty

The author(s) and publisher of this book have used their best efforts in preparing this book and the program contained in it. These efforts include the development, research, and testing of the theories and programs to determine their effectiveness. The author(s) and publisher make no warranty of any kind, expressed ot implied, with regard to these programs or the documentation contained in this book. The author(s) and publisher shall not be liable in any event for incidental or consequential damages in connection with, or arising out of, the furnishing, performance, or use of these programs.

Note to Authors

Have you written a book related to personal computers? Do you have an idea for developing such a project? If so, we would like to hear from you. Brady produces a complete range of books for the personal computer market. We invite you to write to Terrell Anderson, Senior Editor, Simon&Schuster, General Reference Group, 1230 Avenue of the Americas, New York, NY 10020.

Registered Trademarks

IBM, IBM Personal Computer, IBM PC, and IBM 80 CPS Matrix Printer are trademarks of International Business Machines Corporation

Hayes Stack Smartmodem is a trademark of Hayes Microcomputer Products, Inc.

Epson MX-80 and Epson FX-80 are trademarks of EPSON SHINSHU SEIKI CO., LTD.

HANDBOOK OF BASIC
FOR THE IBM PC
REVISED AND EXPANDED

DAVID I. SCHNEIDER
UNIVERSITY OF MARYLAND

Brady Communications Company, Inc., New York, NY 10020
A Simon&Schuster Publishing Company

Copyright © 1985 by Brady Communications Company, Inc.
All rights reserved. No part of this publication may be reproduced or transmitted in any form or by any means, electronic or mechanical, including photocopying and recording, or by any information storage and retrieval system, without permission in writing from the publisher. For information, address Brady Communications Company, Inc., Simon&Schuster Building, 1230 Avenue of the Americas, New York, NY 10020.

Library of Congress Cataloging in Publication Data
Schneider, David I.
  Handbook of BASIC for the IBM PC.
  Includes index.

  1.IBM Personal Computer—Programming. 2. Basic (Computer program language)I.
  Schneider, David I. Handbook of BASIC for the IBM personal computer. II. Title.

QA76.8.I2594S36   1985   001.64'24   84-14530

ISBN 0-89303-510-6

Prentice-Hall of Australia, Pty., Ltd., *Sydney*
Prentice-Hall Canada, Inc., Scarborough, *Ontario*
Prentice-Hall Hispanoamericana, S.A., *Mexico*
Prentice-Hall of India Private Limited, *New Delhi*
Prentice-Hall International (UK) Limited, *London*
Prentice-Hall of Japan, Inc., *Tokyo*
Prentice-Hall of Southeast Asia Pte. Ltd., *Singapore*
Editora Prentice-Hall Do Brasil LTDA., *Rio de Janeiro*
Whitehall Books, Limited, Petone, *New Zealand*

Publishing Director: David Culverwell
Acquisitions Editor: Terrell Anderson
Production Editor: Barbara Werner
Text Design: Paula Huber
Art Director/Cover Design: Don Sellers
Assistant Art Director: Bernard Vervin
Photographer: George Dodson
Manufacturing Director: John Komsa

Typesetter: Shepard Poorman Communication Corp., Indianapolis, IN
Printer: R.R. Donnelley & Sons, Harrisonburg, VA
Typefaces: Baskerville (text & display), OCR-B (programs)

Printed in the United States of America

85 86 87 88 89 90 91 92 93 94 95   2 3 4 5 6 7 8 9 10

CONTENTS

CONTENTS

CONTENTS

ACKNOWLEDGMENTS

Many people have assisted me in writing this book. First of all, the staff of the Brady Communications Company demonstrated how important the publisher is at every stage of the production of a manuscript. Harry Gaines (former president), David Culverwell and Terry Anderson suggested that I undertake this project and provided encouragement and direction. Jessie Katz arranged first class reviews of the manuscript, Bernard Vervin worked closely with me to produce the extensive artwork, and Barbara Werner provided patient editorial assistance.

I am grateful to Larry Goldstein, Roy Myers, Peter Rosenbaum, and Don Withrow for helpful discussions on certain specialized areas of BASIC, and to Don Withrow for writing the appendix on communications and the discussions of the three communications statements. I would like to thank Thomas Bechtold and Mark Ellis for assisting me with checking the manuscript.

Special thanks is reserved for Dan Singer, who revealed to me the full range of the capabilities of BASIC, and to Fred Mosher who proofread the manuscript and fine tuned the accuracy of the book. I acknowledge their contributions with heartfelt gratitude.

David I. Schneider
College Park, Maryland

Books on BASIC are primarily of two types; reference manuals that provide a formal description of each BASIC statement, and textbooks intended to be read from beginning to end. This book combines the best features of both. It has the organization and depth of a reference manual, yet provides the motivation and applications found in textbooks.

The BASIC language, as enhanced for the IBM Personal Computer, has a repertoire of over 180 statements, functions, variables, and commands. Most of these have numerous extensions and variations. I have tried to make each of them accessible by first discussing them in their most used forms, with concrete examples, before proceeding to their subtler and more sophisticated variations.

Concepts are best explained by illustrating them with carefully thought out examples. Therefore, I have included over 650 examples. When a program is presented, the result of executing the program is also shown.

Demonstration programs Most of the programs in this book are intended to illustrate the uses of BASIC statements. On the other hand, there are fifteen programs, referred to as "demonstration programs," which the reader should not necessarily try to analyze but should just type in and run. An example of a demonstration program is the program that displays all of the possible color combinations available in text mode, so that the user can identify those combinations that are the most readable on his monitor.

Prerequisites The reader should have a minimal knowlege of BASIC at the level that can be acquired by reading the first few chapters of a beginning book on BASIC (preferably a book specifically written for the IBM PC). For instance, we assume that the reader can understand short programs using the 9 common BASIC statements PRINT, LET, GOTO, FOR, NEXT, RUN, INPUT, READ, and DATA.

PRELIMINARY MATERIAL

A. DIRECT MODE VERSUS PROGRAM MODE

One way of adding the two numbers 2 and 3 is to type in the statement PRINT 2 + 3 without any line number preceding it and then press the Enter key. (The Enter key is the key on the right side of the typewriter portion of the keyboard that is marked with a hooked arrow.) The result will appear as follows:

```
PRINT 2 + 3
 5
Ok
```

Another way to perform the same operation is to write a one line BASIC program and then run it.

```
10 PRINT 2 + 3
RUN
 5
Ok
```

We say that the statement was executed in direct mode in the first case and in program mode in the second. (Direct mode is also referred to as immediate or command mode and program mode is also referred to as indirect mode.) Every BASIC statement, except CONT, DATA, DEF FN, and ON TIMER can be executed in both modes.

B. ASCII CODES

There are 256 characters that the computer can recognize. These characters have been assigned numbers ranging from 0 to 255, called ASCII values. Appendix A contains a list of these characters and their ASCII values. Most of the characters can be easily displayed on the screen; however, some of them are control characters and as such specify special effects. For instance, the character with ASCII value 28 is the control character corresponding to moving the cursor to the right. See the discussions of CHR$, ASC, and PRINT for further details.

C. MULTIPLE-STATEMENT LINES

More than one statement can be written on the same line in either direct mode or program mode. If this is done, the statements must be separated by a colon. Two examples follow:

```
FOR I = 1 TO 3: PRINT I;: NEXT I
 1  2  3
Ok
```

1

PRELIMINARY MATERIAL

```
10 A$ = "Haste Ma": B$ = "kes Waste"
20 PRINT A$; B$
RUN
Haste Makes Waste
Ok
```

D. Numeric Constants and Variables

There are three sets of numeric constants that are available to the IBM PC: integer constants, single-precision constants, and double-precision constants. The set of integer constants consists of whole numbers from -32768 to 32767. The set of single-precision constants consists of 0, all numbers from 2.938736×10^{-39} to 1.701412×10^{38} with at most 7 significant digits, and the negatives of these numbers. The set of double-precision constants consists of 0, all numbers from about $2.938735877055719 \times 10^{-39}$ to $1.701411834604692 \times 10^{38}$ with at most 17 significant digits, and the negatives of these numbers. (All 17 digits are stored but only 16 are displayed.)

Single- and double-precision constants are sometimes expressed in "scientific" or "floating point" notation; that is, as a number times a power of 10. For single-precision constants, the letter E followed by the integer n denotes 10 raised to the nth power. For double-precision constants, the letter D is used instead of E.

Unless otherwise specified, all constants are assumed to be single-precision. A number is specified as an integer constant by following it with a percent sign (%) and, if given a name, by following the name with a percent sign. A number is specified as a double-precision constant by following it with a number sign (#), writing it with more than 7 digits, writing it in floating point form using the letter D, or if given a name, by following the name with a number sign. An exclamation sign following a number or a numeric variable denotes a single-precision number. Numbers that result from the arithmetic operations +, -, /, and * inherit as their precision the greatest precision of the numbers involved. With versions of BASIC prior to BASIC 2.0, the result of exponentiation, $\wedge$, is always a single-precision number. Beginning with version 2.0, BASIC will do the computation in double-precision provided that at least one of the numbers has double-precision and BASIC has been invoked with the option /D.

Any name assigned to a constant must be of the same precision as the constant if that precision is to be retained. If the variable in a LET statement is numeric and the value is a numeric constant of a different precision than the variable, then the assignment will still be carried out. However, the constant will be converted to the precision of the variable.

E. String Constants and Variables

Any word, phrase, or sentence is a string constant. More generally, *any* sequence of characters to be treated as a single entity may be regarded as a string constant. Most of the time a sequence of characters is surrounded by quotation marks to specify it as a string constant. We usually refer to a string constant as a string.

A string variable is a name ending with a dollar sign to which string constants can be assigned. See the discussion of LET for further details.

F. FILE NAMES AND FILE SPECIFICATIONS

The three types of files that can be created in BASIC are program files, data files, and memory image files. Program files are created when a program is recorded on a disk with the command SAVE. Data files are created with the statement OPEN to store items of information so that they can be accessed by BASIC programs. Memory image files are created by the statement BSAVE to record the contents of a certain portion of memory. Every file has a *filename* consisting of an 8-character (or fewer) primary name followed by an optional period and suffix of at most 3 characters. See the discussion of the command NAME for further details.

With versions of BASIC prior to BASIC 2.0, a file is specified by giving the drive on which it currently resides or will reside, followed by a colon and the file name. (This information is referred to as the *filespec*.) A typical filename is "PAYROLL" and a typical filespec is "B:PAYROLL". If a drive is omitted from a filespec, the drive is taken to be the drive from which BASIC was invoked. See the discussion of SAVE for further details.

BASIC 2.0 and subsequent versions support a hierarchial directory structure. See Appendix D for a description of subdirectories, paths, and current directories. A file is specified by giving the drive on which it currently resides, possibly a path leading from the current directory to the subdirectory containing the file, and the filename. This information is referred to as the *filespec*. If a path is omitted, the file is considered to be in the current directory.

Filespecs can be either a string constant (surrounded by quotation marks) or a string variable.

G. DISPLAY ADAPTERS

There are four different adapters that can be used to connect a display screen to the computer, the IBM Monochrome Display and Printer Adapter, the IBM Color/Graphics Monitor Adapter, the IBM Enhanced Graphics Adapter, and the IBM Professional Graphics Controller. A Monochrome Display can be connected to either a Monochrome Display and Printer Adapter or an Enhanced Graphics Adapter. An RGB color monitor (such as the IBM Color Display) can be connected to either a Color/Graphics Adapter or an Enhanced Graphics Adapter. A composite monitor or TV set can be connected only to a Color/Graphics Adapter. The IBM Enhanced Color Display can only be connected to the Enhanced Graphics Adapter.

H. SCREEN MODES

The word "graphics" refers to pictures and graphs that are drawn on the screen. The IBM PC has a number of special graphics statements, such as

PRELIMINARY MATERIAL

DRAW, LINE, CIRCLE, PSET, and PAINT, that provide excellent graphics capabilities. However, these statements are only available if you are using a graphics monitor attached to the Color/Graphics Monitor Adapter, the Enhanced Graphics Adapter, or the Professional Graphics Controller.

With a graphics monitor, any one of three modes can be specified for the screen: text mode, medium-resolution graphics mode, and high-resolution graphics mode. In text mode, only the characters listed in Appendix A can be displayed on the screen. In medium- and high-resolution graphics mode, the screen is subdivided into many small rectangles called pixels or points. (In medium-resolution graphics mode there are 200 rows, each containing 320 pixels, and in high-resolution graphics mode there are 200 rows, each containing 640 pixels.) Each one of these pixels can be turned on or off to create graphics. Text also can be displayed in both of the graphics modes. However, in medium-resolution graphics mode only 40 characters can be displayed on each line, and in high-resolution graphics mode only 80 characters can be displayed in each line. If the TV set or monitor accepts color, various colors are available in text mode and in medium-resolution graphics mode. The different modes are specified by the SCREEN statement.

I. CONVENTIONS USED IN THIS HANDBOOK

1. We use the word "disk" to refer to either a 5 1/4 inch diskette or a hard disk. We assume that the computer is equipped with at least one disk drive, and that all files will be stored on a disk rather than a cassette. We therefore recommend that the computer be turned on with the DOS diskette in a disk drive and that Disk or Advanced BASIC be invoked.

2. When referring to characters, we use the term "displayable" for those characters that can be easily displayed on the screen (i.e., without having to POKE into memory), and use the word "printable" for those characters that can be printed on the printer.

3. We refer to the person operating the computer as the "user."

4. The word "LET" in LET statements can be omitted. For instance, the statement **LET N = 25** can be abbreviated to **N = 25**. We consistently use the abbreviated form.

5. When we specify two keys separated by a hyphen, we imply that the user will hold down the first key while pressing the second. For instance, the combination Ctrl-Home can be used to clear the screen.

6. Most of the programs in text mode assume that the screen is set to display 80 characters per line. (See the statement WIDTH for further details.) However, these programs are easily adapted to a screen displaying 40 characters per line.

7. When we use the abbreviation *filespec*, we assume that the file specification is a string. For instance, examples of **SAVE filespec** are **SAVE "B:PAYROLL"** and **A$ = "B:PAYROLL": SAVE A$**.

8. INPUT statements request information to be typed by the user. We have underlined this information when it appears during the execution of a program.

9. We often refer to "entering" a program line. The term "enter" means to locate the cursor on the line and press the Enter key.

10. The term "graphics adapter" refers to either the IBM Color/Graphics Monitor Adapter, the IBM Enhanced Graphics Adapter, or the IBM Professional Graphics Controller. The term "Monochrome Adapter" refers to the IBM Monochrome Display and Printer Adapter. The term "graphics monitor" refers to any monitor other than a Monochrome Display.

⌊ABS

The function ABS strips the minus signs from negative numbers and leaves other numbers unchanged; that is, it returns the *absolute value* of the given number. In particular, if x is any number, then the value of

    ABS(x)

is -x when x is negative, and x when x is nonnegative.

COMMENTS

1. Mathematicians write |x| instead of ABS(x).

2. The value of ABS(x) will have the same precision as x, unless x is - 32768 % .

3. The value of ABS(x) is positive whenever x is a nonzero number. The graph of y = ABS(x) is shown in Figure 1.

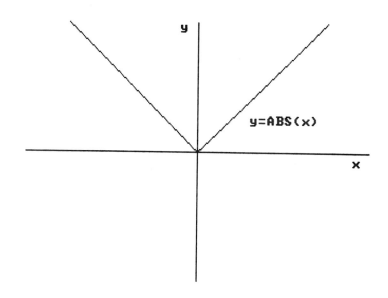

FIGURE 1

EXAMPLES

1. `PRINT ABS(-5); ABS(5); ABS(0)`
   `    5  5  0`
   `    Ok`

```
2.  10 A = -8
    20 B = ABS(A)
    30 PRINT A; B; ABS(B); ABS(A*5); ABS((-2)^5); ABS(1.5)
    RUN
    -8  8  8  40  32  1.5
    Ok
```

APPLICATIONS

1. ABS(A-B) is the distance between the two numbers A and B. For instance, if one person's age is A and another person's age is B then the difference in their ages is ABS(A-B).

2. ABS is used to simplify statements. For instance, we usually write ''ABS(X)<3'' instead of ''-3<X AND X<3''.

3. In certain numerical calculations for which rounding errors can occur, we hesitate to test whether A=B. Instead, we might test whether ABS(A-B)<T where T is an error tolerance we choose. For instance, an error of .00001 might be acceptable and we would test as follows: **IF ABS(A-B)<.00001 THEN 75**.

ASC

Appendix A contains a list of the 256 characters that are recognized by the computer. The ASCII code assigns a number (from 0 to 255) to each character. Most of these characters can be easily displayed on the screen; however, some characters (referred to as control characters) specify special effects. Two examples of control characters are "cursor right" and "carriage return." If c is one of the displayable characters (other than the quotation mark), then the function

    ASC("c")

has as its value the ASCII value of the character c. If A$ is a string, then the value of

    ASC(A$)

is the ASCII value of the first character of the string.

COMMENTS

1.   The function CHR$ is the inverse of ASC. For instance, the value of CHR$(ASC("A")) is A.

2.   The ASC function is not defined for the null string. A statement such as **PRINT ASC("")** results in the message "Illegal function call".

3.   The function ASC actually is defined for the quotation mark. The difficulty arises in specifying a string whose first character is a quotation mark. (The statement **LET A$ = """"** clearly won't work.) One possibility is **LET A$ = CHR$(34)**. Another possibility is **INPUT S$: A$ = MID$(S$,2,1)** with the user responding by typing any string whose second character is a quotation mark. (In general, the value of MID$(S$,n,1) is the string consisting of the nth character of S$.)

EXAMPLES

1.   PRINT ASC("A"); ASC("%"); ASC("IBM"); ASC(","); ASC(" ")
        65 37 73 44 32
     Ok

2.   10 INPUT A$, B$, C$, D$, E$
     20 PRINT ASC(A$); ASC(B$); ASC(C$); ASC(D$); ASC(E$)
     RUN
     ? A, IBM, ",", ;, %
       65 73 44 59 37
     Ok

3.   The following program asks the user to type a name and then displays the name in uppercase letters.

```
10 INPUT "Name"; N$
20 FOR I = 1 TO LEN(N$)
30    L = ASC(MID$(N$,I,1))
40    IF L>96 AND L<123 THEN L = L-32
50    CN$ = CN$ + CHR$(L)
60 NEXT I
70 PRINT CN$
RUN
Name? George H. "Babe" Ruth
GEORGE H. "BABE" RUTH
Ok
```

APPLICATIONS

1. ASC can be used to make a program user-friendly by allowing the user to enter a number without restrictions on using commas. To achieve this the number is input as a piece of string data, and then this string is converted to its equivalent numeric value. Any commas found in the string are simply skipped over. The following program converts A$ to a whole number V:

```
10 PRINT "Enter a whole number: ";: LINE INPUT A$
20 V = 0
30 FOR I = 1 TO LEN(A$)
40   D$=MID$(A$,I,1)
50   IF (D$ >= "0") AND (D$ <= "9") THEN   V = 10*V+
(ASC(D$) - ASC("0"))
60 NEXT I
70 PRINT V
RUN
Enter a whole number: 4,341,728
 4341728
Ok
```

This program is a partial extension (for whole numbers only) of the BASIC function VAL. It can be extended to handle an even greater variety of input by the user.

2. When working with random files, we have to associate a number with each record. One way to accomplish this is to sum up the ASC values of the characters in the "key" of the record, divide this number by some large fixed number, and use the remainder as the record number. (If a record already appears at this location, we say that a *collision* has occurred. Several procedures exist for deciding where to store a record that collides, the simplest of which is to try and store it at the next highest unused location.) Such a procedure is referred to as a *hash* sort.

‖ATN

ATN is the trigonometric function arctangent, the inverse of the tangent function. For any number x, the value of the function

   ATN(x)

is an angle whose tangent is x. The angle is given in radians and lies in the range from -π/2 to π/2 (-1.570797 to 1.570797). See Appendix M for a discussion of radian measure and the definition of the tangent function.

COMMENTS

1.   Figure 1 contains the graph of y = ATN(x).

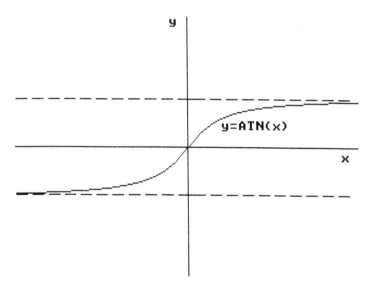

<small>FIGURE 1</small>

2.   In versions of BASIC preceding BASIC 2.0, the value of ATN(x) is always a single-precision number. BASIC 2.0 and subsequent versions provide the option of computing ATN(x) as a double-precision number. To exercise this option, invoke BASIC with the command BASIC/D or BASICA/D. Then, whenever x is a double-precision number, the value of ATN(x) will be computed as a double-precision number.

3.   The function ATN is the inverse of the BASIC function TAN in the sense that if y = ATN(x), then x = TAN(y).

EXAMPLES

Examples 1, 2, and 3 are appropriate with BASIC 2.0 (or later versions) without the /D option, or with earlier versions of BASIC. Example 4 assumes BASIC 2.0 (or a subsequent version) with the /D option.

1. ```
PRINT ATN(3); ATN(-4.8933); ATN(2E+8); ATN(1.23456789)
   1.249046 -1.369211 1.570796 .8899875
Ok
```

2. ```
10 A=2: B#=.5
20 PRINT ATN(A); ATN(B#); ATN(A+B#); ATN(.3^5); ATN(0)
RUN
   1.107149  .4636476  1.19029  2.429995E-03  0
Ok
```

3. ```
PRINT ATN(2%); ATN(2); ATN(2#)
   1.107149 1.107149 1.10714871779409
Ok
```

## APPLICATIONS

1. Surveyors use ATN to determine angles of elevation. For instance, if you are standing at a distance d feet from a building and the building is h feet taller than you, then you must raise your head at an angle of ATN(h/d) radians to look at the top of the building. See Figure 2.

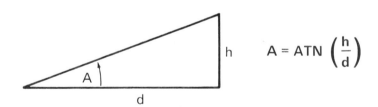

$$A = ATN\left(\frac{h}{d}\right)$$

FIGURE 2

2. The other inverse trigonometric functions can be evaluated using ATN. The formulas are:

arcsin(x) = ATN(x/SQR(1-x*x)
arccos(x) = 1.570796-ATN(x/SQR(1-x*x))
arccot(x) = 1.570796-ATN(x)
arcsec(x) = ATN(SQR(x*x-1))+(x<0)*3.141593
arccsc(x) = ATN(1/SQR(x*x-1))+(x<0)*3.141593

*Notes:* SQR is the square root function. The expression (x<0) takes on the value -1 if x is negative, and 0 otherwise. This is because true statements are
```

ATN

given the value -1 and false statements are given the value 0. There is no universal agreement about the definitions of arcsec and arccsc. We have defined these functions as the inverses of sec and csc when restricted to the domain $-\pi < x < -\pi/2$ and $0 < x < \pi/2$.

The line numbers of a BASIC program can be assigned automatically by giving the command

```
AUTO
```

before typing the program. The lines will be numbered 10, 20, 30, 40, and so forth. As soon as you press the Enter key, the number 10 followed by a space will appear at the beginning of the first line. Each time you press the Enter key the next line will appear properly numbered.

COMMENTS

1. The AUTO command is disabled by a Ctrl-Break. After that you can continue to enter lines manually.

2. You can begin with any line number you like and use any increment between line numbers. The command

```
AUTO n,m
```

gives the first line the number n and increases each subsequent line number by m.

3. If use of the AUTO command generates a line number that has already been assigned, the computer will alert you by printing an asterisk following the line number. To avoid replacing the existing line just press the Enter key.

4. The command

```
AUTO ,m
```

gives the first line the number 0 and increases each subsequent line number by m.

5. The command

```
AUTO n,
```

gives the next line the number n and increases each subsequent line number by whichever increment was used in the most recent AUTO statement and by 10 if there was no prior AUTO statement. If the comma is omitted, 10 always will be taken as the increment.

6. The command

```
AUTO .,m
```

causes the next line to be numbered the same as the most recently entered line (followed by an asterisk). Subsequent line numbers will be incremented by m.

AUTO

7.   Only the current line of the program can be altered while in the AUTO mode. Ctrl-Break must be typed in order to alter other lines.

8.   The key combination Alt-A displays the word AUTO.

9.   If the command AUTO is used in program mode, the program will terminate after AUTO is executed.

EXAMPLE

```
AUTO
10 PRINT
20 PRINT
30 (press Ctrl-Break)
Ok
AUTO ,3
0 PRINT
3 PRINT
6 (press Ctrl-Break)
Ok
AUTO 5,
5 PRINT
8 PRINT
11 (press Ctrl-Break)
Ok
2 PRINT
4 PRINT
AUTO .,7
4* WRITE
11 WRITE
18 WRITE
```

(*Note:* Lines 2 and 4 were entered manually, not AUTOmatically.)

Whenever you turn on the computer you hear a short beep. You can cause a similar sound to occur anywhere you like in a program by using the statement

```
BEEP
```

EXAMPLE

```
10 BEEP
20 INPUT " WHAT IS YOUR NAME ";A$
30 CLS: PRINT A$
```

COMMENTS

1. The beeping sound also can be activated by the command **PRINT CHR$(7)**.

2. The beeping sound also can be produced by pressing Ctrl-G.

3. The duration of the beeping sound is 1/3 second and the frequency is 800 Hz. Sounds of longer duration can be produced by using several BEEP statements. Sounds of other durations and frequencies can be generated with the SOUND statement.

APPLICATIONS

1. BEEP is used to get the attention of the user when the user must respond to a request for information.

2. BEEP often is used to signal the end of a long routine lasting several minutes, during which time the user might have been away from the keyboard.

BLOAD

This discussion assumes an understanding of how memory locations are specified. (See the discussion of DEF SEG for a detailed description.) The BLOAD command is similar to the POKE command, in that it is used to put bytes into specific memory locations. However, whereas POKE fills one memory location at a time, BLOAD will fill as many as 65535 consecutive locations. The bytes that will be placed in these memory locations are stored in a disk file.

Before executing the BLOAD command you must have used a DEF SEG statement to specify a segment containing the consecutive memory locations to be filled. Also, you must have created a disk file (usually with BSAVE) containing the bytes to be put into the memory locations. The command

    BLOAD filespec, m

loads the bytes from the specified file into consecutive memory locations of the specified segment beginning with the location having offset m.

COMMENTS

1. In the event that the filename has the extension ".BAS", this extension can be omitted from the filespec when using BLOAD.

2. BLOAD usually is used in conjunction with the command BSAVE. A portion of memory is saved on a disk using BSAVE and then reloaded (into a possibly different place in memory) with BLOAD. If a portion of memory was saved as a file, then the command

    BLOAD filespec

would load the bytes into the same locations from which they were saved.

EXAMPLES

1. Suppose that a prior DEF SEG statement had specified the 3840th segment as the current segment, and the bytes to be loaded into memory are contained in the file named MEMORY on drive B. The command

    BLOAD "B:MEMORY", 4

would load the contents of the file into consecutive memory locations beginning with absolute memory location 61444. (*Note:* 61444=16*3840+4.)

2. Suppose that a portion of memory had been saved with the command

    BSAVE "B:MEMORY", 4, 9

The command

```
BLOAD "B:MEMORY"
```

would then restore that portion of memory to its original state, even if the portion of memory had been used during the intervening time; provided, of course, that DEF SEG hadn't been invoked.

APPLICATIONS

1. BLOAD is used to load machine language programs.

2. BLOAD is used in conjunction with BSAVE to store and later reproduce the screen. See Application 2 in the discussion of BSAVE.

BSAVE

This discussion assumes an understanding of the way that memory locations are specified. (See the discussion of DEF SEG for a detailed description.) The BSAVE command will store the contents of up to 65535 consecutive memory locations as a disk file.

Before executing the BSAVE command, you must have used a DEF SEG statement to define a segment of the memory. The first memory location to be saved must come from this segment. Choose a name for the file that will hold the data. (For instance, the name might be MEMORY.) Choose the drive to save the file on. (For instance, the file specification B:MEMORY refers to saving the file MEMORY on the disk in drive B.) The command

```
BSAVE filespec,n,m
```

will save, in the specified file, the m consecutive memory locations beginning with the location of offset n in the defined segment.

EXAMPLE

Suppose that a prior DEF SEG statement had specified the 3840th segment as the current segment. (*Note:* 3840*16=61440.) Then the command

```
BSAVE "B:MEMORY",4,6
```

would store the contents of absolute memory locations 61444 to 61449 in a file named MEMORY located on the disk in drive B.

APPLICATIONS

1.   BSAVE is used to save machine language programs.

2.   The contents of the Monochrome Display screen are stored in the 4000 memory locations at the beginning of segment &HB000. The following program saves the screen in the file SCRN on drive B.

```
1000 DEF SEG = &HB000
1010 BSAVE "B:SCRN",0,4000
```

Displays on a graphics monitor are stored in memory beginning at segment &HB800. The text mode screen (invoked with SCREEN 0) uses 4000 memory locations in width 80 and uses 2000 locations in width 40. The graphics screens (invoked by SCREEN 1 and SCREEN 2) use 16K memory locations.

COMMENTS

1.   Files created with BSAVE are referred to as memory image files.

2.   When a picture in medium-resolution graphics mode is BSAVEd, the background color and palette are not saved. When the picture is later

18

BLOADed, the background color and palette then in effect will be used in the picture. Hence, it is quite possible for the picture to have different colors when it is called back.

3. Pictures can be BSAVEd while in medium-resolution graphics mode and then BLOADed while in high-resolution graphics mode or vice versa. In the first case, colors will be converted to shadings, and in the second case, some surprising colors might show up.

4. BSAVE can be used to create displays in medium-resolution graphics mode having characters of two different sizes. The following program produces such a display.

```
10 DEF SEG = &HB800
20 SCREEN 2: CLS
30 LOCATE 12,1
40 PRINT "This line has eighty characters and yet will be
displayed in medium-resolution!!"
50 BSAVE "B:EIGHTY",0,&H4000
60 SCREEN 1: COLOR 1,0
70 BLOAD "B:EIGHTY"
80 LOCATE 14,1
90 PRINT "This line consists of forty characters!!"
```

CALL

There are certain tasks that BASIC cannot perform with an efficient program. This is especially true when manipulating individual bits or bytes of memory, or executing a set of instructions a large number of times. In these cases, it is often better to perform part of the task with a machine language subroutine. The statement

```
CALL offvar (var1,var2,var3, . . . )
```

allows a BASIC program to transfer control to a machine language subroutine. Here, offvar is a numeric variable which serves both to name the subroutine, and to hold the offset address at which the first byte of the subroutine has been placed in memory. For example, the offset might be given as the value of the variable SHIFTLOW8. The variables listed within the parentheses are variables which are needed by the subroutine. We say that the variables are *passed to the subroutine*.

The CALL statement has the offset address of the subroutine ''built in'' via offvar. The segment address is always given by the most recent DEF SEG statement. If no DEF SEG statement has been used prior to executing CALL, then the segment address is taken to be the beginning of BASIC's Data Segment (that is, the default value of DEF SEG).

Examples

1. The following program uses the machine language program contained in lines 130-160 to rotate the lower 8 bits of the binary representation of an integer.

```
10 J=0: B%=0: A%=0
20 DEF SEG
30 DIM B%(7)
40 SHIFTLOW8=VARPTR(B%(0))
50 FOR J=0 TO 15
60    READ B%
70    POKE SHIFTLOW8+J,B%
80 NEXT J
90 INPUT "Input an integer: ", A%
100 CALL SHIFTLOW8 (A%)
110 PRINT "The result is"; A%
120 END
130 DATA &H55, &H8B, &HEC, &H8B
140 DATA &H76, &H06, &H8B, &H04
150 DATA &HD0, &HC0, &H89, &H04
160 DATA &H5D, &HCA, &H02, &H00
RUN
```

```
Input an integer: 259
The result is 262
Ok
```

Line 20 guarantees that offsets will be into BASIC's Data Segment, and not some previously defined segment. The machine language program will be stored in the bytes assigned to the values of the array B%. The starting address of this array is VARPTR(B%(0)). The name for the subroutine was chosen as SHIFTLOW8 to suggest the action carried out. Lines 50 through 80 place the subroutine in memory. Line 100 actually passes control to the subroutine, which then changes the value of A%. Verifying the result, 259 has the binary representation

$$0\,0\,0\,0\,0\,0\,0\,1 \qquad 0\,0\,0\,0\,0\,0\,1\,1$$

Rotating the lower 8 bits to the left 1 gives

$$0\,0\,0\,0\,0\,0\,0\,1 \qquad 0\,0\,0\,0\,0\,1\,1\,0$$

which is the binary representation of 262.

2. See Application 1 in the discussion of VARPTR for another illustration of the use of CALL.

CDBL

The function CDBL is used to convert integer or single-precision numeric constants to double-precision constants. If x is any number, then the value of

    CDBL(x)

is the double-precision number determined by x.

EXAMPLES

1.  ```
    10 A = 123456789
    20 PRINT A; CDBL(A)
    RUN
     1.234568E+08   123456792
    Ok
    ```

In line 10, A was specified as a single-precision numeric constant. Since single-precision constants can have at most 7 significant digits the number was rounded to 123456800 and displayed as 1.234568E+08. (Single-precision constants with more than 7 digits are displayed in floating point notation.) The number CDBL(A) was displayed as 123456792, which is different from either of the other two numbers. Here's how the computation was made. (You might first want to read Appendix B: Binary Representation of Numbers.) The binary representation of 123456789 is

    111010110111100110100010101 (27 digits).

After being rounded to 24 significant digits, the number is

    111010110111100110100011000 (or 123456792).

2.  ```
    10 A = 3.2
    20 PRINT A; CDBL(A)
    RUN
     3.2   3.200000047683716
    Ok
    ```

Many people are unhappy when the computer does this, but here's how it happens. The number 3.2 has the infinite binary expansion 11.001100110011 . . . . The single-precision constant A is stored as a 24-bit binary number that is rounded from the 25-bit number

    11.0011001100110011001100110011

The rounded binary number is

    11.00110011001100110011010 (or 3.200000047683716)

The value of A is obtained by rounding the decimal number to 7 significant digits.

COMMENTS

1.   When the argument of a CDBL function is a numeric expression, the expression is first evaluated and then converted to double-precision.

```
PRINT CDBL(4/3); CDBL(4#/3)
 1.333333373069763   1.333333333333333
Ok
```

In the first case, the number was computed in single-precision and then converted. In the second case, the number was computed in double-precision.

2.   Exercise great care when assigning names to numbers. Otherwise, you unintentionally might do the equivalent of CDBL. Consider the following program:

```
10 A# = 3.2
20 PRINT A#
RUN
 3.200000047683716
Ok
```

The number 3.2, since it was not followed by a # sign, was taken as a single-precision number. Line 10 gave it a double-precision type name, and, since names dominate numbers, the computer converted it to a double-precision number. That is, the computer displayed CDBL(3.2), which is a different number than the double-precision number, 3.2. The programmer might have meant:

```
10 A# = 3.2#
20 PRINT A#
RUN
 3.2
Ok
```

3.   The INPUT statement is a little more forgiving than the LET statement. Consider the following program which at first glance appears to be identical to the first program in Comment 2.

```
10 INPUT A#
20 PRINT A#
RUN
? 3.2
 3.2
Ok
```

The INPUT statement is insisting on a double-precision number and automatically takes 3.2 as such. It does not perform a CDBL.

CDBL

APPLICATIONS

1. CDBL usually is not used to gain greater precision. Generally, this can only be accomplished by specifying the constant originally as a double-precision constant. After first being specified as a single-precision constant, it will not, in general, be accurate to more than 6 significant digits. The only constants that can be converted successfully to true double-precision by CDBL are those with binary representations containing all zeros following their 24 most significant digits.

2. CDBL is used to speed up arithmetic operations, since arithmetic operations are executed fastest when all constants have the same precision level.

The statement

```
CHAIN filespec
```

acts very much like a GOTO statement. However, whereas a GOTO statement causes branching to a designated line of the current program, the CHAIN statement causes branching to the first line of another program (the specified program) that resides on a disk drive. The old program is deleted from memory and the new program is loaded into memory.

EXAMPLE

1.   Suppose that the program CUSTOMER.NY resides on drive B, and the contents of the program are

```
10 PRINT "AL ADAMS"
20 PRINT "BOB BROWN"
```

Now if you run the program

```
10 INPUT "STATE";S$
20 C$ = "B:CUSTOMER."+S$
30 CHAIN C$
```

and answer the question, NY, the output will be:

```
STATE? NY
AL ADAMS
BOB BROWN
Ok
```

COMMENTS

1.   The CHAIN statement can be modified to cause branching to any line of the specified program, not just the first line. The statement

```
CHAIN filespec,n
```

causes branching to line n of the specified program.

2.   Suppose that before branching with a CHAIN statement, values were assigned to certain variables. These values will be lost unless precautions are taken. If you want some of the variables to retain their values, you must list them in a COMMON statement in the original program. (See the discussion of the COMMON statement for further details.) If you want all of the variables to retain their values, modify the CHAIN statement to read

CHAIN

CHAIN filespec,,ALL

3. The statement

CHAIN MERGE filespec,n

is a variation of the CHAIN statement that does not pass control to the specified program but rather causes the lines of the specified program to be merged with the original program. If the same line number appears in both programs, the line from the specified program is used. After the merger, line n is executed. (If n is omitted, the first line of the newly formed program will be executed next. Be careful, when n is omitted an infinite chain loop can easily develop.) As before, precautions must be taken to preserve the values of variables.

4. In order to use CHAIN MERGE, the specified program must have been saved in ASCII format. That is, the specified program must have been saved using the command SAVE filespec, A. In the event that the program was not saved in ASCII format, this is easily corrected by LOADing the program and reSAVEing it with the correct command. (*Note:* When CHAIN is used without MERGE, the specified program can be in any format.)

5. The statement

CHAIN MERGE filespec,,DELETE m - n

causes lines m through n, inclusive, of the original program to be deleted before the specified program is merged. (Line n must exist in the program. Otherwise the error message "Illegal function call" results.)

6. After CHAIN or CHAIN MERGE statements are executed, user-defined functions become undefined, all data is RESTOREd, and event trapping (with statements such as ON ERROR, ON KEY(n), ON PEN, ON STRIG(n), ON PLAY(n), and ON TIMER) is disabled. In graphics modes, the "last point referenced" is set to the center of the screen and the effects of previously executed WINDOW and VIEW statements are voided. In BASIC 2.1, Music Foreground is reset to Music Background. In all other versions of BASIC, Music Background is reset to Music Foreground. DEFtype statements continue to be in effect after CHAIN MERGE statements are executed, but not after pure CHAIN statements. If CHAIN MERGE is executed inside a FOR . . . NEXT or WHILE . . . WEND loop, the loop is forgotten. If it is executed after a GOSUB statement (but not its corresponding RETURN) has been executed, the GOSUB is forgotten and the RETURN statement produces the error message "RETURN without GOSUB" when executed.

FURTHER EXAMPLES

2. Suppose that the program CUSTOMER.NY resides on drive B, and part of the contents of the program are

```
100 PRINT "REQUESTED BY ";N$, D$
110 PRINT "AL ADAMS"
120 PRINT "BOB BROWN"
```

Now if you run the program

```
10 INPUT "YOUR NAME, DATE "; N$, D$
20 INPUT "STATE "; S$
30 C$ = "B:CUSTOMER."+S$
40 CHAIN C$, 100, ALL
```

and answer the questions: JOHN DOE, 1-20-83, and NY, the output will be

```
YOUR NAME, DATE ? JOHN DOE, 1-20-83
STATE ? NY
REQUESTED BY JOHN DOE        1-20-83
AL ADAMS
BOB BROWN
Ok
```

The same output would have been achieved by executing the program

```
10 INPUT "YOUR NAME, DATE"; N$, D$
20 INPUT "STATE"; S$
30 C$ = "B:CUSTOMER."+S$
40 COMMON N$,D$
50 CHAIN C$,100
```

3. The program

```
10 INPUT "YOUR NAME, DATE"; N$, D$
20 INPUT "STATE"; S$
30 C$ = "B:CUSTOMER."+S$
40 CHAIN MERGE C$,100,ALL,DELETE 100-60000
60000 'Program must contain a line 60000
60010 GOTO 20
```

produces the same output as in Example 2, except that the current program is still the original program minus line 60000, and with additional lines added. After displaying the name BOB BROWN, line 20 will be executed and another state requested.

This program can be used to obtain a listing of all the customers in certain states. Shortly before requesting the names of the New York customers, you might have requested the names of the California customers. If so, the Californians' names would have been listed from line 100 on. (There should be a line 60000 in each program even if it holds no data.) The purpose of

CHAIN

DELETEing lines 100-60000 is to get rid of these names before listing the New Yorkers.

APPLICATIONS

1.   The CHAIN statement provides access to other programs. It often is used to link lengthy programs.

2.   The CHAIN MERGE statement can be used to alter a program during operation, usually as a result of a response by the user. The following program allows the user to define a function.

```
10 INPUT "F(X,Y)= ",A$
20 OPEN "TEMP.BAS" FOR OUTPUT AS #1
30 PRINT #1, "60 DEF FNA(X,Y)="+A$
40 CLOSE #1
50 CHAIN MERGE "TEMP.BAS",60
70 PRINT FNA(1.5,4)
RUN
F(X,Y)= 2*X+Y
 7
Ok
LIST
10 INPUT "F(X,Y)= ",A$
20 OPEN "TEMP.BAS" FOR OUTPUT AS #1
30 PRINT #1, "60 DEF FNA(X,Y)="+A$
40 CLOSE #1
50 CHAIN MERGE "TEMP.BAS",60
60 DEF FNA(X,Y)=2*X+Y
70 PRINT FNA(1.5,4)
Ok
```

The command CHDIR is not available in versions of BASIC prior to BASIC 2.0.

BASIC 2.0 and subsequent versions support a hierarchial directory structure in which directories are specified by paths through the structure. See Appendix D for a description of paths and current directories. Initially, the current directory of a disk is the root directory. At any time, the command

```
CHDIR A$
```

where A$ is a string expression for a path, changes the current directory to the directory specified by the path.

EXAMPLES

The following examples refer to the tree diagram presented in Appendix D.

1. Suppose that the disk is in drive C and that the current directory is the root directory. Then the command

```
CHDIR "C:ANN\NOVEL"
```

changes the current directory to NOVEL. If drive C is the default drive, then the command can be written **CHDIR "ANN\NOVEL"**. Since the command is issued with the root directory as the current directory, it is not necessary to write the path as ＼ANN＼NOVEL.

2. Suppose that the disk is in the default drive and that the current directory for that drive is ANN. Then the command in Example 1 can be replaced by

```
CHDIR "NOVEL"
```

3. Suppose that the disk is in the default drive and that the current directory for that drive is NOVEL. The following pair of commands will change the current directory to MATH and list all its entries.

```
CHDIR "..\MATH": FILES
```

This also can be written **CHDIR "\ANN\MATH": FILES**.

COMMENT

The string expression for the path must not be longer than 63 characters.

CHR$

Appendix A lists the characters that are recognized by the computer and their associated ASCII values. If n is a number from 0 to 255, then the value of the function

    CHR$(n)

is the string consisting of the symbol or control character associated with n. The control characters have numbers 7, 9-13, and 28-31. If n is one of these numbers, then the statement **PRINT CHR$(n)** produces the specified effect. Otherwise, the statement displays the associated character on the screen.

The following demonstration programs display the values of CHR$(n) in a rectangular array of 13 rows with 20 symbols in each row except the last. (The first program is appropriate for a graphics monitor and the second for the Monochrome Display.) Characters 0, 32, 255, and each of the control characters display as blank spaces. Press any key to clear the screen.

```
10 REM Graphics Monitor Required
20 ON ERROR GOTO 130
30 CLS: WIDTH 40: KEY OFF
40 LOCATE ,,0: SCREEN 0
50 DEF SEG = &HB800
60 FOR ROW% = 0 TO 12
70 FOR COL% = 0 TO 19
80 A=20*ROW%+COL%
90 IF A=7 OR (A>8 AND A<14) THEN 120
100 IF A>27 AND A<32 THEN 120
110 POKE ROW%*160+COL%*4,COL%+ROW%*20
120 NEXT COL%,ROW%
130 IF INKEY$="" THEN 130 ELSE CLS: END


10 REM Monochrome Display Required
20 ON ERROR GOTO 130
30 CLS: WIDTH 80: KEY OFF
40 SCREEN 0: LOCATE ,,0
50 DEF SEG = &HB000
60 FOR ROW% = 0 TO 12
70 FOR COL% = 0 TO 19
80 A=20*ROW%+COL%
90 IF A=7 OR (A>8 AND A<14) THEN 120
100 IF A>27 AND A<32 THEN 120
110 POKE (ROW%)*320+COL%*8,COL%+ROW%*20
120 NEXT COL%,ROW%
130 IF INKEY$="" THEN 130 ELSE CLS: END
```

CHR$

EXAMPLES

1. ```
PRINT CHR$(49), CHR$(65), CHR$(35), CHR$(34)
1   A   #   "
Ok
```

Notice that the character 1 is displayed without a leading space since it is a string here and not a number.

2. ```
10 A$ = CHR$(34) + "Hello" + CHR$(34)
20 PRINT A$
RUN
"Hello"
Ok
```

3. ```
PRINT "Merry"; CHR$(31); "Xmas"
Merry
      Xmas
Ok
```

## COMMENTS

1. For n > 127, the statement **PRINT CHR$(n)** will normally only display the characters shown in Appendix A if the screen is in text mode. In graphics mode, special characters can be defined corresponding to values of n greater than 127. The following program defines character 128 to be a solid right triangle, character 129 to be the Greek letter sigma, and character 130 to be the fraction 1/3.

```
10 DEF SEG = 0: SCREEN 1
20 POKE 124,0
30 POKE 125,192
40 POKE 126,PEEK(1296)
50 POKE 127,PEEK(1297)
60 DEF SEG
70 CLEAR, 49152
80 FOR I=1 TO 24:' 8 times # of chars.
90 READ A%
100 POKE 49151+I,A%
110 NEXT I
120 '
121 '      Each DATA statement describes
122 '      one character
123 '
128 DATA 2,6,14,30,62,126,254,0: 'solid right triangle
129 DATA 254,64,32,16,32,64,254,0: 'sigma
130 DATA 132,136,158,162,70,130,14,0: 'one-third
RUN
```

31
```

CHR$

```
Ok
FOR I=128 TO 130:PRINT CHR$(I)+" ";:NEXT
◢ Σ ¹/₃
Ok
■
```

This program can be used to define a set of as many as 127 characters. The data for each character consists of a sequence of eight numbers that are selected in exactly the same way that an 8 by 8 tile is specified in high-resolution graphics mode. See the discussion of PAINT for details. (Figure 1 shows the binary representations of the numbers used in the above program to define the character "1/3".) After the DATA statements have been added to the program, the index in line 80 must be adjusted to range from 1 to 8 times the number of characters defined.

132	1 0 0 0 0 1 0 0
136	1 0 0 0 1 0 0 0
158	1 0 0 1 1 1 1 0
162	1 0 1 0 0 0 1 0
70	0 1 0 0 0 1 1 0
130	1 0 0 0 0 0 1 0
14	0 0 0 0 1 1 1 0
0	0 0 0 0 0 0 0 0

FIGURE 1

2.   CHR$ must be used with caution in strings that are to be sent to the printer or modem, since control characters are used to set certain parameters for these devices.

3.   The n in CHR$(n) may be a numeric constant, variable, or expression. If the value of n is not a whole number, CHR$ uses the rounded value of n.

4.   If lines 90 and 100 of the demonstration programs are removed, then special symbols will be displayed at the locations of the array corresponding to the control characters. These symbols can only be produced by POKEing the ASCII values of the control characters into the portion of memory reserved for the screen.

5.   DOS 3.0 and subsequent versions contain a program called GRAF-TABL.COM. If this program is executed before BASIC is invoked, the characters with ASCII values greater than 127 can be displayed in graphics mode with the CHR$ function.

APPLICATIONS

1.   The CHR$ function is used to place into strings both the control characters and the displayable characters that do not appear on the keyboard.

2. The CHR$ function is used extensively to place quotation marks in a string, as in Example 2.

3. The CHR$ function is used in conjunction with the LPRINT statement to affect such printer controls as "compress type", "double strike", and "set vertical tabs." The codes used depend on the printer.

4. The characters with ASCII values 177, 178, 179, and 219 are shaded rectangles of various densities. They can be used with the Monochrome Display as an alternative to color or can be used with a color monitor to produce different shades of a certain color. The following program produces a bar graph comparing monthly sales figures for three different years. (See Fig. 2.)

```
10 SCREEN 0: CLS: KEY OFF
20 FOR I = 1 TO 9
30    READ A(I)
40    FOR J = 1 TO A(I)
50    LOCATE 19-J,4+2*I+6*(INT((I-1)/3))
60    PRINT CHR$(176+I MOD 3)
70 NEXT J,I
80 LOCATE 20,7
90 PRINT "JAN";SPC(9);"FEB";SPC(9);"MAR"
100 PRINT: PRINT
110 PRINT TAB(5); CHR$(177); " 1982";
120 PRINT SPC(5); CHR$(178); " 1983";
130 PRINT SPC(5); CHR$(176); " 1984"
140 DATA 12,15,7,5,3,8,4,7,6
```

5. The characters with ASCII values 179 through 218 can be used to draw single- and double-line boxes. For instance, consider the characters in Figure 3.

CHR$

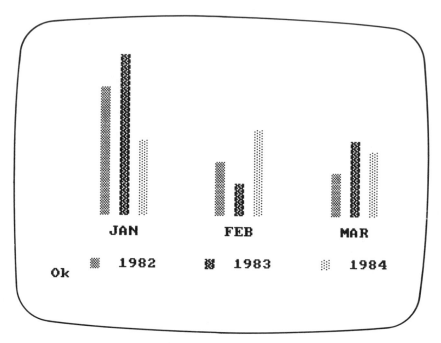

FIGURE 2

218	194	191		196
┌	┬	┐		─

195 ├   ┼   ┤ 180

197

	L	┴	┘		│
	192	193	217		179

FIGURE 3

The CINT function is used to convert single- and double-precision numeric constants to the nearest integer constant. If x is a number strictly between -32768.5 and 32767.5, then the value of the function

```
CINT(x)
```

is the integer constant obtained by rounding x.

EXAMPLES

1. ```
   PRINT CINT(12.63); CINT(1.23456789); CINT(-5.5)
    13  1 -6
   Ok
   ```

2. ```
   10  A = 3: B# = 1.2: C% = 5.5: D = 32767.49
   20  E% = CINT(A): F = CINT(B#): G% = CINT(D)
   30  PRINT E%; F; C%; G%
   RUN
    3  1  6  32767
   Ok
   ```

Note: Let's consider each of the four numbers that were displayed. The number 3 is clearly an integer constant. The number 1 will be stored in memory as a single-precision constant, since it has been assigned to the variable F, whose name does not have a trailing percent sign. The number 6 is an integer constant, even though the CINT function was not used to convert it from 5.5. It was converted when we assigned it to a variable whose name has a trailing percent sign. (In a LET statement, the variable dominates the constant.) The number D = 32767.49 is about the largest number that can be converted with the CINT function. Had the number been 32767.5 or greater, we would have gotten an ''Overflow'' error message when running the program.

APPLICATIONS

1. CINT is used to speed up arithmetic operations. Computations are carried out fastest when all of the constants involved are integer constants.

2. CINT is used to conserve memory space. Integer constants require just 2 bytes for storage, whereas single-precision constants require 4 bytes, and double-precision constants require 8 bytes.

CIRCLE

The CIRCLE statement requires Advanced BASIC and a graphics screen mode.

The CIRCLE statement will draw circles (Figure 1a), ellipses (Figure 1b), or arcs of circles and ellipses (Figures 1c and 1d respectively), in specified colors and with optional radii emanating from the center to the endpoints of each arc (Figures 1e and 1f).

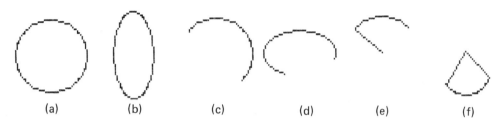

(a)   (b)   (c)   (d)   (e)   (f)

FIGURE 1

PART I   DRAWING CIRCLES AND ELLIPSES

The statement

```
CIRCLE (x,y),r
```

draws the circle with center (x,y) and radius r. The location of the point (x,y) is shown in Figure 2a. The number r gives the distance in points from the center of the circle to the rightmost point, (Figure 2b). The distance in points from the center of the circle to the top of the circle will be 5r/6 in medium-resolution graphics mode (Figure 2c) and 5r/12 in high-resolution graphics mode.

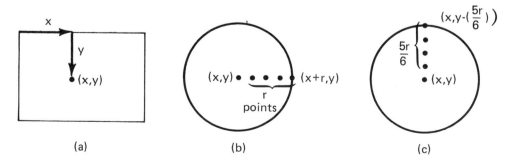

(a)   (b)   (c)

FIGURE 2

CIRCLE

An ellipse is an oval shaped curve. (See Figure 3a.) The longer of the two lines pictured is called the major radius and the shorter is called the minor radius. The ratio

$$\frac{[\text{length of y-radius}]}{[\text{length of x-radius}]}$$

is called the aspect of the ellipse and is denoted by the letter a. (*Note:* Here length is measured in points.) The statement

```
CIRCLE (x,y),r,,,,a
```

draws an ellipse with center (x,y) and aspect a, where r is the length in points of the major radius. So, if a<1, then r is the length of the x-radius, and if a>1, then r is the length of the y-radius. See Figures 3b and 3c.

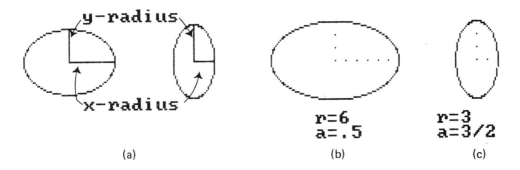

(a)　　　　(b)　　　　(c)

r=6
a=.5

r=3
a=3/2

FIGURE 3

Any circle or ellipse can be drawn in a color, c, by inserting c into the statement. The format is

```
CIRCLE (x,y),r,c
```

Of course in medium-resolution graphics, color must have been enabled and a background color and foreground palette selected. (See the SCREEN and COLOR statements.) The default color is 3. In high-resolution graphics the choices of color are 0 (background) and 1 (foreground) with default color 1.

PART II DRAWING SECTORS AND ARCS

Certain mathematical concepts are needed here. We begin with three paragraphs presenting mathematical preliminaries.

Each radius line of a circle is specified by giving its angle with the x-radius in a counterclockwise direction. See Figures 4a and 4b.

The IBM PC works with angles measured in radians rather than degrees. One radian is approximately 57.3 degrees. Figure 4c shows the radian mea-

CIRCLE

sure associated with various radii of the circle. (*Note:* 360 degrees is approximately 6.28 radians. The exact number is 2 times π, the circumference of the unit circle.) To convert from degrees to radians, multiply by $\pi/180$ (i.e., .01745329 or .0174532925199433). To convert from radians to degrees, multiply by 180/ (i.e., 57.29578 or 57.29577951308232).

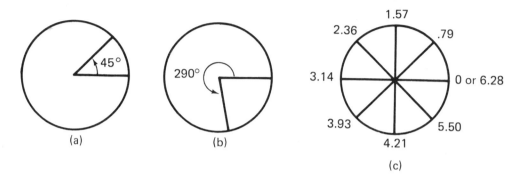

FIGURE 4

Sectors of a circle are specified by giving the pair of radian numbers associated with the boundary radii in a counterclockwise direction, with minus signs before the numbers. See Figures 5a, 5b, and 5c. The minus signs serve a special role here and do not imply that the numbers are negative. To specify just the arc portion of the sector, leave out the minus signs. See Figures 5d and 5e.

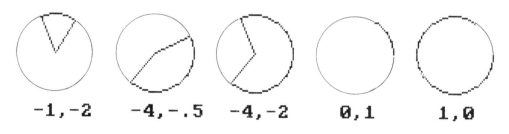

FIGURE 5

If r1,r2 are the pair of radian numbers (prefixed by -) identifying the beginning and ending radii of a sector of a circle or an ellipse, then the statement

```
CIRCLE (x,y),r,,r1,r2
```

draws that sector. To omit one or both of the radii, just omit the corresponding minus sign(s). Omitting both minus signs produces an arc. Any of these geometric objects can be drawn in color by using the same format as for circles.

CIRCLE

EXAMPLES

1.

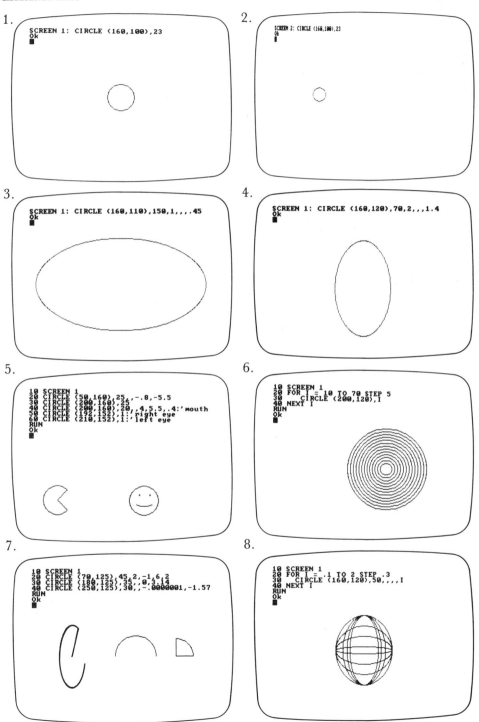

```
SCREEN 1: CIRCLE (160,100),23
Ok
```

2.

```
SCREEN 2: CIRCLE (160,100),23
Ok
```

3.

```
SCREEN 1: CIRCLE (160,110),150,1,,,.45
Ok
```

4.

```
SCREEN 1: CIRCLE (160,120),70,2,,,1.4
Ok
```

5.

```
10 SCREEN 1
20 CIRCLE (50,160),25,,-.8,-5.5
30 CIRCLE (200,160),25
40 CIRCLE (200,160),20,,4,5.5,.4:'mouth
50 CIRCLE (192,152),1:'right eye
60 CIRCLE (210,152),1:'left eye
RUN
Ok
```

6.

```
10 SCREEN 1
20 FOR I = 10 TO 70 STEP 5
30    CIRCLE (200,120),I
40 NEXT I
RUN
Ok
```

7.

```
10 SCREEN 1
20 CIRCLE (70,125),45,2,-1,6,2
30 CIRCLE (180,125),35,,0,3.14
40 CIRCLE (250,125),30,,-.0000001,-1.57
RUN
Ok
```

8.

```
10 SCREEN 1
20 FOR I = .1 TO 2 STEP .3
30    CIRCLE (160,120),50,,,,I
40 NEXT I
RUN
Ok
```

39

CIRCLE

COMMENTS

1.   When PAINTing a sector, don't use the center of the original circle as the starting point, since it is on the boundary.

2.   The IBM PC treats -0 as if it were 0. Hence, in order to draw the x-radius use -.0000001 or -6.28.

3.   The most general circle statement is

```
CIRCLE (x,y),r,c,r1,r2,a
```

4.   The coordinates for the center of the circle or ellipse can be given relative to the last point referenced. The statement would be **CIRCLE STEP (s,t),r,c,r1,r2,a**.

5.   If you intend to draw arcs with just one radius line emanating from the center, do not use BASICA 1.00. Later versions of BASICA correct an error that sometimes draws radii incorrectly.

APPLICATIONS

1.   Pie charts provide an excellent means of graphically representing data. Each region of a pie chart is just a sector of a circle and can easily be drawn with a CIRCLE statement. (See Example 3 in the discussion of PAINT.)

2.   The CIRCLE statement is used in conjunction with the graphics statements DRAW, LINE, PAINT, and PSET to create pictures on the screen.

Whenever you run a program, as soon as you enter the command **RUN**, all variables are cleared from memory. This same result can be accomplished in the middle of a program by giving the command

```
CLEAR
```

The CLEAR command is used to free memory space.

EXAMPLES

1.  ```
    10 A = 12: B(5) = 12.89
    20 CLEAR
    30 PRINT A; B(5)
    RUN
     0  0
    Ok
    ```

2.  ```
    10 DIM A(8000)
    20 FOR I = 1 TO 8000
    30    A(I) = I^3
    40 NEXT I
    50 CLEAR
    60 DIM B(8000)
    70 FOR J = 1 TO 8000
    80    B(J) = J^4
    90 NEXT J
    ```

Let's suppose that this program is run on a computer with 64K (i.e., 65536 bytes) of random access memory. After entering BASIC 1.1, there will be about 35000 bytes of memory free. Lines 10 through 40 will use approximately 32000 bytes of memory, leaving about 3000 bytes. If we hadn't CLEARed the variables in line 50, we would have gotten the error message "Out of memory in line 60".

Note: It takes about two minutes to fill this many array entries; be patient if you run the program. Actually, the memory requirements would be the same if lines 20-40 and 70-90 were deleted. Memory is allocated for numeric arrays when they are initially dimensioned, not when values are assigned to them.

COMMENTS

1.   The CLEAR command not only removes all variables from memory, but also removes all information that has been set with DEF FN and DEFtype statements, closes all open files, RESTOREs all data, and disables event trapping that has been set with statements such as ON ERROR, ON KEY(n), ON PEN, ON STRIG(n), ON PLAY(n), and ON TIMER. In graphics modes, it sets the "last point referenced" to the center of the screen and voids

CLEAR

the effects of previously executed WINDOW and VIEW statements. In BASIC 2.1, Music Foreground is reset to Music Background. In all other versions of BASIC, Music Background is reset to Music Foreground. If CLEAR is executed inside a FOR . . . NEXT or WHILE . . . WEND loop, the loop is forgotten and an error message is produced when the NEXT or WEND statement is reached. If it is executed after a GOSUB statement, but not its corresponding RETURN, has been executed, the GOSUB is forgotten and the RETURN statement produces the error message "RETURN without GOSUB" when executed.

2. The CLEAR command causes all DIMensioned arrays to become undimensioned. For instance, consider the following program, similar to Example 2, but incorporating line 60 into line 10.

```
10 DIM A(4000),B(4000)
20 FOR I = 1 TO 4000
30    A(I) = I^3
40 NEXT I
50 CLEAR
70 FOR J = 1 TO 4000
80    B(J) = J^4
90 NEXT J
RUN
Subscript out of range in 80
Ok
```

The error message resulted since the DIMensioning of the array B(J) was CLEARed, and now the array is only meaningful for $J = 0$ to 10.

3. BASIC has a certain amount of memory available to store programs and data. A variation of the CLEAR command limits the number of bytes available to BASIC for this purpose. The command

```
CLEAR ,n
```

limits BASIC to n bytes. This frees up the remaining bytes for other uses. The function FRE can be used to estimate an upper bound for n.

4. A stack is a last-in, first-out memory, to which you can only add or remove items from the top. Normally 512 bytes of BASIC's portion of memory are allocated to a stack. The size of BASIC's stack can be altered by the command

```
CLEAR ,,m
```

which sets the size of the stack to m bytes.

5. The ERASE statement is a specialized CLEAR statement that removes all specified array variables.

6. The command

    ```
    CLEAR ,n,m
    ```

performs all of the actions mentioned in Comment 1, limits BASIC to n bytes of memory, and sets the size of the stack to m bytes.

FURTHER EXAMPLE

3.
    ```
    10 FOR I = 1 TO 20
    20    PRINT I;
    30    IF I=10 THEN CLEAR
    40 NEXT I
    RUN
     1  2  3  4  5  6  7  8  9  10
    NEXT without FOR in 40
    Ok
    ```

APPLICATIONS

1. The CLEAR command is used to reserve a portion of memory for writing machine language programs.

2. The program in Comment 1 of the discussion of CHR$ uses CLEAR to reserve a portion of memory for a user-defined character set.

3. In BASIC 1.1, certain statements, such as PAINT and GOSUB, make use of BASIC's stack. If you are PAINTing the interior of a complicated region or are using a large number of nested GOSUB routines, you might overflow BASIC's stack. In these situations, use the CLEAR command to enlarge the stack. BASIC 2.0 and subsequent versions do not use the stack for PAINTing.

CLOSE

Data files are created on disks and accessed by OPEN statements. In addition, OPEN statements can be used to access the screen, printer, and keyboard. When a file or a device is OPENed, it is assigned a number and referred to by this number when written to or read from. (See the discussion of OPEN for further details.) Also, each number has a corresponding reserved portion of memory, called its buffer, that holds information on its way to or from the file or device. If a file or device was OPENed with number n, then the statement

    CLOSE #n

sends all of the information currently in n's buffer to the appropriate place and frees up the space allocated as a buffer for n so that it can be used for another file or device.

COMMENTS

1. A single CLOSE statement can simultaneously terminate access to more than one file or device. The statement

    CLOSE

CLOSEs all OPENed files and devices. A statement of the form

    CLOSE #n, #m

CLOSEs the specified files or devices.

2. After a program has finished RUNning, any files that have not been CLOSEd will remain OPEN unless special precautions are taken. (OPEN files may contain information in their buffer that the user wants transferred to a file or device.) These files will be closed, however, if the program terminates with an END statement. Also, these files will be closed by the commands RUN (without the R option), NEW, SYSTEM, CLEAR, LOAD, MERGE, and RESET, or when a program line is entered or deleted.

3. Sequential files can be OPENed in three different modes: OUTPUT, APPEND, and INPUT. It is customary to CLOSE and then reOPEN files each time they will be used in a different mode.

4. Suppose that a sequential file has been OPENed for OUTPUT or APPEND. When the file is CLOSEd, a special end-of-file character is placed in the file. Hence, if the file is never closed, it will have a serious defect. Also, important information about the file will be missing from the directory.

5. The # signs appearing in CLOSE statements can be omitted. For instance, in Example 1, line 30 can be written **30 CLOSE 3**.

EXAMPLES

1.  ```
    10 OPEN "STATES" FOR OUTPUT AS #3
    20 PRINT #3,"Alaska, Alabama"
    30 CLOSE #3
    40 OPEN "STATES" FOR INPUT AS #3
    50 INPUT #3, S$
    60 PRINT S$
    RUN
    Alaska
    Ok
    INPUT #3, S$: PRINT S$
    Alabama
    Ok
    ```

After lines 20 and 30 are executed, the disk contains the two words Alaska and Alabama separated by a comma. Line 50 reads up to the comma. Since we did not CLOSE the file after OPENing it FOR INPUT, we still could access the file in direct mode.

2. Consider the program in Example 1. If line 30 were deleted we would obtain

    ```
    RUN
    File already open in 40
    Ok
    ```

3. Consider the program in Example 1. If **70 END** is added to the program we would obtain

    ```
    RUN
    Alaska
    Ok
    INPUT #3, S$: PRINT S$
    Bad file number
    Ok
    ```
    ```

CLS

Display anything you like on the screen and then press Ctrl-Home. The screen will be cleared and the cursor will move to the upper left-hand corner of the screen. The statement

    CLS

is used to obtain this effect during the execution of a program.

COMMENTS

1. The 25th line of the screen will only be cleared by CLS if the function key display has been turned off by the statement KEY OFF.

2. If a COLOR statement has been invoked, then CLS usually causes the total screen to appear in the background color. The two exceptions are discussed in Comments 4 and 5.

3. In graphics there is a concept called *last point referenced*. This point is usually the point on the screen that was most recently drawn. Certain graphics statements use this point as a starting point. For instance, the statement **LINE −(0,199)** will draw a line from the last point referenced to the lower left-hand corner of the screen. When the computer is first put into graphics mode, the last point referenced is automatically set to be the point in the center of the screen. The CLS statement has the same effect. For instance, in graphics mode, the following program will clear the screen, place a point in the lower right-hand corner of the screen, remove the point after a short pause, and draw a line from the center of the screen to the lower left-hand corner. If line 40 is deleted from the program, the line will be drawn across the bottom of the screen.

```
10 CLS: SCREEN 1
20 PSET (319,199)
30 FOR I = 1 TO 2000: NEXT I
40 CLS
50 LINE −(0,199)
```

4. When we are using a graphics monitor and text mode, the COLOR statement allows us to set a border color. The CLS statement does not affect the color of the border.

5. Suppose that a graphics monitor is being used and the screen is in text mode. Under normal circumstances we work with just one screen. However, the IBM PC has the capability of working with several screens at the same time. These screens often are referred to as *pages*. At any one time, one of these pages is displayed on the monitor and another page (possibly the same as the first) is capable of being written to. If the second page is different from the first, we will not see any characters displayed as we type. However, we

can reverse the roles of the two pages and then see the entire second page at once. (See the discussion of the SCREEN statement for further details.) The CLS statement will clear only the page being written to. To clear all of the pages, toggle the second parameter of the SCREEN statement. For instance, the statements **SCREEN 0,1: SCREEN 0,0** will clear all pages.

6.   With BASIC 2.0 and later versions, if a viewport has been established with the VIEW statement, then CLS will clear only the portion of the screen which lies in the viewport. To clear the entire screen, either use **VIEW:CLS** which cancels the previous VIEW statement, or use Ctrl-Home which will clear the screen, but leave any previous VIEW statement in effect.

7.   The statement **PRINT CHR$(12);** produces the same effect as CLS.

APPLICATIONS

The CLS statement is often used in the first line of a program in order to remove extraneous material from the screen. Also, maximum space is made available for the output of the program before scrolling takes place.

COLOR

The COLOR statement is used to create special effects (e.g. blinking) and to generate colors on the screen.

Several different types of video display screens can be used with the IBM Personal Computer. The Monochrome Display is a special type of monitor that is connected to either a Monochrome Adapter or an Enhanced Color Adapter board. The Monochrome Display is used only in text mode and displays two colors. We shall refer to these colors as white and black. (The actual colors will most likely be either green or amber and black.) Any other type of monitor must be connected to a graphics adapter. Such monitors can produce both text and graphics, and possibly color.

PRELIMINARIES

1. FOREGROUND VERSUS BACKGROUND. With the computer in direct mode, enter the following line of instructions:

```
SCREEN 0: COLOR 0,7: PRINT "Y": PRINT: COLOR 7,0
```

On the screen you should see a rectangle with the letter Y inside. The rectangle is white and the letter Y is black. In this case, we say that the foreground color is black and the background color is white. Actually, whenever the computer displays a character, it always forms a rectangle. Normally the color of the character, known as the foreground color, is white and the color of the rectangle, known as the background color, is black. Since the rest of the screen is also black, we aren't aware of the rectangle.

2. MODES. The IBM PC is capable of displaying both text and graphics on the screen when used with a graphics adapter and an appropriate monitor. However, the computer must first be put into the desired mode by using a SCREEN statement. The three modes and their corresponding SCREEN statements are

> Text mode (SCREEN 0)
> Medium-resolution graphics mode (SCREEN 1)
> High-resolution graphics mode (SCREEN 2)

The IBM Monochrome Display is capable of text mode only with currently existing versions of BASIC. We suspect that future versions of BASIC will allow other modes when the Monochrome display is attached to an Enhanced Graphics Adapter.

When the computer is turned on, it automatically goes into text mode. All keyboard characters can be displayed on the screen along with 150 other characters and symbols that can be displayed via the CHR$ function (See the discussion of CHR$.) The screen is capable of displaying 25 lines. The width of each line is 80 characters on the IBM Monochrome Display, but can also be set to a width of 40 characters on other monitors. (This is accomplished by the statement WIDTH 40. The statement WIDTH 80 can be used to return to the 80 character per line display.)

In the medium-resolution graphics mode, the screen normally can display about half of the different characters and symbols displayable in text mode. As before, 25 lines are available. However, the width of each line will be 40 characters. In addition, various statements (e.g., LINE, CIRCLE, DRAW, and PSET) can be used to draw figures and graphs on the screen. For graphics purposes, the screen is subdivided into 64000 small rectangular regions called pixels or points. Figure 1a shows 1/4 of a square inch of a screen with subdivision into pixels. Horizontally, there are 320 pixels across one line of the screen. Vertically, there are 200 pixels from the top of the screen to the bottom. Each individual pixel can be turned on or off. Graphic displays are formed by turning on the appropriate pixels.

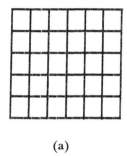

(a)   (b)

FIGURE 1

High-resolution graphics mode functions very much like medium-resolution graphics mode, but with three differences. First, the width of each line of text is 80 characters. Second, the screen is subdivided into 128000 pixels (640 horizontal and 200 vertical). Figure 1b shows 1/4 of a square inch of a screen. Third, whereas different colors can be used in the other two modes, only black and white can be used in the high-resolution graphics mode.

3. COLORS.   We will have 16 colors at our disposal, and each is identified by a number. The colors and their numbers are

0	BLACK	8	GREY
1	BLUE	9	LIGHT BLUE
2	GREEN	10	LIGHT GREEN
3	CYAN	11	LIGHT CYAN
4	RED	12	LIGHT RED
5	MAGENTA	13	LIGHT MAGENTA
6	BROWN	14	YELLOW
7	WHITE	15	HIGH INTENSITY WHITE

COLOR

PART I   IBM MONOCHROME DISPLAY

The IBM Monochrome Display is not capable of displaying colors. The COLOR statement can be used only to produce special effects in text mode.

The following demonstration program displays all of the special effects. (To clear the screen and get back to normal, press any key.)

```
10 CLS: FOR I = 1 TO 8: READ X
20 COLOR X,0: PRINT "YOUR NAME": PRINT
30 NEXT I
40 FOR J = 1 TO 2: READ X
50 COLOR X,7:PRINT "YOUR NAME": PRINT
60 NEXT J
70 IF INKEY$ >< "" THEN COLOR 7,0: CLS: END
80 GOTO 70
90 DATA 7,1,15,9,23,17,31,25,0,16
RUN
YOUR NAME

YOUR NAME
```

YOUR NAME   (high intensity white)

YOUR NAME   (high intensity white)

YOUR NAME   (blinking)

YOUR NAME   (blinking)

YOUR NAME   (high intensity white, blinking)

YOUR NAME   (high intensity white, blinking)

YOUR NAME

YOUR NAME   (letters blinking)

Each of the effects in the demonstration program was created by a statement of the form

```
COLOR f,b
```

where f is a number between 0 and 31, and b is a number between 0 and 15.

When f is between 0 and 7, the statement results in a white foreground and a black background; with three exceptions. The statement COLOR 0,0 results in invisible text (black on black), the statements COLOR 0,7 and COLOR 0,15 result in reverse video (black on white), and the statement

COLOR 1,b , where b is any number from 0 to 15, results in underlined white characters on a black background.

Adding 8 to the value of f in each of the cases discussed in the preceding paragraph changes white foreground colors to high intensity white. In addition, the foreground can be made to blink by adding 16 to the number f. For instance, the statement COLOR 15,0 results in a high intensity white foreground and a black background and the statement COLOR 31,0 gives the same color combination, but with the foreground blinking.

After executing a COLOR statement, the given color combination will stay in effect until a new COLOR statement is executed. For instance, if you clear the screen (with a CLS statement) and the most recent COLOR statement was COLOR 0,7, the entire screen will be in the background color, white.

PART II   COLOR MONITOR (ATTACHED TO A GRAPHICS ADAPTER)

This situation offers the greatest possibilities for the COLOR statement. We will first discuss its use in text mode and then in medium-resolution graphics mode. The COLOR statement cannot be used in high-resolution graphics mode.

A. TEXT MODE

In the discussion of "FOREGROUND VERSUS BACKGROUND" we saw how the text screen is made up of rectangles. Each displayed character is actually the foreground portion of one of these rectangles. The total screen contains either 1000 or 2000 rectangles, depending on whether the width has been set to 40 or 80 characters per line. The COLOR statement provides the capability of choosing the background and foreground colors for each individual rectangle.

The statement

COLOR f,b

causes all further characters displayed on the screen to have a foreground of color f, and a background of color b (i.e., the character itself will have color f and the rectangle containing the character will have color b). Characters placed on the screen prior to this statement retain their original colors. All 16 colors are available as foreground colors. To retain the capability of blinking characters, we must restrict ourselves to colors 0 to 7 as background. Otherwise, all 16 colors can be used for background. Let's consider, for now, the case in which we retain the blinking capability. Later we will show how to obtain the other 8 colors.

Monitors differ considerably in their ability to display colors. Certain color combinations that show quite clearly on one monitor might result in unreada-

COLOR

ble text on another monitor. The following demonstration program will display the 128 possible different color combinations, each labeled with the identification "f,b." We suggest that you write down, on the inside back cover of this book for future reference, the color combinations that are clearest on your monitor.

```
10 SCREEN 0,1: COLOR 15,4,4
20 KEY OFF: WIDTH 40: CLS
30 FOR A=0 TO 15: FOR B = 0 TO 7
40    COLOR A,B
50    A$=RIGHT$(STR$(A),2)
60    B$=MID$(STR$(B),2,2)
70    PRINT A$;:PRINT ",";:PRINT B$;
80    PRINT " ";: NEXT B: NEXT A
90 COLOR 15,4
100 DATA BLACK,BLUE,GREEN,CYAN
110 DATA RED,MAGENT,BROWN,WHITE
120 FOR I = 1 TO 6: FOR J = 1 TO 8
130   READ C$: D$=MID$(C$,I,1)
140   IF D$="" THEN D$=" "
150   PRINT " ";D$;" ";
160 NEXT J: RESTORE: NEXT I
```

EXAMPLES

1. If you execute the statements

   ```
   SCREEN 0,1: COLOR 14,1
   ```

   and then proceed to type, all characters will appear yellow with a blue background. If you clear the screen by pressing Ctrl-Home, the screen will be blue. You can return to the standard colors by executing **COLOR 7,0**.

2. ```
   10 SCREEN 0,1
   20 COLOR 4,7
   30 PRINT "YOUR NAME": PRINT
   40 COLOR 7,4
   50 PRINT "YOUR NAME"
   60 COLOR 7,0
   RUN
   YOUR NAME

   YOUR NAME
   Ok
   ```

The purpose of the SCREEN statement in line 10 is to guarantee that we are in text mode with color enabled. (See the discussion of SCREEN for further

52
   ```

details.) Line 20 causes line 30 to display YOUR NAME in red letters on a white background. Line 40 reverses the two colors. Line 50 uses these colors. Line 60 returns us to white on black. "Ok" will be displayed in white on black, as will all further characters typed.

COMMENTS

1. An embellishment of the COLOR statement will color the border of the screen any color from 0 to 15. The format is

```
COLOR f,b,bd
```

where bd is the number of the border color. For instance, the statement COLOR 4,7,6 will form a brown border. Subsequent typing will display red letters on a white background.

2. Adding 16 to the foreground color causes the foreground color to blink. For instance, the statement COLOR 21,7 will produce blinking magenta letters on a white background.

3. If you are willing to give up the blinking capability, you can gain access to any of the 16 colors as background colors. The procedure to use depends on whether the length of each line is 40 or 80 characters. The statements OUT &H3D8,8 (in WIDTH 40) or OUT &H3D8,9 (in WIDTH 80) enable the use of colors 8 to 15 as background colors. For instance, if you are in WIDTH 80 and execute OUT &H3D8,9: COLOR 23,4, then subsequent typing will produce white letters on a light red background. In general, the statement COLOR f+16,b (where f<16 and b<8) results in a foreground of color f and a background of color b+8. Scrolling or clearing the screen reenables blinking.

B. MEDIUM-RESOLUTION GRAPHICS MODE

The use of the COLOR statement here is much different than in text mode. First, at any one time there will be just one background color for the entire screen. When the background color is changed, the background color of all previously displayed characters changes too. Second, at most 4 different colors can appear on the screen at any one time. The possible colors are grouped into 2 collections, referred to as palette 0 and palette 1.

Palette 0	*Palette 1*
0 Same as background color	0 Same as background color
1 GREEN	1 CYAN
2 RED	2 MAGENTA
3 BROWN	3 WHITE

After selecting a background color and a palette, colors can only be chosen from the four colors in that palette and are identified by the numbers 0, 1, 2, and 3.

COLOR

Monitors differ considerably in their ability to display colors. Certain color combinations that show quite clearly on one monitor might result in unreadable text on another monitor. The following demonstration program displays the 32 different combinations of background colors and palettes.

```
10 CLS: SCREEN 1,0: KEY OFF
20 DATA 30,50,105,125,135,155,210,230,240,260,270,290
30 FOR A = 0 TO 5
40    C = 1 + SQR(A): READ X,Y
50    LINE (X,9)-(Y,109),C,BF
60    LINE (X-10,8)-(Y+10,8),C,BF
70    LINE (X-10,110)-(Y+10,110),C,BF
80 NEXT A
90 FOR B = 0 TO 15: FOR P = 0 TO 1
100   COLOR B,P
110   LOCATE 20,5: PRINT "BACKGROUND COLOR";B
120   LOCATE 22,5: PRINT "PALETTE";P
130   D$=INPUT$(1):IF D$<>CHR$(27) THEN 140 ELSE 150
140 NEXT P: NEXT B: GOTO 90
150 COLOR 0,1: CLS
```

When this program is RUN, the screen will display large roman numerals I, II, III and below them the words ''BACKGROUND COLOR 0'' and ''PALETTE 0.'' The background color will be black, and each roman numeral will be drawn in the corresponding color of palette 0. That is, ''I'' will be green, ''II'' will be red, and ''III'' will be brown. Each time you press a key, you will see another combination of background color and palette. After all 32 combinations have been displayed, the combinations will cycle through again. Press Esc to exit the program. You should write down, in the back inside cover of this book, the color combinations that are clearest on your monitor.

Color combinations are specified by the statement

```
COLOR b,p
```

where b is the number of the background color and p is the number of the palette. For instance, the statement **COLOR 10,1** will change the background color to light green and select palette 1. (Note: In graphics mode the background color is given first. This differs from text mode where the background color is given second.)

Suppose that we have selected a color combination and pressed Ctrl-Home. We then will have a blank screen in the background color. As we type characters, they will appear in the third color of our palette. That is, they will be brown if we selected palette 0, and white if we selected palette 1. (Later, we will show how to display text in other colors. However, at any one time all text appearing on the screen will be in the same color.) Each pixel lit by a graphics statement will have one of the four colors of the selected palette. The specific color will be specified by the graphics statement.

FURTHER EXAMPLES

(*Note:* The following programs require Advanced BASIC.)

3.
```
10 SCREEN 1,0: CLS
20 COLOR 4,1
30 PRINT "YOUR NAME"
40 PSET (160,100),1
50 CIRCLE (160,100),50,2
```

Line 10 puts us in medium-resolution graphics mode and enables color. Line 20 selects red as the background color, and cyan, magenta, and white (palette 1) as the other usable colors. Line 30 prints "YOUR NAME" in white. Line 40 produces a cyan point in the center of the screen. Line 50 draws a magenta circle around the point.

4. Add the lines

```
60 FOR I = 1 TO 9000: NEXT I
70 COLOR 15,0
```

to Example 3. Line 60 causes a pause during which the screen appears as it did in Example 3. Line 70 causes all of the colors on the screen to change. The background color changes to high-intensity white, "YOUR NAME" changes to brown (the third color of palette 0), the point changes to green (the first color of palette 0), and the circle changes to red (the second color of palette 0).

FURTHER COMMENTS

4. Normally, all text characters and symbols are displayed in the third color of the selected palette. If you would rather have them all displayed in the first or second color of the palette, execute the statements **DEF SEG: POKE 78, 1** or **DEF SEG: POKE 78, 2** respectively. The statement **DEF SEG: POKE 78, 3** returns us to the normal situation.

For instance, consider the program of Example 4 above. If we add the line **15 DEF SEG: POKE 78, 2** then "YOUR NAME" will first appear in magenta and later change to red. The point and the circle will have the same colors as before.

5. In medium-resolution graphics mode, the statement **COLOR b,p** is valid for any number p less than 255.5. If the rounded value of p is an even number, palette 0 is specified. If the rounded value of p is odd, palette 1 is specified.

6. We cannot stress too strongly the importance of checking the various combinations of background and palette before using them. Some monitors

COLOR

produce only 8 of the possible background colors. On some monitors, certain color combinations produce illegible text.

7. Executing a COLOR statement in high-resolution graphics mode results in the error message "Illegal function call". However, the forground color can be changed to color n by the statement `OUT 985,n` where n is a number from 1 to 15.

PART III BLACK AND WHITE MONITOR
(ATTACHED TO A GRAPHICS ADAPTER)

In text mode, the screen is capable of producing just black and white (and possibly certain shades of grey) foregrounds, backgrounds, and borders. Characters can be highlighted by blinking them or displaying them in reverse video. Some monitors are also capable of producing grey and high intensity white. The first demonstration program in Part II should be run to identify the best combinations of foreground and background colors. Often, only the values 0, 7, 8, and 15 for f and b will produce legible results.

The second demonstration program of Part II should be run to identify the suitable values of background and palette in medium-resolution graphics mode. Most likely, the best combinations will be a background of 0 or 8, with palette 1.

FURTHER COMMENTS

7. If certain parameters are not specified in a COLOR statement, they assume their most recently assigned values. For instance, the following program results in "YOUR FIRST NAME" being displayed in blinking black on a white background and "YOUR LAST NAME" being displayed in black, also on a white background.

```
10 SCREEN 0,1: COLOR 16,7
20 PRINT "YOUR FIRST NAME"
30 COLOR 0
40 PRINT "YOUR LAST NAME"
```

8. The second parameter of the SCREEN statement is used to enable or disable color. This parameter has no effect on a Monochrome Display or an RGB monitor. However, it does affect TV screens and other types of monitors.

9. Pressing Alt-C displays the word COLOR on the screen.

COLOR

APPLICATIONS

1.   Graphic images are usually more pleasing when colors are used.

2.   Colors can be used to draw attention to a specific part of a display, or set apart various regions.

3.   If an image is drawn in one color, and then drawn in the background color, it will be erased. If it is quickly redrawn in the original color at a nearby location, it will appear to move. This is one means by which images are animated.

COM(n)

The COM(n) statement is used to enable, disable, or suspend trapping of communications events specified in an associated ON COM(n) statement. The COM(n) statement may be used in three forms: COM(n) ON, COM(n) OFF, and COM(n) STOP. Here n is the number (either 1 or 2) of the communications port addressed in the corresponding ON COM(n) statement. (See the discussion of ON COM(n).)

The statement

COM(n) ON

initializes the ON COM(n) statement. It may be placed either before or after its corresponding ON COM(n) statement, but both statements must be executed before communications event trapping will take place.

When a communications event is trapped after the COM(n) ON statement, program control is passed to the GOSUB line of the associated ON COM(n) statement. When a RETURN statement of the subroutine is encountered, trapping is reinitialized.

The COM(n) ON statement is also used to reinitialize event trapping subsequent to the execution of either the COM(n) OFF or COM(n) STOP statements.

The statement

COM(n) OFF

disables communications event trapping when executed. Once this statement is encountered, communications events will not be trapped until a COM(n) ON statement is encountered.

Any communications activity that occurred while COM(n) OFF was effective will be retained in the communications buffer; however, its presence will not be flagged to the program until a COM(n) ON is executed and another communications event occurs. As a result of that communications event, all data in the buffer may be retrieved.

Care must be taken when using the COM(n) OFF statement while a communications buffer is open. Data sent to the communications port will continue to be placed in the buffer even though the COM(n) OFF was executed, however, the presence of that data will not be indicated. Should the buffer become full, an overflow condition and a fatal program error will result.

The characteristics of the statement

COM(n) STOP

are exactly the same as those listed above for COM(n) OFF with one exception. A communications event that occurs subsequent to COM(n) STOP being executed will be remembered. When a COM(n) ON statement is encountered, control will be passed to the GOSUB line of the associated ON COM(n) statement.

COMMENT

Once a communications event is trapped, a COM(n) STOP is automatically executed even though it is not contained in the code. Therefore, trapping will be temporarily suspended until a RETURN statement is executed. A subsequent event occurring before encountering the RETURN statement will be remembered, causing control to be transferred to the GOSUB line of the ON COM(n) statement as soon as the RETURN is executed.

COMMON

BASIC programs can branch to other programs in the middle of the execution of a program. Also, they can merge other programs with the current program while it is running. These actions are accomplished by means of CHAIN statements. However, when CHAINing, variables lose their values unless precautions are taken. A form of the CHAIN statement allows *all* variables to keep their values. However, in order to preserve memory space, we often want to preserve just some of the variables. This is accomplished with a statement of the form

```
COMMON var1, var2,  . . .
```

where the names of the variables to be saved and hence, passed to the new program, are listed and separated by commas.

COMMENTS

1. Three types of variables are endangered by the CHAIN statement: numeric, string, and array variables. DEFtype statements (DEFINT, DEFSNG, DEFDBL, and DEFSTR) continue to be in effect after CHAIN MERGE, but not after pure CHAIN statements.

2. COMMON statements must precede the corresponding CHAIN statements. It is recommended that they appear early in the program.

3. Although several COMMON statements can be used, there should not be any duplication of variables.

4. Array variables are specified in a COMMON statement by expressions such as A( ) or A$( ).

EXAMPLES

1. ```
   200 COMMON A,B$,C()
   210 CHAIN "B:SALES"
   ```

2. ```
   10 INPUT "YOUR NAME"; N$
   20 INPUT "NUMBER OF SALES THIS WEEK"; S
   30 DIM A(S)
   40 FOR I = 1 TO S
   50    PRINT "LIST VALUE OF SALE NUMBER";I
   60    INPUT A(I)
   70 NEXT I
   80 LPRINT N$
   90 COMMON A(), S
   100 CHAIN "B:SALES"
   ```

Suppose that the program SALES resides on a disk in drive B and displays sales figures in a bar chart. Only the sales data need be passed to the program. The name of the salesperson is not needed to construct the chart.

60

The execution of a program will be stopped prematurely if the user presses Ctrl-Break, one of the statements STOP or END is encountered, or an error occurs. After each of these events, the computer will be in direct mode. The command

    CONT

results in the continued execution of the program. In the case of an error, the error first must be corrected in direct mode in order to continue.

COMMENTS

1. CONT causes execution to continue at the statement after the one where the Break, STOP, or END occurred, or at the statement where the error occurred.

2. After the execution of the program has stopped and the computer is in direct mode, you can display and change values of variables and make calculations. However, if you enter or delete a line of the program, or execute one of the statements CLEAR, MERGE, or CHAIN MERGE, then you cannot use CONT to resume execution of the program. If you try, the "Can't continue" message will be displayed. However, you still can continue (with variables lost) by using a GOTO or GOSUB statement.

3. Programs terminate when they encounter certain commands, such as LIST and AUTO. In these cases, CONT cannot be used to continue execution.

4. The statement CONT should not be used in program mode. If so, the message "Can't continue" results. Then executing CONT in direct mode "hangs up" the computer.

5. The word CONT can be displayed by pressing the function key F5.

EXAMPLES

1.  ```
    10 A = 30
    20 PRINT 20
    30 PRINT A
    40 STOP
    50 PRINT 50
    60 END
    70 PRINT 70
    RUN
     20
     30
    Break in 40
    ```
    ```

CONT

```
Ok
A = 40
Ok
CONT
 50
Ok
30 PRINT A+100
CONT
Can't continue
Ok
```

2.
```
10 A = 7654321
20 PRINT CINT(A)
RUN
Overflow in 20
Ok
A = 3.2
Ok
CONT
 3
Ok
```

APPLICATIONS

1. CONT is used in conjunction with STOP to debug programs. After the execution has been halted, the programmer knows the line number at which the Break occurred and, while in direct mode, can have the values of certain variables displayed in order to determine if the program is operating as it should. When satisfied, the programmer can use CONT to resume execution.

2. The CONT command can be used in conjunction with the END or STOP command to prevent information from scrolling off the screen. (See Example 1 in the discussions of END or STOP for a specific illustration.)

COS is the trigonometric function cosine. For an acute angle in a right triangle, the cosine of the angle is the ratio:

$$\frac{\text{length of the side adjacent to the angle}}{\text{length of hypotenuse}}$$

The definition of the cosine function for arbitrary angles and a discussion of radian measure is contained in Appendix M. For any number x, the value of the function

`COS(x)`

is the cosine of the angle of x radians.

COMMENTS

1. Although x can be any number, COS(x) will always be between -1 and 1. Figure 1 contains the graph of y = COS(x).

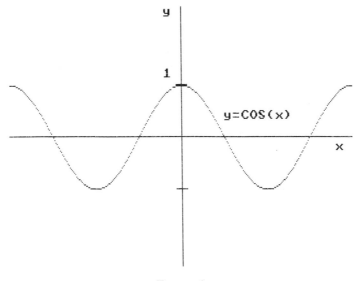

FIGURE 1

2. In versions of BASIC preceding BASIC 2.0, the value of COS(x) is always a single-precision number. BASIC 2.0 and subsequent versions provide the option of computing COS(x) as a double-precision number. To exercise this option, invoke BASIC with the command BASIC/D or BASICA/D. Then, whenever x is a double-precision number, the value of COS(x) will be computed as a double-precision number.

3. The inverse of the cosine function is the function arccosine. This function

COS

is not available directly as a BASIC function. However, it can be defined in terms of ATN and SQR, which are BASIC functions.

$$Arccos(x) = 1.570796\text{-}ATN(x/SQR(1\text{-}x{\wedge}2))$$

Arccos(x) is the angle between 0 and π with cosine x.

EXAMPLES

Examples 1 through 5 apply to BASIC 2.0 (or later versions) without the /D option, or to earlier versions of BASIC. Example 5 assumes BASIC version 2.0 or later, with the /D option.

1. ```
   PRINT COS(1); COS(-5.678); COS(2E+8); COS(1.23456789)
    .5403021   .8223971 -.7359024   .3299291
   Ok
   ```

2. ```
   V = 1.5: PRINT COS(2*3+V); COS(7.5)
    .3466353   .3466353
   Ok
   ```

3. ```
   10 A = 2:B = 7*A:C# = .6435011#:D# = COS(C#)
   20 PRINT COS(A);COS(B);COS(C#);D#
   RUN
   -.4161469   .1367372   .8   .7999999523162842
   Ok
   ```

Note the difference between the results obtained for COS(C#) and D# (which equals COS(C#)). COS(C#) was computed as the single-precision number, .8 . The statement D# = COS(C#) had the effect of converting .8 to double-precision; that is, D# is actually CDBL(COS(C#)).

4. ```
   10 DEF FNARCCOS(X) = 1.570796-ATN(X/SQR(1-X^2))
   20 A = COS(1): B = FNARCCOS(A)
   30 C = FNARCCOS(.5): D = COS(C)
   40 PRINT A; B; C; D
   RUN
    .5403021   .9999999  1.047197   .5000003
   Ok
   ```

In general, for any number x between 0 and π, Arccos(COS(x)) is x, and for any number x between -1 and 1, COS(Arccos(x)) is x.

5. ```
   PRINT COS(2%); COS(2); COS(2#)
   -.4161469 -.4161469 -.4161468365471424
   Ok
   ```

APPLICATIONS

1. Certain periodic phenomena occurring in nature can be modeled with the cosine function. For instance, the tap water temperature (in degrees Fahren-

64
   ```

heit) in Dallas, Texas t days after the beginning of a year, is given approximately by the formula

$$59 + 14*COS((t-208)*\pi/183)$$

where t is between 0 and 365.

CSNG

The function CSNG is used to convert integer and double-precision numeric constants to single-precision constants. If x is a number, then the value of

    CSNG(x)

is the single-precision number corresponding to x.

Examples

1.  ```
    10 A# = 1234567890123456789
    20 PRINT A#;CSNG(A#)
    RUN
     1.234567890123457D+18  1.234568E+18
    Ok
    ```

In line 10, A# was specified as a double-precision numeric constant. Double-precision numbers are stored with 17 significant digits but displayed with at most 16 significant digits. After being rounded to 16 significant digits, A# is 1234567890123457000. Since double-precision numbers are displayed with at most 16 digits, A# must be displayed in floating point notation. When converted to a single-precision number, A# is rounded to 1234568000000000000 and displayed in floating point notation. Single-precision numbers with more than 7 digits always are displayed in floating point notation.

2.  ```
    10 A% = 1234.56
    20 PRINT A%; CSNG(A%)
    RUN
     1235  1235
    Ok
    ```

In line 10, A% was specified as an integer numeric constant. The number 1234.56 is not an integer, but since it was given an integer-type name, it will be rounded to an integer. (The name always dominates the constant.) Now CSNG(A%) is a single-precision number. However, there is no way to recover the accuracy that was lost when 1234.56 was designated as an integer numeric constant.

Applications

1. CSNG is used to speed up arithmetic operations, since computations are executed fastest when all constants have the same precision.

2. CSNG is used to save memory space. Double-precision numbers are stored in 8 bytes of memory, whereas single-precision numbers require only 4 bytes. If 7 significant digits of accuracy is sufficient, then converting numbers to single-precision is more efficient.

CSRLIN

The screen is capable of displaying 25 lines of text, which are numbered from 1 to 25 (beginning at the top of the screen). At any time, the value of the variable

    CSRLIN

will be the number of the line containing the cursor.

EXAMPLES

1. The following program uses the 25th line of the screen to display a reminder to the user. CSRLIN is used to remember where the computer was PRINTing before it temporarily went down to the 25th line.

```
10 A=CSRLIN: KEY OFF: LOCATE 25,1
20 PRINT "Last name only. Type with uppercase letters.";
30 LOCATE A,1
40 INPUT "Who ran the first 4-minute mile"; N$
50 LOCATE 25,1:PRINT SPACE$(79);: LOCATE A,1
60 IF N$<>"BANNISTER" THEN PRINT "Try again": GOTO 10
70 PRINT "Correct"
RUN
Who ran the first 4-minute mile? LANDY
Try again
Who ran the first 4-minute mile? BANNISTER
Correct
Ok
```

2. With the computer in direct mode, the following line of instruction will be erased as soon as it is executed.

    LOCATE CSRLIN-1: LIST

The "-1" was required since pressing the Enter key causes a line feed and advances the cursor one line.

COMMENTS

1. CSRLIN is often used in conjunction with the POS function which gives the number of the cursor's column.

APPLICATIONS

1. CSRLIN, in conjunction with POS and LOCATE, gives the programmer the ability to wander all over the screen and yet return to some location that is specified relative to the starting point. (See Example 1.)

2.   Certain programs request a response from the user, but require that the response be displayed only in a certain region of the screen. CSRLIN can help guarantee that the user stays in this region.

Integer, single-precision, and double-precision constants are stored in 2, 4, and 8 bytes of memory, respectively. Each byte contains a number that can be associated with one of the 256 characters recognized by the computer. (Appendix A lists these characters and their associated numbers, known as ASCII values.) By stringing together the characters associated with the successive bytes storing a number, we can think of the computer as assigning a string to each number.

If A$ is a string of length 2, then the value of the function

```
CVI(A$)
```

is the integer to which the string A$ is assigned. If A$ is a string of length 4, then the value of the function

```
CVS(A$)
```

is the single-precision number to which the string A$ is assigned. If A$ is a string of length 8, then the value of the function

```
CVD(A$)
```

is the double-precision number to which the string A$ is assigned.

EXAMPLE

1.
```
10 PRINT CVI("9W");
20 A$ = "8?}z": PRINT CVS(A$);
30 A# = CVD("AB*34?-}"): PRINT A#
RUN
 22329  1.545697E-02  8.459320813315785D-02
Ok
```

FURTHER DISCUSSION

The function MKI$, which associates strings of length 2 with integer constants, is the inverse of the function CVI. If A$ is a string of length 2, then MKI$(CVI(A$)) has the value A$, and if N is an integer constant, then CVI(MKI$(N)) has the value N. Similarly, the functions MKS$ and MKD$ are inverses of the functions CVS and CVD.

Random files can store only string variables. Numeric data is placed in a random file by using MKI$, MKS$, or MKD$ to convert it into a string. The functions CVI, CVS, and CVD are used later to convert the string back to numeric data after retrieving it from the file. (See Appendix F and the discussion of the functions MKI$, MKS$, and MKD$ for details on accessing random files.)

CVI, CVS, CVD

FURTHER EXAMPLE

2.   The following program establishes a random file to record the area and 1981 population (in thousands) for each state in the USA and enters the data for the first three states. Then this information is read from the file and displayed on the screen.

```
10 OPEN "B:STATES.USA" AS #1 LEN = 8
20 FIELD #1, 2 AS SF$, 4 AS AF$, 2 AS PF$
30 FOR R = 1 TO 3
40    READ X$, Y, Z%
50    LSET SF$ = X$
60    LSET AF$ = MKS$(Y)
70    LSET PF$ = MKI$(Z%)
80    PUT #1, R
90 NEXT R
100 PRINT "State", " Area", "Pop.(000)"
110 FOR R = 1 TO
120    GET #1, R
130    PRINT SF$, CVS(AF$), CVI(PF$)
140 NEXT R
150 CLOSE #1
160 DATA AL, 51705, 3917
170 DATA AK, 591004, 412
180 DATA AZ, 114000, 2794
RUN
State           Area            Pop.(000)
AL              51705           3917
AK              591004          412
AZ              114000          2794
Ok
```

COMMENTS

1.   If A$ is a string of length greater than 2, the function CVI(A$) considers only the first 2 characters of A$. That is, it computes CVI(LEFT$(A$,2)). If the length of A$ is less than 2, then asking for CVI(A$) produces the error message "Illegal function call". Analogous results hold for CVS and CVD.

2.   Notice that in lines 50 to 70 of Example 2, LSET rather than RSET was used to place the numeric data into the file buffer. In this particular program, RSET would have worked just as well. However, if the lengths of the field variables AF$ and PF$ had been greater than 4 and 2, respectively, LSET still would have produced correct results, but RSET would have led to errors. (With RSET, the first character of each numeric string would have been a space.)

70

3. The functions CVI, CVS, and CVD do not change the data; they change only its attribute, that is, how it is handled. See Comment 1 in the discussion of MKI$, MKS$, and MKD$. The function CVI just reverses the process illustrated there.

APPLICATIONS

CVI, CVS, and CVD are used almost exclusively to read numeric data that has been stored in a random file.

DATA

DATA statements are only used in conjunction with READ statements. READ statements call for the next item of a list of constants to be assigned to a variable, and DATA statements store the list. Consider the list

    constant 1
    constant 2
    constant 3

where each entry is a numeric or string constant. (A numeric constant is a number and a string constant is a sequence of characters.) This list is accessed during the execution of a program by including

```
DATA constant 1, constant 2, constant 3
```

as a line of the program. The line can appear anywhere in the program. It needn't precede the READ statement.

EXAMPLES

1.
```
10 DATA 7.8, GABRIEL, " AUGUST 23,1980"
20 READ A, B$, C$
30 PRINT A; B$; C$
RUN
 7.8 GABRIEL AUGUST 23,1980
Ok
```

Note: If line 10 had been numbered 40, the program would have given the same result. Also, the quotation mark surrounding the date was necessary due to the comma and the leading space.

2.
```
10 READ T$, Z
20 READ D, M
30 DATA WASHINGTON, 20015, 8, 23, 1980
40 READ Y
50 PRINT T$; Z; D; M; Y
RUN
WASHINGTON 20015  8  23  1980
Ok
```

COMMENTS

1. Quotation marks surrounding a string constant are optional unless the string constant contains commas, colons, or significant leading or trailing blanks. (The date in line 10 of Example 1 had both a comma and a significant leading blank.) Surrounding quotation marks are not read by READ statements.

2. If an item in a DATA statement is surrounded by quotation marks, then

quotation marks should not appear in the item. They will either be ignored or produce the message "Syntax error".

3. A BASIC program can contain many DATA statements. READ statements will begin by accessing the constants from the DATA statement having the lowest line number and then, after reading all of its items, will proceed to access the constants from the DATA statement with the next higher line number.

4. The maximum number of characters allowed in any BASIC program line is 255. You can include as many constants as you like in a single DATA statement, provided that the total number of characters in the statement doesn't exceed 255.

5. Numeric expressions (e.g., 3+4 or ABS(-2)) and numeric variables cannot be used as numeric constants in DATA statements. Attempts to do so produce the error statement "Syntax error". Similarly, expressions involving strings (e.g., LEFT$("FLORIDA",2)+"A") and string variables should not be used as string constants in DATA statements.

6. See the discussions of READ and RESTORE for further details.

7. The occurrence of two consecutive commas in a DATA statement, is equivalent to having a null string or a zero between the commas.

8. A statement of the form **DATA var1, var2:REM remark** cannot be abbreviated to **DATA var1, var2 'remark**. (DATA is the only BASIC statement that will not recognize this type of abbreviation.) Hence, apostrophes can be used freely in the string constants of DATA statements.

FURTHER EXAMPLES

3. Consider the following list of constants:

United States
2.71828
B:PROG
12,345

This data can be put into the DATA statement

```
10 DATA United States, 2.71828, "B:PROG", "12,345"
```

It was necessary to enclose the third variable in quotation marks due to the colon. Since numeric constants are not allowed to contain commas, the fourth constant had to be treated as a string constant. The DATA statement

```
10 DATA United States, 2.71828, "B:PROG", 12,345
```

would be interpreted as containing a list of five constants; the fourth being 12 and the fifth being 345.

DATA

4. The first DATA statement in Example 3 is equivalent to the pair of DATA statements

```
10 DATA United States, 2.71828
20 DATA "B:PROG", "12,345"
```

provided that there are no intervening DATA statements.

5.
```
   10 U$ = "United States"
   20 DATA U$
   30 READ A$
   40 PRINT A$
   RUN
   U$
   Ok
```

6. In the following program an asterisk is the last data item and signals the end of the data. Such an item is referred to as a *trailer value*, *signal*, or *flag*.

```
   10 READ A$
   20 IF A$="*" THEN 50
   30 PRINT A$,: GOTO 10
   40 DATA E, Pluribus, Unum, *
   50 END
   RUN
   E              Pluribus      Unum
   Ok
```

DATE$

The computer always stores a date in its memory. DATE$ can be used as a statement to set the date or as a variable to read the date.

PART I DATE$ AS A STATEMENT

If D$ is an appropriate string stating a date (See Comment 1) then the statement

```
DATE$ = D$
```

initializes DATE$ to the date given by D$.

COMMENTS

1. The string D$ should consist of a sequence of whole numbers separated by hyphens. The first number, which gives the month, must be from 1 to 12. The next number, which gives the day, must be from 1 to 31. The third should be a number from 1980 to 2099.

2. Single-digit numbers used for the month and the day can be written with leading zeros if desired. The only numbers with less than 4 digits that can be used for the year with all versions of BASIC are 80 to 99 (which are interpreted as 1980 to 1999), and 200 to 209 (which are interpreted as 2000 to 2009).

3. Division signs (/) or hyphens (-) can be used to set the date.

PART II DATE$ AS A VARIABLE

The variable

```
DATE$
```

has as its value a string of 10 characters giving the current date.

FURTHER COMMENTS

4. The value of DATE$ will always have the form mm-dd-yyyy where the first two numbers each consist of 2 digits (with the first digit possibily zero) and the third number consists of 4 digits.

5. When the computer is first turned on the value of DATE$ automatically is set to "01-01-1980". However, this value is often changed by a response to a DOS command requesting the date.

DATE$

EXAMPLES

1. DATE$ = "1-2-84": B$ = DATE$: PRINT B$
   01-02-1984
   Ok

2. A$ = "12/11/2003": DATE$ = A$: PRINT DATE$
   12-11-2003
   Ok

3. The following program assumes that today's date already has been set and that the computer is operating in Advanced BASIC (BASICA).

```
10 ON ERROR GOTO 60
20 C$ = DATE$
30 INPUT "Date of birth"; B$
40 DATE$ = B$
50 IF LEFT$(DATE$,5) = LEFT$(C$,5) GOTO 70
60 DATE$ = C$: END
70 PLAY "CCDCFECCDCGF": GOTO 60
RUN    (suppose that today is April 6th)
Date of birth? 4/6/80
(computer plays "Happy Birthday")
Ok
```

The program uses the DATE$ function to put the "Date of birth" into the same format as today's date before comparing them. DATE$ is restored to its original value before the program ends. (Note: This program is designed only to be used by people born in 1980 or later.)

APPLICATIONS

1. DATE$ can be used to personalize the output of a program by providing the current date for all printed material.

2. DATE$ can be used to maintain a log of the usage of a program. The date and the name of the user can be recorded into a file each time the program is executed.

3. To determine the date N days from now, execute DEF SEG = 0: FOR I = 1 TO N: POKE 1136,1: A$=DATE$: NEXT I: PRINT DATE$. With versions of DOS prior to 3.0, when N is less than 256 the entire FOR . . . NEXT loop can be replaced with POKE 1136, N.

There are four primary types of single-argument functions:

1. Functions that associate numbers with numbers.
2. Functions that associate strings with numbers.
3. Functions that associate numbers with strings.
4. Functions that associate strings with strings.

Some BASIC functions of the first three types are

Function	*Example*
1. SQR	SQR(9) gives 3.
2. CHR$	CHR$(65) results in A.
3. LEN	LEN("COMPUTER") has the value 8.

These three functions involve just one argument. In the first two cases, the argument is a number. In the third case, the argument is a string. (There are no single-argument BASIC functions of the fourth type.) Initially, we will concentrate on functions with just one argument. Later (in Comment 6) we will consider functions of several arguments.

Functions of types 1 and 3 are said to return numbers, and functions of types 2 and 4 are said to return strings. Functions that return strings usually are given names ending in the symbol $. Functions that return numbers *never* have names ending with $.

The DEF FN statement allows us to define functions of any type. In order to define a function we must first give names to the function and the argument. Names corresponding to strings usually end in $. Then we give a rule for determining the value to be returned in terms of the value of the argument. The following list gives, for each primary type of function, sample function names, arguments, and rules.

Function name	*Variable name*	*Rule*
1. CUBE	X	CUBE(X) = X*X*X
2. STARS$	N	STARS$(N) = STRING$(N,"*")
3. ALPHA	X$	ALPHA(X$) = ASC(X$)-64
4. FOUR$	WORD$	FOUR$(WORD$) = LEFT$(WORD$,4)

The first function associates with each number X, the third power of X. The second function associates with each number N, a string of N stars. The third function associates with each string of capital letters X$, the location of the first letter of X$ in the alphabet. The fourth function associates with each string WORD$, the string consisting of the first 4 letters of the original string. Examples of specific values of these functions are

1. CUBE(2) is 8.
2. STARS$(5) is *****.
3. ALPHA("BIT") is 2.
4. FOUR$("Computer") is Comp.

DEF FN

We can define these functions in the beginning of a program with the following statements:

```
10 DEF FNCUBE(X) = X*X*X
20 DEF FNSTARS$(N) = STRING$(N,"*")
30 DEF FNALPHA(X$) = ASC(X$)-64
40 DEF FNFOUR$(WORD$) = LEFT$(WORD$,4)
```

After these functions have been defined, we can use them within the program just as if they were BASIC functions. However, the names must be prefixed by "FN" to show that they are user-defined functions. For instance, consider the following continuation of the program.

```
50 PRINT FNCUBE(2), FNSTARS$(5)
60 PRINT FNALPHA("AT"), FNFOUR$("Print")
RUN
 8            *****
 1            Prin
Ok
```

COMMENTS

1. The names of the arguments are just dummy variables. Changing these names does not change the function. For instance, the statement **DEF FNCUBE(NUMBER) = NUMBER*NUMBER*NUMBER** has the same effect as line 10 in the above program. Also, these names may be the same as the names of other constants that occur elsewhere in the program. Consider the following program:

```
10 Y = 5: M = 4
20 DEF FNA(Y) = Y*Y
30 PRINT FNA(3); FNA(Y); FNA(M)
RUN
 9   25   16
Ok
```

When execution of the program reached line 20, Y was treated as a dummy variable with no meaning whatsoever except as a placeholder in defining the function A. However, in line 30, Y was used as it was designated in line 10.

2. When defining a function, variables with names other than the argument can appear in the rule. Consider this program:

```
10 DEF FNA(X) = X+Y
20 Y = 5
30 PRINT FNA(2)
RUN
```

```
   7
Ok
```

3. A function can be defined without any argument. As an example consider

```
10 DEF FNA = 2*X
20 X = 5
30 PRINT FNA
RUN
 10
Ok
```

4. Functions that return strings usually are given names ending in the symbol $. Such functions also can be specified by using a DEFSTR statement. (See the discussion of DEFtype statements.) The following program defines a function that centers a word on a 40-character line.

```
10 DEFSTR C
20 DEF FNCENTER(W$)=SPACE$((40-LEN(W$))/2)+W$
30 INPUT WORD$
40 PRINT FNCENTER(WORD$)
RUN
? TITLE
                        TITLE

Ok
```

Line 10 assures that every user-defined function whose name begins with the letter C will be regarded as a function that returns strings. Hence, we were able to name our defined function "CENTER" instead of "CENTER$".

5. A numeric function (a function that returns a number) can have a precision specified by adding one of the symbols %, !, or # to the end of the name. The function then will return a number of the specified precision.

   In addition to specifying the precision of the returned number, you most likely also will want to specify the precision of the argument. Unspecified precisions automatically are considered single-precision. The following program illustrates some of the subtleties that arise when specifying precisions.

```
10 DEF FNA#(X#) = X#*X#
20 DEF FNB#(X) = X*X
30 PRINT FNA#(.2#);FNA#(.2);FNB#(.2);FNB#(.2#)
RUN
 .04   .0400000011920929   3.999999910593033D-02
 3.999999910593033D-02
Ok
```

DEF FN

Each of the four numbers displayed is a double-precision number. However, only the first one is accurate. The second number was computed as CDBL(.2)*CDBL(.2) and CDBL(.2) is .2000000029802322. The third number was computed as CDBL(.2*.2), where .2*.2 is a single-precision number. The fourth attempt was a valiant try, but since the argument had a single-precision name, X, there is no way to get the argument to assume a double-precision value. When you want true double-precision, do not spare the number signs. (Of course, DEFDBL can be employed as an alternate to the number signs in some instances.)

6. DEF FN also can be used to define functions of several arguments. All of the conventions for functions of a single argument carry over. The arguments may be all numeric variables, all string variables, or a mixture. Some possibilities are illustrated in the following program.

```
10 SCREEN 0
20 DEF FNA(X,Y,Z) = X*Y*Z
30 DEF FNB(X,Y$) = X*LEN(Y$)
40 DEF FNC$(X,Y$) = CHR$(X)+Y$
50 DEF FND$(X$,Y$) = X$+STRING$(10-LEN(X$),Y$)
60 PRINT FNA(2,3,4), FNB(2,"BYTE")
70 PRINT FNC$(227,"A"), FND$("Yes","!")
RUN
 24             8
πA             Yes!!!!!!!
Ok
```

7. The definition of a function may make use not only of BASIC's built-in functions, but also of user-defined functions that have previously been established by DEF FN statements.

```
10 DEF FNT(X) = SIN(X)*COS(X)
20 DEF FNTT(X) = FNT(X)*FNT(1/X)
30 INPUT A
40 PRINT FNTT(A)
RUN
? 2
-.1592068
Ok
```

8. If an error is typed into a DEF FN statement, the error is not detected until the function is called. The error is then identified as having occurred in the calling line of the program, not in the line of the DEF FN statement. Consider the following program in which a right parenthesis was omitted in line 10.

```
10 DEF FNA(X) = SIN(X
20 PRINT FNA(1)
RUN
Syntax error in 20
Ok
```

9.   The DEF FN statement cannot be used in direct mode. However, if a function is defined during the execution of a program, it can be used in direct mode after the program has ended.

10.   The definitions of user-defined functions are removed by the statements CHAIN, CHAIN MERGE (without the ALL option), CLEAR, LOAD, MERGE, NEW, and RUN or when a program line is entered or deleted.

11.   The following program will not achieve the intended result of allowing the user to define a function while the program is executing. See Application 2 in the discussion of CHAIN MERGE for the proper way to obtain the result.

```
10 INPUT "F(X,Y)=",A$
20 DEF FNA(X,Y)=A$
30 PRINT FNA(1.5,4)
RUN
Type mismatch in 30
Ok
```

APPLICATIONS

Whenever a function occurs more than once in a program, it may be efficient to define it with a DEF FN statement early in the program. The following program is used to find the zeros of a continuous function using the bisection method. The function is specified in line 10. The INPUT statement in line 20 asks for two numbers, A and B, such that the function has values of opposite signs at A and B.

```
10 DEF FNG(X) = X*X*X+X-50
20 INPUT A,B
30 IF SGN(FNG(A)) = SGN(FNG(B)) GOTO 20
40 S = SGN(FNG(B))
50 C = .5*(A+B)
60 IF ABS(FNG(C))<.0001 THEN PRINT C:END
70 IF S*FNG(C)<0 THEN A = C: GOTO 50
80 B = C: GOTO 50
RUN
? 2, 5
 3.59357
Ok
```

DEF SEG

The IBM PC is capable of working with over one million memory locations. In order to be able to move data in and out of specific locations, each location must be given an address. One scheme for assigning these addresses is to number the locations 0, 1, 2, 3, . . . , 1048575. These numbers are then referred to as the *absolute* addresses of the memory locations.

BASIC uses an addressing scheme known as the *segment:offset* method, in which each address consists of a pair of numbers. The memory locations are grouped into overlapping segments of 65536 locations. Segment 0 consists of absolute memory locations 0 to 65535, segment 1 consists of absolute memory locations 16 to 65551, segment 2 consists of absolute memory locations 32 to 65567, ... In general, segment n consists of absolute memory locations n*16 to n*16+65535. Within each segment, the offset of a memory location is its distance from the beginning of the segment. That is, the initial memory location is said to have offset 0, the next is said to have offset 1, . . . , and the last is said to have offset 65535. Since segments overlap, a single memory location can be specified in many different ways. For instance, absolute memory location 100 can be specified as (segment 0:offset 100), or as (segment 1:offset 84), . . . , or as (segment 6:offset 4). To determine the absolute address of a memory location that is given in terms of a segment and an offset, multiply the segment by 16 and add the offset. For instance, the absolute address of the memory location in segment 10 having offset 5 is 10*16+5 or 165.

Each of the statements PEEK, POKE, BLOAD, BSAVE, and CALL contains a parameter that is an offset into the *current* segment of memory. This segment is first specified by a DEF SEG statement. The statement

```
DEF SEG = n
```

specifies the nth segment as the current segment of memory. Until another segment is specified, all offsets refer to this segment. If the number n (and the equals sign) is omitted, then the statement specifies the segment of memory consisting of BASIC's Data Segment.

EXAMPLES

1. The memory location in BASIC's Data Segment having offset 92 contains the number of the last line of the screen that will scroll. Normally, this value is 24. Lines 20 and 30 of the following program specify BASIC's Data Segment as the current segment and then display the value of PEEK(92), the number in the memory location of offset 92 in the current segment. Line 40 then changes the number in this memory location to 25. After running the program, the entire screen will scroll. To return to the standard situation, execute **DEF SEG: POKE 92,24**.

```
10 KEY OFF
20 DEF SEG
30 PRINT PEEK(92);
40 POKE 92,25
50 PRINT PEEK(92)
RUN
 24  25
Ok
```

2.   Absolute memory locations 720896 to 724992 reside on the Monochrome Display Adapter or the Enhanced Graphics Adapter and hold the characters that appear on the Monochrome Display screen. Since $720,896 = 16*45056$, these memory locations are at the beginning of the 45056th segment. The initial memory location holds the ASCII value of the character in row 1 and column 1. The next memory location records its attributes and the one after it holds the ASCII value of the character in row 1 and column 2.

```
10 CLS
20 PRINT "This program requires the Monochrome Display."
30 DEF SEG = 45056
40 PRINT PEEK(0); PEEK(2);
50 PRINT CHR$(PEEK(0)); CHR$(PEEK(2))
RUN
This program requires the Monochrome Display.
 84  104 Th
Ok
```

3.   To adapt Example 2 to a graphics monitor, change the number in line 30 to 47104 and change the words "the Monochrome Display" in line 20 to "a graphics monitor".

COMMENTS

1.   When a RUN command is given, information that has been set with statements such as DEF FN, DEFINT, and DEFSTR is deleted. This is not the case with DEF SEG. Whatever segment was last specified (either in another program or in direct mode) will continue to be the current segment. When BASIC is first invoked, BASIC's Data Segment is the current segment.

2.   Giving a value for n that is not between 0 and 65535 results in the error message "Overflow". The previously specified segment is retained as the current segment.

3.   The numbers used to designate segments and offsets usually are given in hexadecimal form. (See the discussion of the HEX$ function for an explanation of hexadecimal notation.) For instance, the number 65535, which is the largest offset or segment number allowed, is represented as &HFFFF. The

DEF SEG

segment numbers in Examples 2 and 3 are &HB000 and &HB800. Absolute memory location &Hrstu has offset &Hu in segment &Hrst.

4.   The number n in the statement **DEF SEG = n** also can be a numeric variable or expression. For instance, line 30 of Example 2 also can be written **30 A=&HB000: DEF SEG = A**.

The name given to a variable identifies it as being a string variable or a numeric variable. A variable is a string variable if its name ends with a dollar sign. Numeric variables are further identified as integer, single-, or double-precision by the presence of the symbols % , ! , or # , respectively, at the end of the name. (Numeric variables with no terminating symbol are taken as single-precision variables.) The symbols $, % , ! , and # are called *type declaration tags*.

Variables also can have their type declared by the use of a DEFtype statement. Some examples are

```
DEFINT A
DEFSNG B
DEFDBL C
DEFSTR D
```

These statements specify that all variables whose names begin with A, B, C, or D are designated as integer, single-, double-precision numeric variables, or string variables, respectively.

COMMENTS

1.   A DEFtype statement can refer to more than one letter. Consider the following statements:

```
DEFSTR A,B,C
DEFSTR G-M
DEFSTR A,B,C,G-M
```

The first statement declares that all variables whose names begin with the letters A, B, or C are string variables. The second statement declares that all variables whose names begin with the letters G through M are string variables. The third statement has the same effect as the combination of the other two.

2.   DEFtype statements also declare the types of array variables. For instance, after the statement DEFSTR A has been invoked, ADDRESS(1) will be treated as a string.

3.   DEFtype statements usually are placed at the beginning of a program. In particular, they must precede the occurrence of the variables to which they apply.

4.   Type declaration tags override DEFtype instructions. For instance, consider the following program:

```
10 DEFSTR A-C
20 A = "BYTE": B% = 2.75: C! = 2D+08
```

DEFtype

```
30 PRINT A; B%; C!
RUN
BYTE 3   2E+08
Ok
```

Since B% and C! had numeric declaration tags, they were treated as numeric variables even though they had been specified as string variables in line 10. In line 20, the precision of the constant 2.75 was converted to the precision of the variable B%.

5.   It is becoming standard programming practice to DEFine *all* variables.

6.   DEFtype statements will no longer be in effect after any of the statements CHAIN, CLEAR, LOAD, NEW, or MERGE are executed or a program line is entered or deleted. However, DEFtype statements are not affected by CHAIN MERGE statements.

7.   User-defined functions, created with DEF FN statements, return string constants or numeric constants of various precisions. The type of values returned can be specified with DEFtype statements. (See Comment 4 in the discussion of DEF FN for an example.) DEFtype statements can also specify the types and precisions of the arguments of DEF FN statements.

EXAMPLE

```
10 DEFINT A,B,H-M
20 DEFSTR C-G,N-X
30 AXIS=3.2: HEIGHT=4.03: DATE="9/9/83"
40 DIM PERSON(100)
50 PERSON(90) = "GABRIEL"
60 PRINT AXIS; DATE; HEIGHT; PERSON(90)
RUN
 3 9/9/83 4 GABRIEL
Ok
```

APPLICATIONS

The use of DEFtype statements results in programs that are easier to both write and read. The programmer is spared having to add type declaration tags after each variable and the resulting code is not cluttered with the tags.

Problems exist that we would like the computer to solve, yet writing a BASIC program to do the job can prove extremely awkward or, when written, the program can prove to be very slow in executing. This is especially true for programs that manipulate individual bits or bytes of memory, or programs that execute a set of instructions a large number of times. In these cases it is often useful to solve part of the problem using a machine language routine. If n is a digit from 0 to 9, then the statement

```
DEF USRn = L
```

identifies the machine language routine USRn as beginning at offset L into the current memory segment. Subsequent references to the function USRn will transfer control to this machine language routine.

EXAMPLES

1.   Suppose a machine language routine, which takes any string and reverses its characters, has been placed in memory beginning at location &H2000 relative to the beginning of BASIC's Data Segment.

```
10 DEF USR3 = &H2000
20 INPUT A$
30 PRINT USR3(A$)
RUN
? HELLO
OLLEH
Ok
```

2.   Suppose the same machine language routine is placed in memory at location &HF000 relative to the beginning of memory.

```
10 DEF SEG = 0
20 DEF USR3 = &HF000
30 INPUT A$
40 PRINT USR3(A$)
RUN
? WELCOME
EMOCLEW
Ok
```

COMMENTS

1.   In Example 1, the value &H2000 used in DEF USR is taken as the offset into memory from the beginning of BASIC's Data Segment, *provided* that no previous DEF SEGs have occurred. Since DEF SEGs are not erased by com-

DEF USR

mands such as RUN, NEW, and CLEAR, it is always best to include a DEF SEG statement just before using DEF USR. In Example 1 we would add **5 DEF SEG**.

2.   The location L in DEF USRn = L is taken as the offset into memory from the value given by the most recent DEF SEG statement. If, as in Example 2, the location of the machine language routine is relative to the beginning of memory, it is necessary to use the statement **DEF SEG = 0** prior to the DEF USR statement.

3.   Some programmers always prefer to use a zero offset. This can be accomplished by making the appropriate DEF SEG statement. In Example 2, lines 10 and 20 could be changed to read

```
10 DEF SEG = &HF00
20 DEF USR3 = 0
```

4.   The offset assigned to USRn by DEF USRn is not erased by commands such as RUN, NEW, and CLEAR. Only another DEF USRn statement will change the value of the offset assigned to USRn.

There are three ways to remove lines from a program. The NEW command removes all lines. The line numbered n can be removed by entering a blank line numbered n. The DELETE command incorporates and extends these two possibilities. The DELETE command can be used to delete an entire program, a single line, or a sequence of consecutive lines. The command

```
DELETE n
```

deletes the line numbered n. If m is less than or equal to n, the command

```
DELETE m-n
```

deletes all lines with numbers between m and n, inclusive. The command

```
DELETE -n
```

deletes line n and all lines preceding it. The command

```
DELETE .
```

deletes the entered line that was most recently displayed on the screen. (See Example 3 for an illustration of the subtleties of this form of DELETE.) In commands of the forms

```
DELETE .-n
DELETE m-.
DELETE -.
```

the ``.'' is interpreted as the number of the last displayed line.

COMMENTS

1. In the commands described above, the number n must correspond to a line appearing in the program. Otherwise, the error message ``Illegal function call'' results. However, the number m needn't be the number of any line in the program. See Example 2.

2. With versions of BASIC prior to BASIC 2.0, the DELETE command must include a last line number to be deleted. The command

```
DELETE m-
```

results in an ``Illegal function call'' error. This is to prevent the programmer from accidentally erasing most of a program. However, if you really want to delete all lines from line n on, you can do so by entering the line **65529 END**

DELETE

and then giving the command **DELETE m-65529**. (*Note:* 65529 is the largest possible line number.)

3.   In versions of BASIC beginning with BASIC 2.0, the command

   DELETE

removes all lines.

4.   If m is larger than n, the command **DELETE m-n** produces the message "Illegal function call".

5.   DELETE is usually executed in direct mode. When DELETE is executed in program mode, the designated lines are deleted and then the program terminates. At that point, the command CONT cannot be used to resume execution of the program.

6.   After a DELETE command is executed, user-defined functions become undefined, DEFtype and OPTION BASE 1 statements lose their effects, all data is RESTOREd, and event trapping (with statements such as ON ERROR, ON KEY(n), ON PEN, ON STRIG(n), ON PLAY(n), and ON TIMER) is disabled. In graphics modes, the "last point referenced" is set to the center of the screen and the effects of previously executed WINDOW and VIEW statements are voided. In BASIC 2.1, Music Foreground is reset to Music Background. In all other versions of BASIC, Music Background is reset to Music Foreground. If DELETE is executed inside a FOR . . . NEXT or WHILE . . . WEND loop, the loop is forgotten. If it is executed after a GOSUB statement (but not its corresponding RETURN) has been executed, the GOSUB is forgotten and the RETURN statement produces the error message "RETURN without GOSUB" when executed.

7.   The word DELETE can be displayed by pressing Alt-D.

EXAMPLES

1.   ```
10 PRINT "TEN"
20 PRINT "TWENTY"
30 PRINT "THIRTY"
40 PRINT "FORTY"
DELETE 20-35
Illegal function call
Ok
DELETE 20-40
Ok
RUN
TEN
Ok
```

The error message occurred because there is no line 35.

2.   ```
10 PRINT "TEN"
20 PRINT "TWENTY"
```

```
30 PRINT "THIRTY"
40 PRINT "FORTY"
DELETE   15-40
Ok
LIST
10 PRINT "TEN"
Ok
```

3.
```
10 PRINT "TEN"
20 PRINT "TWENTY"
15 PRINT "FIFTEEN"
DELETE .
Ok
RUN
TEN
TWENTY
Ok
15 PRINT "FIFTEEN"
LIST
10 PRINT "TEN"
15 PRINT "FIFTEEN"
20 PRINT "TWENTY"
DELETE .
RUN
TEN
FIFTEEN
Ok
```

DIM

A variable is a name to which the computer can assign a single value. An array variable is a name to which the computer can assign an entire collection of values. The values are thought of as being organized in an array. Two examples of arrays are:

Array B	*Array P*				
563.00	0	0	0	0	0
452.63	0	1	2	3	4
341.16	0	2	4	6	8
228.57	0	3	6	9	12
114.85					
0.00					

Array B is a one-dimensional array. The values are successive balances on a loan of \$563. (The loan, at 12% interest compounded monthly, is paid off with 5 monthly payments of \$116.) If $B(r)$ is the balance after r months, then $B(0) = 563$, $B(1) = 452.63$, $B(2) = 341.16$, $B(3) = 228.57$, $B(4) = 114.85$, and $B(5) = 0$. The array variable B is also referred to as a subscripted variable with subscripts ranging from 0 to 5. The statement

    DIM B(5)

establishes the number of values allowed for this array variable and sets aside space in memory to store the values.

A single column of values is said to form a one-dimensional array. If the values are numbered from 0 to N, and a name is chosen for the array variable to hold these values, then a statement of the form

    DIM arrayname(N)

establishes the total number of values allowed for the array variable and sets aside space in memory to store the values. Since counting starts with 0, there is space for N+1 array values, referred to as arrayname(0), arrayname(1), . . . , arrayname(N).

The rectangular array P above is an example of a two-dimensional array, where the values form part of a multiplication table. Think of the rows as being labeled 0, 1, 2, 3 and the columns as being labeled 0, 1, 2, 3, 4. Let $P(r,c)$ be the entry in the rth row and cth column, which in this example is the product of the numbers r and c. For instance, $P(0,0) = 0$, $P(2,3) = 6$, and $P(3,1) = 3$. The array variable P is sometimes referred to as a double-subscripted variable with the first subscript ranging from 0 to 3 and the second subscript ranging from 0 to 4. The statement

    DIM P(3,4)

specifies the size of this array variable and sets aside space in memory to store its values.

Any rectangular array of values is said to form a two-dimensional array. If the rows are numbered from 0 to M, the columns numbered from 0 to N, and a name chosen for the array variable to hold these values, then the statement

```
DIM arrayname(M,N)
```

is used to specify the size of the array variable. There is space for $(M+1)*(N+1)$ array values. The value in the rth row and cth column will be referred to as arrayname(r,c).

Three-dimensional or higher arrays cannot be easily shown; however, they can be specified. A three-dimensional array variable (or triple-subscripted variable) is specified by a statement of the form

```
DIM arrayname(M,N,R)
```

where the first subscript ranges from 0 to M, the second from 0 to N, and the third from 0 to R. The value for which the first subscript is m, the second is n, and the third is r is referred to as arrayname(m,n,r).

COMMENTS

1.   An array variable must be one of two types: numeric or string. There is no such thing as a mixed array variable. That is, the values must be either all numeric or all string constants.

2.   The rules for naming array variables are the same as the rules for naming ordinary variables. In particular, names ending in $ refer to string array variables; names ending in %, !, or # refer to integer, single-precision, or double-precision numeric array variables, respectively. Integer array variables use less space than single-precision array variables, which in turn, use less space than double-precision array variables. (See Example 2 in the discussion of FRE.)

3.   The type of an array variable and its precision, if numeric, can be specified by a DEFtype statement. (See the discussion of DEFtype statements for further details.) For instance, the statement DEFDBL A, declares that all variables having names beginning with the letter A will be designated as double-precision numeric variables.

4.   A single DIM statement can specify the sizes of several array variables. For instance, the statement

```
DIM A(25), B$(3,7)
```

allocates space for a numeric array variable named A with 26 values referred to as A(0) to A(25), and a two-dimensional string array variable named B$ with 32 values referred to as B$(0,0) to B$(3,7).

DIM

5. Array variables with four or more dimensions must restrict the subscripts to a small range of values. For instance, the error message "Subscript out of range" results from any one of the statements `DIM A#(9,9,9,9)`, `DIM B(11,11,11,11)`, or `DIM C%(6,6,6,6,6)`.

6. An array variable with less than four dimensions can be used without being preceded by a DIM statement to specify its size, provided that all subscripts appearing are between 0 and 10. If so, each subscript will be assumed to range from 0 to 10. However, it is a good idea to DIMension all array variables. So doing conserves memory and makes the program easier for others to follow.

7. Using a subscript outside the range specified by a DIM statement results in the error message "Subscript out of range".

8. An ERASE statement can be used to delete specific array variables and unDIMension them. (See the discussion of the ERASE statement for further details.)

9. All array variables are erased and unDIMensioned by the commands CLEAR, RUN, MERGE, NEW, and LOAD, the statements CHAIN and CHAIN MERGE when used without the ALL parameter or a COMMON statement, or by editing or deleting a program line.

10. Once an array variable has been DIMensioned, we cannot change the range of the subscripts. Our only recourse is to erase the array by one of the methods of Comment 9 and then state the new range with another DIM statement. Employing a second DIM statement without first erasing results in the error message "Duplicate Definition".

11. The amount of available memory determines the maximum size of an array. The subscript in one-dimensional numeric arrays can range up to about FRE(0)/2 for integer arrays, FRE(0)/4 for single-precision arrays, and FRE(0)/8 for double-precision arrays. Attempting to specify a size that would require more space than is available in memory for programs and variables, produces the error message "Out of memory".

12. DIMensioning a numeric array causes space to be allocated for the storage of the numbers assigned to the array. DIMensioning a string array causes space to be allocated for the string pointers. (Each string pointer occupies three bytes of memory.) Space for the strings assigned to the array is not required until the array values are assigned.

13. We can specify that the range of every subscript begin with 1 instead of 0 by first using an OPTION BASE 1 command. (See the discussion of the OPTION BASE command for further details.)

14. The upper limit of a subscript can be specified by an expression. For instance, two allowable statements are `DIM B(8*S+T)` and `DIM A$(LEN(B$))`.

15. Square brackets can be used instead of parentheses in DIM statements. For instance, we can write `DIM B[5]`.

16. The error message "Subscript out of range" is produced if the range N in a one-dimensional DIM statement for a string array exceeds 21844. The corresponding numbers for numeric arrays are 32766, 16383, and 8190, for integer, single-precision, and double-precision numeric arrays. In practice, N must be much lower then these values in order to avoid the message "Out of memory".

EXAMPLES

1. Consider the one-dimensional array presented at the beginning of this discussion. The following program assigns this data to an array variable and provides access to the data.

```
10 DIM B(5)
20 FOR I = 0 TO 5
30   READ B(I)
40 NEXT I
50 DATA 563, 452.63, 341.16, 228.57, 114.85, 0
60 INPUT "NUMBER OF MONTHS"; M
70 PRINT "THE BALANCE AFTER";M;"MONTHS IS";B(M)
RUN
NUMBER OF MONTHS? 3
THE BALANCE AFTER 3 MONTHS IS 228.57
Ok
```

Note: Line 10 was not necessary in this case since the array was one-dimensional and the range of the subscript didn't exceed 10.

2. The chart below assigns personnel in a small business to certain tasks for each day of the week.

	Sun	Mon	Tues	Wed	Thurs	Fri	Sat
Open-up	BOB	AL	TOM	SUE	CARL	JAN	KEN
Clean-up	TOM	CARL	SUE	BOB	AL	KEN	JAN
Lock-up	AL	BOB	CARL	JAN	KEN	SUE	TOM

Think of the three tasks as being numbered 0, 1, and 2, and think of the days of the week as being numbered 0 to 6. The following program assigns this information to an array variable and provides access to the information.

```
10 DIM WHO$(2,6)
20 FOR I = 0 TO 2
30   FOR J = 0 TO 6
40     READ WHO$(I,J)
50   NEXT J
60 NEXT I
```

DIM

```
70 DATA BOB, AL, TOM, SUE, CARL, JAN, KEN, TOM, CARL, SUE,
BOB, AL, KEN, JAN, AL, BOB, CARL, JAN, KEN, SUE, TOM
80 INPUT "Number of task,Number of day"; A,B
90 PRINT WHO$(A,B); " IS ASSIGNED TASK";A;"ON DAY";B
RUN
Number of task,Number of day? 1,3
BOB IS ASSIGNED TASK 1 ON DAY 3
Ok
```

3. Consider the following program:

```
10 A(5) = 123.45
20 DIM A(7)
30 FOR I = 0 TO 7
40    A(I) = I + 10
50 NEXT I
RUN
Duplicate Definition in 20
Ok
```

This program went awry in line 20. Line 10 assigned a value to the array vari-able A without first using a DIM statement. That's allowed, since whenever a one-dimensional array is first mentioned in a program, it is automatically DIMensioned with a range from 0 to 10. It's as if the computer supplied the statement DIM A(10). In line 20, the array variable was reDIMensioned without first being erased.

4.  ```
    10 DIM COST%(15)
    20 FOR I = 0 TO 15
    30    COST%(I) = 5*I + 20
    40 NEXT I
    50 COST%(25) = 123
    RUN
    Subscript out of range in 50
    Ok
    ```
    ```

The DRAW statement requires a graphics monitor. It only can be used with Advanced BASIC; that is, the command BASICA must have been given when BASIC was invoked.

The following demonstration program reveals some of the capabilities of the DRAW statement.

```
10 KEY OFF: CLS: SCREEN 1,0
20 A$=INPUT$(1)
30 DRAW A$: GOTO 20
```

After executing the run command, the screen will be cleared. Now press (and hold down for a few seconds) one of the following keys: U, D, L, R, E, F, G, or H. A moving dot will appear at the center of the screen. The dot will continue to trace out a figure as long as one of the above-mentioned 8 keys is pressed. These keys control the movement of the point as follows:

By varying the pressed key, you will produce drawings on the screen. To terminate the program press Ctrl-Break. Also, pressing a key other than one of the eight mentioned will interrupt the program.

PART I   THE M SUBCOMMAND

You should be familiar with the way that coordinates of points are specified in graphics modes. (See Appendix C for details.) The concept of *last point referenced* is especially important with regard to the DRAW statement. The CLS statement and the RUN command both set the center of the screen as the last point referenced. The center of the screen has coordinates (160,100) in medium-resolution graphics mode and (320,100) in high-resolution graphics mode.

The statement

```
DRAW "M x,y"
```

draws a straight line from the last point referenced to the point with coordinates (x,y). After the statement has been executed, the point (x,y) becomes the new last point referenced. So, for instance, the statements

DRAW

    CLS: DRAW "M 200,50": DRAW "M 300,150"

produce a line from the center of the screen to the point (200,50) and a line from (200,50) to (300,150). The last two statements can be condensed into the single statement

    DRAW "M 200,50 M 300,150"

If the letter M is preceded by the letter N in a DRAW statement, the last point referenced will be the same as it was before the line was drawn. So, for instance,

    CLS: DRAW "NM 200,50 M 300,150"

draws a line from the center of the screen to the point (200,50) and then from the center of the screen to (300,150). (The point (300,150) will be the last point referenced for future DRAW statements.) We often think of the lines as being drawn by a moving point, and say that the point drew the first line and then returned to the original position before drawing the second line.

If the letter M is preceded by the letter B in a DRAW statement, the point moves without drawing the line. That is, the statement DRAW "BM x,y" merely makes (x,y) the new last point referenced. So, for instance,

    CLS: DRAW "BM 200,50 M 300,150"

draws a single line from the point (200,50) to the point (300,150). The statement DRAW "BM x,y" is used extensively to set the starting point before tracing a figure with a DRAW statement.

The coordinates (x,y) also can be specified by statements of the form

    DRAW "M =var1;,=var2;"

where var1 and var2 are numeric variables. So, for instance, the statement DRAW "M 200,50" is equivalent to

    A=200: B=50: DRAW "M =A;,=B;"

The coordinates of the specified point also can be given in relative form. If r and s are nonnegative numbers, then the statement

    DRAW "M +r,s"

draws a line from the last point referenced to the point that is r units to the right and s units down. For instance, in medium-resolution graphics mode,

    CLS: DRAW "M +40,50"

draws a line from the point (160,100) to the point (200,150). The statements
DRAW "M −r,s", DRAW "M +r,−s", and DRAW "M −r,−s" have
analogous interpretations. The presence of the + or − sign in front of the first
coordinate provides the tipoff that relative coordinates are being used.

The relative coordinates r,s also can be specified by statements of the form

    DRAW "M +=var1;,=var2;"

where var1 and var2 are numeric variables. So, for instance, the statement
DRAW "M +40,50" is equivalent to

    A=40: B=50: DRAW "M +=A;,=B;"

In other variations, the expressions inside the quotation marks can be "M
− =A;,=B;", "M +=A;,− =B;", and "M −=A;,− =B;".

EXAMPLES

1. The following statements (in medium-resolution graphics) all draw the
large letter X shown in Figure 1.

    CLS: DRAW "NM 210,50 NM 210,150 NM 110,150 M 110,50"

    CLS: DRAW "BM 110,50 M 210,150 BM 210,50 M 110,150"

    CLS: DRAW "BM 110,50 M +100,100 BM +0,−100 M −100,100"

    CLS:A=100:DRAW "BM 110,50 M +=A;,=A;BM +0,−=A;M −=A;,=A;"

2. The following program draws 64 radii emanating from the center of the
screen.

    10 SCREEN 1: CLS
    20 FOR R = 0 TO 6.3 STEP .1
    30   A = 160+70*COS(R): B = 100+70*SIN(R)
    40   DRAW "NM =A;,=B;"
    50 NEXT R

It would have been incorrect to replace lines 30 and 40 by the single line

    30 DRAW "NM = 160+70*COS(R);, = 100+70*SIN(R);"

Only numeric variables are permitted following the equal signs. Algebraic
expressions are not allowed.

DRAW

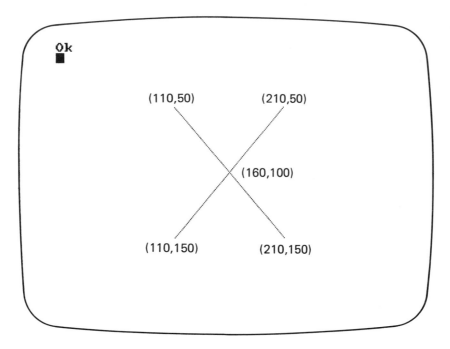

FIGURE 1

PART II   THE SUBCOMMANDS U, D, L, R, E, F, G, AND H

A statement of the form

    DRAW "U n"

where n is a positive integer draws a line by starting at the last point referenced and moving n units up. It is equivalent to the statement **DRAW "M
+0,-n"**. The other subcommands operate as follows:

	Moves	*Equivalent to*
D n	n units down	M +0,n
L n	n units left	M -n,0
R n	n units right	M +n,0
E n	n units NE	M +n,-n
F n	n units SE	M +n,n
G n	n units SW	M -n,n
H n	n units NW	M -n,-n

The prefixes N and B produce the same results as before. For instance, the

100

statement **DRAW "BU20"** results in the last point referenced being changed to the point 20 units above it.

The value n also can be specified by statements of the form

```
DRAW "U =var;"
```

where var is a numeric variable. So, for instance, the statement **DRAW "U 20"** is equivalent to

```
A = 20: DRAW "U =A;"
```

FURTHER EXAMPLES

3. The letter X shown in Figure 1 also can be drawn by the following statements.

```
CLS: DRAW "E50  G100  E50  H50  F100"

CLS: DRAW "NE50  NF50  NG50  H50"

CLS: DRAW "BE50  G100  BU100  F100"

CLS: A = 50: DRAW "NE =A; NF =A; NG =A; H =A;"
```

4. The following program produces the sailboat shown in Figure 2.

```
10 CLS: SCREEN 1: KEY OFF
20 DRAW "L60 E60 D80 L60 F20 R40 E20 L20"
```

PART III   COLOR, ANGLE, AND SCALE

In medium-resolution graphics mode (induced by the statement SCREEN 1), a background color and a palette of 4 colors can be selected using a COLOR statement. If this is done, the statement

```
DRAW "C n"
```

specifies that all subsequent segments be in color n of the palette until another color is specified. The number n can range from 0 to 3. (Zero is the background color and 3 is the foreground color; that is, the color used for text.) Until a color is specified, all figures will be drawn in color 3 of the palette.

Look at the 4 sailboats shown in Figure 3. The top boat was drawn first and then rotated through 90, 180, and 270 degrees counterclockwise about the center of the screen to obtain the other boats. The angle subcommand provides the capability of rotating a figure created with a DRAW statement by 90, 180, or 270 degrees.

DRAW

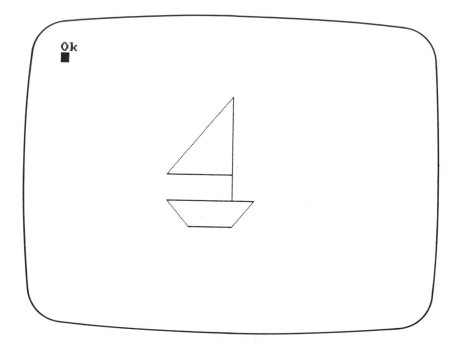

The statement

    `DRAW "A n"`

where n is 0, 1, 2, or 3, specifies that all subsequent figures will be drawn rotated through n*90 degrees.

Figures created with DRAW statements can be enlarged using the scale subcommand. The statement

    `DRAW "S n"`

specifies that all subsequent segments be drawn at n/4 times their stated size until another scale is specified. The number n can range from 1 to 255. For instance, the statement `DRAW "S8 U10 L15 D10 R15"` is equivalent to the statement `DRAW "U20 L30 D20 R30"`. They both draw a rectangle of height 20 and width 30.

The value n in the color, angle, and scale subcommands also can be specified by statements of the form `DRAW "C=var;"`, `DRAW "A=var;"`, or `DRAW "S=var;"` where var is a numeric variable. For instance, the statement `DRAW "C2"` is equivalent to `A = 2: DRAW "C=A;"`

FURTHER EXAMPLES

5. The following program produces the sailboat of Figure 2 with a white background, green sail, and red boat.

```
10 SCREEN 1,0: CLS: KEY OFF
20 COLOR 7,0
30 DRAW "C1 L60 E60 D80 C2 L60 F20 R40 E20 L20"
```

6. The following program uses the angle subcommand to draw a small sailboat and its various rotations. Figure 3 shows all of the possibilities superimposed on one screen.

```
10 CLS: SCREEN 1: KEY OFF: PSET (160,100)
20 INPUT "ANGLE (0-3)"; N
30 DRAW "A=N; BU40 L30 E30 D40 L30 F10 R20 E10 L10"
```

7. The following program uses the scale subcommand to draw sailboats of various sizes. (This particular drawing does not fit the screen for n greater than about 140.)

```
10 CLS: SCREEN 1: KEY OFF
20 INPUT "SCALE (1-255) "; N
30 DRAW "S=N;"
40 DRAW "BM +1,0 L3 E3 D4 L3 F1 R2 E1 L1"
```

PART IV STRINGS AND SUBSTRINGS

DRAW statements consist of the word DRAW followed by a string. The string can be defined as a string constant, and then it can be used to represent the string. For instance, the statement DRAW "U20 L30 D20 R30" is equivalent to

```
A$ = "U20 L30 D20 R30": DRAW A$
```

This string constant also can be incorporated within a DRAW statement as a *substring* by preceding it with an X and trailing it with a semicolon. For instance, the above statement is equivalent to

```
A$ = "U2 L3 D2 R3": DRAW "S40 XA$;"
```

FURTHER EXAMPLE

8. The following program draws the three sailboats of Figure 4.

```
10 CLS: SCREEN 1: KEY OFF
20 A$ = "L60 E60 D80 L60 F20 R40 E20 L20"
```

DRAW

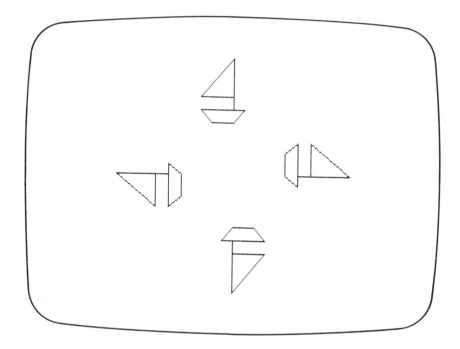

FIGURE 3

```
30 DRAW A$
40 DRAW "BM 75,60 XA$;"
50 DRAW "BM 260,140 XA$;"
60 LOCATE 6,7: PRINT 1
70 LOCATE 11,17: PRINT 2
80 LOCATE 16,30: PRINT 3
```

PART V ENHANCEMENTS IN BASIC 2.0 AND SUBSEQUENT VERSIONS

The angle command, A n, will rotate a figure by 90, 180, or 270 degrees. This feature has been extended in BASIC 2.0 and subsequent versions to allow a figure to be rotated any number of degrees. The statement

```
DRAW "TA n"
```

where n is between -360 and 360, specifies that all subsequent figures will be drawn rotated through n degrees.

The early versions of BASIC were able to color in closed regions of a drawing with the PAINT statement. (See the discusssion of PAINT for further

104

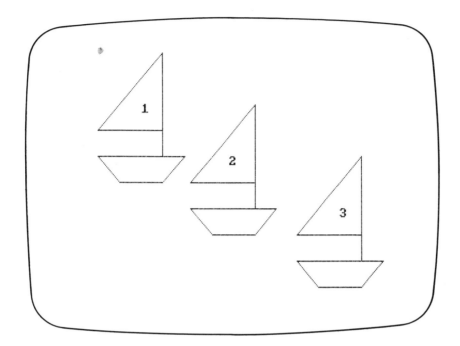

FIGURE 4

details.) Beginning with BASIC 2.0, this capability was incorporated into the DRAW statement. The statement

```
DRAW "P c,b"
```

has the same effect as the statement **PAINT (x,y),c,b** where the point (x,y) is the last point referenced.

FURTHER EXAMPLES

9.   The following program, which requires BASIC 2.0 or subsequent versions, draws the sailboat of Figure 5. The boat has been rotated through a counterclockwise angle of 45 degrees.

```
10 CLS: SCREEN 1: KEY OFF
20 A$ =   "L60 E60 D80 L60 F20 R40 E20 L20"
30 DRAW "TA45" + A$
```

Note: Line 30 could also have been written **30 n=45: DRAW "TA=n;"+A$.**

10.   The following program, which requires BASIC 2.0 or subsequent versions, draws a solid red boat, with a solid green sail, against a white background.

105

DRAW

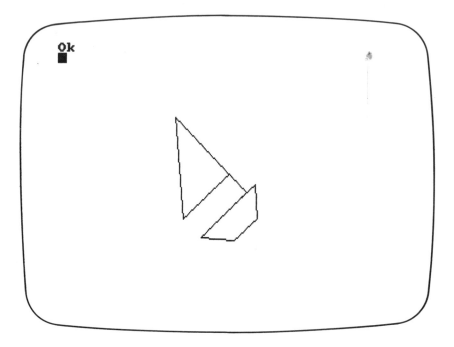

<small>FIGURE 5</small>

```
10 SCREEN 1,0: CLS: KEY OFF: COLOR 7,0
20 A$ = "L60 E60 D80 L60 F20 R40 E20 L20"
30 DRAW A$
40 DRAW "BD5" : DRAW "P 2,3"
50 PSET(150,90),1: DRAW "P 1,3"
```

In line 40, ''BD5'' was used to set a point in the boat as the last point refer-enced. The two statements in line 40 could have been combined as **40 DRAW "BD5 P 2,3"**.

COMMENTS

1. We have consistently used uppercase letters in our DRAW statements and have included spaces to improve readability. Neither of these conventions is necessary. For instance, line 20 of Example 8 could have been written

```
20 A$ = "l60e60d80l60f20r40e20l20"
```

2. Whenever the subcommands U, D, L, R, E, F, G, or H are followed by the number 1, the 1 can be omitted. For instance, line 40 of Example 7 can be written

106

```
40 DRAW "BM +1,0 L3 E3 D4 L3 F R2 E L"
```

3.   In medium-resolution graphics, a horizontal line segment of 6 units and a vertical line segment of 5 units will have the same actual length on the screen. In high-resolution graphics, a horizontal line segment of 12 units and a vertical line segment of 5 will have the same actual length on the screen. For example, the statements **SCREEN 1: DRAW "U50 R60 D50 L60"** and **SCREEN 2: DRAW "U50 R120 D50 L120"** produce squares.

4.   The ''P c,b'' subcommand that is incorporated into DRAW in versions of BASIC beginning with 2.0 does not permit tile painting.

5.   Programs that will be compiled should not use the command ''XA$;'' or any of the other commands involving variables and semicolons. An alternative is provided by the statement VARPTR$. See the discussion of VARPTR$ for further details.

6.   The parameter n in the subcommands U, D, L, R, E, F, G, and H can also assume negative integer values. The results are as expected. For instance, **DRAW "U -9"** has the same effect as **DRAW "D 9"** and **DRAW "E -9"** has the same effect as **DRAW "G 9"**.

EDIT

There are several ways to alter a single line of a program. One way is to use the LIST command to display the line and then, after moving the cursor up to the line, proceed to change the line. These two steps can be accomplished at once with a single EDIT command.

The command

```
EDIT n
```

displays the line numbered n and positions the cursor at the first digit of the line number.

COMMENTS

1.   The EDIT command primarily is used in direct mode. When used in a program, it displays the line to be edited, but prevents the program from continuing with CONT.

2.   If there is no line with the given number, an "Undefined line number" error message is produced.

3.   The command

```
EDIT .
```

produces the entered line that was most recently displayed on the screen. (See Example 2 for an illustration of the subtleties of this form of the EDIT command.)

4.   Editing a program line also clears all variables from memory, removes all information that has been set with DEF FN or DEFtype statements, RESTOREs all data, causes all DIMensioned arrays to become undimensioned, closes all open files, and disables event trapping that has been set with statements such as ON ERROR, ON KEY(n), ON PEN, ON STRIG(n), ON PLAY(n), and ON TIMER. In graphics modes, the "last point referenced" is set to the center of the screen and the effects of previously executed WINDOW and VIEW statements are voided. OPTION BASE 1 is reset to OPTION BASE 0, the speaker is turned off, and lightpens and joystick buttons are deactivated. In BASIC 2.1, Music Foreground is reset to Music Background. In all other versions of BASIC, Music Background is reset to Music Foreground. When a line is edited inside a subroutine, the computer forgets that a GOSUB has occurred; when a line is edited inside a FOR . . . NEXT or WHILE . . . WEND loop, the computer forgets that the loop is active.

EXAMPLES

1.   10 PRINT "TEN"
     20 PRINT "TWENTY"

108

```
EDIT 10
10 PRINT "TEN" (This line displayed automatically.)
```

2.
```
10 PRINT "TEN"
20 PRINT "TWENTY"
15 PRINT "FIFTEEN"
EDIT .
15 PRINT "FIFTEEN" (This line displayed automatically.)
LIST
10 PRINT "TEN"
15 PRINT "FIFTEEN"
20 PRINT "TWENTY"
Ok
EDIT .
20 PRINT "TWENTY" (This line displayed automatically.)
```

END

Traditionally, the last executable line in a BASIC program consists of the statement END to indicate that execution is complete. Programs for the IBM PC do not have to end with END. However, the END statement can be used for other purposes.

Including the statement

```
END
```

in a program causes the program to stop execution at that statement. The letters Ok are displayed, the computer returns to direct mode, and all open files are closed.

COMMENTS

1.   After the execution has been ENDed, there are four options for continuing: CONT, GOTO, GOSUB, and RUN. The CONT command causes the program to continue execution beginning with the statement after the END statement. The statements GOTO m, RUN m, and GOSUB m cause execution to resume at line m. The RUN command reruns the program from the beginning.

2.   After the program ENDs and the computer is in direct mode, you can display and change values of variables and make calculations. However, if you enter or delete a line of the program or execute one of the statements CLEAR, MERGE, or CHAIN MERGE, you cannot use CONT to resume execution of the program. You can continue, however, by using a GOTO or GOSUB statement.

3.   The STOP statement is similar to the END statement. Both cause the program to stop execution and can be followed by CONT, GOTO, GOSUB, or RUN to resume execution. There are two primary differences. STOP leaves all opened files open, whereas END closes them. Also, STOP causes a ''Break in n'' message to be displayed.

EXAMPLES

1.   The following program will display the balance after each month (for 360 months) for a $100,000 mortgage at 12% interest compounded monthly. Upon running the program you will see the balances for the first 12 months, followed by the letters Ok. If you then press the function key F5 (or type CONT and press the Enter key), the next 12 months will be displayed, and so on.

```
10 FOR I = 1 TO 349 STEP 12
20   FOR J = 0 TO 11
30     PRINT I+J,
```

```
45   PRINT USING "##,###.##";102861.26-2861.26*1.01^(I+J)
50   NEXT J
60   END
70 NEXT I
```

Without the END statement, the first 338 months would have flickered by too fast to be read and only the last 22 months would have been clearly displayed.

2.
```
10 A = 30
20 PRINT 20
30 PRINT A
40 END
50 PRINT 50
RUN
 20
 30
Ok
A = 40
Ok
GOTO 30
 40
Ok
CONT
 50
Ok
RUN
 20
 30
Ok
30 PRINT A+100     (This line entered by user.)
CONT
Can't continue
Ok
```

APPLICATIONS

1.   Programmers normally insert an END statement before a subroutine in order to guarantee that the subroutine will only be executed as the result of a GOSUB statement.

2.   The END statement can be used to have two programs in memory at the same time. The first could consist of lines 10-1000, with the last line containing an END statement. The second program could consist of lines 2000-3000. The first program could then be executed with a RUN command and the second program executed with the command RUN 2000.

3.   The END statement is sometimes used to terminate programs containing data files to guarantee that all files will be closed.

END

4.   END can be used to provide an exit from a program by including a line such as `INPUT "Do you want to exit? (Y/N) ",A$: IF A$="Y" THEN END`.

The ENVIRON statement is not valid for versions of BASIC prior to BASIC 3.0.

DOS has an environment table that stores equations of the form "NAME=VALUE". If the computer is turned on with the DOS diskette in drive A, the environment will contain the two equations "PATH= " and "COMSPEC=A:\COMMAND.COM". The first entry in the initial environment table tells the computer to search only the current directory when looking for a command. The second entry tells the computer where the file COMMAND.COM is located. The environment table can be altered by the DOS commands PATH, PROMPT, and SET. The PATH command is used to specify additional directories to be searched when a command or batch file is not found by a search of the current directory. It places an equation of the form "PATH=list of paths" into the environment. The PROMPT command sets a new system prompt and enters an equation of the form "PROMPT=code for prompt" into the environment. The SET command will place *any* equation of the form "NAME=VALUE" into the environment. Programs that we run on the computer can check the environment to see if there are any equations that concern it. See the Disk Operating System Reference Manual for further details.

When BASIC is invoked with the command BASIC or BASICA, an environment table is set up for BASIC. This table initially contains the same equations that were in DOS prior to invoking BASIC. The BASIC statement ENVIRON is used to alter BASIC's environment table in much the same way as PATH, PROMPT, and SET alter DOS's environment. If NAME is a string containing no blanks, then the statement

```
ENVIRON "NAME=;"
```

will remove from BASIC's environment any equation whose left side is identical to NAME. If VALUE is a string, other than the null string or the string ";", then the statement

```
ENVIRON "NAME=VALUE"
```

has one of the following two effects.

1. If there is already an equation in the environment whose left side is identical to NAME, then the right side of the equation is changed to VALUE and the equation is moved to the end of the table.

2. If there is no equation in the environment whose left side is identical to NAME, then the equation "NAME=VALUE" is added to the end of the environment table.

COMMENTS

1. The maximum number of bytes in BASIC's environment table is the multiple of 16 that is equal to or just larger than the number of bytes in

ENVIRON

DOS's environment just before BASIC was invoked. To create space for a large BASIC environment, use SET to create some large equations in DOS's environment and then use the ENVIRON statement with a semicolon to delete them.

2. When the SHELL statement is executed in BASIC, a second copy of COMMAND.COM is loaded into memory and run. This second copy of DOS is referred to as a child of BASIC and inherits BASIC's environment as its own. Hence, a program run under this copy of DOS can make use of strings passed to it from BASIC. Such a program is said to be a child of this copy of DOS. However, when we return to BASIC, BASIC's environment will be the same as it was before the SHELL statement was executed, even if its child's environment was altered. The environment of a child is never passed back to a parent. See the discussion of SHELL for further details.

3. ENVIRON distinguishes between upper and lowercase letters.

4. The equal sign or the semicolon in the equation can be replaced by a space. That is, the statement `ENVIRON "NAME=VALUE"` can also be written `ENVIRON "NAME VALUE"` and the statement `ENVIRON "NAME=;"` can also be written `ENVIRON "NAME="` or `ENVIRON "NAME "`.

5. ENVIRON is a reserved word in BASIC 2.0 and 2.1. Although the statement is not documented in either version, it can be executed in both. However, we suspect that the statement had not been completely debugged when these versions were released.

EXAMPLES

For each of the following examples, suppose that before invoking BASIC, DOS's environment consisted of the following equations.

```
PATH=
COMSPEC=A:\COMMAND.COM
ALPHA=abcdefghijklmnopqrstuvwxyz
BETA=Personal Computer
```

1. ```
   ENVIRON "BETA=;"
   Ok
   ENVIRON "ALPHA=12345"
   Ok
   ENVIRON "xyz=Hello"
   Ok
   ENVIRON "XYZ=;"
   Ok
   ```

At this point, the contents of DOS's environment will be exactly as before, and BASIC's environment will be as follows:

```
PATH=
COMSPEC=A:\COMMAND.COM
```
```

ALPHA=12345
xyz=Hello

2.   The following program illustrates the limitation on the size of BASIC's environment.

```
ENVIRON "Today=Wednesday"
Out of memory
Ok
ENVIRON "ALPHA=;"
ENVIRON "Today=Wednesday"
Ok
```

3.   The following program illustrates the fact that whereas BASIC's environment is passed to the copy of DOS that is its child, it is not passed to the original copy of DOS that is its parent. The DOS command SET, without an equation, displays the contents of DOS's environment.

```
10 ENVIRON "ALPHA=;": REM Make room for another equation
20 ENVIRON "PROMPT=Hello: "
30 CLS
40 SHELL
RUN


The IBM Personal Computer DOS
Version 3.00 (C)Copyright IBM Corp 1981, 1982, 1983, 1984


Hello: SET
PATH=
COMSPEC=A:\COMMAND.COM
BETA=Personal Computer
PROMPT=Hello:


Hello: EXIT
Ok
SYSTEM


A>SET
PATH=
COMSPEC=A:\COMMAND.COM
ALPHA=abcdefghijklmnopqrstuvwxyz
BETA=Personal Computer


A>
```

ENVIRON

APPLICATIONS

1.   Assembly language programs can read environment equations entered by the user and thereby can pass information from program to program.

2.   A statement of the form ENVIRON ''PATH=list of paths'' can be used to designate a list of directories where DOS should search for a specified command after DOS is invoked as a child of BASIC.

ENVIRON$

The ENVIRON$ statement is not valid for versions of BASIC preceding BASIC 3.0.

DOS has an environment table that stores equations of the form "NAME=VALUE". (See the discussion of ENVIRON for a detailed description of environments.) When BASIC is invoked with the command BASIC or BASICA, an environment table is set up for BASIC. This table initially contains the same equations that were in DOS before invoking BASIC. The BASIC statement ENVIRON is used to alter BASIC's environment table, and the function ENVIRON$ is used to read the table. If the equation "NAME=VALUE" is in BASIC's environment, then the value of the function

```
ENVIRON$("NAME")
```

will be the string VALUE. If n is an integer from 1 to 255, then the value of

```
ENVIRON$(n)
```

will be the nth equation in BASIC's environment.

COMMENTS

1. The value of the ENVIRON$ function will be the null string if the argument does not correspond to any equation in the environment.

2. ENVIRON$ distinguishes between upper and lowercase letters.

3. ENVIRON$ is a reserved word in BASIC 2.0 and 2.1. Although the statement is not documented in either version, it can be executed in both. However, we suspect that the statement had not been completely debugged when these versions were released.

EXAMPLES

For each of the following examples, suppose that prior to invoking BASIC, DOS's environment consisted of the following equations.

```
PATH=
COMSPEC=A:\COMMAND.COM
ALPHA=abcdefghijklmnopqrstuvwxyz
BETA=Personal Computer
```

1.  ```
    PRINT ENVIRON$("ALPHA")
    abcdefghijklmnopqrstuvwxyz
    Ok
    ```

2. In the following example, the null string is returned since the ENVIRON$ function treats "beta" as a different word than "BETA".
    ```

ENVIRON$

```
PRINT ENVIRON$("beta")

Ok
```

3.  ```
    10 FOR I = 1 TO 5
    20 PRINT ENVIRON$(I)
    30 NEXT I
    RUN
    PATH=
    COMSPEC=A:\COMMAND.COM
    ALPHA=abcdefghijklmnopqrstuvwxyz
    BETA=Personal Computer

    Ok
    ```
    ```

The EOF function is used when reading a file and tells us if we have reached the end of the file. See Appendix F for a discussion of sequential and random files.

After a sequential file has been OPENed FOR INPUT with reference number n, information can be read from the file, in order, starting at the beginning of the file. At any time, the value of the function

```
EOF(n)
```

will be −1 if the end of the file has been reached and will be 0 otherwise. When a nonempty random file is first OPENed (with reference number n), the value of EOF(n) is 0. After the statement GET #n,r is executed, the value of EOF(n) will be −1 if r is greater than the largest record number and otherwise will be 0.

EXAMPLES

1. Suppose that the file named CITIES resides on the disk in drive B and contains the names and populations of all of the cities in the USA. Also, assume that the information has been entered with statements of the form WRITE #3, C$,P. The following program will search the file for all cities having a population of between 4 and 5 million people.

```
10 OPEN "B:CITIES" FOR INPUT AS #
20 INPUT #3, C$, P
30 IF P>4E+6 AND P<5E+6 THEN PRINT C$,P
40 IF EOF(3) = -1 THEN END
50 GOTO 20
RUN
Detroit        4435051
Philadelphia   4824110
Ok
```

2. The program in Example 1 could have also been written as follows:

```
10 OPEN "B:CITIES" FOR INPUT AS #3
20 WHILE EOF(3) = 0
30   INPUT #3, C$, P
40   IF P>4E+6 AND P<5E+6 THEN PRINT C$,P
50 WEND
60 CLOSE #3
```

Note: There is one slight difference between the programs in Examples 1 and 2. The program in Example 2 will handle the case where CITIES is a null file, that is, one OPENed FOR OUTPUT, never written to, and then closed. In

EOF

this case, the program in Example 1 will produce the error message "Input past end in 20".

COMMENTS

1.   Line 40 of Example 1 could have also been written **40 IF EOF(3) THEN END**. The condition EOF(3) = −1 will be true if the end of the file has been reached and will be false otherwise. False conditions are thought of as having the value zero, and true conditions as having nonzero values. Inserting the number 0 after the word IF has the same effect as inserting a false condition, and inserting the number −1 has the same effect as inserting a true condition. Similarly, line 20 in Example 2 could have been written **20 WHILE NOT EOF(3)**.

2.   The character # should never be used with an EOF function. For instance, requesting the value of EOF(#3) produces the message "Syntax error".

3.   BASIC 2.0 and subsequent versions allow standard output and input to be redirected when BASIC is first invoked. The function EOF(0) returns the end of file condition for the standard input device. For instance, if standard input has not been redirected, then EOF(0) refers to the keyboard.

APPLICATIONS

1.   Usually we do not know how many items of information reside in a certain sequential data file, and therefore, we must rely on the EOF function to tell us when we have reached the end of the file.

2.   EOF also may be used with a communications file. In this case, EOF(1) will be true (value=−1) if the communications buffer is not empty and false (value=0) if the communications buffer is empty.

3.   Executing a GET statement with a record number that is too large does not necessarily produce an error message. The EOF function can be used to detect this occurrence.

120

An ERASE statement is like a selective CLEAR statement. Whereas a CLEAR statement eliminates all variables from memory, an ERASE statement eliminates just designated array variables. The statement

```
ERASE arrayname
```

deletes the specified array. Several arrays can be ERASEd with one ERASE statement by listing all of the names, separated by commas. (See the discussion of the DIM statement for further information about arrays.)

EXAMPLES

1.
```
10 A(5) = 34
20 ERASE A
30 PRINT A(5)
RUN
 0
Ok
```

2.
```
10 SALES(5) = 12: CUST$(5) = "AL ADAMS"
20 Z(5) = 20012: P$(5) = "123-4567"
30 ERASE SALES, CUST$
40 PRINT SALES(5); CUST$(5); Z(5); P$(5)
RUN
 0   20015 123-4567
Ok
```

3.
```
10 DIM A(100,100)          10 DIM A(100,100)
20 DIM B(70,70)            15 ERASE A
RUN                        20 DIM B(70,70)
Out of memory in 20        RUN
Ok                         Ok
```

4. In the program on the left below, we reDIMension the array without first eraseing it.

```
10 A(5) = 23               10 A(5) = 23
20 DIM A(25)               15 ERASE A
RUN                        20 DIM A(25)
Duplicate Definition in 20 RUN
Ok                         Ok
```

APPLICATIONS

1. The ERASE statement is used if we are short of memory space, as in Example 3, or if we want to reDIMension an array, as in Example 4.

ERDEV and ERDEV$

The ERDEV (ERror in DEVice) and ERDEV$ variables are not valid for versions of BASIC preceding BASIC 3.0.

The video screen, keyboard, printer, modem, and disk drives are some examples of devices. The first four are called *character* devices since they process characters serially. Disk drives are called *block* devices since they do random input and output into sectors of the disk. Character devices have names of at most eight characters such as SCRN, CON, LPT1, and AUX. Block devices have two-byte names such as A: , B: , and C: .

When a device error occurs, values are assigned to the variables ERDEV and ERDEV$. The value of

ERDEV

provides information about the type of error and gives certain attributes of the device. The value of

ERDEV$

is the name of the device.

If the device is a character device, the value of ERDEV will be a negative number and the value of ERDEV$ will be an eight-character string containing the name of the device. If the device is a block device, the value of ERDEV will be a positive number and the value of ERDEV$ will be a two-character string containing the name of the device.

The value of ERDEV is an integer from -32768 to 32767, which is stored in two bytes of memory. The two bytes can be determined by executing

```
DEF SEG: A%=ERDEV: B=VARPTR(A%): PRINT PEEK(B); PEEK(B+1)
```

The first byte identifies the type of error as follows:

First Byte	Description of Error
0	Attempt to write on write-protected diskette
1	Unknown unit
2	Drive not ready
3	Unknown command
4	Data error (CRC)
5	Bad request structure length
6	Seek error
7	Unknown media type
8	Sector not found
9	Printer out of paper
10	Write fault
11	Read fault
12	General failure

ERDEV and ERDEV$

To interpret the second byte, first use Appendix K to obtain the binary representation of the byte. The leftmost three bits of the binary representation provide the following information.

Value of Bit	*Information*
leftmost bit = 1	character device
leftmost bit = 0	block device
second bit from left = 1	IOCTL is supported
second bit from left = 0	IOCTL not supported
third bit from left = 1	non IBM format (block only)
third bit from left = 0	IBM format

EXAMPLES

1. When the following program was first executed, the printer was not turned on. The second time that the program was executed, the printer was turned on but was out of paper. The results obtained depend on the printer used. An EPSON FX-80 was used in this example. Had an IBM PC Graphics Printer or an EPSON MX-80 been used, ERDEV would have had the same value for each run, -32759. The number 128 has binary representation 10000000.

```
10 ON ERROR GOTO 100
20 LPRINT "Hello"
30 END
100 PRINT ERDEV; ERDEV$
110 DEF SEG: A%=ERDEV: B=VARPTR(A%)
120 PRINT PEEK(B); PEEK(B+1)
130 RESUME 30
RUN
-32758 LPT1
 10   128
Ok
RUN
-32759 LPT1
  9   128
Ok
```

2. When the first SAVE statement was executed, there was no diskette in drive A. Then a write-protected diskette was placed in drive A. The binary representation of 0 is 00000000.

```
SAVE "A:MYPROGRAM"
Disk not Ready
Ok
```

ERDEV and ERDEV$

```
PRINT ERDEV; ERDEV$
 2 A:
Ok
DEF SEG:A%=ERDEV:B=VARPTR(A%):PRINT PEEK(B);PEEK(B+1)
 2  0
Ok
SAVE "A:MYPROGRAM"
Disk Write Protect
Ok
PRINT ERDEV; ERDEV$
 0 A:
Ok
DEF SEG:A%=ERDEV:B=VARPTR(A%):PRINT PEEK(B);PEEK(B+1)
 0  0
Ok
```

COMMENT

The words ERDEV and ERDEV$ are listed as reserved words in BASIC 2.0 and 2.1, even though the statements are not documented in these versions of BASIC. They can be executed in BASIC 2.0 and 2.1 but we suspect that they might not always perform properly there.

Appendix E lists the error messages that can result when running a program. A subroutine (referred to as an *error handling subroutine*) can be written to take corrective measures instead of displaying error messages. Let's suppose that the error handling subroutine begins on line n. After the statement **ON ERROR GOTO n** is encountered, any error causes the program to branch to line n. (This process is referred to as error trapping.) RESUME statements are located in the error handling subroutine to branch back to other parts of the program. Within the subroutine itself, the variables ERR and ERL are used to identify the type and location of the error.

Most of the error messages in Appendix E have a number. Some of the messages and their numbers are:

    2 Syntax error
    4 Out of DATA
    13 Type mismatch
    15 String too long
    25 Device Fault
    27 Out of paper

When an error is trapped by an error trapping subroutine, the number of the error is assigned to the variable

    ERR

and the number of the line in which the error occurred is assigned to the variable

    ERL

EXAMPLES

```
1.  10 ON ERROR GOTO 50
    20 INPUT "NAME"; N$
    30 PRINT STRING$(250,N$)+N$
    40 END
    50 PRINT ERR; ERL
    60 END
    RUN
    NAME? Dan
    DDDDDDDDDDDDDDDDDDDDDDDDDDDDDDDDDDDDDDDDDDDDDDDDDDDDDDDDDDDDDDDDDDD
    DDDDDDDDDDDDDDDDDDDDDDDDDDDDDDDDDDDDDDDDDDDDDDDDDDDDDDDDDDDDDDDDDDD
    DDDDDDDDDDDDDDDDDDDDDDDDDDDDDDDDDDDDDDDDDDDDDDDDDDDDDDDDDDDDDDDDDDD
    DDDDDDDDDDDDDDDDDDDDDDDDDDDDDDDDDDDDDDDDDDDDDDDDDDDDDDDDDDDDDDDDDDD
    DDDDDDDDDDDDan
    Ok
    RUN
```

ERR and ERL

```
NAME? Amanda
 15  30
Ok
```

Strings cannot have more than 255 characters.

2.   The following program scans a list of numbers and prints those numbers larger than 8. In the event that an item in the list cannot be recognized immediately as a number, the item and its location are printed. When the program was run, the printer was switched on but had no paper in it and was not ON LINE.

```
10 ON ERROR GOTO 60
20 N=0
30 N=N+1: READ A
40 IF A>8 THEN LPRINT A
50 GOTO 30
60 IF ERR=2 THEN READ A$: LPRINT "ITEM";N;"IS ";A$:
   N=N+1: GOTO 140
70 IF ERR=4 THEN END
80 IF ERR=27 GOTO 100
90 IF ERR=25 THEN PRINT "Printer is not ON LINE.":GOTO 120
100 PRINT "Either printer is not turned on"
110 PRINT "or printer is out of paper."
120 PRINT
130 INPUT "Press Enter after checking printer.",E$
140 RESUME
150 DATA 2, 9, ten, 3, 10
RUN
Either printer is not turned on
or printer is out of paper.

Press Enter after checking printer.
Printer is not ON LINE.

Press Enter after checking printer.
Ok
```

After receiving the first news, we put paper into the printer, and after receiving the second, we put the printer ON LINE. The printer typed

```
 9
ITEM 3 IS ten
 10
```

3.   Consider the program of Example 2 with line 150 changed as below:

```
150 DATA $1, 2, 9, ten, 3, 10
```

126

```
RUN
Device Fault in 60
Ok
```

In this case, the problem with the printer occurred while we were in the error handling subroutine, and hence the error was not trapped. So, the error message was displayed on the screen, and the execution of the program was terminated.

4. The errors in the following program arise because the RIGHT$ and LEFT$ functions only operate on strings.

```
10 ON ERROR GOTO 40
20 PRINT LEFT$(1234,3);
30 PRINT RIGHT$(1234,3)
40 IF ERL=20 THEN PRINT 123;: RESUME NEXT
50 IF ERL=30 THEN PRINT 234: END
RUN
 123   234
Ok
```

COMMENTS

1. When errors occur as the result of statements entered in direct mode, the variable ERL is always assigned the number 65535. (The maximum allowable line number in a BASIC program is 65529.) This is illustrated in the following program.

```
PRINT LEFT$(1234, 3)
Type mismatch
Ok
PRINT ERR; ERL
 13   65535
Ok
```

2. The conditions **ERL=m** and **m=ERL** have the same meaning. However, only the first form is affected by a RENUM command. The second form should be used if m is 65535.

APPLICATIONS

The variables ERR and ERL are used primarily in error handling subroutines to sort out the types and locations of errors. Statements of the form **IF ERR=n AND ERL=m THEN RESUME r** are used to take the appropriate course of action.

ERROR

Appendix E lists the error messages that can result from running a program. Most of the error messages have a number. For instance, some of the error messages and their numbers are:

    2   Syntax error
    4   Out of DATA
   13   Type mismatch

In BASIC 2.0 and subsequent versions, the numbers range from 1 to 76, with the exception of 21, 28, 31 through 49, 56, 59, 60, and 65. In earlier versions of BASIC, the numbers 63, 64, and 65 are also skipped. When the statement

    ERROR n

(where n is one of the error message numbers) is encountered during the execution of a program, the effect is exactly the same as if the error corresponding to the number n actually occurred. Execution of the program will terminate and the appropriate error message will be displayed or, if an ON ERROR statement appears in the program, the program will branch to an error handling subroutine. (See the discussion of the ON ERROR statement for further details about error handling subroutines.)

Actually, the statement **ERROR n** is valid for any number from 1 to 255. When n is not one of the error message numbers given above, the corresponding error message is "Unprintable error".

EXAMPLES

1.   `10 ERROR 4`
     `RUN`
     `Out of DATA in 10`
     `Ok`

2.   `10 ON ERROR GOTO 40`
     `20 ERROR 13`
     `30 END`
     `40 PRINT "Computer"`
     `50 END`
     `RUN`
     `Computer`
     `Ok`

The order in which the lines were executed was 10, 20, 40, 50.

3.   `10 INPUT A`
     `20 ERROR A`
     `RUN`
     `? 80`
     `Unprintable error in 20`

```
Ok
RUN
? 2
Syntax error in 20
20 ERROR A
```

4.   After an error is made, the variable ERR is automatically assigned the number of that error. The following program can be used to write words backwards. At first, the program appears to be doing things the hard way. However, this approach employs an interesting programming concept that we discuss in Application 2 below.

```
10 ON ERROR GOTO 50
20 INPUT "PHRASE"; A$
30 ERROR 75
40 END
50 IF ERR=75 THEN GOSUB 70
60 RESUME NEXT
70 FOR I = LEN(A$) TO 1 STEP -1
80    PRINT MID$(A$,I,1);
90 NEXT I
100 RETURN
RUN
PHRASE? computer
retupmoc
Ok
```

APPLICATIONS

1.   When debugging a program, we can temporarily insert an ERROR statement into the program to test an error handling subroutine.

2.   In Example 4, the statement **ERROR 75** operated just like a BASIC statement. It could have appeared several times in the program, and every time it was invoked it would have performed the same task (reversing the letters in whatever string was currently assigned to the string variable A$). It's almost as if we created a new BASIC statement. In general, a program can define and use several new BASIC statements in an analogous manner.

EXP

An exponential function is a function of the form

$$b^x$$

The number b is called the base of the function. The most important exponential function is the one having as base a special number known as "e". The value of "e", to 7 significant digits, is 2.718282, and the value to 16 significant digits is 2.718281828459045. For any number x,

EXP(x)

has the value e^x.

COMMENTS

1. Although x can be any number, the value of EXP(x) will always be a positive number. Figure 1 contains the graph of y = EXP(x).

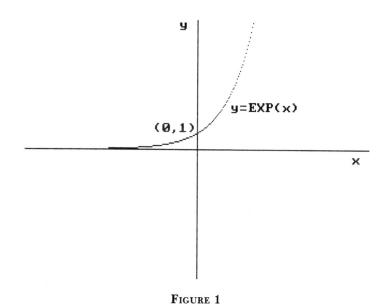

FIGURE 1

2. EXP is the inverse of the BASIC function LOG, the natural logarithmic function. For any x, EXP(x) is the number whose LOG is x. That is, for any number x, the value of LOG(EXP(x)) is x, and for any positive number x, the value of EXP(LOG(x)) is x.

3. Any other exponential function can be expressed in terms of EXP and LOG. For any number x, the value of b^x is EXP(x*LOG(b)).

130

4. In versions of BASIC preceding BASIC 2.0, the value of EXP(x) is always a single-precision number. BASIC 2.0 and subsequent versions provide the option of computing EXP(x) as a double-precision number. To exercise this option, invoke BASIC with the command BASIC/D or BASICA/D. Then, whenever x is a double-precision number, the value of EXP(x) will be computed as a double-precision number.

5. The number 1.701412E+38 is often referred to as *positive machine infinity*. The EXP function grows so fast that it reaches positive machine infinity when x = 88.02970. For x = 88.02970 and on, asking for EXP(x) results in the ''Overflow'' message being displayed and 1.701412E+38 (or 1.701411834604692D+38) being given as the value of EXP(x).

6. Let x be a single-precision number. For x less than or equal to -88.72284, the value of EXP(x) is displayed as 0. For x between -88.72283 and -88.02969 inclusive, asking for EXP(x) results in the ''Overflow'' error message being displayed. However, the value of EXP(x) still will be given correctly.

EXAMPLES

Examples 1 and 2 apply to BASIC 2.0 (or subsequent versions) without the /D option, or to any earlier version of BASIC. Example 3 requires BASIC 2.0 (or subsequent versions) with the /D option.

1. ```
PRINT EXP(0);EXP(1);EXP(2);EXP(-2.345)
 1 2.718282 7.389056 9.584721E-02
Ok
```

2. ```
PRINT EXP(3E-02); EXP(1.23456789)
 1.030455  3.436893
Ok
```

3. ```
10 A = 5: B = 3*A: C# = .123456789: D# = EXP(C#)
20 PRINT EXP(A);EXP(B);EXP(C#);D#
RUN
 148.4132 3269016 1.131401 1.131401062011719
Ok
```

Don't think that the value given for D# is accurate to 16 places. Only the first 6 digits are accurate. EXP(1.23456789) was computed as a single-precision number even though 1.23456789 is a double-precision number. The statement D# = EXP(C#) had the effect of converting 1.131401 to a double-precision number. That is, D# is actually CDBL(EXP(C#)).

4. ```
PRINT EXP(2%); EXP(2); EXP(2\B#)
 7.389056  7.389056  7.38905609893065
Ok
```

APPLICATIONS

1. If $1000 is invested at an interest rate of 12% compounded continuously, then the balance after t years is given by the formula

EXP

```
1000*EXP(.12*t)
```

In general, if P dollars is invested at interest rate r (compounded continuously), then the balance after t years is given by the formula

```
P*EXP(r*t)
```

2.   The decay of radioactive elements is described by the function EXP. For instance, if you start with 2 grams of strontium-90, the amount present after t years is given by the formula

```
2*EXP(-.0244*t)
```

3.   The normal curve of probability has the equation

$$y = (.3989423/s)*EXP(-.5*((x-m)/s)^2)$$

where s is the standard deviation and m is the mean.

Random files consist of ordered sets of records, each with the same length. (See Appendix F and Part II of the discussion of the OPEN statement.) Each of these records is subdivided into blocks of various widths, called fields. In Figure 1, a record of length 34 has been subdivided into 4 fields: NF\$, SF\$, CF\$, and AF\$ with widths of 20, 2, 10, and 2.

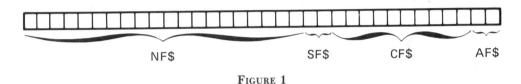

NF\$ SF\$ CF\$ AF\$

FIGURE 1

When setting up a random file, we must choose a width and name for each field. The widths can be any numbers, provided that the sum of the widths does not exceed the record length. The names must be string variables. The FIELD statement specifies the widths and names of the fields. Suppose that a random file has been OPENed AS #n. Then a statement of the form

```
FIELD #n, w1 AS strvar1, w2 AS strvar2, . . .
```

(where w1, w2, . . . are numbers and strvar1, strvar2, . . . are string variables) specifies that the first field of a record will have width w1 and name strvar1, the second field will have width w2 and name strvar2, and so on. For instance, the subdivision shown in Figure 1 corresponds to the statement

```
FIELD #1, 20 AS NF$, 2 AS SF$, 10 AS CF$, 2 AS AF$
```

where we have assumed that the file had been OPENed AS #1 with a record length of at least 34.

The FIELD statement does not write any information into the file nor does it read any information from the file. Information is written into the file by PUT statements and read from the file by GET statements. PUT and GET statements transfer entire records back and forth from the file to a buffer, while the FIELD statement establishes a template for the buffer.

For the moment, think of a buffer as a portion of memory consisting of successive bytes. After a FIELD statement has been executed, the statement **LSET strvar1 = strcon1** will place the string constant strcon1 into the first w1 bytes of the buffer. (If strcon1 has fewer than w1 characters, it will be padded on the right with spaces.) The statement **LSET strvar2 = strcon2** will place strcon2 into the next w2 bytes of the buffer, and so on. A statement of the form **PUT #n,m** then transfers the data in the buffer into the mth record of the actual file. (See the discussion of the PUT statement for further details.)

A statement of the form **GET #n,m** retrieves the mth record from the file

FIELD

and places it into the buffer. Then the data from the record can be accessed one field at a time by referring to each field by the name given in the FIELD statement. (See the discussion of the GET statement for further details.)

EXAMPLE

1.   The following program sets up a random file for Presidents of the United States. Each record consists of 4 fields containing Name, State, College attended, and Age upon taking office.

```
10 OPEN "B:PRES.USA" AS #1 LEN=34
20 FIELD #1, 20 AS NF$, 2 AS SF$, 10 AS CF$, 2 AS AF$
30 LSET NF$ = "George Washington"
40 LSET SF$ = "VA"
50 LSET CF$ = "none"
60 LSET AF$ = "57"
70 PUT #1,1
80 LSET NF$ = "John Adams"
90 LSET SF$ = "MA"
100 LSET CF$ = "Harvard"
110 LSET AF$ = "61"
120 PUT #1,2
130 FOR I = 1 TO 2
140 GET #1,I
150 PRINT NF$,SF$
160 NEXT I
170 CLOSE #1
RUN
George Washington          VA
John Adams                 MA
Ok
```

COMMENTS

1.   The # sign appearing in a FIELD statement can be omitted. For instance, line 20 of Example 1 can be written

```
20 FIELD 1, 20 AS NF$, 2 AS SF$, 10 AS CF$, 2 AS AF$
```

2.   The sum of the widths of the fields specified by a FIELD statement can be less than or equal to the record length given in the OPEN statement. If the sum is greater than the record length, a "Field overflow" error message results.

3.   More than one FIELD statement can be defined for the same file. When more than one FIELD statement is given for a file, all will be in effect at the

134

same time and allow for greater flexibility in accessing the file. (See Example 2.)

4.   If a string variable occurs in a FIELD statement, then we must avoid using it as the destination string in a LET or INPUT statement.(See Example 3 below and Comment 2 in the discussion of LSET and RSET.)

5.   Communications files may be opened as random files. This is especially useful in performing block output or input. The FIELD statement works the same way for communications files as for disk files.

FURTHER EXAMPLES

2.   In Example 1, add the line

```
25 FIELD #1, 22 AS IDENTF$, 12 AS BIOGF$
```

and change line 150 to

```
150 PRINT IDENTF$, BIOGF$
```

When the program is RUN, the output will be

```
George Washington    VA       none      57
John Adams           MA       Harvard   61
Ok
```

3.   In Example 1, add the line

```
25 SF$ = "State"
```

When the program is RUN, the output will be

```
George Washington            MA
John Adams                   MA
Ok
```

As we see, George Washington's home state is incorrect. Here's what happened. As a result of line 25, SF$ was defined as an ordinary string variable, and its value was recorded in the portion of memory known as string space. When line 40 was executed, the value in string space was changed to "VA" and when line 90 was executed, the value in string space was changed to "MA". When line 150 requested a value for SF$, the value from string space, "MA", was assigned to SF$. In order to avoid this type of error, we have included the letter F in the names of all field string variables. It reminds us that these strings must be handled differently than ordinary string variables.

FILES

A disk can be compared to a drawer of a filing cabinet, with its files corresponding to the manila folders. Each file has a name, just as each folder has a name written on its tab. Of course, folders can hold various types of information. For instance, a folder might contain a printout of a BASIC program, an alphabetized membership roll, or a list of tasks to attend to. Files that are created in BASIC are of three types; program, data, and binary files. Program files are created when a BASIC program is saved using the SAVE command. The creation of random and sequential data files is discussed in Appendix F. Memory image files are generally either machine language programs or graphic images that have been stored on the disk with BSAVE.

BASIC 2.0 and subsequent versions provide the capability of organizing files in a hierarchial directory structure. See Appendix D for details. The computer keeps track of a current directory for each drive, with the root directory as the default directory.

For versions of BASIC prior to BASIC 2.0, the FILES command is used to obtain a listing of the files on a diskette. Specifically, the command

```
FILES "B:*.*"
```

produces a list of all the files on the diskette in drive B. The command

```
FILES "B:filename"
```

will echo the filename if there is a file of that name on the diskette in drive B. Otherwise, the message "File not found" is produced.

With BASIC 2.0 and subsequent versions, the commands **FILES "B:*.*"** or **FILES "B:"** produce a list of all the files and sub-directories in the current directory of drive B. A command of the type **FILES "B:path"** echoes the name of the directory on drive B specified by "path", if found. (Otherwise it produces an error message.) A command of the type **FILES "B:path\"** lists the files and sub-directories in the specified directory. The above commands also display the name of the current directory and the number of bytes free on the drive.

COMMENTS

1. BASIC initially was invoked by typing the word BASIC or BASICA following one of the combinations A>, B>, C>, or D>. The combination used identifies the "current drive." For instance, had the screen read **B>BASIC** when BASIC was invoked, then drive B would be the current drive.

For versions of BASIC prior to BASIC 2.0, the command

```
FILES
```

produces a listing of the diskette in the current drive, and the command

136

FILES "DATA.MAY"

determines if a file named DATA.MAY resides on the diskette in the current drive.

In BASIC 2.0 and subsequent versions, the commands **FILES** , **FILES "path"**, and **FILES "path\"** function in an analogous manner with respect to the current drive.

2.   Filenames consist of two parts: a name of at most 8 characters followed by an optional period and extension of at most 3 characters. The two global filename characters   ?   and   *   can be used to specify classes of filenames. The character ? can be thought of as analogous to a wild card in a card game. It can assume any value. For instance, with versions of BASIC prior to BASIC 2.0, the command

FILES "B:D?TA.?AY"

produces a list of all files on the diskette in drive B that have 4-character names beginning with D and ending with   TA , and 3-character extensions ending with AY.

When the character   *   is used in a filename, the string represents any filename which begins with the characters preceding the *. An analogous result holds for extensions. For instance, with versions of BASIC prior to BASIC 2.0, the command

FILES "A:R*.*"

produces a list of all of the files on the diskette in drive A that have names beginning with   R . It will list all such names whether or not they have extensions. (For further examples of the use of the global filename characters, see the IBM Disk Operating System Manual.)

In BASIC 2.0 and subsequent versions, the two global filename characters produce analogous results.

3.   For purposes of naming files, lowercase letters are not distinguished from uppercase letters. However, the computer will always use uppercase letters when displaying file names.

EXAMPLES

In Examples 1, 2, 3, and 4, assume that you are using a version of BASIC prior to BASIC 2.0 and that the diskette in drive B contains the following files: DATA.APR, DATES.123, COLOR.BAS, LINES.BAS, and DIARY.AUG.

```
1.  FILES "B:LINES"
    File not found
    Ok
```

FILES

(*Note:* The entire filename must be given. BASIC automatically adds the extension BAS to any BASIC file or memory image file that does not already have an extension. Forgetting this extension is a common oversight.)

2. FILES "B:Lines.BAS"
   ```
   LINES   .BAS
   Ok
   ```

3. FILES "B:D*.A??"
   ```
   DATA    .APR    DIARY   .AUG
   Ok
   ```

4. FILES "B:DAT?A.APR"
   ```
   File not found
   Ok
   FILES "B:DA*.*"
   DATA    .APR        DATES   .123
   Ok
   ```

5. Assume that you are using BASIC 2.0 (or a later version), and drive C contains the files and directories presented as the example in Appendix D. Suppose that the current directory is ANN.

   ```
   FILES "C:"
   C:\ANN
            .    <DIR>         ..  <DIR> STOCKS  .BAS
   MATH         <DIR> NOVEL        <DIR> ADDRESS .DAT
    173568 Bytes free

   Ok
   ```

Note: The entries . and .. show up in the listing of every directory except the root directory. The entry . identifies the file as a subdirectory, and .. is used to locate the "parent" of this directory.

The function FIX throws away the decimal part of a number. Specifically, if x is a number, then the value of

```
FIX(x)
```

is the whole number of greatest magnitude that lies between x and 0, inclusive.

EXAMPLES

1. ```
   PRINT FIX(2.8); FIX(2/3)
    2  0
   Ok
   ```

2. ```
   PRINT FIX(-4.567); FIX(7.2E+04)
   -4  72000
   Ok
   ```

3. ```
   10 A = 123.456: B = -1.2345678
   20 PRINT FIX(A); FIX(B); FIX(A+B)
   RUN
    123 -1  122
   Ok
   ```

COMMENTS

1. The function FIX preserves the precision of the number on which it operates.

2. For positive numbers, FIX is the same as INT. However, for negative noninteger numbers x, the value of FIX(x) is one more than the value of INT(x).

APPLICATIONS

The following program rounds numbers to 3 decimal places. To round to r decimal places, replace 1000 with 1 followed by r zeros.

```
10 INPUT A#
20 PRINT FIX(1000*A#+.5*SGN(A#))/1000
```
```

FOR and NEXT

A sequence of program lines of the form

```
    :
50 FOR I=A to B
    :
90 NEXT I
    :
```

(where A and B have numeric values with A less than B) make up what is known as a FOR . . . NEXT loop. When line 50 is encountered, the variable I is assigned the value A. Line 90 adds 1 to the value of I and checks to see if the new value of I is greater than B. If so, execution continues with the line following line 90; if not, execution branches to the line following line 50. Hence, the lines between 50 and 90 are performed about B-A+1 times, once with I=A, once with I=A+1, once with I=A+2, etc. (*Note:* The numbers 50 and 90 were selected solely for illustrative purposes.)

EXAMPLES

1.  ```
    10 FOR I=2 TO 6
    20    PRINT I;
    30 NEXT I
    RUN
     2  3  4  5  6
    Ok
    ```

2. The letter I in Example 1 is referred to as the *index* of the FOR . . . NEXT loop. Any integer or single-precision numeric variable can be used as the index.

    ```
    10 PRINT "Outfield of '27 Yankees: ";
    20 FOR J=1 TO 3
    30    READ A$
    40    PRINT A$+" ";
    50 NEXT J
    60 DATA Meusel, Combs, Ruth
    RUN
    Outfield of '27 Yankees: Meusel Combs Ruth
    Ok
    ```

3.  ```
    10 INPUT A
    20 FOR T=A TO 2
    30    PRINT T; T*T,
    40 NEXT T
    RUN
    ```

```
? -1
-1  1          0  0          1  1          2  4
Ok
RUN
? .5
 .5   .25      1.5  2.25
Ok
```

(The last time that line 40 was executed, the value 2.5 was assigned to T. Since 2.5 > 2, the loop was terminated there.)

FURTHER DISCUSSION

So far, successive values of the index have been incremented by 1 each time the loop was traversed. Actually, any number can be used as the increment. In the following FOR . . . NEXT loop, where C is a positive number, line 50 initially sets the value of I to A, and line 90 adds C to the value of I. As before, the loop is repeated until the value of I exceeds B.

```
:
50 FOR I=A TO B STEP C
:
90 NEXT I
:
```

As a further embellishment, a FOR . . . NEXT loop can have its index steadily decreased. If C has a negative value and B is less than A, then line 90 decreases I by the magnitude of C, and the loop is repeated until the value of I is less than B.

COMMENTS

1. Within a single FOR . . . NEXT loop, the statement **NEXT I** should only appear once. The following program attempts to avoid displaying the unlucky number 13.

```
10 INPUT A
20 FOR I=A TO A+3
30    IF I=13 THEN NEXT I
40    PRINT I;
50 NEXT I
RUN
? 11
 11
NEXT Without FOR in 50
Ok
```

FOR and NEXT

The correct program is

```
10 INPUT A
20 FOR I=A TO A+3
30    IF I=13 THEN GOTO 50
40    PRINT I;
50 NEXT I
RUN
? 11
 11  12  14
Ok
```

2.   Every FOR . . . NEXT loop is equivalent to a loop using IF and GOTO statements. For example, the program in Example 1 is equivalent to this program:

```
10 I=2
20 PRINT I;
30 I=I+1
40 IF I<=6 GOTO 20
```

However, FOR . . . NEXT loops are preferable, since they execute faster and are easier for a programmer to decipher than IF and GOTO statements.

3.   The name of the index variable usually can be omitted in the NEXT statement. For instance, in Example 1, the last line of the program could have been **30 NEXT**. The name is only essential if branching takes place inside two FOR . . . NEXT loops. Consider the following program:

```
10 FOR I=1 TO 2
20    PRINT I;
30    GOTO 60
40 NEXT I
50 END
60 FOR J=10 TO 12
70    PRINT J;
75    IF J=11 GOTO 40
80 NEXT J
90 GOTO 40
RUN
 1  10  11  2  10  11
Ok
```

If line 40 is changed to **40 NEXT**, the outcome will be

```
RUN
 1  10  11
```

142

FOR and NEXT

```
NEXT without FOR in 40
Ok
```

Note: This program exhibits bad programming practice since it is not well-structured. One should not branch into the middle of a FOR . . . NEXT loop.

4. FOR . . . NEXT loops execute fastest when the index variable is omitted from the NEXT statement. Consider these programs:

```
10 FOR I=1 TO 10000          10 FOR I=1 TO 10000
20 NEXT I                    20 NEXT
```

On the PC and XT, the program on the left takes 12 seconds to run, whereas the program on the right runs in 9 seconds. On the AT, the programs execute in 5 and 3.6 seconds, respectively. (The same loop written with IF and GOTO statements uses over four times as much running time.)

5. A double-precision variable cannot be used as the index of a FOR . . . NEXT loop. Greatest efficiency is obtained by using an integer variable. For instance, the program on the left in Example 4 would run in 5 seconds on the PC if I was replaced by I%.

6. It is not uncommon for programs to contain time-consuming FOR . . . NEXT loops. To keep the user from thinking that the program has crashed, it is a good idea for the programmer to insert an assuring PRINT statement before entering the loop. Some possibilities are "Computing. Please wait." or "Searching for account. Short delay."

7. Consider a FOR . . . NEXT loop beginning with a statement of the form FOR I=A TO B STEP C. If A is greater than B, with C positive, or if B is greater than A, with C negative, none of the lines inside the loop will be executed and the program will branch to the statement after the statement containing the NEXT statement. If C is zero, an infinite loop will be produced, unless B is equal to A.

8. When using single-precision numbers, certain values of C can produce rounding errors that cause FOR . . . NEXT loops to perform differently than intended. However, precautions can be taken to guarantee the desired result. Consider:

```
10 FOR I=1 to 2 STEP .1
20    PRINT I;
30 NEXT I
RUN
 1  1.1  1.2  1.3  1.4  1.5  1.6  1.7  1.8  1.9
Ok
```

We expected the last number PRINTed to be 2. This can be achieved by

FOR and NEXT

changing line 10 to read **10 FOR I=1 to 2.05 STEP .1** . In general, when working with values of C which are not whole numbers, it is best to give an ending value that is C/2 more than the actual value at which you wish the loop to end.

9. A FOR . . . NEXT loop can contain another FOR . . . NEXT loop within it. However, the second loop must be completely inside the first loop. Schematically:

$$\text{first loop} \left\{ \begin{array}{l} \texttt{100 FOR I=A TO B} \\ \quad \vdots \\ \texttt{200} \qquad \left. \texttt{FOR J=D TO E} \right\} \quad \text{second loop} \\ \quad \vdots \\ \texttt{300} \qquad \texttt{NEXT J} \\ \quad \vdots \\ \texttt{400 NEXT I} \end{array} \right.$$

Such loops are referred to as *nested* loops. If the statements **NEXT J** and **NEXT I** were interchanged, this sequence of statements would not constitute valid nested loops and would produce the error message "NEXT without FOR in 400."

10. Consider the program in Comment 9. If the lines consisting of **NEXT J** and **NEXT I** were adjacent to each other, they could be combined into a single line consisting of the statement:

NEXT J,I

(Here, the order of the letters J and I cannot be reversed.) If there were a third FOR . . . NEXT loop with index variable K nested inside the second loop, and the statement **NEXT K** directly preceded the other two NEXT statements, the three statements could be combined into **NEXT K,J,I**, and so on.

11. The value of the index may be altered within a FOR . . . NEXT loop.

```
10 FOR I%=1 TO 20
20    PRINT I%;
30    IF I%=3 THEN I%=17
40 NEXT I%
RUN
 1  2  3  18  19  20
Ok
```

If the increment or the starting or stopping values are given by variables, the values of these variables may be changed inside the loop without affecting the execution of the loop. This is because the starting and stopping values and the increment are stored in special memory locations when the FOR statement is first encountered.

```
10 L=5: S=2
20 FOR I=1 TO L STEP S
30    PRINT I;
40    L=3: S=1
50 NEXT I
RUN
 1  3  5
Ok
```

12. Be sure to "close out" your loops if you want to provide an early exit. Don't use a routine like the following:

```
110 FOR I = 1 TO 100 STEP 2
120    X = [calculate]
130    IF X=FLAGVAL THEN 160
140    PRINT X
150 NEXT I
160 [continue]
```

Instead, use

```
110 FOR I = 1 TO 100 STEP 2
120    X = [calculate]
130    IF X=FLAGVAL THEN I=100: GOTO 150
140    PRINT X
150 NEXT I
160 [continue]
```

The second program frees up the portion of memory that was set aside to hold the values of the increment and the limits of the index.

13. The limits appearing in the FOR statement can consist of expressions to be computed. For instance, statements such as **FOR I=1 TO LEN(A$)** and **FOR I=SQR(X) TO X*X** are valid.

14. The routines performed by the combination FOR . . . NEXT also can be performed by the combination WHILE . . . WEND. (See the discussion of WHILE . . . WEND for further details.)

15. The computer will forget that it is executing a FOR . . . NEXT loop if one of the commands CHAIN MERGE, CLEAR, MERGE, NEW, or RUN is executed, or if a program line is entered or deleted.

16. A program will operate fastest if the most used variables are initialized

FOR and NEXT

before the others. Therefore, if I appears as the index of a long FOR . . . NEXT loop, then the statement I=0 should appear early in the program.

17. The words FOR and NEXT can be displayed by pressing Alt-F and Alt-N, respectively.

FURTHER EXAMPLE

4. The following program is used to alphabetize a list of members of a baseball team. The statement SWAP interchanges the values of the two string variables.

```
10 FOR I = 1 TO 9: READ A$(I): NEXT
20 FOR I = 1 TO 8: FOR J = 1 TO 8
30    IF A$(J)<=A$(J+1) THEN 50
40    SWAP A$(J),A$(J+1)
50 NEXT J, I
60 FOR I = 1 TO 9: PRINT A$(I)+" "; : NEXT
70 DATA Combs, Koenig, Ruth, Gehrig, Meusel, Lazzeri,
Dugan, Collins, Hoyt
RUN
Collins Combs Dugan Gehrig Hoyt Koenig Lazzeri Meusel Ruth
Ok
```

The program contains four FOR . . . NEXT loops, with the third loop nested inside the second.

APPLICATIONS

1. FOR . . . NEXT statements are among the most often used BASIC statements. The discussions in this handbook of the other BASIC statements reveal that many of them achieve their full power when used in conjunction with FOR . . . NEXT statements.

2. FOR . . . NEXT statements can be used to sort data from lists, prepare tables, graph functions, solve optimization problems, and produce intentional delays.

Each memory location contains a block of 8 binary bits (that is, zeros and ones), referred to as a byte. The number of RAM (Random Access Memory) locations varies from computer to computer. One K of memory consists of 1024 bytes. When BASIC is first invoked, information similar to the following is displayed on the screen:

```
The IBM Personal Computer Basic
Version A1.10 Copyright IBM Corp. 1981, 1982
35454 Bytes free

Ok
```

The third line tells us that there are 35454 memory locations available for use in storing and executing a BASIC program. Actually, we can determine at any time the amount of available bytes by using the function FRE. At any time, the value of

```
FRE(0)
```

is the number of bytes available to BASIC for use at that time.

EXAMPLES

1.  ```
    The IBM Personal Computer Basic
    Version A1.10 Copyright IBM Corp. 1981, 1982
    35454 Bytes free

    Ok
    PRINT FRE(0)
     35454
    Ok
    10 A = 123.45
    PRINT FRE(0)
     35440
    Ok
    RUN
    Ok
    PRINT FRE(0)
     35432
    Ok
    ```

The first time we requested the value of FRE(0), the value returned agreed with the third line of the original display. Then we stored a program into memory using up 14 bytes of memory. The line number required 2 bytes and the statement ''A = 123.45'' required 9 bytes. Two bytes were used to point
    ```

FRE

to the memory location of the next line of the program (or in this case to the end-of-program code), and one byte consisted of the character with ASCII value 0 which is placed at the end of every program line. Next, we ran the program and used an additional 8 bytes to define the variable A and store its value in memory.

2.   The following program illustrates the efficiency of using integer versus single-precision numeric constants.

```
10 PRINT FRE(0)
20 FOR I = 1 TO 10: A(I) = I: NEXT I
30 PRINT FRE(0)
40 FOR J = 1 TO 10: B%(J) = J: NEXT J
50 PRINT FRE(0)
RUN
 35353
 35292
 35253
Ok
```

The numbers 1 to 10 required 61 bytes when stored as single-precision numbers, but only 39 bytes when stored as integers.

FURTHER DISCUSSION

BASIC sets aside a portion of memory, referred to as string space, that is used to store the values of string variables. String space can become fragmented due to the reassigning of different values to the same variable. This results in portions of memory being wasted. Occasionally, BASIC will pause during the execution of a program and reorganize its string space. (In extreme cases this pause can last several minutes.) This procedure is referred to as "housecleaning" or "garbage collection." The FRE function can be used to clean house whenever we like. The value of

```
FRE(" ")
```

is the same as the value of FRE(0). However, requesting that FRE(" ") be computed also causes BASIC to clean house.

FURTHER EXAMPLE

```
3.   10 DIM A$(250)
     20 PRINT FRE(0)
     30 FOR I = 1 TO 250
     40    A$(I) = STRING$(I,"A")
     50 NEXT I
     60 PRINT FRE(0)
```

148

```
70 FOR J = 1 TO 250
80    A$(J) = STR$(J)
90 NEXT J
100 PRINT FRE(0)
110 PRINT FRE(" ")
RUN
 34541
 3158
 2258
 33633
Ok
```

Line 40 assigns to the Ith array variable the string of I letter As. This assignment uses most of the available memory. Line 80 reassigns to each of these variables the much shorter strings consisting of the indices of the variables expressed as strings. Although these new string constants really only require about 900 bytes of memory, string space is so fragmented that most of it is wasted. In line 110, the function FRE(" ") cleans house and frees up the unused bytes of memory.

COMMENTS

1. We invoke housecleaning by merely requiring that FRE(" ") be computed. Its value needn't be displayed. For instance, if line 110 of Example 3 is replaced by **110 A = FRE(" ")**, housecleaning still will occur.

2. The value of FRE(0) is the same as the value of FRE(N), where N is any numeric constant. For instance, line 10 of Example 2 could have been written **10 PRINT FRE(34.5)**. The actual number used is of no consequence.

3. The value of FRE(" ") is the same as the value of FRE(A$), where A$ is any string. For instance, line 110 of Example 3 could have been written **110 PRINT FRE("ABC")**. The actual string used is of no consequence.

APPLICATIONS

1. Programmers use FRE(0) while writing a program to ensure that there is sufficient space in memory to continue the program. If not, they can take certain steps, such as storing the values of array variables in a sequential file instead of in memory, to make more space in memory available.

2. The user of a piece of software might get confused if BASIC pauses to clean house when not expected. The programmer can use the FRE function to clean house at a time when the program is likely to pause anyway, or the programmer can arrange for a message such as "WAIT" to be displayed while housecleaning is taking place.

GET (Files)

Random files consist of ordered sets of records numbered 1, 2, 3, and so on, that reside on disks. Random files are accessed by statements of the form **OPEN filespec AS #n LEN=g**. (See Appendix F and Part II of the discussion of OPEN for further details.) When a file is OPENed, a portion of memory referred to as a *buffer* is set aside to hold records on their way to and from the file. The statement

    GET #n,r

places record number r, of the file with reference number n, into the buffer. (If the number r is omitted, the record after the one most recently transferred by a GET or PUT statement will be moved into the buffer.) Information is usually retrieved from the buffer by first using a FIELD statement to assign names to various sections of the buffer and then requesting these sections by name.

EXAMPLES

1. Suppose that the file "B:PRES" consists of the following consecutive records of length 22 numbered 1, 2, and 3.

    ```
    George Washington    VA
    John Adams           MA
    Thomas Jefferson     VA
    ```

The following program will display the contents of the file along with the number of each record:

```
10 OPEN "B:PRES" AS #1 LEN=22
20 FIELD #1, 22 AS TF$
30 FOR I = 1 TO 3
40    GET #1,I
50    PRINT I; TF$
60 NEXT I
70 CLOSE #1
RUN
 1 George Washington    VA
 2 John Adams           MA
 3 Thomas Jefferson     VA
Ok
```

Line 40 also could have read **40 GET #1**.

2. Consider the file of Example 1. The following program displays the presidents from Virginia.

```
10 OPEN "B:PRES" AS #1 LEN=22
20 FIELD #1, 20 AS NF$, 2 AS SF$
30 FOR I = 1 TO 3
40    GET #1,I
50    IF SF$ = "VA" THEN PRINT NF$
60 NEXT I
70 CLOSE #1
RUN
George Washington
Thomas Jefferson
Ok
```

COMMENTS

1. The # sign appearing in a GET statement can be omitted. For instance, line 40 of Example 1 also can be written as **40 GET 1,I**.

2. In certain situations, records can be read from the buffer by statements of the form **INPUT #n, A\$** and **LINE INPUT #n, A\$**. However, care must be taken to avoid an ''Overflow'' error message. (See the discussions of INPUT# and LINE INPUT# for further details.)

3. GET also may be used with communications files. In this case, the statement **GET #n,m** reads m bytes from the communications file designated as file n. Here m must be less than the number of bytes specified by the LEN option used in the statement OPEN ''COM . . . '' (if this option was used). If the LEN option was not used, then m may be any number up to and including the maximum number of bytes in the file buffer. Also, the parameter m may be omitted, in which case, the statement will read the entire file buffer.

4. In the event that the number r is greater than the largest record number, the statement **GET #n,r** will not produce an error message. However, after such a GET statement is executed the value of EOF(n) will be -1. The string returned by the GET statement will consist of null characters, the characters with ASCII value 0.

5. The LOC function can be used to determine the number of the record that was most recently read or written.

GET (Graphics)

The graphics GET statement is used in conjunction with the graphics PUT statement to make a copy of a rectangular portion of the screen, store it in memory, and reproduce it at a desired location on the screen. (See Appendix C for a discussion of specifying coordinates in graphic modes.)

A rectangular portion of the screen is designated by giving the coordinates of its upper left-hand corner (x1,y1) and its lower right-hand corner (x2,y2). (See Figure 1.) The information about the color of each point of the region will be stored in a numeric array. The statement

```
GET (x1,y1)-(x2,y2), arrayname
```

stores a description of the specified rectangle in the named array. The numerical array can be given a name corresponding to any precision: integer, single-, or double-precision.

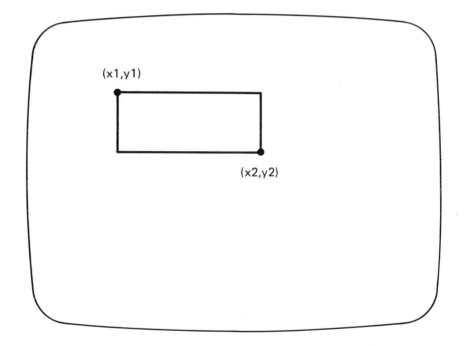

FIGURE 1

The array must first be DIMensioned. (See the discussion of the DIM statement.) In medium-resolution graphics mode, the size, n, of the array is determined in the following manner:

(a) Let h be the number of points in a horizontal side of the rectangle and v be the number of points in a vertical side, (h = x2 - x1 + 1 and v = y2 - y1 + 1).

152

(b) Calculate the number $(2*h + 7)/8$, multiply its integer part by v, and then add 4. Call this number b.

(c) The value of n should be:
   $(b/2) - 1$ for an integer array
   $(b/4) - 1$ for a single-precision array
   $(b/8) - 1$ for a double-precision array.

In high-resolution graphics mode, the procedure for determining the value of n is the same, except that the number 2 in step (b) is replaced by the number 1.

EXAMPLES

1. Determine an appropriate value of n for the following program:

```
10 SCREEN 1
20 DIM A%(n)
30 GET (4,20)-(25,60), A%
```

Solution: Line 10 specifies medium-resolution graphics. Since the name of the array ends with a % sign, it is an integer array.

(a) $h = 25 - 4 + 1 = 22$ $v = 60 - 20 + 1 = 41$

(b) $2*h + 7 = 2*22 + 7 = 51$
   $51/8 = 6.375$, which has integer part 6
   $b = 6*v + 4 = 6*41 + 4 = 250$

(c) $n = (250/2) - 1 = 124$

Therefore, line 20 can read **20 DIM A%(124)**.

2.
```
10 SCREEN 2: CLS
20 LOCATE 1,1: PRINT "B"
30 DIM C%(5)
40 GET (0,0)-(7,7),C%
50 FOR I = 0 TO 5
60    PRINT C%(I);
70 NEXT I
RUN
B
 8  8  26364  31846  26214  252
Ok
```

With integer arrays and high-resolution graphics, the first two entries of the array are the values of h and v. The remaining entries, when translated into a binary configuration, tell us exactly which points must be turned on to form the letter B.

3. The GET statement can be used to form new characters. The following program forms an arrow pointing northeast. Lines 20 through 70 draw the

GET (Graphics)

arrow, lines 80 and 90 encode the arrow into an integer array, lines 110 through 130 display the values of the array, and line 140 places a copy of the arrow on the third line of the screen.

```
10 SCREEN 1: CLS: KEY OFF
20 FOR I=0 TO 7
30    PSET (7-I,I)
40 NEXT I
50 FOR J=3 TO 6
60    PSET (J,0):PSET (7,7-J)
70 NEXT J
80 DIM A%(9)
90 GET (0,0)-(7,7),A%
100 CLS
110 FOR K = 0 TO 9
120    PRINT A%(K);
130 NEXT K
140 PUT (160,16),A%
RUN
 16  8 -253  3840  13056 -15616  771
 12  48  192
Ok                          /
```

COMMENTS

1. The statement GET requires Advanced BASIC. That is, the command BASICA must have been given when BASIC was invoked.

2. The three-step procedure given above for determining the number n actually gives the smallest acceptable size of the array. The array also can be DIMensioned with any number larger than n.

3. Normally, arrays with n less than 11 do not have to be specifically DIMensioned. However, such is not the case if the array will be used with a GET statement.

4. The rectangle to be stored can also be specified by giving its lower left-hand and upper right-hand corners.

APPLICATIONS

1. See the discussion of the PUT graphics statement to see how GET and PUT are used in computer animation.

2. In Example 2 we used GET to form an array for the letter B. By using the proper PUT statement, we can place this letter anywhere we like on the screen, not just in the locations allowed by the LOCATE statement. For instance, if we decide to label a point of a graph with the letter B, we can place the label exactly where it should be.

154

3.   In Example 3, we constructed a new character and used GET to encode it in an array. Now that we know the entries in that array, we can display the arrow on the screen whenever and wherever we like. The following program places the arrow emanating from the center of the screen.

```
10 SCREEN 1
20 DIM B%(9)
30 FOR I = 0 TO 9
40    READ D%: B%(I)=D%
50 NEXT I
60 DATA 16,8,-253,3840,13056,-15616,771,12,48,192
70 PUT (160,93),B%
```

GOSUB and RETURN

GOSUB statements act like GOTO statements, but with an important embellishment. When the statement

    GOSUB n

is encountered, the program branches to line n; that is, line n will be the next line executed. However, the computer remembers where it branched from, and when it encounters the statement

    RETURN

it branches back to the statement immediately following the GOSUB statement.

COMMENTS

1. A subroutine is a relatively small program that resides inside a larger program. The subroutine performs some specific task that may have to be repeated many times while running the main program. Subroutines that are entered by GOSUB statements must contain RETURN statements. The GOSUB statement branches to the first line of the subroutine. This explains the choice of name for the GOSUB statement.

2. In the event that several GOSUB statements are executed before a RETURN is encountered, the program will branch back to the statement following the most recent GOSUB statement. The next RETURN encountered causes a branching to the statement following the next most recent GOSUB, and so on. As a result, it is possible for one subroutine to call another.

3. There must be a line in the program having the line number specified in the GOSUB statement. Otherwise, the error message ''Undefined line number'' results.

4. Computed GOSUB statements (e.g., **A=100: GOSUB A**) are not allowed.

5. GOSUB, like RUN and GOTO, can be used in direct mode to start the execution of a program at any line. Unlike RUN, however, GOSUB will not clear memory of all variables, arrays, etc. And, unlike GOTO, if RETURN is encountered, the computer returns to direct mode without giving an error message. Thus, GOSUB can be used conveniently from direct mode to debug subroutines.

6. Executing one of the commands CLEAR, CHAIN, CHAIN MERGE, LOAD, MERGE, or NEW, or editing or deleting a program line causes BASIC to forget about any active GOSUB statements (i.e., GOSUB statements that have not been matched with RETURN statements).

    10 GOSUB 40
    20 PRINT 20

156

```
30 END
40 PRINT 40
50 CLEAR
60 RETURN
RUN
 40
RETURN without GOSUB in 60
Ok
```

7. See the discussion of the RETURN statement for further embellishments of RETURN.

EXAMPLES

1.
```
10 PRINT "One ";
20 GOSUB 100
30 PRINT "Three"
90 END
100 PRINT "Two ";
110 RETURN
RUN
One Two Three
Ok
```

We can think of lines 100 and 110 as consisting of a simple subroutine. Line 90 ensures that the subroutine cannot be entered accidentally. (If line 90 is deleted, the word Two will be printed a second time.)

2. The sequence in which the lines below are executed is 10, 20, 100, 110, 200, 210, 120, 130, 30, 90.

```
10 PRINT "One ";
20 GOSUB 100
30 PRINT "Five"
90 END
100 PRINT "Two ";
110 GOSUB 200
120 PRINT "Four ";
130 RETURN
190 END
200 PRINT "Three ";
210 RETURN
RUN
One Two Three Four Five
Ok
```

3. In the following program, the RETURN statement branches back to the statement after the GOSUB statement, not the line after the line containing the GOSUB statement.

157

GOSUB and RETURN

```
10 PRINT "One ";: GOSUB 100: PRINT "Three ";
20 PRINT "Four"
90 END
100 PRINT "Two ";:RETURN
RUN
One Two Three Four
Ok
```

APPLICATIONS

1. GOSUB statements allow programs to be written in blocks that can be saved and used in other programs.

2. It is good programming practice to break down a large program into smaller routines. In BASIC programming, each of these routines becomes a subroutine which is accessed by a GOSUB statement. With appropriate REM statements labeling each GOSUB statement, the main body of a program can be very easy to write and, more importantly, easy to verify. In turn, each subroutine should be simple enough so that it too is easy to understand and verify. This technique of programming is termed *top-down* or *structured* programming.

The statement

```
GOTO n
```

where n is the number of a line of the current program, causes line n to be the next line executed.

EXAMPLES

1.  ```
    10 PRINT "One ";
    20 GOTO 40
    30 PRINT "Three ";
    40 PRINT "Four ";
    50 PRINT "Five"
    RUN
    One Four Five
    Ok
    GOTO 30
    Three Four Five
    Ok
    ```

2.  ```
    10 INPUT A
    20 PRINT A; "squared is"; A*A
    30 GOTO 10
    RUN
    ? 8
      8 squared is 64
    ? -1
    -1 squared is 1
    ?
    Break in 10
    Ok
    ```

After the third question mark, we pressed Ctrl-Break.

COMMENTS

1. GOTO is frequently used with the IF statement in

    ```
    IF condition GOTO n
    ```

Whenever the condition following the word IF is true, line n of the current program will be the next line to be executed.

2. In direct mode, the statement **GOTO n** is similar to the statement **RUN n**. Both cause the program to be executed beginning with line n. However, the RUN statement automatically clears all variables from memory, removes all

GOTO

information that has been set with DEF FN and DEFtype statements, causes all DIMensioned arrays to become undimensioned, and closes all open files. The GOTO statement does none of these.

3. The statement GOTO should be used with moderation. Many programmers try to avoid its use entirely. Using GOTO for long jumps makes the program difficult to follow, modify, or debug.

4. Computed GOTOs are not permitted. For example, the statements **A=5: GOTO A** and **GOTO 4+5** produce the error message "Undefined line number."

5. The word GOTO can be displayed by pressing Alt-G.

FURTHER EXAMPLES

3.
```
10 INPUT "Did you chop down the cherry tree"; A$
20 IF A$ = "no" GOTO 10
RUN
Did you chop down the cherry tree? no
Did you chop down the cherry tree? yes
Ok
```

4.
```
10 A = 3
20 PRINT A + B
RUN
 3
Ok
B = 4: RUN
 3
Ok
B = 4: GOTO 10
 7
Ok
```

5. The following program, which requires Advanced BASIC, turns the computer into a simple musical instrument capable of playing the 7 notes A through G when the corresponding keys are pressed. Line 10 assigns the value of the pressed key to the variable A$ and line 20 plays this value. Line 30 then causes the process to repeat. To terminate this program press Ctrl-Break or any letter after G.

```
10 A$ = INKEY$
20 PLAY A$
30 GOTO 10
```

6. The following program functions as a 10-second timer. Line 10 resets the computer's clock. The clock will start ticking and the variable TIME$ will steadily change. When line 40 is encountered, if the seconds portion of the

time is 10, line 50 will be executed. Otherwise, line 30 is executed, the time is PRINTed, and so on.

```
10 TIME$ = "00:00:00"
20 CLS
30 LOCATE 10,30: PRINT TIME$
40 IF VAL(RIGHT$(TIME$,2)) < 10 THEN GOTO 30
50 LOCATE 10,30: PRINT TIME$: BEEP
```

```
7. 10 PRINT "Infinite loop  ";
   20 GOTO 10
   RUN
   Infinite loop   Infinite loop   Infinite loop   Infinite loop
   Infinite loop   Infinite loop   Infinite loop
   Break in 10
   Ok
```

This program will PRINT the words "Infinite loop" indefinitely. To get out of the program press Ctrl-Break.

APPLICATIONS

1. The GOTO statement allows us to repeat a process as long as we like. In Example 6, we kept PRINTing the time for 10 seconds. In Example 5, we PLAYed notes until we decided to stop.

2. When used in direct mode, the GOTO statement is a powerful debugging tool. We can set the values of the variables to whatever we like and then start the execution of the program at any point.

3. The GOTO statement can be used during program development to branch around time-consuming routines in order to test a new part of the program.

4. Suppose that a program produces graphics and we do not want to have the cursor and the prompt (Ok) appear at the end. This can be accomplished by making the last line of the program something like **999 GOTO 999**.

HEX$

The function HEX$ is used to convert whole numbers from their base 10 representations to their base 16 representations.

MATHEMATICAL PRELIMINARIES

Normally, we write integers in their decimal, that is base 10, representations. For instance, if r, s, t, u, v are digits from 0 to 9 then

$$rstuv$$

represents the number

$$r*10000 + s*1000 + t*100 + u*10 + v$$

or
$$r*10^4 + s*10^3 + t*10^2 + u*10 + v$$

In the hexadecimal representation of numbers, the number 16 plays the role of 10. Also, the digits 0 to 9 are supplemented with 6 additional digits called A, B, C, D, E, and F, which stand for the numbers 10, 11, 12, 13, 14, and 15, respectively. In hexadecimal notation

$$rstuv$$

represents the number

$$r*16^4 + s*16^3 + t*16^2 + u*16 + v$$

or
$$r*65536 + s*4096 + t*256 + u*16 + v$$

Some decimal numbers and their hexadecimal equivalents are:

18	12	(18 = 1*16 + 2)
60	3C	(60 = 3*16 + 12)
2890	B4A	(2890 = 11*256 + 4*16 + 10)
65535	FFFF	(65535 = 15*4096 + 15*256 + 15*16 + 15)

The following demonstration program converts hexadecimal representations to decimal representations.

```
10 INPUT "HEXADECIMAL NUMBER"; X$
20 Y = VAL("&H"+X$)
30 IF Y>=0 THEN PRINT Y: END
40 PRINT Y+65536
RUN
```

```
HEXADECIMAL NUMBER? B4A
 2890
Ok
```

FURTHER DISCUSSION

If n is a whole number (in decimal form) between 0 and 65535, then the value of

```
HEX$(n)
```

is the string consisting of the hexadecimal representation of n. If x is *any* number between 0 and 65535.49, then the value of

```
HEX$(x)
```

is the string consisting of the hexadecimal representation of the whole number obtained by rounding x.

COMMENTS

1. If $x \geq 65535.5$ or $x \leq -32768.5$, then HEX$(x) results in an ''Overflow'' error message or an erroneous result.

2. If x is a negative number greater than -32768.5, then HEX$(x) is the same as HEX$(65536+x).

EXAMPLES

1.
```
PRINT HEX$(23),HEX$(60.6)
 17              3D
Ok
```

Notice that the number 17 was not printed with a space preceding it. This is so since the output of HEX$ is a string variable, not a numeric variable.

2.
```
10 A = 2890: B$ = HEX$(2.3 + 33.8)
20 PRINT HEX$(A),B$
RUN
B4A             24
Ok
```

APPLICATIONS

For certain purposes, memory locations are grouped in blocks of 16, and it is often convenient to give hexadecimal addresses to these blocks. (See the discussion of the DEF SEG statement for further details.)

IF

IF statements provide the capability to make decisions. A statement of the form

```
IF condition THEN action
```

causes the program to take the specified action if the stated condition is true. If the condition is false, the action is not taken and the next *line* is executed.

Some common types of conditions involve the following relationships between numbers or strings.

Relationship	Numbers	Strings
=	is equal to	is identical to
<	is less than	precedes alphabetically
>	is greater than	follows alphabetically
< >	is not equal to	is not identical to
< =	is less than or equal to	precedes alphabetically or is identical to
> =	is greater than or equal to	follows alphabetically or is identical to

(When strings are alphabetized, ASCII values are used to determine the order of each pair of characters.) The most common types of actions are GOTO, GOSUB, PRINT, and LET statements. However, any BASIC statement can specify the action to be taken.

EXAMPLES

1.
```
10 PRINT "When did Darwin publish"
20 INPUT "his 'Origin of Species'"; Y
30 IF Y=1859 THEN GOTO 70
40 IF Y<1859 THEN PRINT "After that."
50 IF Y>1859 THEN PRINT "Before that."
60 INPUT "Try again: ", Y: GOTO 30
70 PRINT "That's correct."
RUN
When did Darwin publish
his 'Origin of Species'? 1850
After that.
Try again: 1859
That's correct.
Ok
```

2. The following program alphabetizes two words. (The SWAP statement interchanges the values of the two string variables.)

```
10 INPUT "Type  word, word: ", A$, B$
20 IF A$ <= B$ THEN GOTO 40
30 SWAP A$, B$
40 PRINT A$, B$
RUN
Type  word, word: byte, bit
bit              byte
Ok
```

FURTHER DISCUSSION

An extension of the "IF condition THEN action" statement is

```
IF condition THEN action 1 ELSE action 2
```

This statement causes the program to take action 1 if the stated condition is true and to take action 2 if the condition is false.

FURTHER EXAMPLE

3.
```
10 PRINT "What horse won the"
20 INPUT "Triple Crown in 1973"; H$
30 IF H$ ="Secretariat" THEN PRINT
"Correct" ELSE PRINT "No, Secretariat."
RUN
What horse won the
Triple Crown in 1973? Citation
No, Secretariat.
Ok
```

COMMENTS

1. Statements of the form IF condition THEN GOTO n are so common that BASIC has provided the following four ways to abbreviate them:

```
IF condition THEN n
```

```
IF condition GOTO n
```

```
IF condition GOTO n ELSE action
```

```
IF condition THEN n ELSE action
```

2. The action part of an IF . . . THEN . . . statement can consist of multiple BASIC statements separated by colons. The sequence

```
IF condition THEN statement 1: statement 2
```

IF

should be thought of (but not written) as

IF condition THEN (statement 1: statement 2)

That is, in the event that the condition is false, neither statement 1 nor statement 2 will be executed. This is also true for IF . . . THEN . . . ELSE . . . statements.

3. The action part of an IF statement can consist of other IF statements. Some imbedded statements and their interpretations are

```
IF cond 1 THEN IF cond 2 THEN action
```
IF cond 1 THEN (IF cond 2 THEN action)

```
IF cond 1 THEN action 1 ELSE IF cond 2 THEN action 2
```
IF cond 1 THEN action 1 ELSE (IF cond 2 THEN action 2)

```
IF cond 1 THEN IF cond 2 THEN action 1 ELSE action 2
```
IF cond 1 THEN (IF cond 2 THEN action 1 ELSE action 2)

In the third case, ELSE was associated with the closest THEN preceding it. The lines containing the parentheses are strictly for illustrative purposes. They are not valid BASIC lines.

4. Conditions consisting of expressions involving numeric constants and variables often can be written without using any relationships (such as = and < >). When used in an IF statement, such conditions are considered to be false if the number obtained from evaluating the expression is 0 and are considered to be true otherwise. So, for instance, the statement IF A-5 THEN GOTO 99 has exactly the same meaning as the statement IF A<>5 THEN GOTO 99. (They both branch to line 99 only when the variable A has a value different than 5.)

5. Complex conditions can be constructed from simple conditions by using logical operators such as AND, OR, and NOT. (Appendix G contains a detailed discussion of logical operators.) Just like arithmetic operators (+, -, *, /, ∧), logical operators are performed in a specific order. NOT is performed first, then AND, and finally OR. Also, arithmetic operators are evaluated before relationships, and both take precedence over logical operators. Some possibilities and their interpretations are:

```
NOT cond 1 AND cond 2 OR cond 3
```
((NOT cond 1) AND cond 2) OR cond 3

```
cond 1 OR NOT cond 2 AND cond 3
```
cond 1 OR ((NOT cond 2) AND cond 3)

```
C<A+B AND A-5
```
$(C<(A+B))$ AND $(A-5)$

6. The words THEN and ELSE are not BASIC statements and can only be used in conjuction with IF as illustrated in this discussion.

7. Pressing Alt-T (or Alt-E) displays the word THEN (or ELSE) on the screen.

8. Due to rounding errors, the condition A=B where A and B are single-precision numbers sometimes should be replaced by a condition such as ABS(A-B)<.005 to check the ''absolute error'' between the two numbers A and B, or ABS((A-B)/A)<.0002 to check the ''relative'' error of B with respect to A.

9. The ON statement allows the branching caused by several IF statements to be combined together, and is often easier to interpret. See the discussion of ON . . . GOSUB and ON . . . GOTO for details.

FURTHER EXAMPLES

4.
```
10 PRINT 10;: A=2: B=3
20 PRINT 20;: IF A>1 GOTO 40
30 PRINT 30;: IF B-A=1 GOTO 50 ELSE BEEP
40 PRINT 40;: IF B=6/2 THEN 30
50 PRINT 50
RUN
 10   20   40   30   50
Ok
```

5. The following program can be used by a brokerage firm to compute commissions. The commission on gold purchases is 6% for amounts from $50 to $300. For purchases exceeding $300, the firm charges 2% of the amount purchased plus $12.

```
10 INPUT "Amount of gold: ", GOLD
20 IF GOLD<50 THEN PRINT "Amount too low
 for purchase.": END
30 PRINT "Commission is $";
40 IF GOLD<300 THEN PRINT .06*GOLD ELSE
PRINT .02*GOLD+12
RUN
Amount of gold: 1234
Commission is $ 36.68
Ok
```

Notice that the END statement in line 20 was not executed.

6.
```
10 INPUT "Pitcher, Catcher"; P$, C$
20 IF P$="Hoyt" THEN IF C$="Collins"
THEN PRINT "A winning combination":END
ELSE PRINT "We want Collins":END
```

```
30 PRINT "Ho Hum"
RUN
Pitcher, Catcher? Hoyt, Roberts
We want Collins
Ok
RUN
Pitcher, Catcher? Hoyt, Collins
A winning combination
Ok
```

7.
```
10 INPUT "denominator"; D
20 IF D THEN PRINT 3.14/D ELSE GOTO 10
RUN
denominator? 0
denominator? 2.7
 1.162963
Ok
```

8. The following program will hire anyone who understands computers or who has both a doctorate and 5 years of work experience.

```
10 INPUT "Do you have a Ph.D. (Y/N)"; D$
20 PRINT "How many years of work"
30 INPUT "experience do you have"; E
40 INPUT "Do you use computers (Y/N)"; C$
50 IF D$="Y" AND NOT E<5 OR C$="Y" THEN
   PRINT "Hired." ELSE PRINT "Forget it."
```

INKEY$ is used to read a key from the keyboard. The following program takes about 12 seconds to run. Suppose that while it is still running, we type the letters A, B, and C.

```
10 FOR I = 1 TO 10000
20 NEXT I
RUN
Ok
ABC_
```

The keyboard has a buffer which can save up to 15 characters when the computer is busy elsewhere. The three letters were stored in the keyboard buffer and were displayed on the screen after the program finished running. Now add two additional lines and proceed exactly as before.

```
10 FOR I = 1 TO 10000
20 NEXT I
30 A$ = INKEY$
40 PRINT A$
RUN
A
Ok
BC_
```

In line 30, INKEY$ read the letter A from the keyboard buffer and assigned it to the string variable A$. Line 40 PRINTed the value of A$ onto the screen before the program ended. Then, as in the previous program, all remaining letters in the buffer were displayed.

In general, the program line

```
stringvar = INKEY$
```

takes one of three actions, depending on the state of the keyboard buffer.

1. If the buffer is empty, the string variable is assigned the empty string. The situation is the same as if the statement `stringvar = ""` had been executed.

2. If the buffer is not empty and its first character is one of the characters numbered from 1 to 255 in the ASCII Code table of Appendix A, then the string variable is assigned this character and the character is removed from the buffer. In this case, the string variable will have length 1.

3. There are certain special keys and key combinations that, when pressed, send a 2-character string (with the null character as the first character) to the keyboard buffer. For instance, pressing the Home key results in

INKEY$

CHR$(0)+"G", pressing Alt-N results in CHR$(0)+"1", and pressing Ctrl-Pg Dn results in CHR$(0)+"v". Hence, if we RUN the program shown above and press Ctrl-Pg Dn while the program is executing the result will be as follows:

```
RUN
 v
Ok
```

Notice that the string CHR$(0)+"v" was displayed as a space followed by the letter v. (Had we asked the computer to **PRINT LEN(A$)**, we would have gotten a 2.) In this case, a 2-character string was assigned to the string variable and the two characters were removed from the buffer. Such 2-character strings are referred to as *extended codes*. A complete table of extended codes is contained in Appendix N. This table gives the ASCII code for the second character of each 2-character string.

EXAMPLES

1. The following program poses a multiple-choice question. The program displays a question and waits for the user to press A, B, C, or D. As soon as a key is pressed, the computer responds. The user does not have to press the Enter key.

```
10 PRINT "The world's longest river is:"
20 PRINT
30 PRINT "   A.   Mississippi"
40 PRINT "   B.   Yangtze"
50 PRINT "   C.   Nile"
60 PRINT "   D.   Amazon"
70 PRINT
80 PRINT "(Type A, B, C, or D)"
90 A$ = INKEY$
100 IF A$ = "" GOTO 90
110 IF A$="C" OR A$="c" THEN PRINT
"Correct, the Nile": END
120 PRINT "Try another answer": GOTO 90
```

2. The following program makes use of extended codes to assign a special task to the combination Ctrl-Pg Dn. Press Ctrl-Break to stop the program.

```
10 PRINT "(Press Ctrl-Pg Dn to beep.)"
20 A$ = INKEY$: IF A$ = "" GOTO 20
30 IF LEN(A$)=2 AND RIGHT$(A$,1)="v"
   THEN BEEP
40 GOTO 20
```

170

INKEY$

COMMENTS

1. Unlike the INPUT statement, the INKEY$ variable has no provision to produce a question mark or a prompt to tell the user that a response is being requested. The cursor doesn't even appear. A prompt can be produced by a separate PRINT statement, and the statement LOCATE,,1 can be used to turn on the cursor. Characters read by the INKEY$ statement will not be displayed on the screen as they are typed, unless a PRINT statement is added for this purpose.

2. With the computer in text and direct modes, try the following. Hold down the Alt key, press 227 on the numeric keypad, and then let up the Alt key. The Greek letter pi will appear on the screen. Consult Appendix A, and you will see that the Greek letter pi has ASCII value 227. Actually, any character in the list with ASCII values 32 to 254, except 127, and many of the characters with ASCII values less than 32 can be displayed on the screen in this way.

Consider the following program.

```
10 CLS: LOCATE ,,1
20 A$ = INKEY$: IF A$="" GOTO 20
30 PRINT A$;
40 GOTO 20
```

Line 10 clears the screen and turns on the cursor. Striking the typewriter portion of the keyboard produces the standard results. However, the sequence "Hold down Alt, press 3 on numeric keypad, release Alt" causes a heart to appear on the screen. Any displayable character in Appendix A can be produced in this manner.

3. The INPUT$(1) function is in some ways similar to the INKEY$ variable. There are two differences between them. The INPUT$(1) function waits until a character is available from the keyboard buffer before allowing the program to continue. The INKEY$ variable looks to see if a character is available from the keyboard buffer and, if not, just assigns the empty string to the string variable and lets the program move on. The second difference is that the INKEY$ variable can recognize not only the characters listed in the ASCII value list, but also can tell if certain special keys and key combinations, such as Num Lock and Ctrl-Pg Dn, have been pressed.

4. Extended codes usually are identified by their ASCII values. For instance, if the combination Ctrl-Pg Dn is pressed, and the line A$ = INKEY$ is executed, then LEN(A$)=2 and ASC(RIGHT$(A$,1))=118.

5. INKEY$ also can be used as a statement. For instance, the statement WHILE INKEY$ = "":WEND causes the execution of a program to pause until a key is pressed, and the statements WHILE INKEY$<>"":WEND purge the keyboard buffer.

INKEY$

APPLICATIONS

1. Whenever an event is being trapped in a program, INKEY$, rather than INPUT, should be used to request a response from the user. See Example 2 in the discussion of ON TIMER.

2. Sometimes the programmer wants to keep the standard keyboard free for entering copy, and yet he or she needs many other keys available to initiate special operations. The capability of INKEY$ to recognize extended codes meets this need. Special keys or key combinations can be used to branch to subroutines.

The micro-processor receives data from and sends data to the various parts of the computer through mechanisms known as *ports*. For instance, there are ports associated with the keyboard, the disk drives, the speaker, and the screen. A piece of data consists of a byte (corresponding to an integer from 0 to 255), and each port has a number assigned to it. The value of the function

```
INP(n)
```

is the value of the byte read from port n.

EXAMPLE

1. Port 97 is associated with the speaker.

```
10 PRINT INP(97)
20 BEEP
30 PRINT INP(97)
RUN
 76
 79
Ok
```

Note: Your results might differ from those above.

COMMENTS

1. The value of n must be in the range 0 to 65535.

2. The statement OUT is used to *send* data to various ports.

3. INP and OUT are not affected by DEF SEG statements since they apply to ports, not memory locations.

APPLICATIONS

1. The INP function is used in communications software to monitor the status of communications ports. The determination is more direct than can be obtained with other BASIC statements. Also, INP is not destructive, as opposed to INPUT$ and LINE INPUT#.

2. Port 957 is associated with the printer. If INP(957) has the value 223, then the printer is on-line.

INPUT

The INPUT statement is used to request information from the user of the program. A statement of the form

    INPUT var

where var is a variable, causes the computer to display a question mark and a space. It then pauses until the user types in a value to be assigned to the variable and presses the Enter key.

Usually we want to tell the user the type of information requested by displaying a prompting message. A statement of the form

    INPUT "prompt"; var

will display the message contained inside the quotation marks. The message will be followed by a question mark and a space. The variation

    INPUT "prompt", var

suppresses both the question mark and the space.

EXAMPLES

1.  ```
    10 INPUT C$
    20 PRINT "***"+C$
    RUN
    ? USA
    ***USA
    Ok
    ```

After entering RUN, the user will see a question mark and the cursor on the next line. Since Ok hasn't appeared, the user knows that the computer has paused.

2.  ```
    10 INPUT "COUNTRY: ", C$
    20 PRINT "***" + C$
    RUN
    COUNTRY: USA
    ***USA
    Ok
    ```

3.  ```
    10 INPUT N
    20 PRINT N*5
    RUN
    ? 23
     115
    Ok
    ```

174
    ```

COMMENTS

1. If the variable specified in the INPUT statement is a numeric variable, then the response to the request must be a numeric constant. Otherwise, a "?Redo from start" message results and the request is repeated. In the event that the numeric constant has a different precision than the variable, the constant is converted to the precision of the variable. Of course, the constants must be of appropriate magnitudes for the corresponding variables. If integer variables are assigned numbers outside the range from -32768 to 32767, or single- and double-precision variables are assigned numbers greater than machine infinity ($1.701412E+38$), an "Overflow" message results. If the precision of the variable is lower than the precision of the constant, the constant will be rounded.

2. Expressions are not allowed in response to an INPUT statement. For instance, in Example 1 the responses "US"+"A" and LEFT$ ("USAmerica",3) would be rejected, and in Example 3 the responses 1/3 and EXP(5) would be rejected.

3. If the variable specified in the INPUT statement is a string variable, then the response should be a string constant. The string constant usually need not be enclosed in quotation marks. If it is, the quotation marks will be stripped from the constant. However, the string constant should be enclosed in quotation marks if it contains leading blanks, trailing blanks, or commas. (Leading and trailing blanks not inside quotation marks will be lost.) Also, if the leading character is a quotation mark, the string must not contain interior quotation marks.

4. If the variable is a string variable and we respond with a number, the number will be treated as a string. Later it can be converted back to a number with the VAL function.

5. If we respond to the request for information by pressing the Enter key, the null string or 0 will be assigned to the variable, as is appropriate.

6. Suppose that line n contains an INPUT statement. If we respond to the request for information by pressing Ctrl-Break, the message "Break in line n" is displayed. The computer will be in direct mode. We can resume execution of the program at line n by entering the command CONT, and will again be prompted for the requested input.

7. In each of the examples presented above, the cursor moved to the next line after the information from the user was received. This can be prevented by placing a semicolon immediately following the word INPUT. In Example 2, for instance, so altering line 10 results in

```
10 INPUT; "COUNTRY: ", C$
20 PRINT "***" + C$
RUN
COUNTRY: USA***USA
Ok
```

INPUT

8. With the computer in text and direct modes, hold down the Alt key, push the sequence 225 on the numeric keypad, and then release the Alt key. The Greek letter beta will be displayed on the screen. Consulting the table of ASCII values in Appendix A, we see that beta has ASCII value 225. Any character with an ASCII value from 32 to 255 (except 127) can be displayed on the screen using the Alt key and the numeric keypad. The response to INPUT's request for a string constant can consist of characters entered using the Alt key and the numeric keypad.

9. One INPUT statement can be used to request values for several variables. A statement of the form

```
INPUT var1, var2, var3
```

requests a response of three constants. These constants must be separated by commas and each should be of the same type as the corresponding variable.

10. The INPUT statement has some characteristics in common with LINE INPUT, INPUT$, and INKEY$. The LINE INPUT statement allows us to respond to a request for a string constant with *any* sequence of characters, including commas and quotation marks. The INPUT$ function automatically processes the response after a specified number of characters have been typed. INKEY$ assumes the value of the first character pending in the keyboard buffer. See the discussions of these statements for further details.

11. "Redo from start" is not an error message and cannot be trapped by the ON ERROR statement.

12. If the response to a request for a string consists of 255 or more characters, only the first 254 will be included in the string.

13. The word INPUT can be displayed by pressing Alt-I.

FURTHER EXAMPLES

4.
```
10 INPUT "AGE"; A
20 PRINT 7+A/2
RUN
AGE? FORTY
?Redo from start
AGE?
```

Since A is a numeric variable, the computer could not assign the string constant FORTY to it.

5.
```
10 INPUT "AGE"; A%
20 PRINT A%
RUN
AGE? 40.5
 41
Ok
```

176

Here, the numeric constant 40.5 was rounded when converted to the integer constant 41.

6.  ```
    INPUT A$: PRINT A$
    ? "TOY"
    TOY
    Ok
    ```

7.  ```
    INPUT A$: PRINT A$
    ? "(1,2)"
    (1,2)
    Ok
    ```

The quotation marks are necessary because of the comma.

8.  ```
    INPUT A$: PRINT A$
    ? "A "two-headed" dime"
    ?Redo from start
    ? A "two-headed" dime
    A "two-headed" dime
    Ok
    ```

9.  ```
    10 INPUT "SALARY"; S$
    20 PRINT S$
    RUN
    SALARY? 12000
    12000
    Ok
    ```

We can tell from the way 12000 was displayed that it is being stored as a string constant. Had it been a numeric constant, it would have been displayed with a leading space. If we want to do computations with this number, we can execute the statement S = VAL(S$) and compute with S.

10. ```
    INPUT A: PRINT A+5
    ?
     5
    Ok
    ```

The Enter key was pushed in response to the question mark. As a result, the number 0 was assigned to the variable A.

11. ```
    10 INPUT "INCOME"; I$
    20 PRINT I$
    RUN
    INCOME? (user pressed Ctrl-Break)
    Break in 10
    Ok
    PRINT 12000+1234.56
     13234.56
    Ok
    CONT
    ```

INPUT

```
INCOME? 13234.56
 13234.56
Ok
```

After the first request, the user decided to employ the computer as an adding machine to total the two sources of income.

12.   In the following program, the letter è was typed by holding down the Alt key, pushing 130 on the numeric keypad, and then releasing the Alt key.

```
10 INPUT "What is your favorite liqueur"; L$
20 PRINT "I will get you some "; L$; " now."
RUN
What is your favorite liqueur? crème de menthe
I will get you some crème de menthe now.
Ok
```

13.
```
10 INPUT "NAME,PHONE NO.,ZIP CODE: ", N$, P$, Z
20 IF Z>5000 THEN PRINT N$, P$
RUN
NAME,PHONE NO.,ZIP CODE: Doe, John, 123-4567, 76543
?Redo from start
NAME,PHONE NO.,ZIP CODE: John Doe, 123-4567, 76543
John Doe        123-4567
Ok
```

The comma in "Doe, John" was treated as a delimiter. Since numeric constants cannot contain hyphens, the phone number is a string constant. The message "?Redo from start" was the result of there being both more constants than variables and a type mismatch (the computer would try to assign 123-4567 to Z).

14.
```
10 FOR I = 1 TO 3
20     INPUT "NAME, AGE: ", N$(I), A(I)
30 NEXT I
40 FOR I = 1 TO 3
50     IF A(I) > 40 THEN PRINT N$(I)
60 NEXT I
RUN
NAME, AGE: AL ADAMS, 54
NAME, AGE: BOB BROWN, 35
NAME, AGE: CAROL COE, 41
AL ADAMS
CAROL COE
Ok
```

APPLICATIONS

1.   The INPUT statement is one of the most frequently used statements in BASIC. One of the main uses of computers is the processing of data, and the

178

INPUT statement can be used, as in Example 13, to enter the data into the computer.

2.   Programmers make use of the INPUT statement when debugging a subroutine of a program. An INPUT statement is inserted temporarily in the subroutine to allow the programmer to assign values to the variables and observe the effects.

3.   The INPUT statement can be used to stop execution of a program until the user is ready to continue. Suppose that the screen has been almost completely filled with data that the user should read before the program proceeds. The statement

```
INPUT "Press Enter key to continue", C
```

allows the user to take some time to absorb the material before continuing.

INPUT#

A sequential data file is a sequence of pieces of information residing on a disk. Appendix F and the discussions of WRITE# and PRINT# explain how information is entered into sequential files and how files look on the disk. In addition to the items of information inserted by the user, the files also contain assorted quotation marks and commas, and three characters that we refer to as CR, LF, and AR.

In the standard usage of PRINT# and WRITE#, the characters CR (carriage return) and LF (line feed) occur only as a pair with CR first. We denote this pair by <CR/LF>. Also, the character AR (arrow character with ASCII value 26 denoting end of file) normally appears only at the end of a file. We shall assume that both of these conditions hold for the files discussed here.

After the statement **OPEN "filespec" FOR INPUT AS #n** is executed, information can be read from the file, in order, starting at the beginning of the file. The statement

> **INPUT #n, A$**

will assign to the string variable A$ a certain amount of information from the beginning of the file according to the following rules:

(a) The computer looks for the first character that is not a space.

(b) If the character determined in (a) is CR, and hence the first part of the pair <CR/LF>, then the empty string is assigned to A$. That is, the result is the same as when the statement **A$=""** is executed. Subsequent input with either INPUT#, LINE INPUT#, or INPUT$ will continue with the next character after the pair <CR/LF>.

(c) If the character determined in (a) is a quotation mark, the computer reads *all* characters until it encounters either a second quotation mark or the character AR, or until 255 characters have been read. It then assigns to A$ the string consisting of the characters between (but not including) the two quotation marks, or the first quotation mark and AR, or the quotation mark and the 256th character, respectively. In the first case, a <CR/LF> or comma trailing the second quotation mark (along with possible intervening spaces) will be ignored by the next INPUT# or LINE INPUT# statement.

(d) If the character determined in (a) is not a CR or a quotation mark, the computer reads all characters until it encounters either a comma, the pair <CR/LF>, or AR, or until 255 characters have been read. It then assigns to A$ the string consisting of all of the characters preceding the comma, the pair <CR/LF>, or AR, or the string of 255 characters, respectively. Subsequent input will begin with the next character after the comma or the pair <CR/LF>, or with the 256th character.

INPUT#

The statement

```
INPUT #n, A
```

will assign a number to the numeric variable, A, according to the following rules:

    (a) The computer looks for the first character that is not a space.

    (b) If the character determined in (a) is CR, and hence the first part of the pair $<CR/LF>$, then 0 is assigned to A. Subsequent input begins with the next character after the pair $<CR/LF>$.

    (c) If the character determined in (a) is not CR, then the computer reads consecutive characters until it encounters a space, CR, AR, or comma, or until 255 characters have been read. The computer analyzes these consecutive characters (not including the terminating space, CR, AR, or comma) and, if it finds a number, assigns that number to A. In the event that the first character is not a digit, the value 0 will be assigned to A. In the event that the first character is a digit, but some of the characters are not digits, then the value of the number that precedes the first non-digit character will be assigned to A. Subsequent input begins with the next character after the space, $<CR/LF>$ pair, or comma, or with the 256th character.

EXAMPLES

1.   Suppose that the sequential file shown below is named RIVERS.

```
"Nile",4160<CR/LF><AR>

10 OPEN "RIVERS" FOR INPUT AS #2
20 INPUT #2,N$
30 PRINT N$
40 INPUT #2, L
50 PRINT #2, L
60 CLOSE #2
RUN
Nile
 4160
Ok

10 OPEN "RIVERS" FOR INPUT AS #2
20 INPUT #2, A
30 PRINT A
40 CLOSE #2
RUN
 0
Ok
```

INPUT#

2. Suppose that the sequential file shown below is named NUMBERS.

```
3.14159  "pi"<CR/LF> 2.71828    "e"<CR/LF><AR>

10 OPEN "NUMBERS" FOR INPUT AS #3
20 INPUT #3, N
30 PRINT N
40 CLOSE #3
RUN
 3.14159
Ok

10 OPEN "NUMBERS" FOR INPUT AS #3
20 INPUT #3, A$
30 PRINT A$
40 CLOSE #3
RUN
3.14159  "pi"
Ok
```

3. Suppose that the sequential file shown below is named STATES.

```
Alabama  Montgomery   51,705   3,917<CR/LF><AR>

10 OPEN "STATES" FOR INPUT AS #2
20 INPUT #2, S$
30 INPUT #2, N
40 PRINT S$, N
50 CLOSE #2
RUN
Alabama  Montgomery   51      705
Ok
```

This program is poorly suited to read the file. It can be improved by replacing lines 20 and 30 by **20 LINE INPUT #2, T$** and line 40 by **40 PRINT T$**. (See the discussion of LINE INPUT#.)

4. Suppose that the sequential file shown below is named CHEER.

```
49ers,hooray<CR/LF><AR>

10 OPEN "CHEER" FOR INPUT AS #1
20 INPUT #1, A
30 INPUT #1, B$
40 PRINT A; B$
50 CLOSE #1
```

```
RUN
 49 hooray
Ok
```

FURTHER DISCUSSION

After the initial INPUT# statement is executed, the computer begins reading the information for the next INPUT# statement as stated above. The criteria for assigning strings or numbers to variables are the same as before.

A single INPUT# statement can assign values to several variables at once.
The variables must be separated by commas.

INPUT# statements also can be used to read string characters from the
buffer of a random file. (See the discussion of GET (Files) for the details of
how records are retrieved from random files and placed into buffers.)
Although this is not the standard way to retrieve data from the buffer, it has
its uses. For instance, we could create a random file in which each record was
structured like a short sequential file. This would combine the best features of
both modes of access. We could jump around to any record desired and also
efficiently pack data into each record. If we intend to use INPUT# to read the
buffer, we must plan ahead and store the data with delimiters, such as commas and quotation marks.

FURTHER EXAMPLES

5. Suppose that the sequential file shown below is named RIVERS.

```
Nile, 4160 <CR/LF>Amazon, 4080 <CR/LF><AR>

10 OPEN "RIVERS" FOR INPUT AS #2
20 FOR I = 1 TO 2
30    INPUT #2, N$, L
40    PRINT N$, L
50 NEXT I
60 CLOSE #2
RUN
Nile          4160
Amazon        4080
Ok
```

6. Suppose that the sequential file shown below is named NUMBERS.

```
 3.14159  "pi"<CR/LF> 2.71828    "e"<CR/LF><AR>

10 OPEN "NUMBERS" FOR INPUT AS #3
20 FOR I = 1 to 3
30    INPUT #3, N, N$
40    PRINT N; N$;
```

INPUT#

```
50 NEXT I
60 CLOSE #3
RUN
 3.14159 pi 2.71828 e
Input past end in 30
Ok
```

7.   The following program creates a random file and uses INPUT# to retrieve information.

```
10 OPEN "HEIGHTS" AS #1 LEN = 31
20 FIELD #1, 31 AS PRESF$
30 C$ = CHR$(13) + CHR$(10)
40 LSET PRESF$="George Washington"+C$+"6 ft  2 in"+C$
50 PUT #1, 1
60 LSET PRESF$ ="John Adams"+C$ +"5 ft  7 in" +C$
70 PUT #1, 2
80 FOR I = 1 TO 2
90   GET #1, I
100  INPUT #1, P$, H$
110  PRINT P$, H$
120 NEXT I
130 CLOSE #1
RUN
George Washington          6 ft  2 in
John Adams     5 ft  7 in
Ok
```

Line 30 defined C\$ as <CR/LF>. If C\$ had not been used in lines 40 and 60, line 100 would have produced the error message ''FIELD overflow in 100'' since there would be no delimiter for P\$.

COMMENTS

1.   In the event that the character with ASCII value 0 appears in a file, it will be ignored by INPUT#.

2.   The pair <LF/CR> is ignored by INPUT#, as is a single occurrence of <LF> that is not adjacent to a <CR>.

3.   INPUT# is usually used to retrieve data that have been recorded with WRITE#.

184

The INPUT$ function is related to the INPUT statement. Both provide means for the user to interact with the program while it is running. The statement **INPUT "", A$** (the comma suppresses the question mark) causes a pause until the user types in a string and presses the Enter key, after which the string is assigned to the variable A$. The INPUT$ function operates in a similar manner, except that there is no need to press the Enter key. However, the computer must be told the length of the string in advance. The statement

```
A$ = INPUT$(n)
```

(where A$ is a string variable and n is a positive integer) causes the program to pause until the user types n characters. Then the string of n characters is assigned automatically to the string variable. In most uses of the INPUT$ function, n has the value 1.

EXAMPLES

1. The following program poses a multiple-choice question. The program displays the question and waits for the user to press A, B, or C. As soon as a key is pressed, the computer gives its response. There is no need to press the Enter key.

```
10 PRINT "The most common last name in the USA is:
20 PRINT
30 PRINT "    A.   Jones"
40 PRINT "    B.   Williams"
50 PRINT "    C.   Smith"
60 PRINT
70 A$ = INPUT$(1)
80 IF A$ = "C" THEN PRINT "Correct, Smith": END
90 PRINT "Try another answer": GOTO 70
```

2. The following program requires that the computer be operating in Advanced BASIC. The statement BASICA must have been used to invoke BASIC from DOS.

```
10 A$ = INPUT$(1)
20 PLAY A$
30 GOTO 10
```

This program turns the computer into a very elementary musical instrument. The user can produce music by successively pressing keys between A and G. For instance, pressing the sequence C, C, D, C, F, E produces the first bar of Happy Birthday. If a key outside of the range A to G is pressed, the error

INPUT$

message "Illegal function call in 20" results and execution is terminated. If line 10 is changed to **A$ = INPUT$(5)**, the computer will wait until a sequence of 5 keys are pressed and then play them one after another.

COMMENTS

1. Unlike the INPUT statement, the INPUT$ function has no provision to produce a question mark or a prompt to tell the user that a response is being requested. The cursor doesn't even appear. A prompt can be produced by a separate PRINT statement, and the statement **LOCATE,,1** can be used to turn on the cursor.

2. When a response to an INPUT$ function is typed on the keyboard, no characters appear on the screen. If desired, a PRINT statement can be included to display the typed characters. For instance, if the program in Example 2 is given the additional line **25 PRINT A$**, the notes will be displayed on the screen as they are PLAYed.

3. With the computer in direct mode, try the following sequence of events. Hold down the Alt key, press 227 on the numeric keyboard, and then let up the Alt key. The Greek letter pi will appear on the screen. Consulting Appendix A (ASCII Character Codes) we see that the Greek letter pi has ASCII value 227. Actually, any character in the list with ASCII value 32 or greater, except for the character with ASCII value 127, can be displayed on the screen in this manner. The INPUT$ function, however, provides the capability of placing all characters except "heart" and "null" in a string.

Consider the following program:

```
10 CLS: LOCATE ,,1
20 A$ = INPUT$(1)
30 PRINT A$;
40 GOTO 20
```

Line 10 clears the screen and turns on the cursor. Striking the typewriter portion of the keyboard produces the standard results. However, the sequence "Hold down Alt, press 4 on numeric keyboard, release Alt" causes a diamond to appear on the screen. Hence, we see that the INPUT$ function has greater versatility than the INPUT statement, in that the former can use more characters in its strings.

4. Consider the following program.

```
10 FOR I = 1 TO 5000: NEXT I
20 PRINT "Type the first letter of your name"
30 N$ = INPUT$(1)
40 PRINT N$
```

The execution of line 10 takes about 6 seconds. Suppose that during those 6 seconds the user presses several keys. These characters will be stored in the keyboard buffer, and when the program arrives at line 30, the first letter that was pressed will be assigned to N$. The buffer can store up to 15 letters. The programmer might want to take steps to clear the buffer before using INPUT$. This can be accomplished by adding the line **25 WHILE INKEY$<>"": WEND.**

5. The INPUT$(1) function is similar to the INKEY$ variable. There are two differences. The INPUT$(1) function waits until a character is available from the keyboard buffer before allowing the program to continue. The INKEY$ variable looks to see if a character is pending in the keyboard buffer and, if not, just assigns the empty string, """, to the string variable and lets the program move on. The second difference is that the INKEY$ variable can recognize not only the 256 characters listed in Appendix A (ASCII Character Codes), but also can tell if certain special keys and key combinations, such as Num Lock and Ctrl-Pg Dn, have been pressed.

6. The INPUT$ function can also be used to read characters from a file. Let's say that a file has been OPENed FOR INPUT AS #m. Then the function

```
A$ = INPUT$(n,m)
```

assigns the next n characters of the file to the string variable A$. Since INPUT$ recognizes carriage returns and line feeds, which occur frequently in files, they will appear as characters in the string. This feature of INPUT$ is put to good use in the demonstration program in Appendix F.

APPLICATIONS

1. The INPUT$ function allows the user to control the program from the keyboard. For instance, the program might display a menu consisting of various tasks that could be performed. The user could indicate a choice by typing in a command to be read by the INPUT$ function.

2. The INPUT$ function is used in computer assisted instruction programs. Often a multiple choice question is asked, and the response is recorded by the INPUT$ function. The program then can branch to one of various subroutines, depending on the answer to the question.

3. At the completion of a graphics picture or a text display, we sometimes want to suppress the intrusion of the cursor and the prompt ''Ok''. This can be accomplished by including an INPUT$ statement after the picture or display is completed.

4. Since all characters are usually significant in communications, INPUT$ is useful when reading data from the communications buffer. See Appendix L for further details.

INSTR

We say that one string has a second string as a substring with offset m if the second string appears (as consecutive characters) beginning with the mth character of the first string. For instance, "Washington" has "ngt" as a substring with offset 6; "July 4, 1776" has "1776" as a substring with offset 9; and "Warren Gamaliel Harding" has " " (the string consisting of a single space) as a substring twice (first with offset 7 and then with offset 16). The INSTR function is used to determine if one string has another string as a substring and, if so, to determine the offset. If A$ and B$ are strings, then the value of

INSTR(A$,B$)

is

    0, if the string B$ is not a substring of A$,

and otherwise

    m, where m is the first offset of B$ in A$.

So, INSTR("Washington","ngt") is 6, INSTR("Washington","DC") is 0, and INSTR("Warren Gamaliel Harding"," ") is 7.

As a refinement, we can also ask for the first occurrence of a substring with offset beyond a certain point. In particular,

INSTR(n,A$,B$)

is

    0, if B$ does not occur as a substring of A$ with offset n or greater, or

    m, where m is the first offset of B$ in A$, such that m is greater than or equal to n.

So, the value of INSTR(8,"Warren Gamaliel Harding"," ") is 16 and the value of INSTR(7,"Washington","ngt") is 0.

COMMENTS

1. Be careful to include all the spaces when counting the characters in a string. After a positive number has been converted to a string, it has a space as its first character. If this character is overlooked, the interpretations of INSTR will be incorrect.

2. If B$ is the null string ("") and A$ is not the null string, then INSTR(A$,B$) is 1 and INSTR(n,A$,B$) is n.

3. If n is greater than the length of A$, INSTR(n,A$,B$) is 0.

4. If A$ is the null string, then INSTR(A$,B$) and INSTR(n,A$,B$) will both be zero.

188

5.   The number n in INSTR(n,A$,B$) must be between 1 and 255 inclusive. Otherwise, the error message ''Illegal function call'' results.

EXAMPLES

1.   The character e has ASCII value 101. Hence, CHR$(101) is the string consisting of the character e.

```
10 A$ = "College Park, MD 20742"
20 B$ = "20742": C$ = ",": D$ = "d": E$ = CHR$(101)
30 PRINT INSTR(A$,B$); INSTR(A$,C$); INSTR(A$,D$);
   INSTR(A$,E$); INSTR(6,A$,E$)
RUN
 18  13  0  5  7
Ok
```

2.
```
10 INPUT B$
20 A$ = "Hence CHR$(101) is the string consisting of
the character e."
30 M = INSTR(A$,B$): PRINT M: GOTO 10
RUN
? "101"
 12
? 101
 12
? e
 2
? CHR$(101)
 7
?        (the Enter key was pressed)
 1
?
```

When INPUT is followed by a string variable, the INPUT statement automatically makes a string out of everything handed to it. So at the second input, 101 was converted to ''101'', and at the fourth input CHR$(101) was converted to ''CHR$(101)''. (*Note:* Press Ctrl-Break to stop this program.)

3.   The following program determines the number of parts of a name.

```
10 INPUT "Your full name: ", A$
20 F = INSTR(A$," ")
30 IF F=0 THEN N=1: GOTO 90
40 G = INSTR(F+1,A$," ")
50 IF G=0 THEN N=2: GOTO 90
60 H = INSTR(G+1,A$," ")
70 IF H = 0 THEN N=3: GOTO 90
```

INSTR

```
80 PRINT "You have 4 or more parts to your name.": END
90 PRINT "You have"; N; "parts to your name."
RUN
Your full name: Victoria C. Woodhull
You have 3 parts to your name.
Ok
```

4.   The following piece of a program asks for a number and then checks to see if the user included dollar signs or commas. If so, the string is sent to a subroutine that strips the dollar sign and commas. (Such a subroutine is presented in the discussion of LEN.)

```
10 LINE INPUT "Salary? "; S$
20 IF INSTR(S$,"$")<>0 OR INSTR(S$,",")<>0 THEN
   GOSUB 1000
30 S# = VAL(S$)
```

If S\$ is the string \$23,456, then S# will be the number 23456.

APPLICATIONS

1.   The INSTR function is vital to data processing, where it is used to split strings into component parts. For instance, the program in Example 3 can be expanded to sort out a person's first name.

2.   The INSTR function is useful in making a program user-friendly. For instance, the program in Example 4 will help tolerate a wide range of user responses.

If x is any number, then

```
INT(x)
```

is the greatest whole number less than or equal to x. On the number line, INT(x) is either x itself, or the first whole number to the left of x. See Figure 1.

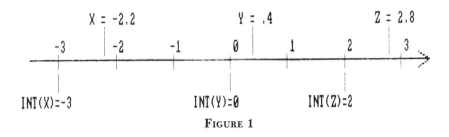

FIGURE 1

EXAMPLES

1.  ```
    PRINT INT(2.6); INT(-1.3); INT(1234D-2)
     2 -2  12
    Ok
    PRINT INT(3); INT(1/4); INT(87654321.218)
     3  0  87654321
    Ok
    ```

2.  ```
    10 A = 45.67: B = -3.1
    20 PRINT INT(A); INT(B); INT(A+B); INT(6*B)
    RUN
     45 -4  42 -19
    Ok
    ```

COMMENTS

1. The function INT preserves the precision of the number on which it operates. Because of its name, one might think that INT returns only integer numeric constants. It returns whole numbers of any precision. In the last item of Example 1, INT returned a double-precision constant.

2. For positive numbers, INT is the same as FIX. However, for negative numbers x that are not whole numbers, the value of INT(x) is one less than the value of FIX(x).

3. The INT function will operate on any number that the computer recognizes. On some other computers, the numbers are restricted to range from −32768 to 32767.

191

INT

APPLICATIONS

1. Certain formulas involve the INT function. For instance, the cost in cents of mailing a letter of weight x ounces is

```
22 + 17*INT(x)
```

2. INT is often used to interpret user input. For example, when asked his or her age, the user might enter 23.6. In this case, the value of INT(23.6) will most likely be more useful than either 23.6 or its rounded value.

IOCTL and IOCTL$

The IOCTL (Input/Output ConTroL) statement and the IOCTL$ function, which allow BASIC to send control data to a device driver and to read input from the device, are not valid for versions of BASIC preceding BASIC 3.0.

Some examples of devices are the video screen, keyboard, printer, communication lines, and disk drives. PC-DOS comes with standard programs, called device drivers, that communicate with these devices. Many non-standard peripheral devices, such as certain types of fixed disks not produced by IBM, can be attached to the PC. However, the manufacturer must supply a device driver on disk to manage communication between the PC and the device. Installation of the device driver involves typing a sequence of characters and perhaps copying some disk files.

Each device driver is a .COM file with all of the code in it to implement the associated device. It is possible to talk to the driver without talking to the device. For instance, we might tell the device driver of an asychronous communications device to change the baud rate. Or, we might ask the device driver of a printer if the printer is currently printing.

Suppose that a device has been OPENed with reference number n, and that A$ is a control data string that the driver recognizes. Then the statement

```
IOCTL #n, A$
```

sends the string to the driver. At any time, the value of the function

```
IOCTL$(n)
```

is a control data string read from the device driver.

COMMENTS

1. The control data string can have a length of at most 255 characters. The string can contain multiple commands separated by semicolons.

2. Not all device drivers are equipped to handle IOCTL and IOCTL$. If so, the error message "Illegal function call" results. To determine if a device driver can handle IOCTL, use DEBUG to load the driver and then examine the sixth bit of the sixth byte. If this bit is 1, then IOCTL is supported.

3. The name of a user-installed device driver can be the same as the name of an existing driver, such as LPT2. If so, the user-installed device driver will take precedence over the one that comes with DOS.

4. The words IOCTL and IOCTL$ are listed as reserved words in BASIC 2.0 and 2.1, eventhough the statements are not documented in these versions of BASIC. They can be executed in BASIC 2.0 and 2.1. However, we suspect that they might not always perform properly there.

IOCTL and IOCTL$

EXAMPLE

Suppose that a plotter has been attached to the PC and its device driver (which accepts IOCTL) has been installed.

```
10 OPEN "PLOTTER" FOR OUTPUT AS #3
20 IOCTL #3, "BEGIN";CHR$(0)+CHR$(15)
30 PRINT IOCTL$(3)
40 CLOSE #3
```

APPLICATIONS

1.   The IOCTL$ function can be used to obtain information about the configuration of a device. For instance, it can determine the baud rate of an asychronous communications device.

2.   After an IOCTL statement has been executed, an IOCTL$ function can be used to confirm that the command has been implemented.

The left part of the keyboard contains ten keys labeled F1 to F10 and known as the "soft" or "function" keys. These keys can be assigned any 15-character string. If n is one of the numbers from 1 to 10 and A$ is a string of length 15 or less, the statement

```
KEY n, A$
```

assigns the string A$ to the soft key Fn. Afterwards, pressing the specified key causes the string to be displayed on the screen. For instance, the statement **KEY 6, "Your Name"** assigns the string "Your Name" to key F6. (While in direct mode, enter the statement and then press the function key F6 several times.)

The 25th row of the screen identifies the strings assigned to the soft keys by displaying the first six characters of each string. For a WIDTH 40 screen, only the first five soft keys are identified. The statement

```
KEY OFF
```

turns off this display and the statement

```
KEY ON
```

turns it back on.

Appendix A lists the 256 characters recognized by the computer and their associated ASCII values. The characters with ASCII values 32 to 126 appear on the white keys in the center of the keyboard. If m is a number from 32 to 126, the statement **KEY n, CHR$(m)** assigns to the nth soft key the string consisting of the character with ASCII value m. For instance, the statement **KEY 4, CHR$(36)** assigns a dollar sign to the soft key F4. For many values of m from 0 to 31, the statement **KEY n, CHR$(m)** converts the nth soft key into a control key. For instance, after the statement **KEY 2, CHR$(6)** is executed, the soft key F2 will operate just like the combination Ctrl-cursor right. The cursor will jump to the beginning of the next word. Comment 6 contains the controls associated with some of the numbers from 0 to 31. For values of m from 128 to 255, the statement **KEY n, CHR$(m)** assigns to the nth soft key the character having ASCII value 128 less than m. For instance, the statement **KEY 7, CHR$(164)** assigns a dollar sign to the soft key F7. In all of the above cases, the 25th line will show the character having ASCII value m when the statement **KEY n, CHR$(m)** is executed. For instance, the statement **KEY 2, CHR$(6)** produces a spade next to the number 2 on the 25th line, and the statement **KEY 7, CHR$(164)** produces an ñ next to the number 7.

When BASIC is first invoked, the soft keys are programmed to produce the strings shown below. (The arrow symbol stands for carriage return, or Enter.)

F1 LIST
F2 RUN ←——

KEY

F3 LOAD”
F4 SAVE”
F5 CONT ◄—
F6 ,”LPT1:” ◄—
F7 TRON ◄—
F8 TROFF ◄—
F9 KEY
F10 SCREEN 0,0,0 ◄—

The statement

    KEY LIST

causes the computer to display the strings assigned to each of the 10 soft keys. For instance, if this statement is entered in direct mode just after BASIC is invoked, the listing from the previous paragraph results.

COMMENTS

1. If a quotation mark is to appear in a string, it must be assigned via its ASCII value. For instance, the statement KEY 6, "," + CHR$(34) + "LPT1:" + CHR$(34) + CHR$(13) produces the standard string that is assigned to KEY 6.

2. If the string appearing in a KEY statement has more than 15 characters, *only the first 15* will be assigned to the soft key.

3. The LOCATE statement is used to place characters at specified locations of the screen. However, characters may not be placed on the 25th line until it has been first cleared with a KEY OFF statement.

4. The statement KEY n, "" assigns the null string to the nth soft key. We say that the key has been *disabled* as a soft key.

5. The INKEY$ function provides a way for the computer to identify keys that are pressed during the execution of a program. If a soft key has not been disabled, pressing that key causes the INKEY$ function to return the first letter of the associated string. However, if the soft key Fn has been disabled, the INKEY$ function returns a string of length two, whose first character is CHR$(0) and whose second character is the character with ASCII value 58 greater than n. See Example 4.

6. For certain values of m between 0 and 31, the statement KEY n, CHR$(m) programs the soft key Fn to perform a control function.

m	*Response from Pressing the Key*
2	cursor moves to previous word (i.e., same as pressing Ctrl-cursor left).
3	cursor moves to beginning of next line

196

5 erases from the current cursor position to the end of the logical line (i.e., same as pressing Ctrl-End).

6 cursor moves to next word (i.e., same as pressing Ctrl-cursor right).

7 beeping sound produced by speaker (i.e., same as the combination Ctrl-G).

8 destructive backspace (i.e., same as pressing the backspace key).

9 tab

11 cursor moves to upper left-hand corner of the screen (i.e., same as pressing Home.)

12 screen is cleared and cursor is moved to upper left-hand corner (i.e., same as the combination Ctrl-Home).

13 carriage return (i.e., same as the Enter key).

14 cursor moves to the end of the logical line (i.e., same as End).

18 insert mode is set (i.e., same as pressing Ins).

27 logical line containing the cursor is erased (i.e., same as Esc).

28 cursor moves one position right (i.e., same as pressing the cursor right key).

29 cursor moves one position left (i.e., same as pressing the cursor left key).

30 cursor moves one position up (i.e., same as pressing the cursor up key).

31 cursor moves one position down (i.e., same as pressing the cursor down key).

7. The word KEY can be displayed by pressing the function key F9.

EXAMPLES

1. The following program assigns the first 10 BASIC statements to the soft keys and displays these statements on the 25th line of the screen.

```
10 FOR N = 1 TO 10
20    READ A$
30    KEY N, A$+" "
40 NEXT N
50 KEY ON
60 DATA ABS, ASC, ATN, AUTO, BEEP
70 DATA BLOAD, BSAVE, CHR$, CALL, CDBL
```

2. After the statement

```
KEY 1, CHR$(12) + "LIST" + CHR$(13)
```

is executed, pressing the soft key F1 clears the screen, prints the word LIST, and causes a carriage return (thereby listing the entire program currently in memory).

KEY

3. Suppose that a program initially contains many lines that begin with the BASIC statement LPRINT. After the statement

```
KEY 4, CHR$(13) + "LPRINT " + CHR$(34): AUTO
```

has been entered, pressing KEY 4 enters the current line of the program, AUTOmatically numbers the next line, and displays LPRINT " after the number.

4. The following program displays the two-character string that is returned by the INKEY$ function when a disabled soft key is pressed. After the program was started by executing RUN, the 10 soft keys were pressed one at a time in order. (Press Ctrl-Break to terminate the program.)

```
10 FOR N = 1 TO 10: KEY N, "": NEXT N
20 A$ = INKEY$: IF A$ = "" THEN 20
30 PRINT A$;
40 GOTO 20
RUN
 ; < = > ? a A B C D
```

5. The following program lines cause the computer to wait until the soft key F8 is pressed.

```
10 KEY 8, ""
20 A$ = INKEY$: IF A$ <> CHR$(0)+"B" THEN 20
```

FURTHER DISCUSSION

The ON KEY(n) statement allows us to write programs which can be interrupted and caused to branch to a special subroutine. The 10 soft keys, F1 to F10, and 4 cursor control keys provide 14 function keys which can be "trapped" by the ON KEY(n) statement, with values of n ranging from 1 to 14. (See the discussion of ON KEY(n).) In BASIC 2.0 and subsequent versions, we can define an additional 6 function keys, "F15" to "F20," which then can be "trapped" by the ON KEY(n) statement.

Each key on the keyboard has a scan code number ranging from 1 to 83. (See Appendix J.) Some keys and their scan codes are listed below.

Key	Scan code
# / 3	4
P	25
A	30
V	47
Pg Up	73

If n is a number from 15 to 20, then the statement

```
KEY n, CHR$(0) + CHR$(k)
```

defines the function key "Fn" to be the regular keyboard key with scan code k. If this statement, along with **KEY(n) ON** and **ON KEY(n) GOSUB m** are executed, then pressing the key with scan code k initiates a GOSUB to line m. For instance, the following program will PLAY the first bar of a familiar song when the key P is pressed. (This program requires Advanced BASIC. Press Ctrl-Break to terminate the program.)

```
10 KEY 15, CHR$(0) + CHR$(25)
20 KEY(15) ON
30 ON KEY(15) GOSUB 50
40 GOTO 40
50 PLAY "CDEC"
60 RETURN
```

FURTHER COMMENTS

8. The normal function keys and the cursor control keys cannot be redefined as key "Fn"; that is, the scan code values 59 through 68, 72, 75, 77, and 79 should not be used for k.

9. If the Caps Lock or Num Lock key is active, or the Shift, Alt, or Ctrl key is pressed together with the key to be trapped, then trapping will not occur for keys "F15" to "F20" which were defined using CHR$(0) + CHR$(k). See Comments 10 and 11 below.

10. The KEY n statement can define the keys "F15" to "F20" to be a combination of any of the non-function keys with one or more of the latched keys, Caps Lock, Num Lock, Alt, Ctrl, or Shift. The statement

```
KEY n, CHR$(s) + CHR$(k)
```

defines the function key "Fn" to be the combination of the key whose scan code is k, together with one or more of the latched keys according to the value of s. The values of s associated with each of the latched keys are given below

Key	Value
Caps Lock	64
Num Lock	32
Alt	8
Ctrl	4
Shift	1, 2, or 3

For example, **KEY 18, CHR$(32) + CHR$(25)** defines function key "F18" as the combination Num Lock-P. With the appropriate ON KEY and KEY ON statements, trapping will occur when the Num Lock key is active and the key P is pressed.

KEY

For key combinations involving more than one latched key, the value used for s is just the sum of the values for each of the desired latched keys. For example, to define function key 20 as the combination Alt-Ctrl-P, use `KEY 20, CHR$(12) + CHR$(25)`.

11.   The latched keys Caps Lock and Num Lock are toggle keys; that is, once pressed they remain active until pressed again. This fact must be taken into account when trying to trap a key defined by KEY n. If a function key is not defined as including the keys Caps Lock or Num Lock, but these keys happen to be active, then no trapping will occur.

APPLICATIONS

1.   Suppose that a program being written will use a certain word or phrase many times. The word or phrase can be assigned to one of the soft keys and then displayed with just a single keystroke.

2.   Many pieces of software have a menu giving the different tasks that the software can perform. Often the user is asked to press an appropriate soft key in order to initiate a task. The KEY statement is used to assign the names of the tasks to the soft keys and to display these names on line 25 of the screen. The statement `ON KEY(n)` is used to cause branching to a subroutine when a soft key is pressed.

The left part of the keyboard consists of 10 keys labeled F1 to F10. The numeric keypad on the right of the keyboard has 4 white cursor control keys. For purposes of this discussion, these cursor control keys are called F11 (Cursor Up), F12 (Cursor Left), F13 (Cursor Right), and F14 (Cursor Down).

The computer has the ability to respond to the pressing of the keys F1 to F14 by branching to a subroutine. This process is referred to as *trapping* a key. The statement

    KEY(n) ON

is used in conjunction with the statement ON KEY(n) GOSUB m to trap the key Fn. The statement KEY(n) ON causes the computer to constantly check the status of the key Fn for possible trapping, and the statement ON KEY(n) GOSUB m instructs the computer to respond to the pressing of that key by branching to line m. We say that KEY(n) ON enables trapping of the key. The statement

    KEY(n) OFF

disables trapping of the key. (See the discussion of the statement ON KEY(n) for further details.)

The statement

    KEY(n) STOP

enables a delayed trapping of the key Fn. The combination of this statement and ON KEY(n) GOSUB m results in the computer remembering if the key has been pressed, but delaying branching until the statement KEY(n) ON is executed. See Example 2.

EXAMPLES

1.
```
10 KEY(3) ON
20 ON KEY(3) GOSUB 90
30 PRINT "Press key F3"
40 IF A=0 THEN 40
50 KEY(3) OFF
60 PRINT "Press it again"
70 FOR I = 1 TO 4000: NEXT I
80 END
90 BEEP
100 A=1
110 RETURN
```

Line 40 will be executed repeatedly until key F3 is pressed. Then the speaker will beep and lines 40, 50, and 60 will be executed once. Line 70 produces a

KEY(n)

delay of 5 seconds to allow you to press the key again. However, this time no beeping sound is heard since trapping was disabled in line 50.

```
2.  10 CLS
    20 ON KEY(14) GOSUB 90
    30 LOCATE 12,9: PRINT "The time is"
    40 KEY(14) STOP
    50 LOCATE 12,21
    60 PRINT TIME$
    70 KEY(14) ON
    80 GOTO 40
    90 T=T+1: LOCATE 1,1
    100 PRINT "The key has been pressed"; T; "times"
    110 RETURN
```

This program turns the computer into a clock. Also, the first row of the screen counts the number of times that the Cursor Down key is pressed. This count is updated by the subroutine in lines 90 through 110, which is entered every time the key is pressed. Line 40 guarantees that the subroutine will not be entered right after line 50. If this were to happen, the computer would PRINT the key data on row one and then RETURN to line 60 and PRINT the current time on row two. To see this occur, change line 80 to GOTO 50 and press the Cursor Down key repeatedly.

COMMENTS

1. The statements discussed here can only be used with Advanced BASIC. That is, the command BASICA must have been given when BASIC was invoked.

2. This statement is quite different from the KEY statement, which is primarily used to assign strings to the soft keys or to turn on and off the display of these strings on the 25th line of the screen.

3. BASIC 2.0 and subsequent versions allow the trapping of 6 additional keys or key combinations with values of n ranging from 15 to 20. See the discussion of KEY for the details of how these key combinations are specified.

4. Trapping of all keys is deactivated whenever any of the commands CHAIN, CHAIN MERGE, CLEAR, LOAD, MERGE, or RUN are executed, or when a program line is deleted or entered.

APPLICATIONS

See the discussion of ON KEY(n).

The KILL command is used to erase a program, data, or memory image file located on a disk. The command

    KILL filespec

erases the specified file.

COMMENTS

1.   BASIC was invoked from DOS by typing the word BASIC or BASICA following A>, B>, C>, or D>. The expression used identifies the "default drive". For instance, had the screen read **B>BASIC** or **B>BASICA** when BASIC was invoked, then drive B: would be the default drive.

When using the KILL command, you have the option of not specifying the drive. If so, the named file is erased from the default drive. (With BASIC 2.0 and subsequent versions, it is erased from the current directory of the default drive.)

2.   Filenames consist of two parts—a name of at most 8 characters followed by an optional period and an extension of at most 3 characters. Files that have the extension BAS can be LOADed and RUN by referring to them without their extension. However, to KILL a file, you must give the entire name. (Note: When a program or memory image file is created in BASIC and SAVEd with a name having at most 8 characters, the extension BAS is automatically added to the name. It is not unusual for programmers to forget to use the extension and therefore get a "File not found" error message.)

3.   With versions of BASIC preceding BASIC 2.0, you can only KILL one file at a time. The global filename characters "*" and "?" that can be used with the FILES command are not accepted by the KILL command. If you want to erase several files at once, return to DOS and use ERASE. ERASE will accept global filenames. With versions of BASIC beginning with 2.0, the global filenames *can* be used with KILL.

4.   The KILL command will not erase a sequential or random file that is open. (See the discussion of the OPEN statement.) Attempting to do so invokes a "File already open" error message.

5.   Once a file has been KILLed, there is no way to recover it using BASIC. However, on the disk only the first letter of the name of the file in the directory is changed to tell the computer that the space allocated to this file can be reused. Utility programs that recover the file are available commercially.

6.   The KILL command will not erase a directory. This can only be done with the RMDIR command.

KILL

1. SAVE "A:SALES"
    Ok
    KILL "A:SALES"
    File not found
    Ok
    KILL "A:SALES.BAS"
    Ok

2. SAVE "RECORDS.MAY"
    Ok
    FILES "RECORDS.MAY"
    RECORDS .MAY
    Ok
    KILL "RECORDS.MAY"
    Ok
    FILES "RECORDS.MAY"
    File not found
    Ok

If A\$ is a string and n is a positive whole number, then

```
LEFT$(A$,n)
```

is the string consisting of the leftmost n characters of A\$.

COMMENTS

1.   There are 256 different characters that can be used in strings. These characters and their ASCII values are listed in Appendix A. All of these characters are counted when they appear in a string; even the control characters, such as carriage return, beep, and cursor down. All spaces are counted, even leading and trailing spaces.

2.   Although the LEFT\$ function is defined only for strings, it can be used indirectly to extract a specified number of digits from a number. For instance, if A is a positive whole number, then STR\$(A) is the string consisting of a leading space followed by the digits corresponding to the value of A. Thus, taking into account the leading space, the n most significant digits of A are VAL(LEFT\$(STR\$(A),n+1)). See Example 1.

3.   The LEFT\$ function creates a new string, but does not destroy the original string.

4.   The value of n in LEFT\$(A\$,n) can be any number between 0 and 255.4999. If n is not a whole number, it will be rounded to the nearest whole number. If the (rounded) value is 0, LEFT\$ will return the empty string, "". If the value is greater than the number of characters in A\$, then LEFT\$ will return the entire string A\$.

5.   The functions RIGHT\$ and MID\$ are analogous to the LEFT\$ function. MID\$(A\$,1,n) has the same value as LEFT\$(A\$,n).

EXAMPLES

1.   ```
PRINT LEFT$("Matthew Webb",7)
Matthew
Ok
PRINT VAL(LEFT$(STR$(1875),3))
 18
Ok
```

2.   ```
10 T$ = "Very"+CHR$(13)+"Truly Yours"
20 PRINT LEFT$(T$,10)
RUN
Very
Truly
Ok
```

(*Note:* CHR\$(13) is the undisplayable character carriage return.)

LEFT$

3.  ```
    10 INPUT "Is La Paz the highest city in the world"; A$
    20 B$ = LEFT$(A$,1)
    30 IF B$="Y" OR B$="y" THEN PRINT "Incorrect": GOTO 50
    40 PRINT "Correct"
    50 PRINT "Lhasa, Tibet is the highest city in the world."
    RUN
    Is La Paz the highest city in the world? yup
    Incorrect
    Lhasa, Tibet is the highest city in the world.
    Ok
    ```

By using LEFT$, the program was able to tolerate many different responses to the question such as Yes, yes, and Yeah.

4. The following program isolates a person's first name from his full name. In line 20, the value of A will be the location of the first space in the name.

```
10 INPUT "Full name: ", N$
20 A = INSTR(N$," ")
30 F$ = LEFT$(N$,A-1)
40 PRINT "Your first name is "; F$; "."
RUN
Full name: William Archibald Spooner
Your first name is William.
Ok
```

APPLICATIONS

The LEFT$ function can help make programs user-friendly, as in Example 3, and to manipulate strings, as in Example 4.
```

If A\$ is a string, then the value of

```
LEN(A$)
```

is the number of characters in the string.

COMMENTS

1. There are 256 different characters that can be used in strings. These characters along with their ASCII values are listed in Appendix A. All of these characters are counted when they appear in a string, even control characters such as carriage return, beep, and cursor down. All spaces are counted, even leading and trailing spaces.

2. Although the LEN function is defined only for strings, it can be used indirectly to determine the number of digits in a number. For instance, if N is a positive whole number (not displayed in floating point form), then STR\$(N) is the string consisting of the digits in N plus the leading space. Thus, the number of digits in N is LEN(STR\$(N))-1.

EXAMPLES

1.  ```
    PRINT LEN("1 byte"); LEN(" *** ")
       6  5
    Ok
    ```

2.  ```
    PRINT  LEN("ring"+CHR$(7))
       5
    Ok
    ```

(*Note:* CHR\$(7) is the undisplayable character "beep.")

3.  ```
    10 A$ = "U. S. Grant": B = LEN(A$)
    20 C = 1822: D$ = STR$(C)
    30 PRINT B; LEN(D$)-1
    RUN
     11  4
    Ok
    ```

We cannot compute LEN(C) since C is a numeric variable, not a string variable. Attempting to do so results in the error message "Type mismatch". Since positive numbers automatically carry a leading space with them, STR\$(C) is the string " 1822".

4.  ```
    10 INPUT "Phone number"; P$
    20 IF LEN(P$)=8 THEN PRINT "Include area code": GOTO 10
    30 IF LEN(P$)<>12 GOTO 10
    RUN
    Phone number? 123-4567
    ```

LEN

```
Include area code
Phone number? 555-123-4567
Ok
```

APPLICATIONS

1. LEN is used extensively when manipulating strings.

2. LEN is often used to obtain the terminating value of a FOR . . . NEXT loop. The following program can be used to convert an amount of money written in its standard form into a number. Numeric form is needed in order to perform calculations with the amount.

```
10 LINE INPUT "Amount: "; A$
20 C$ = ""
30 FOR I=1 TO LEN(A$)
40   B$=MID$(A$,I,1)
50   IF B$="," OR B$="$" THEN GOTO 70
60   C$=C$+B$
70 NEXT I
80 A#=VAL(C$): PRINT A#
RUN
Amount: $12,345,678.55
 12345678.55
Ok
```

A variable is a name to which the computer can assign a value. Variables are of two types: numeric and string. Furthermore, numeric variables can be of three different precisions: integer, single-, and double-precision. The type of a variable can be specified by a DEFtype statement (DEFINT, DEFSNG DEFDBL, or DEFSTR), or one of the type declaration tags %, !, #, or $. If var is a variable, and val is a value of the same type, then the statement

```
LET var = val
```

assigns the value to the variable.

EXAMPLE

1.  ```
    10 LET A = 5
    20 LET B$ = "BOY"
    30 LET A# = 123456789
    40 LET SSN$(4) = "217-34-8087"
    50 PRINT A; B$; A#; SSN$(4)
    RUN
     5 BOY 123456789 217-34-8087
    Ok
    ```

COMMENTS

1.   If the variable is a string variable and the value is a string constant, then the value must be enclosed in quotation marks.

2.   If the variable is a numeric variable and the value is a numeric constant of a different precision, then the assignment will be carried out, if possible. However, the constant will be converted to the precision of the variable. (An example of an assignment that cannot be carried out is **LET A%=80000**. This statement produces the error message "Overflow".)

3.   Attempts to assign numeric values to string variables, or vice versa, result in the error message "Type mismatch".

4.   LET statements can be used to assign expressions to variables. These expressions can be combinations of constants and/or variables. See Example 5.

5.   Variable names must begin with a letter. The other characters, except possibly the last, must be letters, numerals, or decimal points. If the name consists of more than 40 characters (in addition to the type declaration tag), only the first forty characters will be significant.

6.   Caution must be taken to avoid using *reserved words* for names of variables. Appendix I contains a list of reserved words.
    ```

LET

7. LET statements can omit the word LET. For instance, line 10 of Example 1 could have been written **A = 5**. In this handbook, we usually omit the word LET.

8. If a double-precision numeric variable is assigned a value with more than 16 significant digits, 17 digits will be stored in memory and, when displayed, this 17-digit value will be rounded to a 16-digit number. However, calculations use the full 17 digits stored in memory.

```
10 LET A# = 1234567890123456.2
20 PRINT A#
30 PRINT A#-1000000000000000
RUN
 1234567890123456
 234567890123456.2
Ok
```

9. When the computer is given a statement of the form **LET var = expression**, the expression is evaluated first, then the answer assigned to the variable. Thus LET statements like LET A=A+2 make sense; A+2 is calculated, then this new value replaces the old value of A. Note then that LET statements do *not* set up an equation for the computer to solve. The statement **LET X=2*X+1** does not mean "If X equals 2*X+1 then what is X?", but instead, "Replace the current value of X by 2*(the current value of X)+1."

10. For good programming style, variable names should indicate the type of information that the variable will hold.

11. If a certain variable is to be used often in a program, it should be assigned a value early. (Executing a statement such as **LET A=0** is referred to as *initializing* the variable.) Each time that a variable is used, the computer searches for it in a list of variables. Time is saved if frequently used variables are near the top of the list.

FURTHER EXAMPLES

2.  ```
    LET ADDRESS$ = HOME: PRINT ADDRESS$
    Type mismatch
    Ok
    ```

3.  ```
    LET A% = 5.8: PRINT A%
     6
    Ok
    ```

The single-precision constant 5.8 was rounded to the integer constant 6.

4.  ```
    LET A = "ADAM": PRINT A
    Type mismatch
    Ok
    ```
    ```

5.  ```
    10 LET A = 2*3+4
    20 LET B = 5
    30 LET B = B+1
    40 LET C = 2*3+B
    50 PRINT A; B; C
    RUN
     10  6  12
    Ok
    ```

6.  ```
    10 NOM$ = "ADAM": AGE = 25
    20 PRINT NOM$, AGE
    RUN
    ADAM              25
    Ok
    ```

Note: Had line 10 read **NAME$ = "ADAM": AGE = 25**, the message "Syntax error in 10" would have resulted, since NAME is a reserved word.

7.  ```
    10 DEFSTR N
    20 NOM = "ADAM"
    30 PRINT NOM
    RUN
    ADAM
    Ok
    ```

Line 10 declared that all variables beginning with the letter N be string variables.

8.  ```
    10 DEFINT H
    20 LET HEIGHT! = 5.8
    30 PRINT HEIGHT!
    RUN
     5.8
    Ok
    ```

Did you expect to see 6 PRINTed? LET statements take precedence over DEFtype statements, and the LET statement specified that the variable be a single-precision constant.

9.  ```
    A# = .2: B# = .2#: PRINT A#; B#
     .2000000029802322   .2
    Ok
    ```

In the first case, the single-precision number .2 was converted to a double-precision number when assigned to the variable A#. See the discussion of CDBL for details.
    ```

LINE

The LINE statement is used in graphics modes to draw straight lines (Figure 1a), open rectangles (Figure 1b), or solid rectangles (Figure 1c).

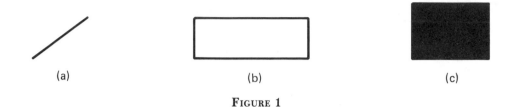

(a)　　　　　　　　　　(b)　　　　　　　　　　(c)

FIGURE 1

We assume that the reader is familiar with the way that coordinates of points are specified in graphics modes. (See Appendix C for details.) The statement

```
LINE (a,b)-(c,d)
```

draws a straight line segment joining the two points (a,b) and (c,d). The statement

```
LINE (a,b)-(c,d),,B
```

draws an open rectangle having the points (a,b) and (c,d) as diagonally opposite corners. The statement

```
LINE (a,b)-(c,d),,BF
```

draws a solid rectangle having the points (a,b) and (c,d) as diagonally opposite corners.

In medium-resolution graphics mode with color enabled (invoked by the statement SCREEN 1,0), a background color and a palette of 4 colors can be selected via a COLOR statement. If so, the statements

```
LINE (a,b)-(c,d),k
LINE (a,b)-(c,d),k,B
LINE (a,b)-(c,d),k,BF
```

each draw their figures in color k of the current palette. The number k can range from 0 to 3. Zero is the background color and 3 is the foreground color. If no color is specified, the foreground color is used.

EXAMPLES

1. `CLS: LINE (25,150)-(200,40)`

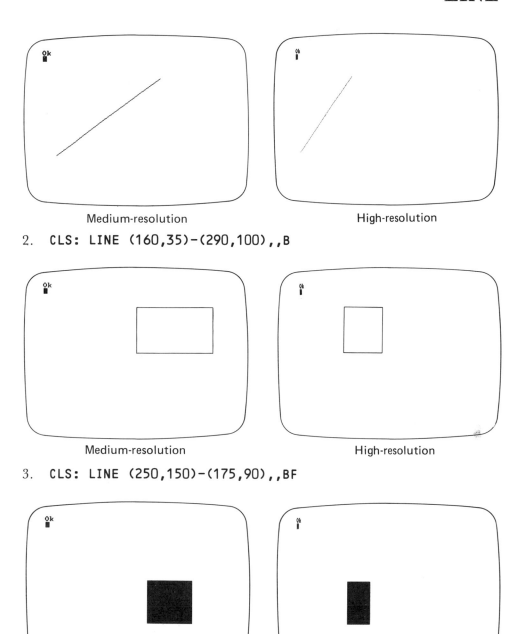

Medium-resolution   High-resolution

2. `CLS: LINE (160,35)-(290,100),,B`

Medium-resolution   High-resolution

3. `CLS: LINE (250,150)-(175,90),,BF`

Medium-resolution   High-resolution

COMMENTS

1. The LINE statement requires a graphics monitor.

LINE

2.   The first pair of coordinates in a LINE statement can be omitted. If so, the last point referenced is used as the first point.

3.   Either pair of coordinates can be given in relative form, that is, as STEP (s,t). If the second coordinate is in relative form, then the first coordinate is used as the last point referenced.

4.   After a LINE statement is executed in a program, the second point becomes the last point referenced.

5.   The statement PAINT can be used to obtain rectangles whose boundaries have a different color than their interiors.

FURTHER EXAMPLES

4.
```
10 CLS: SCREEN 1,0
20 LINE -(80,180)
```

```
10 CLS: SCREEN 1,0
20 LINE -(80,180)
30 LINE -(300,150)
```

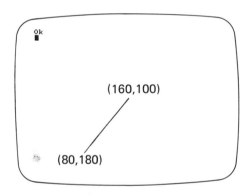

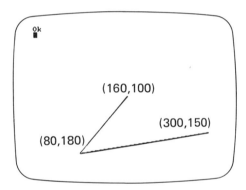

In line 20, the center of the screen is taken as the last point referenced. In line 30, the point (80,180) is used as the last point referenced.

5.
```
10 CLS: SCREEN 1,0: KEY OFF
20 LINE (20,20)-(50,150)
30 LINE STEP (50,-50)-(150,50)
40 LINE (200,50)-STEP (50,-50)
50 LINE STEP (50,50)-STEP (0,50)
RUN (See Figure 2.)
```

6.   The following program draws a bar graph that displays 6 months of data. (See Figure 3)

```
10 CLS: SCREEN 1: KEY OFF
20 LINE (24,16)-(24,160)
30 LINE -(300,160)
40 LOCATE 22,8
50 PRINT "J    F    M    A    M    J"
60 FOR M=0 TO 5
```

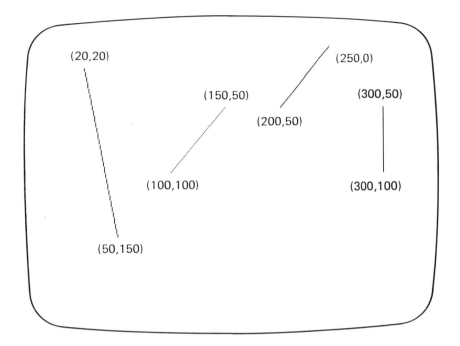

FIGURE 2

```
70      READ A
80      LINE (45+M*40,160)-(75+M*40,160-10*A),,BF
90      LOCATE 19-1.25*A,7+5*M
100     PRINT A
110 NEXT M
120 DATA 3,14,7,9,6,12
```

7. The following program creates a line graph for the data of Example 6.
(See Figure 4)

```
10 CLS: SCREEN 1: KEY OFF
20 LINE (24,16)-(24,160)
30 LINE -(300,160)
40 LOCATE 22,8
50 PRINT "J    F    M    A    M    J"
60 READ A: PSET (60,160-10*A)
70 FOR M=1 TO 5
80     READ A
90     LINE -(60+40*M,160-10*A)
100 NEXT M
110 DATA 3,14,7,9,6,12
```

LINE

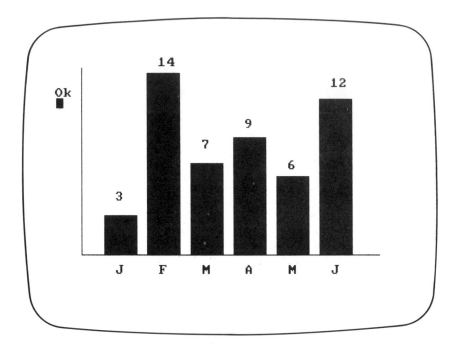

FIGURE 3

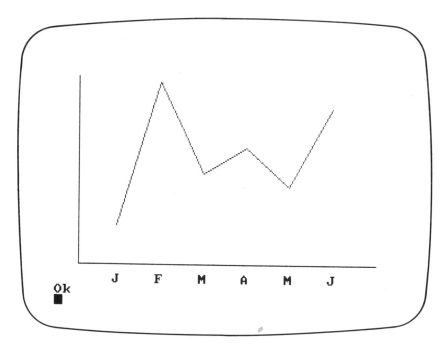

FIGURE 4

8. The following program draws a magenta line from the upper left-hand corner of the screen to the lower right-hand corner and draws a cyan solid rectangle in the upper right-hand quarter of the screen.

```
10 CLS: SCREEN 1,0: KEY OFF
20 COLOR 0,1
30 LINE (0,0)-(319,199),2
40 LINE (319,0)-(160,100),1,BF
```

FURTHER DISCUSSION

BASIC 2.0 and subsequent versions provide two enhancements to the line statement: *line clipping* and *style*.

Consider a statement of the form LINE (a,b)-(c,d) where the point (c,d) is off the screen. We can think of the point (c,d) as being located in some large coordinate system containing the screen. BASIC 2.0 (and subsequent versions) will imagine the line connecting the two points as being drawn in the large coordinate system and will display the portion of the line that lies on the screen. That is, it "clips" off a portion of the imaginary line. Earlier versions of BASIC just replaced the point (c,d) with some point on the edge of the screen and drew the line connecting these two points. Also, BASIC 2.0 (and subsequent versions) retain the point (c,d) as the last point referenced, whereas earlier versions of BASIC take a point on the edge of the screen as the last point referenced.

Instead of being limited to drawing just solid lines between two points, the user can draw patterned, or "styled," lines with BASIC 2.0 and subsequent versions. Some examples are shown in Figure 5. The style consists of a 16 point pattern that is repeated as many times as necessary.

To draw a styled line from (a,b) to (c,d), we consider the pixels lying on the straight line between the two specified points and turn on some of these pixels. Suppose that we begin with the point (c,d) and, of the first 16 pixels, we turn on the 1st, 5th, 10th, and 14th pixels. We can represent this pattern by the 16-tuple

    1000100001000100

Counting from left to right, this 16-tuple has 1s in its 1st, 5th, 10th, and 14th positions and 0s elsewhere. The 16-tuple is the binary representation of the decimal number 34884 and the hexadecimal number &H8844. The statement

    LINE (a,b)-(c,d),,,34884

or the statement

    LINE (a,b)-(c,d),,,&H8844

draws the line from (a,b) to (c,d) beginning at (c,d) with the first 16 pixels as described above and then repeating the same pattern in each successive 16-

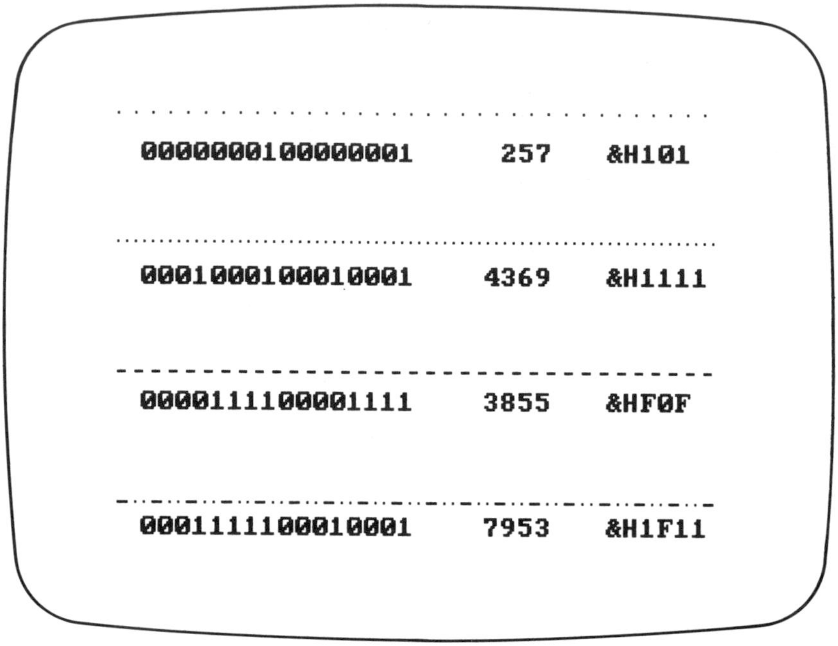

LINE

```
. . . . . . . . . . . . . . . . . . . . . . . . . . . . . .
      0000000100000001            257      &H101

      ...............................................
      0001000100010001           4369      &H1111

      - - - - - - - - - - - - - - - - - - - - - - -
      0000111100001111           3855      &HF0F

      - - .- - .- - - .- - .- - - - .- - .- - - -
      0001111100010001           7953      &H1F11
```

FIGURE 5

tuple until the point (a,b) is reached. In general, if s is a whole number from 0 to 65535, then the statement

```
LINE (a,b)-(c,d),,,s
```

draws the line from (a,b) to (c,d) with the pattern determined by the 16-tuple binary representation of s. The number s is referred to as the *style* of the line. Figure 5 shows 4 different patterns of lines with the associated 16-tuple and style of each. Both the decimal and hexadecimal forms of the styles are shown.

FURTHER EXAMPLES

9. The following program produced different results when run with different versions of BASIC. BASIC 1.1 produced Figure 6a, and BASIC 2.0 produced Figure 6b. With BASIC 1.1, the first line was drawn to the point (319,0). With BASIC 2.0, a line was imagined as being drawn to the point (600,0) and then the portion contained on the screen was displayed. Also, the effect of line 30 demonstrates that after line 20 was executed, the last point referenced was taken as (319,0) in BASIC 1.1 and as (600,0) in BASIC 2.0.

```
10 SCREEN 1: CLS: KEY OFF
20 LINE (0,199)-(600,0)
30 LINE -(159,199)
```

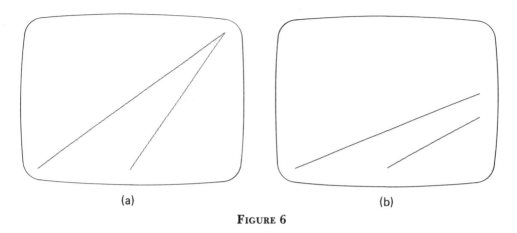

(a)   (b)

FIGURE 6

10. The following program draws the last styled line in Figure 5 and displays the numbers shown below. The POINT function has the value 3 if the indicated pixel is on, and the value 0 if it is off. The pattern of 0s and 3s is the same as the pattern of 0s and 1s appearing in the binary representation of 7953. *Note:* The number 7953 appearing in line 20 could have been written as &H1F11.

```
10 CLS: SCREEN 1
20 LINE (20,170)-(300,170),,,7953
30 FOR I = 0 TO 15
40 PRINT POINT(300-I,170);
50 NEXT I
RUN
 0  0  0  3  3  3  3  3  0  0  0  3  0  0  0  3
Ok
```

FURTHER COMMENTS

6. As mentioned above, in versions of BASIC preceding 2.0, points off the screen are replaced by points on the edge of the screen. In BASIC 1.1, negative coordinates of such points are replaced by 0, second coordinates greater than 199 are replaced with 199, and positive out of range first coordinates are replaced by either 319 (in medium-resolution graphics) or 639 (in high-resolution graphics).

7. The following procedure can be used to determine the style of a pattern in decimal form:

  (a) Write down the 16-tuple of 0s and 1s.
  (b) Split the 16-tuple into two 8-tuples.
  (c) Use Appendix K to find the decimal number associated with each 8-tuple.

219

LINE

<ol start="8">
<li>
<ol type="a" start="4">
<li>The number s is computed as 256*[number associated with left 8-tuple] + [number associated with right 8-tuple].</li>
</ol>
</li>
</ol>

8. To determine the style of a number in hexadecimal form, replace steps (c) and (d) in Comment 7 as follows:

   (c) Use Appendix K to find the hexadecimal number associated with each 8-tuple. If the number associated with the right 8-tuple consists of a single digit, append a 0 to the left of it.

   (d) The number s is obtained by writing down "&H", then [the number associated with the left 8-tuple], and then [the number associated with the right 8-tuple].

9. The parameter k can be inserted into a line statement to draw a styled line in color and the parameter B can be inserted to draw a styled rectangle. However, the parameter BF cannot be used with a styled line.

10. When a styled line is drawn, the pixels associated with 1s in the pattern are turned on, and the pixels associated with 0s are left alone. Hence, if the line is being drawn over a busy background, it might not turn out as expected. One way of handling this situation is to first draw a solid line in one color, and then superimpose the styled line on top of it in another color.

APPLICATIONS

In addition to its obvious uses in graphics, the LINE statement can also be used to clear a rectangular portion of the screen. For instance, in high-resolution graphics mode, the statement `LINE (0,0)-(320,100),0,BF` clears the upper-left quarter of the screen.

LINE INPUT

The LINE INPUT statement is used to request information from the user. A statement of the form

```
LINE INPUT A$
```

where A$ is a string variable, causes the computer to pause until the user types in a sequence of up to 254 characters and pushes the Enter key. This sequence is then assigned to the string variable and the program continues running.

Usually we want to tell the user the type of information that is being requested by displaying a prompt message. A statement of the form

```
LINE INPUT "prompt"; A$
```

will display the message contained inside the quotation marks.

EXAMPLES

1.  ```
    10 LINE INPUT C$
    20 PRINT "***"+C$
    RUN
    USA
    ***USA
    Ok
    ```

After entering RUN, the user will see a blinking cursor on the next line. Since Ok hasn't appeared, the user knows that the computer has paused. The user then can type in whatever he or she pleases.

2.  ```
    10 LINE INPUT "COUNTRY: "; C$
    20 PRINT "***" + C$
    RUN
    COUNTRY: USA
    ***USA
    Ok
    ```

3.  ```
    10 LINE INPUT "? "; A$
    20 PRINT A$
    RUN
    ? "JOHN SMITH,III"
    "JOHN SMITH,III"
    Ok
    ```
    ```

LINE INPUT

COMMENTS

1. The LINE INPUT statement isn't discriminating. It will assign to the string variable any sequence of characters, exactly as typed. In particular, as seen in Example 3, it will take quotation marks and commas. Although it does not take trailing spaces, it will take leading spaces.

2. If the response to a LINE INPUT statement is a number, the number will be treated like a string. Later it can be converted back to a number using the VAL function.

3. If we respond to the request for information by pressing the Enter key, the null string will be assigned to the variable.

4. Suppose that line n contains a LINE INPUT statement. If we respond to the request for information by pressing Ctrl-Break, the message "Break in line n" is displayed. The computer then will be in direct mode. We can resume execution of the program at line n by entering the command CONT.

5. In each of the examples presented above, the cursor moved to the next line after receiving the information from the user. This can be prevented by placing a semicolon immediately following the words LINE INPUT. For instance, in Example 2 so altering line 10 results in

```
10 LINE INPUT; "COUNTRY: "; C$
20 PRINT "***" + C$
RUN
COUNTRY: USA***USA
Ok
```

6. With the computer in text and direct modes, hold down the Alt key, push the sequence 225 on the numeric keypad, and then release the Alt key. The Greek letter beta will be displayed on the screen. Consulting the table of ASCII values in Appendix A, we see that beta has ASCII value 225. Any character with ASCII value from 32 to 255 (except 127) can be displayed on the screen using the Alt key and the numeric keypad. The response to LINE INPUT's request for a string constant can consist of characters entered using the Alt key and the numeric keypad.

7. The LINE INPUT statement has some characteristics in common with INPUT, INPUT$, and INKEY$. The INPUT statement allows us to request several pieces of information at one time, and the information can be both strings and numbers. The INPUT$ function automatically processes the response after a specified number of characters have been received. INKEY$ accepts as information only the character currently available from the keyboard buffer. (See the discussions of these statements for further details.)

8. The statement **LINE INPUT "prompt", A\$** is equivalent to the statement **LINE INPUT "prompt"; A\$**.

FURTHER EXAMPLES

4.  ```
    10 LINE INPUT "SALARY? "; S$
    20 PRINT S$
    RUN
    SALARY? 12000
    12000
    Ok
    ```

We can tell from the way that 12000 was PRINTed that it is being stored as a string constant. Had it been a numeric constant, it would have been PRINTed with a leading space. If we want to do computations with this figure, we can LET S = VAL(S$) and compute with S.

5.  ```
    10 LINE INPUT "INCOME?"; I$
    20 PRINT I$
    RUN
    INCOME?     (User presses Ctrl-Break)
    Break in 10
    Ok
    PRINT 12000+1234.56
     13234.56
    Ok
    CONT
    INCOME? 13234.56
    13234.56
    Ok
    ```

After the first request, the user decided to use the computer as an adding machine and total the various sources of income.

6.  ```
    10 LINE INPUT "What is your favorite liqueur? "; L$
    20 PRINT "I will get you some "; L$; " now "
    RUN
    What is your favorite liqueur? crème de menthe
    I will get you some crème de menthe now.
    Ok
    ```

The character è was typed by holding down the Alt key, pushing 130 on the numeric keypad, and then releasing the Alt key.

APPLICATIONS

1. The LINE INPUT statement often provides the safest way to request information. For instance, consider Example 4. The user could have res-
    ```

LINE INPUT

ponded 12000, 12,000, $12000, or $12,000. All of these responses would have been accepted. Also, we can easily design a subroutine that would convert them to their numeric values. If we really had to, we could even design a subroutine that would deal with a response such as TWELVE THOUSAND DOLLARS.

2. The INPUT statement is the best known BASIC statement for requesting information. However, it cannot be used if the response might either contain a comma or begin with a quotation mark and contain other quotation marks within the string. In such cases, the LINE INPUT statement must be used.

LINE INPUT#

A sequential data file is a sequence of pieces of information that reside on a disk. Appendix F and the discussions of WRITE# and PRINT# explain how information is entered into sequential files and how it looks on the disk. In addition to the items of information inserted by the user, the files also contain assorted quotation marks and commas, and 3 characters that we refer to as CR, LF, and AR.

In the standard usage of PRINT# and WRITE#, the characters CR (carriage return) and LF (line feed) occur only as a pair with CR first. We denote this pair by <CR/LF>. Also, the character AR (arrow character denoting end of file) normally appears only at the end of a file. We shall assume that both of these conditions hold for the files discussed here.

After the statement **OPEN "filespec" FOR INPUT AS #n** is executed, the information can be read from the file, in order, starting at the beginning of the file. The statement

```
LINE INPUT #n, A$
```

will assign to the string variable A$ a certain amount of information from the file having reference number n. The computer reads successive characters until it encounters the pair <CR/LF>, the character <AR>, or until it has read 255 characters, and then assigns these characters to the string variable A$. The pair of characters <CR/LF> are not included in the string.

Subsequent input with either LINE INPUT#, INPUT#, or INPUT$ will begin with the next character after the <CR/LF> pair or with the 256th character. The criteria for reading further strings is the same as before.

LINE INPUT# statements also can be used to extract strings from the buffer of a random file. (See the discussion of GET (Files) for the details of how records are retrieved from random files.) However, if we intend to use LINE INPUT# to read information from random files, we must plan ahead and place <CR/LF> pairs at appropriate places in the buffer.

EXAMPLES

1. Suppose that the sequential file shown below is named FILMS.

```
"Coquette",Pickford<CR/LF> "The Champ",Beery<CR/LF/AR>

    10 OPEN "FILMS" FOR INPUT AS #3
    20 LINE INPUT #3, A$
    30 PRINT A$
    40 LINE INPUT #3, B$
    50 PRINT B$
    60 CLOSE #3
    RUN
    "Coquette",Pickford
```

225

LINE INPUT#

```
    "The Champ",Beery
Ok
```

Notice that the commas and quotation marks did not serve as delimiters for LINE INPUT#. Also, the leading space before "The Champ" was not skipped over.

2.   The following program creates a random file in which each record lists several cities in a single state. Then the program reads the second record.

```
10 OPEN "B:STATES" AS #1 LEN = 27
20 FIELD #1, 24 AS DF$, 3 AS EF$
30 C$ = CHR$(13) + CHR$(10)
40 LSET EF$ = "*" + C$
50 LSET DF$ = "Birmingham" + C$ + "Mobile" + C$
60 PUT #1, 1
70 LSET DF$ = "Anchorage" + C$ + "Juneau" + C$
80 PUT #1, 2
90 LSET DF$ = "Phoenix" + C$ + "Tucson" + C$ + "Tempe" + C$
100 PUT #1, 3
110 GET #1, 2
120 FOR I = 1 TO 3
130    LINE INPUT #1, A$
140    IF RIGHT$(A$,1) = "*" THEN 170
150    PRINT A$
160 NEXT I
170 CLOSE #1
RUN
Anchorage
Juneau
Ok            .
```

In line 30, C$ is assigned the pair of characters CR and LF. In line 40, an asterisk and <CR/LF> are placed at the end of each buffer where they will remain permanently. In essence, each record is a short sequential file. If we had relied on fields to insert and retrieve data, we would only have been able to place two cities in each record. However, with our current system, we can occasionally pack three cities into a single record.

COMMENTS

1.   LINE INPUT# usually is used to retrieve information from a sequential file that has been placed into the file with a PRINT# statement.

2.   The # sign in a LINE INPUT statement can trail the word INPUT without an intervening space. For instance, line 20 in Example 1 could have been written 20 LINE INPUT#3, A$.

3.   LINE INPUT# can also be used to read from the buffer of a communications file. However, its use should be limited to situations in which you can guarantee that the incoming data has <CR/LF> pairs in appropriate places.

4.   In the event that the character with ASCII value 0 appears in a file, it will be totally ignored by LINE INPUT#.

LIST

The LIST command is used to obtain a listing of the current program in proper order. Variations of the command produce listings of single lines or sequences of consecutive lines.
The command

    LIST

displays each line of the program in proper order.
The command

    LIST n

lists the line numbered n. If m < =n, the command

    LIST m-n

lists all lines with numbers between m and n inclusive. The command

    LIST -n

lists all lines up to and including line n. The command

    LIST m-

lists line m and all lines following it. The command

    LIST .

lists the entered line that was most recently displayed on the screen. See Example 2 for an illustration of the subtleties of this form of the LIST command. For commands of the forms

    LIST .-n
    LIST m-.
    LIST -.
    LIST .-

the "." is interpreted as the number of the last displayed line.

COMMENTS

1.   If more than 22 lines of a program are requested by a LIST command, they will not all fit on the screen at one time, and scrolling will take place. The displaying can be interrupted at any time by pressing Ctrl-Num Lock. To

continue, just press any key. Also, you can abort the LISTing at any time by pressing Ctrl-Break.

2. The line numbers (n and/or m) appearing with a LIST command needn't correspond to actual existing lines in the program. The command still carries out the spirit of the request by listing all existing lines that meet the specified criteria.

3. The line numbers referred to must be between 0 and 65529. Otherwise you will receive a ''Syntax error'' message.

4. The word LIST can be displayed by pressing the F1 key.

5. The LIST command is used primarily in direct mode. While it can be used in a program, it will cause the execution of the program to terminate as soon as the LISTing is completed. At that point, CONT cannot be used to resume execution of the program.

6. The LIST command has some important variations that open up interesting possibilities. These variations allow the output of the command to go to a printer, a disk file, a communications adapter, or to the screen.

The command **LIST m-n, "LPT1:"** results in lines m through n being printed on the first printer. It has the same effect as the statement **LLIST m-n**. However, if you have more than one printer, then the LIST command has greater flexibility, since it allows you to print on any printer.

A command such as **LIST m-n,"B:PROGRAM"** saves lines m-n on drive B: and gives it the name PROGRAM. The file will be in a format known as ASCII format. This format allows the file to be MERGEd with other programs or to be accessed by word processing software. This variation can be thought of as an extension of the command **SAVE "B:PROGRAM",A**. Whereas SAVE saves the entire program, the LIST variation allows the flexibility of saving the entire program or just a part of it.

A command such as **LIST m-n,"COM1:1200,N,8"** sends lines m-n to the first communications adapter.

The command **LIST m-n,"SCRN:"** displays lines m-n on the screen.

EXAMPLES

1.
```
10 PRINT "TEN"
20 PRINT "TWENTY"
30 PRINT "THIRTY"
40 PRINT "FORTY"
LIST 15-30
20 PRINT "TWENTY"
30 PRINT "THIRTY"
Ok
```

2.
```
10 PRINT "TEN"
20 PRINT "TWENTY"
15 PRINT "FIFTEEN"
```

LIST

```
LIST .
15 PRINT "FIFTEEN"
Ok
LIST
10 PRINT "TEN"
15 PRINT "FIFTEEN"
20 PRINT "TWENTY"
Ok
LIST .
20 PRINT "TWENTY"
Ok
```

APPLICATIONS

1. The LIST command is essential when writing and debugging programs, since it puts lines in their proper order and allows us to look at any part of the program.

2. Suppose that we have written a program and want to use a portion of it in another program. We can employ the variation **LIST m-n, filespec** to save that portion. The portion can be incorporated into another program later via the MERGE command. (See the discussion of MERGE for further details.)

3. When debugging a program, we often use the combination of STOP and CONT to interrupt the execution of the program and check that everything is working properly up to that point. However, if after STOPping the execution at line numbered m we alter or add a program line, then we can't use CONT to continue. However, if we know the next line number after line m, then we can use a GOTO n statement in direct mode to continue execution at that line. We can determine that next line number via the command **LIST m-**. (Caution: With this technique, important variables will have to have their values reassigned.)

4. A simple way to copy statements from one part of a program to another is to LIST on the screen the lines to be copied, and then simply change the line number of each line and press the Enter key. The old lines will be unaffected.

The LLIST command is similar to the LIST command except that, whereas LIST displays program lines on the screen, LLIST prints them on the printer. The variations

```
LLIST n
LLIST m-n
LLIST -n
LLIST m-
LLIST .
LLIST .-n
LLIST m-.
LLIST -.
LLIST .-
```

produce the same results as the corresponding LIST commands. (See the discussion of LIST for details.)

COMMENTS

1. Printing can be interrupted at any time by pressing Ctrl-Num Lock. To continue, just press any key. Also, you can abort the printing at any time by pressing Ctrl-Break.

2. The line numbers (m and/or n) appearing with an LLIST command needn't correspond to actual existing lines in the program. The command still carries out the spirit of the request by printing all existing lines that meet the specified criteria.

3. The line numbers referred to must be between 0 and 65529. Otherwise you will receive a ''Syntax error'' message.

4. The computer returns to direct mode after execution of the LLIST command.

5. The LLIST command is used primarily in direct mode. When used in a program line, it will cause the execution of the program to terminate as soon as the LLISTing is completed.

6. The variations of the LIST command that allow output to various devices do not apply to the LLIST command.

LLIST

EXAMPLES

1. *Screen*

```
10 PRINT "TEN"
20 PRINT "TWENTY"
30 PRINT "THIRTY"
40 PRINT "FORTY"
LLIST 15-30
Ok
```

Printer

```
20 PRINT "TWENTY"
30 PRINT "THIRTY"
```

2. *Screen*

```
10 PRINT "TEN"
20 PRINT "TWENTY"
15 PRINT "FIFTEEN"
LLIST .
Ok
LIST
10 PRINT "TEN"
15 PRINT "FIFTEEN"
20 PRINT "TWENTY"
Ok
LLIST .
Ok
```

Printer

```
15 PRINT "FIFTEEN"
20 PRINT "TWENTY"
```

APPLICATIONS

1. The LLIST command is helpful when writing and debugging programs, since it puts lines in their proper order and prints out any part of the program. We can look over the printout, mark it up, and proceed to alter the program. LLIST has an advantage over LIST, in that we can look at more than 22 lines at one time with LLIST.

2. We always save important programs on disk and should back up the disk with another disk. The cautious programmer also keeps a hard copy as backup. This is best accomplished with LLIST.

LOAD

In order to work with a program that resides on a disk, the program must first be read into the RAM (random access memory). This is accomplished by using the command

```
LOAD filespec
```

The program then can be edited or run. A variation of the LOAD command,

```
LOAD filespec,R
```

results in the specified program being LOADed and then run.

COMMENTS

1. The LOAD command clears all variables from memory, removes all information that has been set with DEF FN or DEFtype statements, causes all DIMensioned arrays to become undimensioned, closes all open files, and disables event trapping that has been set with statements such as ON ERROR, ON KEY(n), ON PEN, ON STRIG(n), ON PLAY(n), and ON TIMER. In graphics modes, the "last point referenced" is set to the center of the screen and the effects of previously executed WINDOW and VIEW statements are voided. OPTION BASE 1 is reset to OPTION BASE 0, the speaker is turned off, and lightpens and joystick buttons are deactivated. In BASIC 2.1, Music Foreground is reset to Music Background. In all other versions of BASIC, Music Background is reset to Music Foreground.

2. The R option keeps all open data files open. Hence, the command LOAD filespec,R is similar to the command RUN filespec,R.

3. Pressing the function key F3 causes the word LOAD, followed by a quotation mark, to be displayed on the screen.

4. The LOAD command with the R option can be used within a program to pass control to another program. Hence, it is similar to a CHAIN command. CHAIN commands have the advantage that values previously assigned to variables can be preserved by the use of the ALL option or a COMMON statement.

5. If the name of the specified file to be LOADed has the extension BAS, it's not necessary to use the extension when designating the file.

6. The specified program can be represented by a string variable. This allows one program to LOAD a second, which is chosen based on a name INPUT by the user. For example:

```
10 PRINT "The available games are:"
20 PRINT "Hangman"
30 PRINT "Tictac"
```

LOAD

```
40 PRINT "Maze"
50 PRINT
60 INPUT "Select a game: ", A$
70 LOAD A$, R
```

7. If the specified file is not present on the disk or is not a BASIC program file, executing the LOAD command results in the message "File not found."

EXAMPLES

The following examples hold for all versions of BASIC. However, with BASIC 2.0 (and subsequent versions), we make the assumption that the programs are in the current directory.

1. Suppose that the program named PROG.BAS consists of the two lines

```
10 PRINT "MY ";
20 PRINT "COMPUTER"
```

and resides on the disk in drive B.

```
LOAD "B:PROG"
LIST
10 PRINT "MY ";
20 PRINT "COMPUTER"
Ok
```

2. Let the program PROG.BAS be as in Example 1.

```
LOAD "B:PROG",R
MY COMPUTER
Ok
```

The LOC function keeps track of our position in a file while writing data into or reading data from the file. See Appendix F for a general discussion of sequential and random files.

PART I   SEQUENTIAL DATA FILES

A sequential data file is a sequence of items of information residing on a disk. The items of information can only be read from the file in order, from beginning to end. Similarly, items are entered into the file in order, beginning with the first entry. Additional items can be added only to the end of the file. The OPEN statements

```
OPEN filespec FOR INPUT  AS #n
OPEN filespec FOR OUTPUT AS #n
OPEN filespec FOR APPEND AS #n
```

must precede reading from, entering original items to, and adding items to the end of an existing file, respectively. See the discussion of OPEN for further details.

If we could look at a file residing on a disk, we would see a sequence of characters. These characters consist of the data items and commas, quotation marks, carriage returns, and line feeds inserted by the computer to delimit the data. Think of the characters as being partitioned into blocks of 128 characters. The first block contains characters 1 to 128, the second block contains characters 129 to 256, and so on. Whenever we are reading from or writing to a sequential file (OPENed AS #n), the value of the function

```
LOC(n)
```

depends on the mode in which the file was OPENed and the quantity of data processed since it was OPENed.

OUTPUT mode: LOC(n) is the number of complete blocks (of 128 characters) which have been written. When a file is first OPENed FOR OUTPUT, LOC(n) will be 0, and will remain so until 128 characters have been written to the file. LOC(n) then becomes 1, and will remain so until 256 characters have been written. LOC(n) then becomes 2, and so on.

APPEND mode: In BASIC 1.1, LOC(n) is the number of complete newly completed blocks (of 128 characters) which have been written to the file. In BASIC 2.0 and subsequent versions, LOC(n) is the number of complete new sets of 128 characters that have been written to the file.

INPUT mode: LOC(n) is the number of the block (of 128 characters) from which we are currently reading. When a file is first OPENed FOR INPUT, LOC(n) will be 1. LOC(n) will remain 1 until we read the 129th character, at

LOC

which time LOC(n) becomes 2. LOC(n) becomes 3 when the 257th character is read, and so on.

EXAMPLE

1. The following program creates a sequential file named SEQFILE and records strings of 78 As, Bs, Cs, and Ds. The file is then CLOSEd and reOPENed For APPEND, at which time a string of 78 Es are recorded. (*Note:* Each PRINT #2 statement actually records 80 characters, since carriage return and line feed characters are automatically inserted at the end of each string.) The file is then CLOSEd and reOPENed FOR INPUT, at which time the entire contents of the file are read. The value of LOC(2) is regularly displayed. BASIC 3.0 produced the output shown below.

```
10 OPEN "SEQFILE" FOR OUTPUT AS #2
20 FOR I = 1 TO 4
30    PRINT #2, STRING$(78, 64+I)
40    PRINT LOC(2);
50 NEXT I
60 CLOSE #2
70 PRINT
80 OPEN "SEQFILE" FOR APPEND AS #2
90 PRINT #2, STRING$(78,69)
100 PRINT LOC(2)
110 CLOSE #2
120 OPEN "SEQFILE" FOR INPUT AS #2
130 FOR I = 1 TO 5
140    INPUT #2, A$
150    PRINT LOC(2);
160 NEXT I
170 CLOSE #2
RUN
 0  1  1  2
 0
 1  2  2  3  4
Ok
```

Note: When the above program is run with a version of BASIC preceding 2.0, the number in the second line of output is 1 instead of 0.

PART II   RANDOM FILES

A random file can be thought of as an ordered set of records numbered 1, 2, 3, and so on. These records pass into and out of the file through a portion of memory referred to as a buffer. Records are copied from the buffer to the file by PUT statements and are copied from the file into the buffer by GET statements. (For complete details, see the discussions of GET and PUT.)

A random file is accessed by a statement of the form **OPEN filespec AS #n LEN = g**, which assigns a number to the file. At any time, the value of the function

```
LOC(n)
```

is the number of the record that has most recently been copied into or out of file n, using a PUT or GET statement.

FURTHER EXAMPLE

2. The following program creates a random file named RANFILE where each record contains 10 characters. Lines 40 and 50 enter the word "one" into record 1, lines 70 and 80 enter the word "two" into record 2, and lines 100 and 110 enter the word "five" into record 5. Then lines 130 and 150 retrieve and display the contents of record 2. The value of LOC(1) is displayed regularly.

```
10 OPEN "RANFILE" AS #1 LEN = 10
20 FIELD #1, 10 AS DF$
30 PRINT LOC(1);
40 LSET DF$ = "one"
50 PUT #1,1
60 PRINT LOC(1);
70 LSET DF$ = "two"
80 PUT #1
90 PRINT LOC(1);
100 LSET DF$ = "five"
110 PUT #1,5
120 PRINT LOC(1);
130 GET #1,2
140 PRINT LOC(1)
150 PRINT DF$
160 CLOSE #1
RUN
 0  1  2  5  2
two
Ok
```

COMMENTS

1. The character # should never be used with a LOC function. For instance, requesting the value of LOC(#2) produces the message "Syntax error".

LOC

2.   The function LOC also can be used with communications files. At any time, the value of LOC(n) is the number of bytes waiting to be read in the communications file buffer with reference number n.

3.   The number 128 that occurs in the discussion of sequential files can be changed to another number if desired. However, the decision must be made at the time that BASIC is invoked. If BASIC is invoked with a statement of the form BASIC /S:*m*, then the number *m* will play the role of the number 128. For instance, if BASIC 3.0 is invoked with the statement **BASIC /S:64**, then the output of Example 1 will be

```
RUN
 1  2  3  5
 1
 2  3  4  5  7
Ok
```

APPLICATIONS

Users often enters records into a random file without keeping track of the record numbers. The LOC function provides the capability of going back and changing the most recently entered record.

The screen is capable of displaying 25 lines of text, each line 80 characters long. We think of the screen as subdivided into 25 rows (numbered from 1 to 25 from the top of the screen), and 80 columns (numbered from 1 to 80 starting at the left of the screen). In Figure 1, we see that the position in the rth row, cth column is obtained by moving r units down and c units to the right. (We say that the position has text coordinates r,c.)

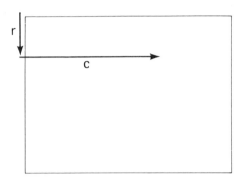

FIGURE 1   POSITIONS OF CHARACTERS

The following demonstration program plots positions after being given their coordinates. Press any letter to request a new position, and press Ctrl-Break to terminate the program.

```
10 KEY OFF: CLS: SCREEN O: WIDTH 80
20 INPUT "Coordinates";A,B
30 IF A<1 OR A>25 OR B<1 OR B>80 THEN GOSUB 100
40 IF B>35 GOTO 70
50 CLS
60 LOCATE A,B: PRINT CHR$(219); A; CHR$(44); B;: GOTO 90
70 LOCATE A,B-10:PRINT A; CHR$(44); B
80 LOCATE A,B: PRINT CHR$(219)
90 A$ = INPUT$(1): GOTO 10
100 IF A<1 OR A>25 THEN PRINT
    "Row numbers must be between 1 and 25."
110 IF B<1 OR B>80 THEN PRINT
    "Column numbers must be between 1 and 80."
120 RETURN 20
```

The statement

```
LOCATE r,c
```

LOCATE

moves the cursor to the position with coordinates r,c.

Normally, the cursor only appears during the running of a program when an INPUT or LINE INPUT statement is being executed. However, in text mode it can be made to appear at other times by executing the statement

```
LOCATE ,,1
```

Subsequently, the statement

```
LOCATE,,0
```

returns the situation to the normal state of affairs.

EXAMPLES

1.  ```
    LOCATE 15,5: PRINT "A"
          A         (line 15)
    Ok
    ```

2.  ```
    10 CLS: TIME$ = "0"
    20 PRINT "Elapsed seconds = "
    30 LOCATE 1,18
    40 PRINT RIGHT$(TIME$,2): GOTO 30
    RUN
    Elapsed seconds = 05
    ```

The number shown here, 05, is just for illustrative purposes. The number will change every second. Press Ctrl-Break to terminate the program. If line 30 is deleted from the program and GOTO 30 is changed to GOTO 20, the numbers will scroll and be unreadable.

3.  ```
    10 SCREEN 0
    20 PRINT "Normally the cursor is invisible"
    30 PRINT "while FOR . . . NEXT loops execute."
    40 FOR I = 1 TO 2000: NEXT I
    50 LOCATE ,,1
    60 PRINT "We have just turned the cursor on."
    70 FOR I = 1 TO 2000: NEXT I
    80 LOCATE ,,0
    90 PRINT "We have turned the cursor back off."
    100 FOR I = 1 TO 2000: NEXT I
    ```

FURTHER DISCUSSION

The statements SCREEN 0: PRINT CHR$(219) produce a solid rectangle. Looking closely at the screen we see that this rectangle is actually made up of horizontal line segments. The number of line segments will be 14 on the Monochrome Display (labelled 0 to 13) and 8 when using another monitor (labelled 0 to 7). See Figure 2.

240
    ```

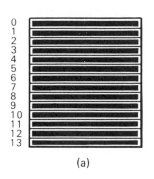
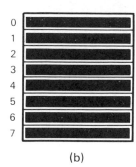

(a)   (b)

FIGURE 2

The standard text mode cursor is composed of segments 12 and 13 on the Monochrome Display and segment 7 on other monitors. The LOCATE statement can be used to change the text mode cursor to certain sequences of horizontal line segments. If $I <= J$, then the statement

```
LOCATE,,1,I,J
```

changes the cursor to the rectangle consisting of line segments numbered I to J. If $I > J$, then the above statement results in a two-part cursor consisting of the line segments with numbers less than or equal to J, or greater than or equal to I. The following program will display any possible cursor.

```
10 SCREEN 0
20 INPUT "Beginning segment (0,1,2,etc.):"; B
30 INPUT "Ending segment (0,1,2,etc.):"; E
40 LOCATE ,,1,B,E
```

The first row of the screen is not capable of displaying a two-part cursor. Run the above program and respond with the numbers 6 and 2. A two-part cursor is produced. Now press Ctrl-Home to clear the screen and move the cursor to the first row. You will notice that only the bottom part of the cursor appears. Use the cursor control keys to move the cursor around the screen. Both parts of the cursor will be visible whenever the cursor is away from the first row.

In text mode, the statement

```
LOCATE r,c,n,I,J
```

moves the cursor to the location with coordinates r,c, gives it the shape specified by I,J, and turns the cursor on during program execution if n is 1, and off during program execution if n is 0.

LOCATE

Comments

1. LOCATE can be used to PRINT on the 25th line of the screen. However, before doing so, the statement **KEY OFF** must be used to turn off the soft key display on line 25.

2. The standard cursor for the IBM Monochrome Display consists of line segments numbered 12 and 13, and hence is invoked by the statement **LOCATE,,1,12,13**. The standard cursor for other monitors is invoked by the statement **LOCATE ,,1,7**.

3. In the general LOCATE statement, if J is present, then I must also be present. Otherwise, any of the five parameters can be omitted. If r or c is omitted, it assumes the value associated with the current position of the cursor. If n is omitted, the cursor stays on if it is currently on and stays off if it is currently off. If both I and J are omitted, the cursor keeps its present shape. If I is present but J is missing, then the cursor will consist of the single line segment numbered I.

4. There is a major difference between the way that coordinates of characters and coordinates of points are specified. For coordinates of characters, the horizontal position is given first; whereas, for coordinates of points, the vertical coordinate is given first.

5. Only the first two parameters in a LOCATE statement have an effect in graphics mode.

6. When a graphics monitor is being used, the statement **LOCATE,,,8** will turn off the cursor in all situations.

Applications

1. LOCATE is used in conjunction with PRINT to put text exactly where we want it on the screen.

2. LOCATE can be used to prevent scrolling, as in Example 2.

3. LOCATE can be used to erase a single line from the screen. The statement **LOCATE r,1: PRINT SPACE$(80)** deletes line r.

4. The statement **LOCATE r,(80-LEN(A$))*.5: PRINT A$** displays the string A$ in the center of row r.

5. Cursor shapes are often changed to indicate to the user that special processes are in effect. For instance, the IBM PC uses a special cursor shape for the insertion of characters.

The LOF function keeps track of the size of a data file while writing information into or reading information from the file. See Appendix F for a general discussion of sequential and random files.

PART I   SEQUENTIAL DATA FILES

A sequential data file is a sequence of items of information residing on a disk. The items of information can only be read from the file in order, from beginning to end. Similarly, items are entered into the file in order, beginning with the first entry. Additional items can be added only to the end of the file. The OPEN statements

```
OPEN filespec FOR INPUT AS #n
OPEN filespec FOR OUTPUT AS #n
OPEN filespec FOR APPEND AS #n
```

must precede reading from, entering original items to, and adding items to the end of an existing file, respectively. (See the discussion of OPEN for further details.)

If we could look at a file residing on a disk, we would see a sequence of characters. These characters consist of the data items and commas, quotation marks, carriage returns, and line feeds inserted by the computer to delimit the data. Think of the characters as being partitioned into blocks of 128 characters. The first block contains characters 1 to 128, the second block contains characters 129 to 256, and so on. After a sequential file has been OPENed (say, as #n), the value of the function

```
LOF(n)
```

depends on the current length of the file and the mode in which the file was OPENed.

In BASIC 1.1, the value of LOF(n) is as follows:

OUTPUT and APPEND modes: At any time, the value of LOF(n) is 128*(the number of blocks of 128 characters of data which have been written with PRINT #n or WRITE #n statements). LOF(n) will be 0 until 128 characters have been written, at which time LOF(n) becomes 128. LOF(n) will remain 128 until 2 full blocks, a total of 256 characters, have been written, at which time LOF(n) becomes 256, and so on.

(b) INPUT mode: The value of LOF(n) is always 128*(the number of blocks into which data have been written). If 257 characters are written to a file and the file closed, the number of blocks written is 3. (The file is using 3 blocks, though the third block only contains one character.)

LOF

In BASIC 2.0 and subsequent versions, the value of LOF(n) is exactly the number of characters which have been written into the file. In all modes, OUTPUT, APPEND, and INPUT, LOF(n) gives the Length Of File in bytes (characters).

EXAMPLE

1. The following program creates a sequential file named SEQFILE and records strings of 78 As, Bs, Cs, and Ds. The file is then CLOSEd and reOPENed FOR APPEND, at which time a string of 78 Es is recorded. (*Note:* Each PRINT #2 statement actually records 80 characters, since carriage return and line feed characters are automatically inserted at the end of each string.) The file is then CLOSEd and reOPENed FOR INPUT, at which time the entire contents of the file are read. The value of LOF(2) is regularly displayed.

```
10 OPEN "SEQFILE" FOR OUTPUT AS #2
20 FOR I = 1 TO 4
30    PRINT #2, STRING$(78, 64+I)
40    PRINT LOF(2);
50 NEXT I
60 CLOSE #2
70 OPEN "SEQFILE" FOR APPEND AS #2
80 PRINT #2, STRING$(78,69)
90 PRINT LOF(2)
100 CLOSE #2
110 OPEN "SEQFILE" FOR INPUT AS #2
120 INPUT #2, A$
130 PRINT LOF(2);
140 CLOSE #2
```

When this program is run in BASIC 1.1, we get the following:

```
RUN
 0  128  128  256  384
 512
Ok
```

When this program is run in BASIC 2.0 (or a later version) we get the following output:

```
RUN
 80  160  240  320  400
 401
Ok
```

244

The 401st character counted by LOF(2) is the end of file character placed in the file when it was closed.

PART II   RANDOM FILES

A random file can be thought of as an ordered set of records numbered 1, 2, 3, and so on. These records pass into and out of the file through a portion of memory referred to as a buffer. Records are copied from the buffer to the file by PUT statements and are copied from the file into the buffer by GET statements. (For complete details, see the discussions of GET and PUT.)

A random file is accessed by a statement of the form **OPEN filespec AS #n LEN = g**, which assigns a number to the file and sets the length of each record. For versions of BASIC prior to 2.0, the value of the function

```
LOF(n)
```

will be as follows:

If the record length, g, is 128 then LOF(n) is 128*(the highest record number). If the record length is different than 128, then the value of LOF(n) is the multiple of 128 that is equal to or just greater than g*(the highest record number). The following table shows the value of LOF(n) for various record lengths and highest record number.

Record length	Highest record number	LOF(n)
128	4	512
32	8	256
20	30	640

In BASIC 2.0 and subsequent versions, if a random file is OPENed with LEN=g, then the value of LOF(n) is always g*(the highest record number.) For the 3 sets of record length and highest record number given above, the value of LOF(n) would be 512, 256, and 600.

FURTHER EXAMPLE

2.   The following program creates a random file named RANDFILE where each record contains 100 characters. Lines 40 and 50 enter the word "one" into record 1, lines 70 and 80 enter the word "two" into record 2, and lines 100 and 110 enter the word "five" into record 5. Then lines 130 and 150 retrieve and display the contents of record 2. The value of LOF(1) is displayed regularly.

```
10 OPEN "RANDFILE" AS #1 LEN = 100
20 FIELD #1, 100 AS TF$
30 PRINT LOF(1);
```

LOF

```
40 LSET TF$ = "one"
50 PUT #1,1
60 PRINT LOF(1);
70 LSET TF$ = "two"
80 PUT #1
90 PRINT LOF(1);
100 LSET TF$ = "five"
110 PUT #1,5
120 PRINT LOF(1);
130 GET #1,2
140 PRINT LOF(1)
150 PRINT TF$
160 CLOSE #1
```

When run in BASIC 1.1, we get the following:

```
RUN
 0   128   256   512   512
two
Ok
```

When run is BASIC 2.0 or a later version, we get the following:

```
RUN
 0   100   200   500   500
two
Ok
```

COMMENTS

1.   The character # should never be used with a LOF function. For instance, requesting the value of LOF(#2) produces the message "Syntax error".

2.   The function LOF also can be used with communications files. The value of LOF(n) equals the number of bytes currently unused in the communications file buffer with reference number n.

3.   The number 128 occurs in this discussion because the sequential file buffer has a capacity of 128 bytes.

APPLICATIONS

Users often enter records into a random file without keeping track of the record numbers. The LOF function provides the capability of determining the highest record number.

For any positive number x, the value of

    LOG(x)

is the natural logarithm (or log to the base e) of x.

MATHEMATICAL PRELIMINARIES

The most familiar logarithmic function is $LOG_{10}(x)$, known as the common logarithmic function, or the log to the base 10. For any positive number x, $LOG_{10}(x)$ is the exponent to which 10 must be raised in order to get x. For instance, $LOG_{10}(100) = 2$, $LOG_{10}(1,000,000) = 6$, and $LOG_{10}(.001) = -3$. Values of this function usually are obtained from a table or a calculator.

Logarithms can be defined to bases other than 10. If b is any number, then $LOG_b(x)$ is the exponent to which b must be raised in order to get x. For instance, $LOG_2(8) = 3$, $LOG_{64}(8) = .5$ and $LOG_{.5}(2) = -1$.

The most important logarithm, called the natural logarithm, is the one having as its base the number known as "e". The value of "e" to 7 significant digits is 2.718282. Whenever we write LOG(x) without referring to a base, it is implied that the base is "e". Hence, LOG(x) is the exponent to which "e" must be raised in order to get x. Values of the natural logarithmic function are obtained by using the LOG function.

COMMENTS

1. LOG(x) is defined only for positive values of x. Figure 1 contains the graph of y = LOG(x).

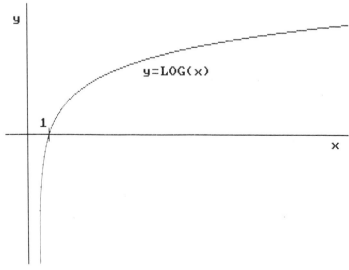

FIGURE 1

LOG

2. LOG is the inverse of the function EXP. That is, for any positive number x, EXP(LOG(x)) has the value x, and for any number x, LOG(EXP(x)) has the value x.

3. In versions of BASIC preceding BASIC 2.0, the value of LOG(x) is always a single-precision number. BASIC 2.0 and subsequent versions provide the option of computing LOG(x) as a double-precision number. To exercise this option, invoke BASIC with the command BASIC/D or BASICA/D. Then, whenever x is a double-precision number, the value of LOG(x) will be computed as a double-precision number.

4. The logarithm to the base b can be obtained from LOG by using the formula

$$LOG_b(x) = LOG(x)/LOG(b)$$

In particular,

$$LOG_{10}(x) = LOG(x)/LOG(10)$$
$$= LOG(x)/2.302585$$
$$= .4342945*LOG(x)$$

In double-precision, $LOG_{10}(x) = .4342944819032518*LOG(x)$

5. The most frequently used abbreviations for the natural (base e) and common (base 10) logarithmic functions are ln and log, respectively. For instance, these abbreviations usually appear on calculators. Our BASIC function LOG is actually the function ln.

6. If x is not positive, requesting LOG(x) results in the message "Illegal function call".

EXAMPLES

Examples 1, 2, and 3 are appropriate for BASIC 2.0 (or later versions) without the /D option or earlier versions of BASIC.

```
1.  PRINT LOG(3);LOG(.5);LOG(3.2D+12);LOG(5+2^4);LOG(2.718282)
     1.098612 -.6931473  28.79417  3.044522  1
    Ok

2.  10 A = 1234: B# = 4.3#: C# = LOG(B#)
    20 PRINT LOG(A);LOG(2*A+B#);LOG(B#);C#
    RUN
     7.118016  7.812904  1.458615  1.458615064620972
    Ok
```

The last number displayed is a double-precision number. However, it is no more accurate as a value of LOG(4.3) than the single-precision number preceding it. Since LOG(B#) is computed as a single-precision number, C# is really the same as CDBL(LOG(B#)). (See the discussion of CDBL for an explanation of the conversion.)

248

3.
```
10 T = .4342945
20 INPUT "Positive number"; X
30 PRINT "The common log of the number is ";T*LOG(X)
RUN
Positive number? 2
The common log of the number is    .30103
Ok
```

4. The following statement was executed using BASIC 3.0 with the /D option.

```
PRINT LOG(2%); LOG(2); LOG(2#)
 .6931471  .6931471  .6931471805599453
Ok
```

APPLICATIONS

1. Money invested at the interest rate of 12% compounded continuously will double after

```
LOG(2)/.12
```

years. In general, the number of years required for money to increase n-fold when invested at the interest rate r compounded continuously is

```
LOG(n)/r
```

2. Scientists use the LOG function for many calculations. It is involved in measuring the intensities of earthquakes, determining the age of ancient artifacts, and predicting the temperatures of cooling objects.

3. Logarithms were invented to reduce the multiplication of numbers to addition: LOG(x*y) = LOG(x)+LOG(y). With a modern computer, this is no longer necessary unless the result of the multiplication is larger than machine infinity or smaller than "machine zero," in which case logarithms may be useful. (By "machine zero" we mean the smallest positive number that the computer can represent.)

LPOS

The printer contains a buffer that stores characters until it has a full line of characters or until it receives a line feed. This feature provides the capability of printing in both directions. For the moment, however, pretend that the printer has no buffer, but prints data as soon as it receives LPRINT statements, in the same way the screen displays data as soon as PRINT statements are executed. At any time, the value of

```
LPOS(1)
```

would be the location of the print head on the line. Locations are numbered from 1 to the width of a line. This hypothetical model of the printer allows us to determine where items will be printed on the page. In actuality, LPOS(1) is the current location of the print head within the buffer.

EXAMPLE

```
10 LPRINT "1234567890123"
20 PRINT LPOS(1);
30 LPRINT "12345";
40 PRINT LPOS(1);
50 LPRINT SPC(4) "ten";
60 PRINT LPOS(1);
70 LPRINT
80 PRINT LPOS(1);
RUN
 1  6  13  1
Ok
```

In line 50, the statement SPC(4) causes the print head to move 4 spaces to the right. The printout was

```
1234567890123
12345    ten
```

COMMENTS

1. Often it will be the case that after a program has run the value of LPOS(1) will be different from 1. This would have occurred in the example had line 70 been omitted. If so, turning the printer OFF and ON will not reset LPOS(1) to 1. As shown, this can be accomplished using the statement LPRINT.

2. LPOS(0) has the same meaning as LPOS(1). If more than one printer is connected to the computer, then LPOS(2) and LPOS(3) give the analogous information for the second and third printers.

250

APPLICATIONS

1. LPOS(1) can be used to guarantee that an item is printed on the left side of the page. For instance, suppose that lines have width 80. Then the statement

```
IF LEN(A$)>41-LPOS(1) THEN LPRINT:LPRINT A$;:ELSE LPRINT A$;
```

will print the string A$ on the next line if it won't fit on the left half of the page.

LPRINT and LPRINT USING

The LPRINT and LPRINT USING statements cause data to be sent to the printer in the same way that PRINT and PRINT USING cause data to be displayed on the screen. In addition, LPRINT is used to set various print modes, such as type size and vertical line spacing. If A$ is a string, N is a number, and F$ is a format string, then the statements

```
LPRINT A$

LPRINT N

LPRINT USING F$; A$

LPRINT USING F$; N
```

cause their respective items to be printed.

The IBM 80 CPS Matrix Printer and the EPSON MX-80 printer have the following four different print sizes.

```
normal                                    10 characters per inch
normal-double width              5 char/in
compressed                                16.5 characters per inch
compressed-double width     8.25 characters per inch
```

When the printer is first turned on, it will be in normal mode. The statement **LPRINT CHR$(15)** turns on compressed mode, and the statement **LPRINT CHR$(18)** turns off compressed mode. The statement **LPRINT CHR$(14)** turns on double-width. Double-width turns off automatically after the next carriage return. However, it can be turned off in the middle of a line with **LPRINT CHR$(20)**.

EXAMPLES

1. The following program turns the printer into a memory typewriter that types an entire line at a time. After entering RUN, type a line and then press the Enter key and watch the line print out on the printer. You can then type another line, and so on. Press Ctrl-Break to terminate.

```
10 LINE INPUT A$
20 LPRINT A$
30 GOTO 10
```

2. ```
10 LPRINT "This is the normal print size."
20 LPRINT CHR$(14);
30 LPRINT "normal-double width"
40 LPRINT "We automatically return to normal size."
```
```

LPRINT and LPRINT USING

```
50 LPRINT CHR$(14); "WIDE "; CHR$(20); "NORMAL"
60 LPRINT CHR$(15);
70 LPRINT "This is the compressed print size."
80 LPRINT CHR$(14);
90 LPRINT "compressed-double width"
100 LPRINT "We automatically return to compressed size."
110 LPRINT CHR$(14);"COMP-DBL WIDTH "; CHR$(20);"COMPRESSED"
120 LPRINT CHR$(18);
130 LPRINT "We have returned to the normal print size."
RUN
```

```
This is the normal print size.
normal-double width
We automatically return to normal size.
WIDE  NORMAL
This is the compressed print size.
compressed-double width
We automatically return to compressed size.
COMP-DBL WIDTH  COMPRESSED
We have returned to the normal print size.
```

COMMENTS

1. Appendix A lists all of the characters recognized by the computer. Of these characters, only those with ASCII values 32 to 126 can be printed with LPRINT on all printers. These are the characters that appear in the white "typewriter" portion in the center of the keyboard. Certain printers allow 64 different graphics fonts to be printed. These graphics fonts are invoked by using CHR$(N) for N = 160 to 223. The following demonstration program will print these fonts on the appropriate printers.

```
10 WIDTH "LPT1:",80: LPRINT CHR$(18)
20 FOR I = 160 TO 223
25    IF I MOD 8 = 0 THEN LPRINT
30    LPRINT I; CHR$(I); SPC(2);
40 NEXT I: LPRINT
```

2. When commas and semicolons are used within an LPRINT statement, they function just as in PRINT statements. Commas cause the next item printed to appear in the next print zone, and semicolons cause the next item to appear in the next position. Internal spaces are treated like semicolons. Commas and semicolons at the end of LPRINT statements suppress carriage returns and line feeds. This is true even for LPRINT statements that just change the print mode. For instance, in Example 2, if the semicolon at the end of line 20 is removed, there will be a blank line between the first two printed lines of the printout.

LPRINT and LPRINT USING

3.   The program in Example 2 could have been written more compactly. For instance, lines 20 and 30 could have been combined into the single line

```
20 LPRINT CHR$(14); "normal-double width"
```

4.   The IBM 80 CPS Matrix Printer and the Epson MX-80 and FX-80 printers are capable of typing a line 8 inches long. This means that the maximum number of characters that can be typed in a single line is:

normal	80 char per line
normal double-width	40 char per line
compressed	132 char per line
compressed double-width	66 char per line

When changing type sizes, the WIDTH statement should be used to alter the maximum line length. For instance, the statement **WIDTH "LPT1", 132** enables the printer to fill an entire 8-inch line with compressed characters.

5.   Turning the printer OFF and ON resets the print size to normal. However, it does not change the line width.

6.   Any LPRINT statement, including those that just alter print size, can be executed in direct mode.

7.   Spaces will have the same size as any other characters. For instance, in normal double-width mode, the spaces will be twice the size as in normal mode. This should be kept in mind when using TAB, SPC, and SPACE$, and when using commas to direct the printing to specified print zones.

8.   The following table provides a useful reference for the statements that affect print size:

	on	*off*
double-width	CHR$(14)	CHR$(20)
compressed	CHR$(15)	CHR$(18)

FURTHER DISCUSSION

There are many possible vertical line spacings. Three standard spacings are:

normal	6 lines per inch
tight	8 lines per inch
tighter	72/7 (approx. 10.3) lines per inch

When printing uppercase letters, the space between lines will equal 5/7 of the size of an uppercase letter for normal spacing, and 2/7 for tight spacing. Tighter spacing results in no space at all between lines.

Normal spacing is invoked when the printer is turned on. Otherwise, the following statements are used to invoke the various spacings:

LPRINT and LPRINT USING

normal	LPRINT CHR$(27) "2"
tight	LPRINT CHR$(27) "0"
tighter	LPRINT CHR$(27) "1"

After one of these statements is executed, the line feed will cause the paper to advance by the specified spacing.

FURTHER EXAMPLE

```
3.  10 A$ = "ABCDEFGHIJKLMNOPQRSTUVWXYZ"
    20 LPRINT CHR$(27) "2";
    30 LPRINT A$
    40 LPRINT CHR$(27) "0";
    50 LPRINT A$
    60 LPRINT CHR$(27) "1";
    70 LPRINT A$
    80 LPRINT CHR$(27) "2";
    90 LPRINT A$
    100 LPRINT A$
    RUN
```

```
ABCDEFGHIJKLMNOPQRSTUVWXYZ
ABCDEFGHIJKLMNOPQRSTUVWXYZ
ABCDEFGHIJKLMNOPQRSTUVWXYZ
ABCDEFGHIJKLMNOPQRSTUVWXYZ
ABCDEFGHIJKLMNOPQRSTUVWXYZ
```

Line 20 guaranteed normal spacing. In line 30 the alphabet was printed and, since there was no semicolon or comma at the end of line 30, a line feed caused the paper to advance normally to the next line. Line 50 printed the alphabet and then a line feed caused the paper to advance by the amount specified in line 40, the amount associated with tight spacing, and so on.

FURTHER DISCUSSION

We now consider some of the additional features of the printer.

PAGE LENGTH AND FORM FEED

When the printer is first turned on, the location of the print head is regarded as being on line 1 of a page of 66 lines. Usually, we set the print head just below a perforation before turning on the printer. If the ON LINE button is toggled and the FF button pressed, the paper will advance and the print head will be located at the same position on the next sheet of paper.

The number of lines per page can be set to any value N from 1 to 66 by the statement **LPRINT CHR$(27) "C" CHR$(N)**. Thereafter the printer treats each N lines as a page. So, for instance, if the print head is on line 1 and FF is pressed, the paper advances N lines. If the print head is on line 2 and FF is

LPRINT and LPRINT USING

pressed, the paper advances N-1 lines, and so on. Form feeds can also be invoked within a program by the statement `LPRINT CHR$(12);`.

EMPHASIZED AND DOUBLE STRIKE MODE

When EMPHASIZED mode is invoked, each letter is struck twice (with a slight right shift) during a single pass of the print head. When DOUBLE STRIKE mode is invoked, each letter is struck twice (with a slight vertical shift) during two passes of the print head. The statements for using these modes are:

	ON	OFF
EMPHASIZED	LPRINT CHR$(27) "E"	LPRINT CHR$(27) "F"
DOUBLE STRIKE	LPRINT CHR$(27) "G"	LPRINT CHR$(27) "H"

HORIZONTAL AND VERTICAL TABS

Horizontal tabs are set at positions M and N by the statement

    LPRINT CHR$(27) "D" CHR$(M) CHR$(N) CHR$(0)

Afterwards, a statement of the form

    LPRINT CHR$(9) A$

results in A$ being printed at the next horizontal tab stop. The printer starts counting positions on a line with 0. The total number of tabs that can be set is as large as the width of a line.

Vertical tabs are set at lines M and N by the statement

    LPRINT CHR$(27) "B" CHR$(M) CHR$(N) CHR$(0)

Afterwards, a statement of the form

    LPRINT CHR$(11) A$

results in A$ being printed at the next vertical tab stop. If the printer head has already passed the line called for, it will proceed to that line on the next page.

PRECISE LINE SPACING

Earlier, we discussed the method used to set the line spacing to 6, 8, or 72/7 lines per inch. (*Note:* 6 is 72/12 and 8 is 72/9.) That is, we know how to set the line spacing at 72/N lines per inch where N is 12, 9, or 7. Actually, line spacing may be set at 72/N lines per inch where N is any number from 1 to 85. When N is 1 the lines will overlap considerably and when N is 85 there will be more than an inch between lines. To set the stage for precise line spacing with value N, execute the statement

```
LPRINT CHR$(27) "A" CHR$(N);
```

The new spacing will take effect when the statement

```
LPRINT CHR$(27) "2";
```

is executed. The first of these two statements changed the default line spacing (which had been 72/12) to 72/N. The statements **LPRINT CHR$(27) "0";** and **LPRINT CHR$(27) "1";** retain their original meanings. To revert back to 72/12 line spacing, execute the statement **LPRINT CHR$(27) "A" CHR$(12);**.

MISCELLANEOUS FEATURES

The printer has a buzzer that is activated briefly by the statement **LPRINT CHR$(7);**.

The statement **LPRINT CHR$(141);** results in a carriage return without a line feed. This feature provides the possibility of printing characters on top of other characters.

The printers mentioned earlier have the capability of printing 63 Japanese characters, or 9 special French, German, British, or American characters. However, switches inside the printer must be flipped in order to use these characters.

FURTHER EXAMPLES

We recommend turning the printer OFF and then ON before running each of these programs.

```
4.  10 LPRINT CHR$(27) "C" CHR$(5);
    20 LPRINT "first line of page 1"
    30 LPRINT "second line of page 1"
    40 LPRINT CHR$(12);
    50 LPRINT "first line of page 2"
    60 LPRINT "second line of page 2"
    RUN
                    first line of page 1
                    second line of page 1



                    first line of page 2
                    second line of page 2
```

LPRINT and LPRINT USING

```
5. 10 LPRINT CHR$(27) "E";
   20 LPRINT "EMPHASIZED mode"
   30 LPRINT CHR$(27) "G";
   40 LPRINT "both EMPHASIZED and DOUBLE STRIKE modes"
   50 LPRINT CHR$(27) "F";
   60 LPRINT "DOUBLE STRIKE mode"
   70 LPRINT CHR$(27) "H";
   80 LPRINT "ordinary letters"
   RUN

            EMPHASIZED mode
            both EMPHASIZED and DOUBLE STRIKE modes
            DOUBLE STRIKE mode
            ordinary letters


6. 10 LPRINT "012345678901234567890123456789012345678901234567890123456789"
   20 LPRINT CHR$(27) "D" CHR$(5) CHR$(22) CHR$(40) CHR$(0);
   30 LPRINT CHR$(9) "1st tab" CHR$(9) "2nd tab" CHR$(9) "3rd tab"
   RUN

    012345678901234567890123456789012345678901234567890123456789
            1st tab               2nd tab              3rd tab

7. 10 LPRINT CHR$(27) "B" CHR$(3) CHR$(6) CHR$(8) CHR$(0);
   20 LPRINT "1st line"
   30 LPRINT CHR$(11) "3rd line" CHR$(11) "6th line" CHR$(11)
   "8th line"
   RUN

       1st line


       3rd line



       6th line

       8th line

8. 10 ALPHA$ = "ABCDEFGHIJKLMNOPQRSTUVWXYZ"
   20 LPRINT CHR$(27) "A" CHR$(18);
   30 LPRINT ALPHA$
   40 LPRINT CHR$(27) "2";
   50 LPRINT ALPHA$
   60 LPRINT CHR$(27) "A" CHR$(4); CHR$(27) "2";
   70 LPRINT ALPHA$: LPRINT ALPHA$
   RUN
```

LPRINT and LPRINT USING

```
ABCDEFGHIJKLMNOPQRSTUVWXYZ
ABCDEFGHIJKLMNOPQRSTUVWXYZ
ABCDEFGHIJKLMNOPQRSTUVWXYZ
```

FURTHER COMMENTS

9. With the Epson MX-80 and FX-80 printers, precise line spacing is invoked as soon as the statement **LPRINT CHR$(27) "A" CHR$(N);** is executed, and the statement **LPRINT CHR$(27) "2";** results in a return to normal line spacing. The following program produces output on the Epson printers identical to that obtained in Example 8 on the IBM 80 CPS printer.

```
10 ALPHA$ = "ABCDEFGHIJKLMNOPQRSTUVWXYZ"
20 LPRINT ALPHA$
30 LPRINT CHR$(27) "A" CHR$(18);
40 LPRINT ALPHA$
50 LPRINT CHR$(27) "A" CHR$(4);
60 LPRINT ALPHA$: LPRINT ALPHA$
```

10. The printer contains a buffer that stores a full line of characters before printing them on the paper. This feature gives it the capability of printing in both directions. However, even if the buffer is not full, a carriage return or a line feed results in the contents of the buffer being printed. Care must be taken to guarantee that the last line of a printout is not left in the buffer. This can be done by assuring that each block of information sent to the printer ends with a carriage return.

11. If A$ is a string with the same number of characters as the width of a line, then the statement **LPRINT A$;** induces a line feed, even though a semicolon is at the end of the statement.

12. Precise spacing can be used to obtain double-spaced (N=24) or triple-spaced (N=36) printouts.

13. To understand exactly what spacing will occur between two lines, consider the following:

The printer advances the paper vertically in increments of 1/72 of an inch. The print head itself uses 9 pins, each 1/72 of an inch apart vertically, to print out all the various characters. Capital letters use the top 7 pins exclusively, and so are 7/72 of an inch high. The bottom two pins in the print head give the bottom extenders on various characters, such as the lower case letters g, j, p, q, and y.

When the statement **LPRINT CHR$(27) "A" CHR$(N)** is in use, the printer advances the paper N/72 of an inch (N of the basic unit of vertical spacing) after it prints the line. If, for example, we are using N=12, then the

259

LPRINT and LPRINT USING

printer will advance the paper 12/72·of an inch for each line feed. Thus, when printing capital letters, which will be 7/72 of an inch high, the printer leaves a space of 12/72 - 7/72, or 5/72 of an inch after each line of type.

As another example, suppose you wish to have exactly 1/2 inch of spacing after each line. The line of type (for capital letters) will need 7/72 of an inch. The spacing desired is 36/72 of an inch. Thus, since 7/72 + 36/72 = 43/72 of an inch of vertical paper advance is required, use N = 43.

14.   If the printer is turned off, the statement LPRINT produces the message ''Out of paper'', whereas if the printer is disconnected, the message ''Device Timeout'' is produced.

APPLICATIONS

1.   LPRINT USING produces data in chart form. Often there are so many columns and rows of data that condensed printing and tight spacing must be used.

LSET and RSET

Suppose that A\$ is a string variable to which a string constant of length n has been assigned. If D\$ is a string, the statement

```
LSET A$ = D$
```

assigns to the variable A\$ a new string of length n. If the length of D\$ is n or more, A\$ is assigned the string consisting of the first n characters of D\$. Otherwise, A\$ is assigned the string consisting of D\$ followed by spaces. We say that D\$ has been left-justified into a string of n spaces. The statement

```
RSET A$ = D$
```

operates in the same manner except that when the length of D\$ is less than n, D\$ is right-justified into a string of n spaces.

EXAMPLES

1.
```
10 A$ = "ABCDEFG"
20 PRINT A$
30 LSET A$ = "123456789"
40 PRINT A$
50 LSET A$ = "abcd"
60 PRINT A$, LEN(A$)
70 RSET A$ = "123456789"
80 PRINT A$
90 RSET A$ = "ABCD"
100 PRINT A$, LEN(A$)
RUN
ABCDEFG
1234567
abcd            7
1234567
    ABCD        7
Ok
```

Note: Line 50 could have been written `50 N$ = "abcd": LSET A$ = N$`.

2. In the following program, LSET and RSET are used to help format and efficiently pack the names and disciplines of the 1982 Nobel Prize winners.

```
10 A$ = SPACE$(10): B$ = SPACE$(4)
20 FOR I = 1 TO 9
30   READ D$,E$
40   RSET A$ = D$
50   LSET B$ = E$
60   PRINT A$ + "  " + B$ + "    ";
```

261

LSET and RSET

```
70 NEXT I
80 DATA Stigler, Economics, Marquez, Literature
90 DATA Myrdal, Peace, Robles, Peace, Wilson, Physics
100 DATA Klug, Chemistry, Vane, Physiology or Medicine
110 DATA Bergstrom, Physiology or Medicine
120 DATA Samuelsson, Physiology or Medicine
RUN
      Stigler  Econ        Marquez  Lite        Myrdal  Peac
       Robles  Peac         Wilson  Phys           Klug  Chem
         Vane  Phys      Bergstrom  Phys      Samuelsson  Phys
Ok
```

FURTHER DISCUSSION

There are two types of string variables. Ordinary string variables have their values stored in a portion of memory referred to as string space. Field string variables have their values stored in the buffer of a random file. (See Appendix F for a general discussion of random files.)

Random files can be thought of as sets of numbered records residing on a disk. Records are entered into the file by a four-step procedure:

1. A statement of the form **OPEN filespec AS #n LEN = g** sets up a g-byte portion of memory, referred to as a buffer for the file.

2. The buffer is subdivided into sections called fields, whose widths and names are specified by a FIELD statement. The name of each field is a string variable. (See the discussion of FIELD for further details.)

3. The statements LSET and RSET are used to place information into the individual fields. For instance, if AF$ is a field variable of width w, the value of AF$ is always a string of length w residing in the w-byte section of the buffer assigned to AF$. Therefore, a statement of the form **LSET AF$ = D$** places the string D$ (truncated or left-justified) into the field named AF$.

4. A PUT statement is used to copy the characters in the buffer into a designated record of the file.

FURTHER EXAMPLES

3.
```
10 OPEN "B:TEST" AS #1 LEN = 10
20 FIELD #1, 5 AS AF$, 5 AS BF$
30 LSET AF$ = "abc"
40 RSET BF$ = "ABC"
50 FIELD #1, 10 AS TF$
60 PRINT TF$
70 CLOSE #1
RUN
abc****ABC (Asterisks are used here to denote spaces.)
Ok
```

262

Lines 50 and 60 result in the entire contents of the buffer being displayed on the screen. There are 4 spaces between abc and ABC in the display.

4. Consider the program in Example 3 with the following choices for lines 30 and 40. (Asterisks again denote spaces.)

```
30 LSET AF$ = "abc"
40 LSET BF$ = "ABC"
RUN
abc**ABC**
Ok
```

```
30 RSET AF$ = "abc"
40 LSET BF$ = "ABC"
RUN
**abcABC**
Ok
```

```
30 RSET AF$ = "abc"
40 RSET BF$ = "ABC"
RUN
**abc**ABC
Ok
```

```
30 LSET AF$ = "abcdefg"
40 RSET BF$ = "ABCDEFG"
RUN
abcdeABCDE
Ok
```

COMMENTS

1. Numeric data can be placed into the fields of a random file. However, the data must be converted to strings via MKI$, MKS$, or MKD$ functions before it can be assigned to field string variables by LSET or RSET statements.

2. A string variable is defined by a three-byte string descriptor. The first byte consists of the length of the string. The second and third bytes point to the location in string space (a portion of memory) where the actual text of the string is stored.

The statement **A$=D$** finds space in string space that is free and big enough to hold the text of D$, moves the text from D$'s text area in string space to the new space, and changes the three-byte descriptor of A$ to point to the new copy of the text. In the process, part of the free string space is used up and the old text, which was previously pointed to by A$, is now ''orphaned'' — no

263

LSET and RSET

string descriptor points to it. The orphaned text becomes ''garbage'' cluttering string space.

The statement **LSET A$=D$** does not change the contents of either string descriptor. The old text pointed to by A$ is located and becomes the destination of the text of the string D$. The text is moved — as it was in the previous example — but this time *on top of* old text, not in new free string space. The length of A$ does not change. The text move halts when the old text is completely overlaid. If D$ was shorter, after the move blanks pad out the rest to completely wipe out the old text of A$.

In summary, **A$=D$** moves the data into unused free string space and changes A$'s string descriptor to point to new data. **LSET A$=D$** moves the data into a previously defined text area and no string descriptors are changed. This is why LSET must be used with random files to put data into strings defined by FIELD statements. FIELD statements define the string descriptors to point to areas of text not in string space, but in the buffer itself. You do not want to clobber those string descriptors! LSET moves the data to where the descriptor points, that is, moves the data into the buffer.

APPLICATIONS

1. LSET and RSET are used primarily to enter data into random files.

2. LSET and RSET can be used to minimize string space fragmentation, by avoiding the creation of ''garbage.''

3. LSET and RSET can be used as in Example 2 to justify data.

The MERGE command is used to splice together two programs. Suppose that one program is currently in memory, and another program (with different line numbers from the first) resides on a disk. Then the command

```
MERGE filespec
```

(where filespec is the file specification of the second program) results in all of the lines of the second program being appended to the first program.

EXAMPLE

1. Suppose that a program named CUSTOMER.NY resides on drive B and consists of the lines

```
100 DATA NEW YORK
110 DATA AL ADAMS, BOB BROWN, CAROL COLE
```

Also, suppose that the following program currently resides in memory.

```
10 READ S$ : PRINT "STATE-";S$
20 FOR I = 1 TO 3
30    READ N$ : PRINT N$,
40 NEXT I
```

Then, the command

```
MERGE "B:CUSTOMER.NY"
```

results in the program

```
10 READ S$ : PRINT "STATE-";S$
20 FOR I = 1 TO 3
30    READ N$ : PRINT N$,
40 NEXT I
100 DATA NEW YORK
110 DATA AL ADAMS, BOB BROWN, CAROL COLE
```

as the program residing in memory. Upon RUNning the program, we would obtain

```
STATE-NEW YORK
AL ADAMS       BOB BROWN       CAROL COLE
Ok
```

The program CUSTOMER.NY still resides on drive B.

MERGE

Comments

1. When we SAVE programs onto a disk drive, we specify a format for the way that the program is recorded. The two most used formats are known as compressed binary and ASCII. The ordinary SAVE command results in the program being recorded in compressed binary format. Following the SAVE command by a comma and the letter A, results in the program being saved in ASCII format. Only programs that have been SAVEd in ASCII format can be MERGEd. Attempting to MERGE a program that was SAVEd in compressed binary format results in the error message "Bad file mode."

If you want to MERGE a program that is in compressed binary format, follow the following steps:

> SAVE program M, the program currently in memory.
> LOAD program D, the program originally on disk.
> SAVE program D in ASCII format with the command **SAVE "D",A**.
> LOAD program M.
> MERGE program D.

The first step is needed to keep from losing program M.

2. If the two programs have some line numbers in common, then the lines from the program on the disk drive will replace the corresponding lines from the program in memory.

3. In the event that the name of the file to be MERGEd has the extension BAS, the extension can be omitted when specifying the file.

4. The command MERGE is similar to the statement CHAIN MERGE. MERGE is normally used in direct mode and CHAIN MERGE is usually used within a program. If MERGE is used within a program, the program will execute up to the MERGE command, the MERGE will then be carried out as if it had been entered in direct mode, and *no* further statements of the newly created program will be executed.

5. The MERGE command clears all variables from memory, removes all information that has been set with DEF FN or DEFtype statements, RESTOREs all data, causes all DIMensioned arrays to become undimensioned, closes all open files, and disables event trapping that has been set with statements such as ON ERROR, ON KEY(n), ON PEN, ON STRIG(n), ON PLAY(n), and ON TIMER. In graphics modes, the "last point referenced" is set to the center of the screen and the effects of previously executed WINDOW and VIEW statements are voided. OPTION BASE 1 is reset to OPTION BASE 0, the speaker is turned off, and lightpens and joystick buttons are deactivated. In BASIC 2.1, Music Foreground is reset to Music Background. In all other versions of BASIC, Music Background is reset to Music Foreground. When MERGE is executed inside a subroutine, the computer forgets that a GOSUB has occurred, and when it is executed inside a FOR . . . NEXT or WHILE . . . WEND loop, forgets that the loop is active.

6.   See Comment 10 in the discussion of SAVE for a suggestion that will pre-vent MERGEing the wrong kind of file.

FURTHER EXAMPLES

2.   Consider these two programs:

```
10 PRINT "TEN"                        5 PRINT "CINC"
20 PRINT "TWENTY"                     10 PRINT "DIX"
```

Suppose that the first program is currently in memory and that the second program resides (in ASCII format) on a disk in drive B and has the name FRENCH.BAS.

```
MERGE "B:FRENCH"
Ok
LIST
5 PRINT "CINC"
10 PRINT "DIX"
20 PRINT "TWENTY"
Ok
```

3.   Consider the same situation as in Example 2 with the exception that the second program is in compressed binary format.

```
MERGE "B:FRENCH"
Bad file mode
Ok
SAVE "B:ENGLISH"
Ok
LOAD "B:FRENCH"
Ok
SAVE "B:FRENCH",A
Ok
LOAD "B:ENGLISH"
Ok
MERGE "B:FRENCH"
Ok
```

Notice that it was not necessary to SAVE the program ENGLISH in ASCII format.

APPLICATIONS

1.   The MERGE command is frequently used to insert a standard program into another program as a subroutine.

⎸MID$

MID$ can be used as a function to extract a portion of a string, or as a statement to replace a portion of a string.

PART I MID$ AS A FUNCTION

If A$ is a string and b and L are positive whole numbers, then

    MID$(A$,b,L)

will be the string consisting of L successive characters of A$ beginning with the bth character. The number L can be omitted. If so,

    MID$(A$,b)

will be the string consisting of all of the characters of A$ from the character in location b on.

EXAMPLES

1. PRINT MID$("Chester Alan Arthur",9,4); MID$("1830",2,1)
   Alan8
   0k

2. 10 A$ = "Yellow submarine": C$ = MID$(A$,4): B = 4: L = 7
   20 PRINT C$, MID$(A$,B,L), A$
   RUN
   low submarine low sub   Yellow submarine
   0k

Notice that even though the MID$ function extracted a portion of the string A$ to form a new string, the value of A$ was not changed.

3. The INPUT statement will not accept a fraction as a response unless the fraction is treated as a string. The following program converts the string to a number. In line 20, the value of S will be the location of the division sign.

```
10 INPUT "Type a fraction: ", F$
20 S = INSTR(F$,"/")
30 F = VAL(MID$(F$,1,S-1))/VAL(MID$(F$,S+1))
40 PRINT F
RUN
Type a fraction: 17/25
 .68
0k
```

268

MID$

COMMENTS

1. MID$(A$,b,L) will be the same string as MID$(A$,b) if there are fewer than L characters to the right of the bth character of A$.

2. Since 255 is the maximum number of characters in a string, neither b nor L can exceed 255. If b is greater than the number of characters in A$, then MID$(A$,b,L) will be the null string, "".

3. There are 256 different characters that can be used in a string. These characters, along with their ASCII values, are listed in Appendix A. All of these characters are counted when they appear in a string; even the undisplayable characters, such as carriage return, beep, and cursor down. All spaces are counted, including leading and trailing spaces.

4. The MID$ function creates a new string, but does not destroy the original string. (See Example 2.)

5. The functions LEFT$ and RIGHT$ are similar to the MID$ function.

PART II   MID$ AS A STATEMENT

If A$ is a string variable, S$ is a string, and b and L are positive whole numbers, then the statement

```
MID$(A$,b,L) = S$
```

replaces the characters in the string value of A$, beginning with the bth character, with the first L characters of S$. The number L can be omitted. If so, all of the characters of S$ are used, provided that there is enough room to accommodate them.

FURTHER EXAMPLES

4. ```
A$ = "123 567": MID$(A$,5,2) = "smile": PRINT A$
123 sm7
Ok
```

5. ```
10 A$ = "abcdefghij"
20 C$ = "FGHIJKLMNOP"
30 INPUT B
40 MID$(A$,B,4) = C$
50 PRINT A$: GOTO 10
RUN
? 6
abcdeFGHIj
? 9
abcdefghFG
?
```

269

MID$

6. The following program capitalizes all lowercase letters in a string.

```
10 INPUT A$
20 FOR I = 1 TO LEN(A$)
30   B = ASC(MID$(A$,I,1))
40    IF 96<B AND B<123 THEN MID$(A$,I,1) = CHR$(B-32)
50 NEXT I
60 PRINT A$
RUN
? 1600 Penn. Ave
1600 PENN. AVE
Ok
```

7. The variable DATE$ has as its value the current date in the format MM-DD-YYYY. The following program uses MID$ both as a statement and a function to convert the date to the format YY-MM-DD. The second format is convenient for sorting purposes.

```
10 D$ = "YY-MM-DD"
20 MID$(D$,1,2) = MID$(DATE$,9,2)
30 MID$(D$,4) = MID$(DATE$,1,5)
40 PRINT DATE$
50 PRINT D$
RUN
06-12-1984
84-06-12
Ok
```

FURTHER COMMENTS

6. The number of characters in A$ will not change, even if B+L exceeds the number of characters in A$ and S$ has lots of characters.

7. The numbers b and L cannot exceed 255. If they do, the error message "Illegal function call" results. Also, b must be no greater than LEN(A$). Otherwise, the same error message results.

8. A statement of the form MID$("string",b,L) = S$ results in the message "Syntax error". A variable representing the string, not the string itself, must be used.

9. MID$ can be used as a statement in much the same way as LSET to avoid the creation of "garbage." See Comment 2 in the discussion of LSET.

APPLICATIONS

MID$ is used to make programs user-friendly and to manipulate strings. It is essential for processing text information.

The command MKDIR is not available in versions of BASIC prior to BASIC 2.0.

BASIC 2.0 and subsequent versions support a hierarchial directory structure in which files and directories are specified by paths through the structure. See Appendix D for a detailed discussion of directories and paths. If A$ is a string expression for a path, then the command

```
MKDIR A$
```

creates a directory with the location and name specified by the path.

EXAMPLES

The following examples refer to the tree diagram presented in Appendix D.

1. When the disk was first formatted, the directories might have been created as follows. (Here we assume that the disk is in drive C.)

```
MKDIR "C:ANN"
MKDIR "C:BOB"
MKDIR "C:ANN\MATH"
MKDIR "C:ANN\NOVEL"
MKDIR "C:BOB\BASEBALL"
```

If drive C was the default drive, then the C: could have been omitted from each of these commands. Also, note that since the root directory was the current directory, it was not necessary to precede the names ANN and BOB with back-slashes.

2. Suppose that the disk is in the default drive, and that the current directory for that drive is BASEBALL. Then the command

```
MKDIR "NATIONAL"
```

will create a sub-directory of BASEBALL named NATIONAL.

3. With the situation as in Example 2, the command

```
MKDIR "..\HOCKEY"
```

or the command

```
MKDIR "\BOB\HOCKEY"
```

will create a new sub-directory of BOB named HOCKEY.

MKDIR

COMMENTS

1.   The string expression for the path must not be longer than 63 characters.

2.   When a directory is created with the MKDIR command, BASIC makes 2 entries in this new directory. If the FILES command is used to list the entries in a directory, the 2 entries " . <Dir> " and " .. <Dir> " always appear. BASIC uses these two entries to work with the directory hierarchy. You need not be concerned with them.

3.   Directories are removed with the command RMDIR, and the current directory is changed with the command CHDIR.

4.   Complex tree structures are difficult to keep track of and slow down disk access time. Some experienced users recommend placing all directories onto the disk's root directory.

APPLICATIONS

1.   Tree structures are intended for hard disk systems in which the disk has the capacity to contain over a thousand files.

2.   A root directory is fixed in size. A sub-directory is a kind of file, and so there is no limit to the number of entries (filenames) in a sub-directory, other than the limit imposed by the amount of disk space available to hold the data. The root directory of a single-sided diskette can hold at most 64 files and the root directory of a double-sided diskette can hold at most 112 files. By using sub-directories with diskettes, the maximum number of files can be increased about fivefold.

MKI$, MKS$, MKD$

Integer numeric constants are stored in two bytes of memory. If the two bytes contain the numbers r and q, then the integer n equals

$$r + 256*q \qquad \text{if } q < 128$$
$$r + 256*q - 65536 \qquad \text{if } q >= 128$$

If n is an integer, then the value of

```
MKI$(n)
```

will be the string CHR$(r)+CHR$(q).

Single- and double-precision numeric constants are stored in 4 and 8 bytes of memory respectively. The procedures for determining the values of the bytes are rather complicated. If x is a single-precision number, then the value of

```
MKS$(x)
```

will be the string of length 4 having as characters the characters whose ASCII values are the numbers in the 4 bytes storing x. If x is a double-precision number, then the value of

```
MKD$(x)
```

will be the string of length 8 having as characters the characters whose ASCII values are the numbers in the 8 bytes storing x.

EXAMPLES

1. ```
   PRINT MKI$(12875)
   K2
   Ok
   ```

The characters K and 2 have ASCII values 75 and 50, respectively, and 75 + 256*50 = 12875.

2. ```
   10 A% = -7327
   20 PRINT MKI$(A%)
   RUN
   aπ
   Ok
   ```

The characters a and π have ASCII values 97 and 227, respectively, and 97 + 256*227 - 65536 = -7327.

MKI$, MKS$, MKD$

FURTHER DISCUSSION

A random file can be thought of as a set of numbered records residing on a disk. (See Appendix F for a general discussion of random files.) Records are entered into the file by a four-step procedure:

1. A statement of the form **OPEN filespec as #n LEN = g** sets up a g-byte portion of memory, referred to as a buffer.

2. The buffer is subdivided into sections called fields, whose widths and names are specified by a FIELD statement. The name of each field is a string variable. (See the discussion of FIELD for further details.)

3. The statements LSET and RSET are used to place information into the individual fields. For instance, if AF$ is a field variable of width w, the value of AF$ is always a string of length w residing in the w-byte section of the buffer assigned to AF$. A statement of the form **LSET AF$ = D$** places the string D$ (possibly truncated or left-justified) into the field named AF$.

4. A PUT statement is used to copy the characters in the buffer into a designated record of the file.

Since the fields of the buffer can only contain strings, any numeric data must be converted into string format before being placed into the buffer. This conversion is accomplished by the functions MKI$, MKS$, and MKD$. The strings can be converted back into numbers by the functions CVI, CVS, and CVD.

FURTHER EXAMPLE

```
3.  10 OPEN "B:NUMBERS" AS #3 LEN=14
    20 FIELD #3, 2 AS INTF$, 4 AS SINGF$, 8 AS DOUBF$
    30 LSET INTF$ = MKI$(22329)
    40 LSET SINGF$ = MKS$(.02822886)
    50 LSET DOUBF$ = MKD$(.2258308750154971#)
    60 PRINT INTF$, SINGF$, DOUBF$
    70 PRINT CVI(INTF$);
    80 PRINT CVS(SINGF$);
    90 PRINT CVD(DOUBF$);
    100 CLOSE #3
    RUN
    9W              6ag{              txyz5ag~
     22329   2.822886E-02   .2258308750154971
    Ok
```

Note: RSET could have been used instead of LSET in lines 30 through 50. However, if the fields were wider than designated in line 20, it would have been essential to use LSET.

MKI$, MKS$, MKD$

COMMENTS

1. The functions MKI$, MKS$, and MKD$ do not change the bytes representing a number; they changed only the number's attribute, that is, the way it is handled. For example, the integer A%=260 is in memory as the following sequence of six bytes:

2	type=integer
65	ASCII value of A
0	ASCII value of null character
0	ASCII value of null character
4	the integer itself, least significant byte
1	the integer itself, most significant byte

The actual data are the last two bytes, 4 and 1.

After the statement B$=MKI$(A%) has been executed, the string B$ is in memory as the following sequence of seven bytes:

3	type=string
66	ASCII value of B
0	ASCII value of null character
0	ASCII value of null character
2	length of string
x	first byte of pointer
y	second byte of pointer

The last three bytes constitute the string descriptor. The last two bytes point to a new area in free string space where the new two-character string consisting of the two bytes 4 and 1 has been moved. The data bytes have not changed, we just now call them "string characters." These two characters can be moved like any string. In particular, the statement **LSET CF$=B$** is valid, where CF$ was defined as a string variable of length 2.

2. The function STR$ also creates a string out of a number. However, STR$ is inappropriate for use with random files, since the lengths of the strings created by STR$ vary. Unlike the MKI$, MKS$, and MKD$ functions, STR$ creates a string out of a number by converting the binary representation of the number into the ASCII code values for the base 10 digits, decimal point, etc. that make up the number as it is displayed by the PRINT statement. For an integer value this can be anywhere from 2 to 6 characters. For a double-precision number, up to 22 characters can be returned by STR$.

3. If MK_$ is given a value of a non-matching precision, that value is first changed to the precision of MK_$ and then stored as character data.

MOTOR

A cassette player can be connected to the computer by a cable plugged into the round connector to the right of the keyboard connector at the back of the computer. When the cassette player is initially set to the play mode and turned on, nothing will happen. The statement

    MOTOR 1

turns on the motor, and the statement

    MOTOR 0

turns off the motor.

EXAMPLE

Suppose that the cassette player contains a recording of the overture to the opera William Tell.

```
10 INPUT "Would you like to hear the William Tell
Overture? (Y/N) ", A$
20 IF A$ = "Y" THEN MOTOR 1 ELSE END
30 PRINT "Hit any key to stop the music."
40 S$ = INPUT$(1)
50 MOTOR 0
```

The statement in line 40 causes the execution of the program to pause until a key is pressed.

COMMENTS

1. The statement MOTOR n turns on the cassette player motor if n is a positive number, and turns it off if n is zero. (A negative value of n produces the error message "Illegal function call.") If n is an algebraic expression, the expression will be evaluated to determine the appropriate action. For instance, the statement A = 2: MOTOR A*A-4 turns off the motor.

2. The statement MOTOR, without any number following it, alters the current state of the motor.

3. The IBM Personal Computer XT does not have a cassette connector.

APPLICATIONS

With appropriate special hardware, the cassette port can be used to turn *any* electrical device on or off at specified times. Hence, the computer can control

276

the lights in your house while you are away, or turn on a coffee pot in the morning. The following program will turn on an electrical device for 3 minutes at 7:00 A.M.

```
10 IF TIME$ = "07:00:00" THEN MOTOR 1
20 IF TIME$ = "07:03:00" THEN MOTOR 0
```

NAME

The NAME command is used to change the name of a file. The format of the command is

```
NAME filespec1 AS filespec2
```

For instance, if the disk in drive B contains a file named SALES, then the command **NAME "B:SALES" AS "B:INCOME"** will change its name to INCOME. (Here we assume that, for BASIC 2.0 and subsequent versions, the file is in the current directory of B. See Appendix D.)

COMMENTS

1.   The NAME command only changes the name of the file. It leaves the file exactly where it was on the disk. Hence it cannot be used alone to create a second copy of a file or to move a file from one disk to another.

2.   BASIC was initially invoked from DOS by typing the word BASIC or BASICA following A>, B>, C>, or D>. The combination used identifies the "default drive." For instance, had the screen read **B> BASIC** when BASIC was invoked, then drive B would be the default drive.

When using the NAME command, you have the option of not specifying the drive. If you don't, the default drive is taken as the drive containing the file.

3.   If the first named file does not exist in the specified location, a "File not found" message results. If the new name is the same as the name of a file that already exists in the location, a "File already exists" message results.

4.   Filenames consist of two parts—a name of at most 8 characters followed by an optional extension consisting of a period and at most 3 characters. Files that have the extension ".BAS" can be LOADed and RUN by referring to them without their extension. However, in order to reNAME a file you must give the entire name. (Note: When a program or memory image file is created in BASIC and SAVEd with a name having at most 8 characters, the extension ".BAS" is automatically added to the name. Programmers sometimes forget to use the extension and therefore get a "File not found" message.) Also, the NAME command will not automatically add the extension ".BAS" to the new name.

5.   The following characters are allowed in filenames in all versions of BASIC.

```
A through Z
0 through 9
&   !   -   @   '   `   ~
(   )   {   }   __   #   $   %
```

6. For purposes of specifying and naming files, lowercase letters are not distinguished from uppercase letters.

EXAMPLES

For purposes of these examples, assume that the disk in drive A contains the files ACCOUNTS and ARROW.BAS, and the disk in drive B contains the files BALANCE, BROWN, and BLUE.BAS. Also, assume that drive A is the default drive and BASIC 1.1 is being used. The results of these programs will differ slightly with BASIC 2.0 and subsequent versions.

1.
```
NAME "B:BALANCE" AS "B:SALES"
Ok
FILES "B:*.*"
SALES          BROWN          BLUE      .BAS
Ok
```

Note: With versions of BASIC prior to BASIC 2.0, ''B:SALES'' can be written ''SALES''.

2.
```
NAME "ARROW.BAS" AS "VECTORS"
Ok
FILES
ACCOUNTS          VECTORS
Ok
```

3.
```
NAME "B:BLUE" AS "B:GREEN"
File not found
Ok
```

4.
```
NAME "B:BLUE.BAS" AS "B:BROWN"
File already exists
Ok
```

NEW

Suppose that you have been working with a program and decide to abandon it and start all over again. The command

    NEW

will delete the current program from memory and clear all values assigned to variables.

COMMENTS

1.   The NEW command clears all variables from memory, removes all information that has been set with DEF FN or DEFtype statements, causes all DIMensioned arrays to become undimensioned, closes all open files, and disables event trapping that has been set with statements such as ON ERROR, ON KEY(n), ON PEN, ON STRIG(n), ON PLAY(n), and ON TIMER. In graphics modes, the "last point referenced" is set to the center of the screen and the effects of previously executed WINDOW and VIEW statements are voided. OPTION BASE 1 is reset to OPTION BASE 0, the speaker is turned off, lightpens and joystick buttons are deactivated, and tracing with TRON is terminated. In BASIC 2.1, Music Foreground is reset to Music Background. In all other versions of BASIC, Music Background is reset to Music Foreground.

2.   The NEW command does not alter any information that has been set with DEF SEG or DEF USR.

3.   The NEW command is usually used in direct mode. Executing the NEW command within a program terminates the program.

EXAMPLE

```
10 PRINT "TEN"
20 A = 20: PRINT 20
30 B$ = "THIRTY": PRINT B$
RUN
TEN
 20
THIRTY
Ok
NEW
Ok
40 PRINT "FORTY"
50 PRINT A
60 PRINT B$
RUN
```

```
FORTY
  0

Ok
```

The NEW command reset the value of the numeric variable A to 0, reset the value of the string variable B\$ to the null string, and caused the original program consisting of lines 10 through 30 to be deleted from memory.

OCT$

The function OCT$ is used to convert integers from their base 10 representations to their base 8 representations.

Mathematical Preliminaries

Normally, we write integers in their decimal (base 10) representations. For instance, if r, s, t, u, v are digits from 0 to 9, then

    rstuv

represents the number

$$r*10000 \; + \; s*1000 \; + \; t*100 + \; u*10 \; + \; v$$
$$\text{or} \quad r*10^4 \quad + \quad s*10^3 \quad + \quad t*10^2 + \quad u*10 \; + \quad v$$

In the octal representation of numbers, the number 8 plays the role of 10. In octal notation

    rstuv

represents the number

$$r*8^4 \quad + \quad s*8^3 \quad + \quad t*8^2 \; + \quad u*8 \; + \quad v$$
$$\text{or} \quad r*4096 \; + \quad s*512 \; + \quad t*64 \; + \quad u*8 \; + \quad v$$

Some decimal numbers and their octal equivalents are:

18	22	$(18=2*8 + 2)$
60	74	$(60=7*8 + 4)$
2891	5513	$(2891=5*512 + 5*64 + 1*8 + 3)$
65535	177777	$(65535=1*32768 + 7*4096 + 7*512 + 7*64 + 7*8 + 7)$

Discussion

If n is a whole number (in decimal form) between 0 and 65535, then

    OCT$(n)

will be the string consisting of the octal representation of n. If x is *any* number between 0 and 65535.49, then

    OCT$(x)

will be the string consisting of the octal representation of the whole number obtained by rounding x.

Comments

1. If x is a negative number not less than -32768.49, then OCT$(x) is the same as OCT$(65536+x).

282

2. If $x > 65535.49$ or $x < -32768.49$, then OCT$(x) results in an "Overflow" error message or an erroneous result.

3. Due to a bug in BASIC, OCT$(x) results in an "Overflow" error message if $32767.49 < x < 32768$.

EXAMPLE

1.  ```
    PRINT OCT$(23),OCT$(138.6)
    27           213
    Ok
    ```

Notice that the number 27 was not displayed with a space preceding it. This is so since the output of OCT$ is a string variable, not a numeric variable.

2.  ```
    10 A = 2891: B$ = OCT$(2.3 + 33.8)
    20 PRINT OCT$(A),B$
    RUN
    5513          44
    Ok
    ```

3. Octal numeric constants are recognized by the arithmetic unit of the computer provided they are between 0 and 177777 and preceded by & or &O. The following program converts octal representations to decimal representations.

```
10 INPUT "OCTAL NUMBER";A
20 IF A>=0 THEN PRINT A: END
30 PRINT A+65536
RUN
OCTAL NUMBER? &5513
 2891
Ok
```

ON COM(n)

The occurrence of a communications event can be trapped in a manner similar to trapping of errors and keys with their respective statements of ON ERROR and ON KEY(n). The format for the ON COM(n) statement is similar to the other event trapping statements, which is:

```
ON COM(n) GOSUB line
```

The communications port is designated by n, which has the value 1 or 2. As a result of data from COMn: being placed in its associated file buffer, program control will be transferred to the line indicated by the GOSUB statement.

The ON COM(n) statement must be used in conjunction with the COM(n) statement.

Nothing is executed when the ON COM(n) statement is encountered, even after communications event trapping has been enabled with the COM(n) ON statement. The ON COM(n) statement is executed when data is placed in the communications buffer, regardless of where within the program processing is occurring. When the communications event occurs, ON COM(n) causes control to be passed to the GOSUB line and processing to continue there until a RETURN statement is encountered. At that point, processing will be resumed with the statement following the last statement processed when the communications event occurred.

EXAMPLE

```
 10 OPEN "COM1:300,E,7,1" AS #1
 20 ON COM(1) GOSUB 2000
 30 COM(1) ON
     .
     .
     .
100 PRINT "This is line # 100."
110 PRINT "This is line # 110."
120 PRINT "This is line # 120."
     .
     .
     .
2000 ' * * * COMMUNICATIONS MANAGER * * *
2010 PRINT "This is line # 2010."
     .
     .
     .
2100 RETURN
```

Line 10 opens the communications buffer associated with communications port #1. Line 20 instructs the program to transfer processing control to line

2000 at the occurrence of a communications event (if communications event trapping for that buffer has been turned "on"). Line 30 turns on communications event trapping for buffer #1. The remaining lines of the program are self-explanatory.

When the program was executed, if the communications event occurred just as line 110 was processed, the video screen output would look like this:

> This is line # 100.
> This is line # 110.
> This is line # 2010.
> This is line # 120.

COMMENTS

1. The ON COM(n) statement is a feature of advanced BASIC (BASICA) and will cause a syntax error if execution is attempted with Cassette or Disk BASIC.

2. The ON COM(n) and COM(n) ON statements may be listed in the program in any order; however, communications event trapping for COMn: will not be in effect until both statements are executed.

3. At the occurrence of the communications event, trapping for that communications buffer is temporarily suspended until a RETURN statement is encountered. The effect is the same as when the COM(n) STOP statement is executed. That is, the occurrence of a subsequent communications event when trapping is suspended will be remembered, and cause the subroutine to be executed again immediately after the RETURN is encountered. Only one event may be remembered at any time.

4. The RETURN statement of the subroutine addressed by ON COM(n) may be in the form of RETURN or RETURN line. Either form will exit the subroutine and reactivate the ON COM(n) statement.

5. The ON COM(n) statement may be disabled by using the COM(n) OFF statement.

ON ERROR

Appendix E lists the error messages that can appear when running a program. A subroutine (referred to as an *error handling subroutine*) can be written to take corrective measures instead of having an error message displayed and the program terminated. Suppose that the error handling subroutine begins on line n. After the statement

    ON ERROR GOTO n

is encountered, any error (other than "Division by zero") causes the program to branch to line n. This process is referred to as *error trapping*.

EXAMPLE

1. The following program counts the number of items in a DATA statement.

```
10 ON ERROR GOTO 60
20 N=0
30 READ A
40 N=N+1
50 GOTO 30
60 PRINT N
70 END
80 DATA 20, 864, 218, 10, 299
RUN
 5
Ok
```

Without line 10, the error message "Out of DATA in 30" would have been displayed, and the number 5 would not have been displayed. The error handling subroutine consists of lines 60 and 70.

COMMENTS

1. In Example 1, the error handling subroutine terminated the program with an END statement. Usually, however, the last line of the subroutine contains a RESUME statement that branches back to the statement in which the error occurred, a RESUME NEXT statement that branches to the statement following the statement in which the error occurred, or a RESUME t statement that branches to line t. (See the discussion of the RESUME statement for further details.)

2. Error trapping can be disabled at any time with the statement

    ON ERROR GOTO 0

3. If ON ERROR is not disabled by **ON ERROR GOTO 0**, it will remain active even after the program has ended. For instance, after such a program finishes running, if you type and enter RUB (instead of RUN) the error trapping routine will take over.

4. Error trapping will be disabled if any of the commands CHAIN, CHAIN MERGE, CLEAR, LOAD, MERGE, NEW, or RUN are executed or if a program line is entered or deleted.

5. If a second error occurs within the error handling subroutine itself (that is, before a RESUME statement has been executed), the error cannot be trapped but must result in an error message and termination of the program. If the statement **ON ERROR GOTO 0** is encountered within the error handling subroutine, the message corresponding to the error being trapped will be displayed, and execution of the program will stop.

6. Just as with other subroutines, it is good practice to precede error handling subroutines by an END or STOP statement so that they are not entered accidentally.

7. Consider Example 1. If one of the items in the DATA statement had been a string constant, a syntax error rather than a logical error would have resulted. Since the error handling subroutine ends with END, the program would have terminated after executing the error handling subroutine and line 80 would have been presented in a form for editing.

8. An inappropriate response to an INPUT statement cannot be trapped by an ON ERROR statement. Instead the message "Redo from start" appears on the screen and the INPUT statement is executed again.

FURTHER EXAMPLES

2. In the following program, the number of items in a DATA statement is counted and then alphabetized. The alphabetizing procedure used is known as a *bubble sort*.

```
10 REM BUBBLE SORT
20 N=0
30 ON ERROR GOTO 70
40 READ W$
50 N=N+1
60 GOTO 40
70 RESUME 80
80 RESTORE: DIM A$(N)
90 ON ERROR GOTO 0
100 FOR I = 1 TO N: READ A$(I): NEXT I
110 FOR I = 1 TO N-1
120    FOR J = 1 TO N-1
130       IF A$(J)<=A$(J+1) THEN 150
```

287

ON ERROR

```
140        SWAP A$(J),A$(J+1)
150     NEXT J
160 NEXT I
170 FOR I = 1 TO N: PRINT A$(I),: NEXT I
180 DATA PAT, VAT, CAT, MAT, HAT
RUN
CAT             HAT             MAT             PAT             VAT
Ok
```

The error handling subroutine consists of line 70. The statement, **RESUME 80**
was necessary since error handling subroutines should either terminate the
program or end with a RESUME statement. For instance, had the statement
in line 70 been **GOTO 80**, then line 90 would have terminated the program
and produced the message ''Out of DATA in 40.'' *Note:* This program can
be used to alphabetize any list of words. Just place the words in DATA
statements.

3.
```
10 ON ERROR GOTO 90
20 A$ = "one" : B = 2
30 C$ = A$+B
40 PRINT C$
50 ON ERROR GOTO 0
60 C$= B+A$
70 PRINT C$
80 END
90 B$ = STR$(B)
100 C$ = A$+B$
110 LPRINT A$, B
120 RESUME NEXT
RUN
one 2              (Printer produced ''one         2'')
Type mismatch in 60
Ok
```

The order in which the statements were executed was 10, 20, 30, 90, 100,
110, 120, 40, 50, 60.

4. Suppose that in Example 3 line 50 was renumbered as line 115.

```
RUN
Type mismatch in 30
Ok
```

In this case the printer would have produced the same result as in Example 3.
The order in which the statements were executed was 10, 20, 30, 90, 100,
110, 115.

5. Suppose that in Example 3 we forgot to turn on the printer.

```
RUN
Out of paper in 110
Ok
```

There is nothing we can do to prevent the program from terminating when an error takes place inside the error handling subroutine.

6. For further examples see the discussions of RESUME, ERR and ERL, and ERROR.

APPLICATIONS

1. Error handling subroutines are essential when writing software for users who are not well versed in BASIC. They will not have the foggiest idea of what to do if an error message appears. Also, we should try to anticipate their errors and make appropriate provisions.

2. Suppose that a program asks the user for the name of a file to be accessed by the program. If the user mistypes the file name, or if the wrong disk is in the disk drive, the program will ordinarily terminate with the message "File not found". An error trapping subroutine can permit the user to retype the filename.

ON . . . GOSUB and ON . . . GOTO

The ON . . . GOSUB and ON . . . GOTO statements are really composites of the statements IF, GOSUB, and GOTO. (If you are unfamiliar with any of these three statements, refer to them before proceeding.)

ON . . . GOSUB and ON . . . GOTO statements involve a numeric variable (call it I), which normally assumes values like 1, 2, or 3, and a sequence of line numbers. A statement of the form

```
ON I GOTO m,n,r
```

causes the program to **GOTO** m if the value of I is 1, **GOTO** n if the value of I is 2, and **GOTO** r if the value of I is 3. That is, the statement is equivalent to the sequence of statements

```
IF I=1 GOTO m
IF I=2 GOTO n
IF I=3 GOTO r
```

We are not limited to branching to just three lines, but can allow branching to as many lines as we like. A statement of the form

```
ON I GOSUB m,n,r
```

has an analogous meaning to the statement discussed above.

EXAMPLES

1.
```
   10 INPUT I
   20 ON I GOTO 40, 50
   30 PRINT "Thirty": GOTO 10
   40 PRINT "Forty ";
   50 PRINT "Fifty": GOTO 10
   RUN
   ? 1
   Forty Fifty
   ? 2
   Fifty
   ? 3
   Thirty
   ?
```

Notice that no branching resulted when I was assigned the value of 3. (Press Ctrl-Break to terminate this program.)

2.
```
   10 INPUT J
   20 ON J GOSUB 100, 200, 300, 400
   30 PRINT 30
```

ON . . . GOSUB and ON . . . GOTO

```
40 GOTO 10
90 END
100 PRINT 100;: RETURN
200 PRINT 200;: RETURN
300 PRINT 300;: RETURN
400 PRINT 400;: RETURN
RUN
? 4
  400   30
? 2
  200   30
?
```

COMMENTS

1. The value of the variable in an ON . . . GOSUB or ON . . . GOTO statement can be any nonnegative number less than 255.5. In the event that the value of the variable is not a whole number, the value will be rounded to the closest whole number. If the value is 255.5 or more, or is negative, the error message "Illegal function call" results. For instance, consider the following outcomes from RUNning the program in Example 1.

```
RUN
? 1.7
Fifty
? 2.25
Fifty
? 256
Illegal function call in 20
Ok
```

2. If the (rounded) value of the variable in an ON . . . GOSUB or ON . . . GOTO statement is 0, or is greater than the number of line number options provided in the statement, program execution continues with the next statement.

3. An expression can be used in place of the variable in an ON . . . GOSUB or ON . . . GOTO statement. Some examples are

```
ON 10*I+3 GOTO 100, 200
ON INT(I) GOSUB 100, 200, 300
ON INSTR("YyNn",A$)/2 GOTO 100, 200
```

4. The numbers m, n, r, etc., in an ON . . . GOSUB or ON . . . GOTO statement must be numeric constants. Computed GOSUBs or GOTOs using variables or expressions for m, n, r, etc., are not allowed. For instance, the statements `ON I GOTO A,B,C` and `ON I GOSUB 2*50,INT(20.8)` are not valid.

ON . . . GOSUB and ON . . . GOTO

FURTHER EXAMPLES

3.   The following program uses the function SGN. SGN(A) is 1, 0, or -1 depending upon whether A is positive, zero, or negative.

```
10 INPUT "Total taxes"; T
20 INPUT "Amount of prepaid taxes"; A
30 ON 2+SGN(A-T) GOTO 40, 50, 60
40 PRINT "Balance due: $"; T-A: END
50 PRINT "You have prepaid all taxes.": END
60 PRINT "Amount overpaid: $"; A-T: END
RUN
Total taxes? 9876.54
Amount of prepaid taxes? 12345.67
Amount overpaid: $ 2469.13
Ok
```

In this case, A-T was a positive number, SGN(A-T) was 1, and 2+SGN (A-T) was 3.

4.   The following incomplete program is an outline of a program to access a list of names and addresses. Each subroutine would perform its designated task.

```
10 PRINT "    MENU"
20 PRINT "1. Add entry"
30 PRINT "2. Delete entry"
40 PRINT "3. Change entry"
50 PRINT "4. Display entry"
60 PRINT "5. Quit": PRINT
70 INPUT "Selection"; SELECT
80 ON SELECT GOSUB 100, 200, 300, 400, 500
90 PRINT: GOTO 10
99 END
100 'Add entry subroutine code
  :
199 RETURN
200 'Delete entry subroutine code
  :
299 RETURN
300 'Change entry subroutine code
  :
399 RETURN
400 'Display entry subroutine code
  :
499 RETURN
500 END
```

ON . . . GOSUB and ON . . . GOTO

```
RUN
        MENU
1. Add entry
2. Delete entry
3. Change entry
4. Display entry
5. Quit

Selection?
```

5. Insurance premium rates are determined by age groups. Suppose that a policy has the following rate schedule:

AGE	RATE
20 - 39	76.54
40 - 59	98.76
60 - 79	123.45

```
10 INPUT "Age last birthday"; A
20 ON INT(A/20) GOTO 40, 50, 60
30 PRINT "We don't insure persons under 20 or over 80.": END
40 PRINT "Your annual rate is $76.54": END
50 PRINT "Your annual rate is $98.76": END
60 PRINT "Your annual rate is $123.45"
RUN
Age last birthday? 45
Your annual rate is $98.76
Ok
```

ON KEY(n)

The leftmost part of the keyboard contains 10 keys labeled F1 to F10 and known as the "soft" or "function" keys. The numeric keypad on the right side of the keyboard has 4 arrow keys that are used to move the cursor. For purposes of this discussion, refer to these cursor control keys as F11 (Cursor Up), F12 (Cursor Left), F13 (Cursor Right), and F14 (Cursor Down).

The statement **KEY(n) ON** causes the computer to check key Fn after execution of each BASIC statement to see if it is being pressed. Suppose that a KEY(n) ON statement is followed by the statement

```
ON KEY(n) GOSUB m
```

Nothing will happen immediately. However, as soon as key Fn is pressed, the program will branch to line m; that is, line m will be the next line executed. This process is referred to as *trapping* the nth function key. The computer will remember where it branched from and as soon as it encounters the statement **RETURN**, it will branch back to that point in the program.

EXAMPLES

1. While the following program is running, press key F4 several times. The screen will keep a record of the number of times the key is pressed. When other individual keys are pressed nothing happens. (Press Ctrl-Break to terminate the program.)

```
10 CLS: KEY(4) ON
20 ON KEY(4) GOSUB 40
30 GOTO 30
40 T = T + 1
50 LOCATE 12,1
60 PRINT "You have pressed key F4" T "times"
70 RETURN
```

2. In the following program, an airplane appears on line 12 of the screen. Pressing key F13 (the Cursor Right key) causes the airplane to move to the right. Pressing the soft key F10 causes the airplane to drop a bomb. (Press Ctrl-Break to terminate the program.)

```
10 CLS: KEY OFF: WIDTH 80
20 KEY(10) ON: ON KEY(10) GOSUB 100
30 KEY(13) ON: ON KEY(13) GOSUB 200
40 A$ = "  >==>  "
50 LOCATE 12,1,0: PRINT A$
60 GOTO 60
```

```
100 B = C+4
110 FOR I = 13 TO 23
120    LOCATE I,B: PRINT CHR$(157)
130    FOR J=1 TO 25: NEXT J
140    LOCATE I,B: PRINT " "
150 NEXT I
160 RETURN
200 IF C<72 THEN 230
210 LOCATE 12,C: PRINT "         "
220 C=1: GOTO 240
230 C=C+2
240 LOCATE 12,C: PRINT A$
250 RETURN
```

(*Note:* Wait until bombs reach the ground before moving the airplane. In Example 4, we shall improve the program and remove this restriction.)

COMMENTS

1.   The ON KEY(n) statement can only be used with Advanced BASIC. That is, the command BASICA must have been given when BASIC was invoked.

2.   The KEY(n) ON statement does not have to precede the ON KEY(n) statement. However, the ON KEY(n) statement will not be enabled until the KEY(n) ON statement is executed.

3.   Suppose that a program branches to a subroutine due to an ON KEY(n) statement, and that the indicated key is pressed while the subroutine is being executed. This event will not cause an immediate branch to the beginning of the subroutine. Instead, the computer will remember that the key was pressed and will reexecute the subroutine as soon as RETURN is reached. See Example 4.

4.   Suppose that your program contains ON KEY(n) and KEY(n) ON statements, but that there is a sequence of lines that you do not want interrupted. Precede the lines by the statement **KEY(n) STOP** and follow the lines by the statement **KEY(n) ON**. If the indicated key is pushed during the execution of these lines, the computer will take no action but will remember that the key was pushed and will branch to the subroutine as soon as the KEY(n) ON statement is reached. (See Example 2 in the discussion of the KEY(n) statement.)

5.   The RETURN statement following the subroutine can refer to a specific line. The statement **RETURN t** results in a branch back to line t rather than to the statement that would have been executed next if the key hadn't been pressed.

6.   The trapping routine for the key identified by the number n can be disabled by the statement **KEY(n) OFF** or the statement **ON KEY(n) GOSUB 0**. Trapping of all keys is disabled whenever any of the commands CHAIN,

ON KEY(n)

CHAIN MERGE, CLEAR, LOAD, MERGE, or RUN are executed or when a program line is deleted or entered.

7. INPUT, LINE INPUT, and INPUT$ cause the execution of a program to be suspended until the user responds. If an ON KEY(n) statement is active at this time, the computer does an automatic KEY(n) STOP and then an automatic KEY(n) ON when execution resumes.

8. BASIC 2.0 and subsequent versions allow the trapping of 6 additional keys or key combinations with values of n ranging from 15 to 20. See the discussion of KEY for the details of how they are specified.

FURTHER EXAMPLES

```
3.   10 KEY OFF: CLS
     20 A=0
     30 ON KEY(5) GOSUB 70
     40 KEY(5) ON
     50 PRINT "Press key F5": GOTO 50
     60 END
     70 A=A+1
     80 PRINT "We have executed the subroutine" A "times."
     90 FOR I = 1 TO 3600: NEXT I
     100 BEEP
     110 RETURN
```

The words "Press key F5" will scroll by quickly until you press the F5 key. Then you will enter the subroutine. The subroutine takes about 6 seconds to be executed and ends with a beep. If you press the key F5 during that 6 seconds, nothing will happen until after the beep. At that time the subroutine will be executed again.

4. The program in Example 2 can be improved by adding the following four lines.

```
     115 KEY(13) STOP
     125 KEY(13) ON
     135 KEY(13) STOP
     145 KEY(13) ON
```

These lines guarantee that lines 120 and 140 will not be interrupted in the middle. Now you can move the airplane even while a bomb is falling.

APPLICATIONS

1. Programs often present the user with a list, or "menu," of the different tasks that the program can perform. The user is told to press F1 to perform the first task, F2 to perform the second task, and so on. ON KEY(n) statements are used to interrupt the program and branch to the subroutine that carries out the requested task.

This statement involves light pens (see the first two paragraphs of the discussion of PEN) and subroutines (see the discussion of GOSUB and RETURN). The statement **PEN ON** causes the computer to check the light pen after the execution of each BASIC statement to see if the pen is active. Suppose that the PEN ON statement is followed by the statement

```
ON PEN GOSUB n
```

Nothing will happen immediately. However, as soon as the light pen is activated, the program will branch to line n; that is, line n will be the next line executed. This process is referred to as *trapping* the light pen. The computer will remember where it branched from and, as soon as it encounters the statement **RETURN**, it will branch back to that point in the program.

EXAMPLES

1. The following program turns the computer into a clock. Whenever the light pen is activated, the program will branch to line 100 and cause the speaker to emit a short beeping sound. The subroutine consists of line 100. Line 110 returns us back to whatever line the computer would have executed if the pen hadn't been activated. Line 90 is not essential here; however, it is good practice to always precede subroutines by END statements. Press Ctrl-Break to terminate the program.

```
10 SCREEN 0,1: COLOR 15,1: WIDTH 40
20 CLS: KEY OFF
30 PEN ON
40 ON PEN GOSUB 100
50 LOCATE 12,9
60 PRINT "The time is"
70 LOCATE 12,21: PRINT TIME$
80 GOTO 70
90 END
100 BEEP
110 RETURN
```

2. The following program draws a rectangle and paints it in a color selected by the light pen. Touch one of the colors with the pen and then activate the pen. Now, deactivate the pen and try another color. Press Ctrl-Break to terminate the program.

```
10 SCREEN 1,0: COLOR 1,0: KEY OFF: CLS
20 LINE (40,40)-(280,100),,B
30 LOCATE 20,1: PRINT "GREEN"
```

ON PEN

```
40 LOCATE 20,19: PRINT "RED"
50 LOCATE 20,37: PRINT "BLUE"
60 ON PEN GOSUB 90:PEN ON
70 GOTO 70
80 END
90 IF PEN(7)<7 THEN PAINT(160,50),1,3: GOTO 120
100 IF PEN(7)>35 THEN PAINT(160,50),0,3: GOTO 120
110 PAINT (160,50),2,3
120 RETURN
```

COMMENTS

1. The PEN ON statement does not have to precede the ON PEN statement. However, the ON PEN statement will not be enabled until the PEN
ON statement is executed.

2. Suppose that a program branches to a subroutine due to an ON PEN
statement, and that the pen is activated while the subroutine is being executed. This event will not cause an immediate branch to the beginning of the
subroutine. Instead the computer will remember that the pen was activated
and will re-execute the subroutine as soon as RETURN is reached. See
Example 3.

3. Suppose that your program contains ON PEN and PEN ON statements,
but that there is a sequence of lines that you do not want interrupted. Precede
the lines by the statement **PEN STOP** and follow the lines by the statement
PEN ON. If the light pen is activated during the execution of these lines, the
computer will take no action but will remember that the pen was activated
and will branch to the subroutine as soon as the PEN ON statement is
reached. See Example 5.

4. In Example 2, we used the value of PEN(7) that was set when the light
pen was activated. We could have used any of the other PEN functions except
for PEN(0). The trapping procedure results in PEN(0) being set incorrectly.

5. The RETURN statement following the subroutine can refer to a specific
line. The statement **RETURN m** results in a branch back to line m rather than
to the line that would have been executed next if the light pen hadn't been
activated. See Example 4.

6. The light pen trapping routine can be disabled in various ways. To disable just the trapping routine but leave the pen operative, execute the statement **ON PEN GOSUB 0**. The statement **PEN OFF** disables all functioning of
the light pen. Also, all functioning is disabled by the commands CHAIN,
CHAIN MERGE, CLEAR, LOAD, MERGE, and RUN, and by entering
or deleting a program line.

7. The ON PEN statement can only be used with Advanced BASIC. That
is, the command BASICA must have been given when BASIC was invoked.

8.   INPUT, LINE INPUT, and INPUT$ cause the execution of the program to be suspended until the user responds. If an ON PEN statement is active at this time, the computer does an automatic **PEN STOP** and then an automatic **PEN ON** when execution resumes.

FURTHER EXAMPLES

3.
```
10 SCREEN 0,1: COLOR 15,1: KEY OFF: CLS
20 A=0
30 ON PEN GOSUB 70
40 PEN ON
50 PRINT "activate pen": GOTO 50
60 END
70 A=A+1
80 PRINT "We have executed the subroutine" A "times."
90 FOR I = 1 TO 3000: NEXT I
100 BEEP
110 RETURN
```

The words "activate pen" will scroll by rapidly until you activate the light pen. Then you will enter the subroutine. The subroutine takes about 5 seconds to be executed. It ends with a beep. If you activate the light pen during that 5 seconds, nothing will happen until after the beep. At that time the subroutine will be executed again.

4.   We have added a few more lines to Example 3 to illustrate a RETURN to a specific line.

```
10 SCREEN 0,1: COLOR 15,1: KEY OFF: CLS
20 A=0
30 ON PEN GOSUB 70
40 PEN ON
50 PRINT "activate pen": GOTO 50
55 PRINT "we've returned"
56 FOR J=1 TO 1000: NEXT
57 GOTO 50
60 END
70 A=A+1
80 PRINT "We have executed the subroutine" A "times."
90 FOR I = 1 TO 3000: NEXT I
100 BEEP
110 RETURN 55
```

5.   The following is a variation of the program in Example 1. The first row of the screen keeps a running count of the number of times that the light pen has been activated.

ON PEN

```
10 CLS: SCREEN 0,1: COLOR 15,1
20 ON PEN GOSUB 90
30 LOCATE 12,9: PRINT "The time is"
40 PEN STOP
50 LOCATE 12,21
60 PRINT TIME$
70 PEN ON
80 GOTO 40
90 T=T+1: LOCATE 1,1
100 PRINT "The pen has been activated"; T; "times"
110 RETURN
```

Line 40 guarantees that the subroutine will not be entered immediately after line 50. If this were to happen, the time would be PRINTed on row 2. To see this occur, change line 80 to **80 GOTO 50** and activate the light pen repeatedly.

ON PLAY(n)

The statement ON PLAY is not available with versions of BASIC preceding BASIC 2.0. This discussion assumes a familiarity with the PLAY statement, particularly, the Music Background (MB) mode, and actually involves four statements: PLAY ON, ON PLAY(n), PLAY OFF, and PLAY STOP.

The MB command of the PLAY statement sets up a music buffer capable of storing up to 32 notes and pauses so that the program can continue to execute while music is being played in the background. The statement

```
PLAY ON
```

causes the computer to check the music buffer after execution of each BASIC statement. Suppose that a PLAY ON statement is followed by the statement

```
ON PLAY(n) GOSUB m
```

and that n or more notes are placed in the music buffer by a PLAY statement. Nothing will happen immediately. However, as soon as the number of notes in the buffer changes from n to n-1, the program will branch to line m; that is, line m will be the next line executed. The computer will remember where it branched from and, as soon as it encounters the statement **RETURN**, will branch back to that point in the program. This process is referred to as *trapping* the music buffer.

EXAMPLE

The following program asks the user to name the song playing in the background. The ON PLAY(n) statement allows the program to terminate the music shortly after the user responds.

```
10 PLAY ON
20 ON PLAY(2) GOSUB 120
30 GOSUB 120
40 PRINT "The name of this song is:"
50 PRINT "1. Merry Christmas"
60 PRINT "2. Twinkle, Twinkle, Little Star"
70 PRINT "3. Jingle Bells"
80 A$ = INKEY$: IF A$ = "" THEN 80
90 IF A$ = "3" THEN PRINT "Correct": GOTO 110
100 PRINT "Nice try, but no cigar."
110 END
120 F = F+1
130 ON F GOTO 140,150,160,170,180
140 PLAY "MB O3 L8 EE E4 EE E4": GOTO 190
150 PLAY "EG C. D16 E4 P4": GOTO 190
```

ON PLAY(n)

```
160 PLAY "FF F. F16 F EE L16 EE": GOTO 190
170 PLAY "L4 GGFD C1": GOTO 190
180 PRINT "Time is up": GOTO 110
190 RETURN
```

COMMENTS

1.   The ON PLAY(n) statement can only be used with Advanced BASIC. That is, the command BASICA must have been given when BASIC was invoked.

2.   The PLAY ON statement does not have to precede the ON PLAY(n) statement. However, the ON PLAY(n) statement will not be enabled until the PLAY ON statement is executed.

3.   Suppose that a subroutine is branched to due to an ON PLAY(n) statement, and that the number of notes in the music buffer decreases from n to n-1 while the subroutine is being executed. This event will not cause an immediate branch to the beginning of the subroutine. Instead, the computer will remember that the event occured and will reexecute the subroutine as soon as RETURN is reached.

4.   Suppose that your program contains ON PLAY(n) and PLAY ON statements, but that there is a sequence of lines that you do not want interrupted. Precede the lines by the statement

PLAY STOP

and follow the lines by the statement **PLAY ON**. If the number of notes in the music buffer decreases from n to n-1 during the execution of these lines, the computer will take no action but will remember that the event occurred and will branch to the subroutine as soon as the PLAY ON statement is reached.

5.   The RETURN statement following the subroutine can refer to a specific line. The statement **RETURN t** results in a branch back to line t rather than to the statement that would have been executed next if the number of notes in the music buffer hadn't decreased from n to n-1

6.   The trapping routine can be disabled by the statement

PLAY OFF

or the statement **ON PLAY(n) GOSUB 0**. Trapping is also disabled if one of the commands CHAIN, CHAIN MERGE, CLEAR, LOAD, MERGE, or RUN is executed, or if a program line is entered or deleted.

7.   The statements INPUT, LINE INPUT, and INPUT$ cause the execution of the program to be suspended until the user responds. If an ON PLAY(n) statement is active at that time, the computer does an automatic PLAY STOP and then an automatic PLAY ON when execution resumes.

8.   The music buffer can hold up to 32 notes and pauses. When music is being played in either Music Normal or Music Staccato modes, pauses are inserted between each pair of notes. Hence, in these modes the music buffer will hold only 16 notes at any one time.

9.   If an ON PLAY(n) statement is active and fewer than n notes are placed in the buffer, trapping will take place immediately.

APPLICATIONS

ON PLAY(n) is used to play continuous background music. Long compositions are broken up into small pieces that are fed into the music buffer one at a time.

ON STRIG(n)

This statement involves joysticks (see the first two paragraphs of the discussion of STRIG) and subroutines (see the discussion of GOSUB and RE-TURN). The statement **STRIG(0) ON** causes the computer to check the lower button of the joystick after the execution of each BASIC statement to see if it is currently pressed. Suppose that this statement is followed by the statement

```
ON STRIG(0) GOSUB m
```

Nothing will happen immediately. However, as soon as the lower button is pressed the program will branch to line m. That is, line m will be the next line executed. This process is referred to as *trapping* a joystick button. The computer will remember where it branched from and, as soon as it encounters the statement **RETURN**, will branch back to that point in the program. The statements **STRIG(4) ON** and **ON STRIG(4) GOSUB m** have an analogous effect with respect to the upper joystick button.

EXAMPLES

1. The following program uses the lower joystick button to trigger the release of a bomb from an airplane. Press Ctrl-Break to terminate the program.

```
10 CLS: KEY OFF
20 STRIG(0) ON
30 ON STRIG(0) GOSUB 60
40 LOCATE 12,20,0: PRINT ">==>"
50 GOTO 40
60 FOR J = 13 TO 23
70    LOCATE J,21: PRINT CHR$(157)
80    FOR K = 1 TO 95: NEXT K
90    LOCATE J,21: PRINT " "
100 NEXT J
110 RETURN
```

2. The following program is a combination of Example 1 above and Example 1 from the discussion of the STICK function. The joystick lever moves an airplane around the screen and the lower button releases bombs.

```
10 CLS: SCREEN 0: WIDTH 80: KEY OFF
20 A$ = ">==>"
30 STRIG(0) ON
40 ON STRIG(0) GOSUB 120
50 X = 1: Y = 1
60 X1 = X: Y1 = Y
```

```
70 X = STICK(0)/4: Y = 1+STICK(1)/11
80 LOCATE Y1,X1: PRINT "    "
90 LOCATE Y,X: PRINT A$
100 FOR I =1 TO 95: NEXT I
110 GOTO 60
120 FOR J = Y+1 TO 23
130     LOCATE J,X+1: PRINT CHR$(157)
140     FOR K=1 TO 95: NEXT K
150     LOCATE J,X+1: PRINT " "
160 NEXT J
170 RETURN
```

3.   The following program provides an embellishment to Example 3 from the discussion of the STICK function. Moving the joystick lever traces a drawing on the screen. Pushing the lower button changes the background color, and pushing the upper button clears the screen. This program requires a graphics monitor.

```
10 SCREEN 1,0: COLOR 1,1: CLS: KEY OFF
20 A = 1
30 STRIG(0) ON
40 STRIG(4) ON
50 ON STRIG(0) GOSUB 120
60 ON STRIG(4) GOSUB 150
70 PSET(STICK(0),STICK(1))
80 X = STICK(0)
90 Y = STICK(1)
100 LINE -(X,Y)
110 GOTO 80
120 A=A+1
130 COLOR A,0
140 RETURN
150 CLS
160 PSET(STICK(0),STICK(1))
170 RETURN
```

COMMENTS

1.   The ON STRIG(n) statement can only be used with Advanced BASIC. That is, the command BASICA must have been given when BASIC was invoked.

2.   Actually, two joysticks can be connected to the computer. If so, the statements ON STRIG(2) and ON STRIG(6) play the same role with respect to the second joystick as ON STRIG(0) and ON STRIG(4) do for the first joystick. (*Note:* This feature is not available with BASIC 1.00 and BASIC 1.05)

3. The STRIG(n) ON statement does not have to precede the ON STRIG(n) statement. However, the ON STRIG(n) statement will not be enabled until the STRIG(n) ON statement is executed.

4. Suppose that a program branches to a subroutine due to an ON STRIG(n) statement, and that the indicated button is pressed while the subroutine is being executed. This event will not cause an immediate branch to the beginning of the subroutine. Instead, the computer will remember that the button was pressed and will reexecute the subroutine as soon as RETURN is reached. See Example 4.

5. Suppose that your program contains ON STRIG(n) and STRIG(n) ON statements, but that there is a sequence of lines that you do not want interrupted. Precede the lines by the statement **STRIG(n) STOP** and follow the lines by the statement **STRIG(n) ON**. If the indicated button is pushed during the execution of these lines, the computer will take no action, but will remember that the button was pushed and will branch to the subroutine as soon as the STRIG(n) ON statement is reached. (See Example 2 in the discussion of the STRIG(n) statement.)

6. The RETURN statement following the subroutine can refer to a specific line. The statement **RETURN t** results in a branch back to line t rather than to the statement that would have been executed next if the button hadn't been pressed. See the right hand program in Comment 7.

7. Consider the following pair of programs.

```
10 CLS: STRIG ON                  10 CLS: STRIG ON
20 FOR I = 1 TO 2000: NEXT        20 FOR I = 1 TO 2000: NEXT
30 LOCATE 1,1                     30 STRIG(0) ON
40 PRINT STRIG(0); STRIG(1)       40 ON STRIG(0) GOSUB 70
RUN                               50 GOTO 50
 -1 -1                            60 END
Ok                                70 LOCATE 1,1
                                  80 PRINT STRIG(0); STRIG(1)
                                  90 RETURN 60
                                  RUN
                                   0 -1
                                  Ok
```

In both cases, the lower button of the joystick was held down throughout execution of the program. In line 40 of the program on the left, the STRIG(0) and STRIG(1) functions performed as expected. In line 80 of the program on the right the STRIG(1) function performed normally, but the STRIG(0) function did not return the value -1 as usual. In general, whenever pressing a button causes branching to a subroutine, that particular pressing will not generate the usual values of STRIG(0), STRIG(2), STRIG(4), or STRIG(6).

8. The trapping routine for the button identified by the number n can be disabled by the statement **STRIG(n) OFF** or the statement **ON STRIG(n)**

GOSUB 0. The trapping of all buttons is disabled if one of the commands CHAIN, CHAIN MERGE, CLEAR, LOAD, MERGE, or RUN is executed, or if a program line is entered or deleted.

9.   INPUT, LINE INPUT, and INPUT$ cause the execution of the program to be suspended until the user responds. If an ON STRIG(n) statement is active at this time, the computer does an automatic `STRIG(n) STOP` and then an automatic `STRIG(n) ON` when execution resumes.

FURTHER EXAMPLE

```
4.   10 KEY OFF: CLS
     20 A=0
     30 ON STRIG(0) GOSUB 70
     40 STRIG(0) ON
     50 PRINT "Press lower button quickly": GOTO 50
     60 END
     70 A=A+1
     80 PRINT "We have executed the subroutine"; A; "times."
     90 FOR I = 1 TO 3000: NEXT I
     100 BEEP
     110 RETURN
```

The words "Press lower button quickly" will scroll by rapidly until you press the lower button. Just give the button a light tap. Then you will enter the subroutine. The subroutine takes about 5 seconds to be executed. It ends with a beep. If you press the button normally during that 5 seconds, nothing will happen until after the beep. At that time the subroutine will be executed again.

APPLICATIONS

Joysticks are used primarily for games. The players move objects around the screen with the lever and use the buttons to initiate certain actions, as in Examples 1, 2, and 3.

ON TIMER

The statement ON TIMER is not available with the versions of BASIC preceding BASIC 2.0.

This discussion actually involves the four statements ON TIMER, TIMER ON, TIMER OFF, and TIMER STOP. The statement **TIMER ON** "resets" an internal timer and causes the computer to check the number of seconds recorded on this internal timer after the execution of each BASIC statement. Suppose that a TIMER ON statement is followed by the statement

```
ON TIMER(n) GOSUB m
```

where n is a number from 1 to 65535. Nothing will happen immediately. However, whenever the elapsed time recorded on the internal timer is a multiple of n, the computer will branch to line m. That is, once every n seconds, line m will be executed. The computer will remember where it branched from and as soon as it encounters the statement **RETURN**, it will branch back to that point in the program. This process is referred to as *trapping* the clock.

EXAMPLE

1. The following program updates the time every 10 seconds. Press Ctrl-Break to terminate this program.

```
10 CLS: TIMER ON
20 PRINT "The time is now " ; TIME$
30 PRINT
40 PRINT "The time will change at the tone every 10
seconds."
50 ON TIMER(10) GOSUB 70
60 GOTO 60
70 BEEP
80 LOCATE 1,17: PRINT TIME$
90 RETURN
RUN
The time is now 01:15:48

The time will change at the tone every 10 seconds.
```

COMMENTS

1. The ON TIMER statement can be used only with Advanced BASIC. That is, the command BASICA must have been given when BASIC was invoked.

2. The TIMER ON statement does not have to precede the ON TIMER statement. However, the ON TIMER statement will not be enabled until the TIMER ON statement is executed.

3. Suppose that a program branches to a subroutine due to an ON TIMER statement, and that the indicated number of seconds elapses while the subroutine is being executed. This event will not cause an immediate branch to the beginning of the subroutine. Instead, the computer will remember that the time has elapsed and will reexecute the subroutine as soon as RETURN is reached.

4. Suppose that your program contains ON TIMER and TIMER ON statements, but that there is a sequence of lines that you do not want interrupted. Precede the lines by the statement **TIMER STOP**, and follow the lines by the statement **TIMER ON**. If the indicated number of seconds elapses during the execution of these lines, the computer will take no action but will remember that the time has elapsed and will branch to the subroutine as soon as the TIMER ON statement is reached. (The TIMER ON statement also resets the internal timer. Future branches to the subroutine will occur at n second intervals counted from the point at which the TIMER ON was executed.)

5. INPUT, LINE INPUT, and INPUT$ cause the execution of the program to be suspended until the user responds. If an ON TIMER statement is active at this time, the computer does the equivalent of a TIMER STOP and then, when execution resumes, a TIMER ON, with the exception that the timer is not reset.

6. The RETURN statement following the subroutine can refer to a specific line. The statement **RETURN t** results in a branch back to line t rather than to the statement that would have been executed next if the time hadn't elapsed.

7. The trapping routine can be disabled by the statement **TIMER OFF** or the statement **ON TIMER GOSUB 0**. (See Example 2.) It is also disabled when one of the commands CHAIN, CHAIN MERGE, CLEAR, LOAD, MERGE, or RUN is executed, or when a program line is entered or deleted.

8. The parentheses in the ON TIMER statement can contain a numeric expression. See Example 3.

FURTHER EXAMPLES

2. The following program asks a question and then gives a hint if the correct answer is not given within 10 seconds. Line 110 guarantees that the hint will only be given once. The INKEY$ function in line 70 reads the keyboard.

```
10 TIMER ON
20 ON TIMER(10) GOSUB 100
30 PRINT "Who was the seventh president of the US?"
40 PRINT "1. Andrew Jackson"
50 PRINT "2. Franklin Pierce"
60 PRINT "3. John Quincy Adams"
70 A$ = INKEY$: IF A$="" THEN 70
80 IF A$ = "1" THEN PRINT "Correct": END
```

ON TIMER

```
90 PRINT "Wrong, try again.": GOTO 70
100 PRINT "Hint: He was born in South Carolina."
110 TIMER OFF
120 RETURN
RUN
Who was the seventh president of the US?
1. Andrew Jackson
2. Franklin Pierce
3. John Quincy Adams
Hint: He was born in South Carolina.
Wrong, try again. (The user answered 3.)
Correct (The user answered 1.)
Ok
```

3.  ```
    10 INPUT "Pick a positive number. ", N
    20 TIMER ON
    30 ON TIMER(2*N + 1) GOSUB 60
    40 PRINT "A tone will sound in"; 2*N + 1; "seconds."
    50 GOTO 50
    60 BEEP
    70 END
    RUN
    Pick a positive number. 3
    A tone will sound in 7 seconds.
    Ok
    ```
    ```

The OPEN statement is used primarily to initiate access to files on disks. (See Appendix F for a general discussion of sequential and random files.) However, it also can be used to access the printer, screen, and keyboard.

In order to create a disk file, we must decide which disk drive to write the file to, give the file a name, and choose a number (normally from 1 to 3) that will temporarily be used to refer to the file. The combination of the disk drive specification and the name of the file is referred to as the *filespec*. For instance, two possible filespecs are "A:ACCOUNTS.MAY" and "B:NAMES". In BASIC 2.0 and subsequent versions, we can create a hierarchical directory structure. If so, the filespec will consist of the drive, the path identifying the directory containing the file, and the filename.

PART I   SEQUENTIAL FILES

If n is a number from 1 to 3, the statement

```
OPEN filespec FOR OUTPUT AS #n
```

creates a file on the specified drive having the name given by filespec. This file will be temporarily referred to as file n. Also, a section of memory, called a buffer, is set aside for the file. Having OPENed the file FOR OUTPUT we now may write information into the file using the statements PRINT#n, PRINT#n USING, and WRITE#n. When we have finished writing information to the file, the statement **CLOSE #n** should be given. From this point on, the file can only be referred to by its filespec; the temporary reference number n will no longer identify the file.

If a certain file already has been created with reference number n, and we want to add information to the end of the file, we gain access to the file with the statement

```
OPEN filespec FOR APPEND AS #n
```

(The temporary reference number n can differ from the one used to create the file.) We then record the information and CLOSE the file as before. From the time that the file is OPENed FOR APPEND until it is CLOSEd, we refer to it not by its filespec but by the number n.

If a certain file already has been created, and we want to read information from the file, we gain access to the file with a statement of the form

```
OPEN filespec FOR INPUT AS #n
```

(The temporary reference number n can differ from the one used to create the file.) Having OPENed the file FOR INPUT, we may now read information

OPEN

from the file using the statements INPUT #n, LINE INPUT #n, and INPUT$(m,n). When we have finished reading information from the file, the statement **CLOSE #n** should be executed. From this point on, the file can be referred to only by its filespec.

EXAMPLE

1.  ```
    10 OPEN "B:PRES.USA" FOR OUTPUT AS #2
    20 PRINT#2, "George Washington"
    30 CLOSE#2
    40 OPEN "B:PRES.USA" FOR APPEND AS #1
    50 PRINT#1, "John Adams"
    60 CLOSE#1
    70 OPEN "B:PRES.USA" FOR INPUT AS #2
    80 INPUT#2, A$, B$
    90 PRINT A$, B$
    100 CLOSE #2
    RUN
    George Washington          John Adams
    Ok
    ```

COMMENTS

1. Each of the above OPEN statements has an alternate form, shown below:

    ```
    OPEN filespec FOR OUTPUT AS #n
        OPEN "O", #n, filespec

    OPEN filespec FOR APPEND AS #n
        OPEN "A", #n, filespec

    OPEN filespec FOR INPUT AS #n
        OPEN "I", #n, filespec
    ```

Actually, the strings "O", "A", and "I" can be replaced by any string beginning with the letters O, A, and I, respectively. For instance, line 40 of Example 1 also can be written as **40 OPEN "A", #1, "B:PRES.USA"** or as **40 OPEN "ABC", #1, "B:PRES.USA"**.

2. The # signs appearing in the OPEN statements can be omitted. For instance, line 40 of Example 1 also can be written as **40 OPEN "B:PRES.USA" FOR APPEND AS 1**. (*Note:* The # signs appearing in lines 20, 50, and 80 are essential.)

3. BASIC was first invoked from DOS by typing the word BASIC (or BASICA) following A>, B>, C>, or D>, which identified the current drive or default drive. For instance, had the screen read **B>BASIC** when BASIC was invoked, then drive B would be the current drive. The filespec of
    ```

a file can consist solely of the name of the file. If so, the specified disk drive will be taken as the current drive.

4. Normally, at most three files can be open at any one time, with each identified by a number: 1, 2, and 3. We can raise this limit to 15 files when we invoke BASIC. While in DOS, the statement **BASIC /F:m** invokes BASIC with an allowable limit of m files.

5. Normally, after a file has been OPENed for one mode of access, it should be CLOSEd before it is accessed in another mode. For instance, if line 30 were omitted from Example 1, an error message would result.

6. If a file has been OPENed FOR OUTPUT or APPEND under one number, then (without first being CLOSEd) it can be OPENed for INPUT under another number. However, care must be taken to avoid INPUTting more information than has actually been recorded in the file. (See the discussion of CLOSE for further details.)

7. A file can be OPENed for INPUT with two different reference numbers. For instance, one number might be used to "look ahead" with INPUT$ before using the other number to read in an entire data item with INPUT#.

8. CAUTION: If a file has already been created and its filespec is used in an OPEN FOR OUTPUT statement, the file will automatically be erased. An existing file can only be OPENed FOR APPEND or INPUT without destroying its contents.

9. If the file referred to in an OPEN FOR APPEND statement does not exist, then a new file will be created. That is, the statement will have the same effect as an OPEN FOR OUTPUT statement. However, if the file referred to in an OPEN FOR INPUT statement does not exist, the error message "File not found" results.

PART II   RANDOM FILES

Random files consist of an ordered set of records all having the same length.

If n is a number from 1 to 3, the statement

```
OPEN filespec AS #n LEN = g
```

creates a random file on the specified drive with the name given by filespec. This file will be temporarily referred to as file n and each record will have length g. Also, a section of memory will be set aside as an input/output buffer. We can then proceed to write to and read from the file. The statement **CLOSE #n** should be executed when we are finished working with the file. From the time that the file is OPENed until the file is CLOSEd, we refer to it not by its filespec but by the number n. After the file is CLOSEd, it can be referred to only by its filespec; the temporary reference number n no longer will identify

OPEN

the file. The next time that we want to use the file, we reOPEN it with the same OPEN statement given above. However, we can change the reference number to another number, if we so desire. (See the discussions of FIELD, GET, LSET/RSET, and PUT for the details of writing to and reading from a random file.)

FURTHER EXAMPLE

```
2.  10 OPEN "B:PRES" AS #1 LEN=22
    20 FIELD #1, 20 AS N$, 2 AS A$
    30 LSET N$ = "George Washington"
    40 LSET A$ = "57"
    50 PUT #1
    60 GET #1,1
    70 PRINT N$,
    80 PRINT A$
    90 LSET N$ = "James Monroe"
    100 LSET A$ = "58"
    110 PUT #1,5
    120 CLOSE #1
    RUN
    George Washington            57
    Ok
```

In lines 30 to 50, we wrote information into the file. In lines 60 to 80, we read information from the file and PRINTed this information on the screen. In lines 90 to 110, we wrote more information into the file. Unlike the situation for sequential files, we did not have to CLOSE and reOPEN the file when changing back and forth from writing to reading.

FURTHER COMMENTS

10. The OPEN statement for random files has the alternate form

```
OPEN "R", #n, filespec, g
```

For instance, line 10 of Example 2 also can be written as **10 OPEN "R", #1, "B:PRES2", 22**. Actually, the string "R" can be replaced by any string beginning with the letter R.

11. Comments 2, 3, and 4 above also apply to random files.

12. Record length can routinely be set at any number from 1 to 128. If no length is given in the OPEN statement, the record length is automatically set to 128. If we decide to have the length greater than 128, we must first invoke BASIC from DOS with the statement **BASIC /S:m** where m is any number up to 32767. Thereafter, the maximum allowable record length will be m. Since each sector of a disk consists of 512 bytes, the greatest efficiency results from using record length 512.

PART III SCREEN AND PRINTER AS FILES

The statements PRINT and WRITE output data to the screen and the statement LPRINT outputs data to the printer. The screen and printer also can be specified as sequential files in OUTPUT mode. If this is done, data can be sent to them with PRINT# and WRITE# statements. The statement

```
OPEN "SCRN:" FOR OUTPUT AS #n
```

designates the screen as file #n, and the statement

```
OPEN "LPT1:" FOR OUTPUT AS #n
```

designates the first printer as file #n.

FURTHER EXAMPLE

3.   The following program allows the user to specify the device on which to exhibit the sentence "Dr. Livingstone, I presume?" If the user types SCRN:, the sentence will be displayed on the screen, and if the user types LPT1:, the sentence will be printed by the printer.

```
10 INPUT "SCRN: or LPT1: "; D$
20 CLS
30 OPEN D$ FOR OUTPUT AS #1
40 PRINT #1, "Dr. Livingstone, I presume?"
50 CLOSE #1
RUN
SCRN: or LPT1: ?
```

PART IV THE KEYBOARD AS A FILE

The statement

```
OPEN "KYBD:" FOR INPUT AS #n
```

designates the keyboard as file #n and allows the statements INPUT# and LINE INPUT# to access the keyboard.

FURTHER EXAMPLE

```
4.   10 OPEN "KYBD:" FOR INPUT AS #1
     20 LINE INPUT #1, A$
     30 PRINT A$
     40 CLOSE #1
```

OPEN

After the program is RUN, the user should type a message on the keyboard. Nothing will happen until the Enter key is pressed or until 255 characters have been typed, at which time the entire message will be displayed on the screen.

FURTHER COMMENTS

13.   The statements LOC and LOF are not valid for use with the screen, printer, or keyboard as files.

14.   The screen and printer cannot be OPENed FOR APPEND or INPUT, and the keyboard cannot be OPENed FOR OUTPUT or APPEND.

15.   In addition to the statements PRINT#, PRINT# USING, and WRITE#, the statement WIDTH may be used after the printer has been OPENed as a file.

16.   The printer also can be OPENed as a random file with a statement of the form **OPEN "LPT1:" AS #n**. This is often done in order to suppress line feeds. (See Comment 7 in the discussion of WIDTH.)

17.   In BASIC 3.0 and subsequent versions support the statements IOCTL and IOCTL$ which access device drivers. However, device drivers must first be OPENed as files before these statements can be executed. See the discussions of IOCTL and IOCTL$ for further details.

APPLICATIONS

1.   One of the primary uses of computers is the processing of data, which usually is stored on disks. The OPEN statement provides access to this data.

2.   Suppose that a programmer is writing a program that will print information with tricky formatting. Instead of writing the program with LPRINT statements, he or she might OPEN the printer as a file and use PRINT# statements instead. By so doing, the programmer can change the device in the OPEN statement to ''SCRN:'' and see the output displayed on the screen before printing it.

OPEN "COM . . .

The OPEN COM statement opens a communications buffer, associates it with a communications port, designates the communications parameters to be used, and establishes the communications line monitoring parameters. The format for this statement is:

OPEN "COMn:baud rate,parity,data bits,stop bits,line
     parameters" AS #m LEN=g

Where:

n is the number (either 1 or 2) of the communications port.

Baud rate is the transmission/reception speed of data between the computer and the modem. Typical speeds for data communications with BASIC are 300 and 1200 baud using modems and normal telephone lines. However, higher speeds are possible over better than normal grade telephone lines or by directly connecting two computers between their serial ports without the use of a modem. Possible baud rates are: 75, 110, 150, 300, 600, 1200, 1800, 2400, 4800, and 9600. The default baud rate is 300.

Parity is a single character indicating the type of parity checking to be used during communications. Each character transmitted or received is contained within eight bits. When parity checking is used, the highest bit is used as the parity bit. There are five methods of parity checking possible. The same type of parity checking must be used by both the transmitting computer and the receiving computer. The default is EVEN parity checking. The following options are available for parity checking:

E EVEN: The parity bit is used to make the sum of all eight bits even.

O ODD: The parity bit is used to make the sum of all eight bits odd.

N NONE: The parity bit is not used for parity checking. In this case all eight data bit are used to transmit the character. (See data bits below.)

S SPACE: The parity bit is not used for parity checking and is always transmitted as zero (0).

M MARK: The parity bit is not used for parity checking and is always transmitted as one (1).

Data bits is a positive integer number indicating the number of data bits to be used in transmitting each character. The typical number of data bits used is either seven or eight. Seven data bits can be used to transmit all of the basic ASCII character set, however, numeric data and graphics characters require eight data bits for transmission. When using eight data bits, N must be specified for parity. Other valid numbers of data bits are four, five, or six. The default is seven data bits.

Stop bits are used to indicate to the receiving computer that transmission of the character is completed. The number of stop bits required depends upon the baud rate or the number of data bits. Typically only one stop bit is

OPEN "COM . . .

required. However, at baud rates of 110 and below, two stop bits are required. When using five or less data bits, 1 1/2 stop bits are required and are indicated by specifying two stop bits in the communications parameters. The only valid entries for stop bits are 1 and 2. The default is 1.

Line parameters are optional entries used to tell BASIC how to react to some of the line signals from the communications port. There are six different parameters that may be used:

RS   suppresses the Request to Send (RTS) line. When an OPEN COM statement is executed the RTS line is turned on unless the RS parameter is used.

CS[n]   controls the Clear to Send (CTS) line. The CTS line is normally on when the system is booted. BASIC checks the CTS when an OPEN COM statement is executed and will issue an error interrupt if the CTS line is off. This parameter will not turn the line on or off but will allow the checking of it to be suppressed or specify a delay before issuing the error interrupt. The argument n may be a number from 0 to 65535 and is used to specify the number of milliseconds to wait before issuing the interrupt if the line is off. (1000 milliseconds = 1 second). Checking of the CTS line may be suppressed by using CS or CS0. The default is 1 second (equivalent to CS1000) unless RS was specified. If RS was specified, the default is to suppress checking of the CTS (equivalent to CS or CS0.)

DS[n]   controls the Data Set Ready (DSR) line. As with the CTS line, the DSR line is normally on when the system is booted and if not on will cause an error in the execution of any BASIC communications statement. Testing of this line may also be tailored by using the argument n following DS. The n is used the same with DS as it is with CS. The default is 1 second (equivalent to DS1000).

CD[n]   controls the Carrier Detect (CD) line. Typically, the Carrier Detect line is not checked by communications software. When an OPEN COM statement is executed, the CD line is not checked unless the CD parameter is used and n is greater than 0. If the CD line is off when checked, an error interrupt will be issued. The default is no checking of the CD line (equivalent to CD or CD0).

PE   enables parity checking. (Available from BASIC 2.0 on.) The default is no parity checking. Earlier versions of BASIC did not have this feature and, therefore, the default with those versions was with parity checking. This parameter affects the incoming data only. Outgoing data is not checked, but is treated in the manner specified by the parity parameter. When parity checking is specified and an error in parity is detected, a device I/O error will be issued.

LF   sends a line feed following each carriage return. This parameter is not normally used with modem communications, but is necessary when using one of the communications ports to send data to a serial printer. When using a parallel printer and the LPRINT statement, a carriage return and line feed are automatically sent at the end of each line unless specifically suppressed. When sending data to a serial printer through the communications port, a carriage return will automatically be sent at the end of each line unless specifically suppressed, but not a line feed. This parameter, when specified, allows printing to a serial printer to be equivalent to printing to a parallel printer.

#m is the file number of the file buffer to be used for communications. This number may be from 1 to the maximum number of the file buffers specified when invoking BASIC with the /F: switch. This buffer number will continue to be associated with the specified communications port until the file is closed. It is used to direct all input and output statements through the proper buffer and, therefore, the proper communications port. For example, the statement `OPEN "COM1:1200,N,8,1,CD" AS #2` assigns file buffer #2 to communications port number 1. Data may be sent to the port in the variable A$ by executing `PRINT #2,A$`. The statements PRINT# and INPUT# always transfer data to and from the file buffer, not the communications port.

g, if used, sets the record length of the communications buffer and, therefore, the maximum number of characters that can be read or written to the communications buffer with PUT and GET statements. The default is 128 characters. GET and PUT have limited use with communications.

EXAMPLES

1.   The statement

```
OPEN "COM1:" AS #1
```

opens file buffer #1 and associates it with communications port number 1. It also sets all communications and line monitoring parameters to their respective default parameters: baud = 300, parity = E, data bits = 7, stop bits = 1, RTS line on, CTS line is checked with CS1000, DSR line is checked with DS1000, CD line is not checked, parity checking is disabled with BASIC 2.0 and enabled with earlier versions, and line feeds are not sent at the end of each line.

2.   The statement

```
OPEN "COM2:1200,N,8,CD3000" AS #3
```

opens file buffer #3 and associates it with communications port number 2. It also sets all communications and line monitoring parameters to their respec-

OPEN "COM . . .

tive default parameters with the exception that baud = 1200, parity = None, data bits = 8, and the CD line is checked and will cause an error interrupt 3 seconds after the line is off (carrier is lost).

COMMENTS

1.   When using BASIC 2.0 and parity of EVEN or ODD, the PE parameter should always be selected unless some other method of error checking is used within the program such as the XMODEM or Cyclic Redundancy Checking protocols. When using parity of NONE, SPACE, or MARK, do not use the PE parameter. Use of PE with these parity parameters will only waste time in the execution of the program.

2.   The recommended communications parameters are NONE parity, 8 data bits, and 1 stop bit. This will allow the transmission of numeric data, non-ASCII files and the IBM extended ASCII set (graphics characters). Transmission of these data requires the use of all 8 bits to represent the character being transmitted. If an 8 bit character is transmitted using, for instance, EVEN parity, 7 bit data bits, and 1 stop bit, the high bit of the character would be altered and interpreted as the parity bit. Therefore, IBM-extended ASCII character number 227, the Greek letter pi, would be transmitted as "c" which has ASCII value 99. This happens because the numeric value of the high bit is 128 and if it is used as a parity bit for character number 227, then the character transmitted has an ASCII value 128 less than intended, or in this case, 99.

3.   The effectiveness of the line-monitoring parameters depends upon the line signals supported by the modem and the RS-232C cable used. Check the modem instruction manual and inspect the cable to see which line signals are supported, before relying on the reactions of these parameters. The parameters are associated with the following pin assignments:

RS	RTS line	Pin #4
CS	CTS line	Pin #5
DS	DSR line	Pin #6
CS	CD line	Pin #8
PE	not applicable	
LF	not applicable	

The best way to ensure that all of these pins are supported is to use a complete 25 conductor cable. Most modems have the capability of supporting these pins, although some are controlled by the internal DIP switches (refer to the modem instruction manual for details).

OPTION BASE

The range of the subscripts of an array variable normally begins with 0. See the discussion of the DIM statement for details. Invoking the statement

```
OPTION BASE 1
```

(before any array variables have been DIMensioned) causes the ranges of the subscripts of all array variables to begin with 1 instead of 0.

COMMENTS

1.   Some computers use the statement OPTION BASE n, where n is any integer, to set the beginning of the subscript range at the number n. For the IBM PC the only acceptable values of n are 0 and 1. However, since the range normally begins with 0, there is really no need to use the statement OPTION BASE 0. Using a value of n other than 0 or 1 results in the error message "Syntax error."

2.   Once OPTION BASE 1 has been invoked, we cannot switch back to beginning the ranges of subscripts with zero unless we first CLEAR all variables. ERASEing all existing array variables is not sufficient. See Example 6.

3.   The OPTION BASE 1 condition is reset to the standard OPTION BASE 0 condition when one of the commands CLEAR, LOAD, MERGE, NEW, or RUN is executed, or when a program line is entered or deleted.

EXAMPLES

1.
```
10 OPTION BASE 1
20 DIM A(23)
30 A(0) = 5
RUN
Subscript out of range in 30
Ok
```

2.
```
10 OPTION BASE 1
20 DIM A(25)
30 CLEAR
40 A(0) = 5
RUN
Ok
```

3.
```
10 OPTION BASE 1
20 DIM B$(3,7)
30 B$(2,0) = "TOM"
RUN
Subscript out of range in 30
```

OPTION BASE

4.   In the programs below, the value of FRE(0) will be the number of unused bytes in memory that are available to BASIC at that time. Four bytes are required to hold the value of a single-precision number.

```
10 M = FRE(0)            10 M = FRE(0)
20 DIM A(100)            20 OPTION BASE 1
30 PRINT M-FRE(0)        30 DIM A(100)
RUN                      40 PRINT M-FRE(0)
 413                     RUN
Ok                        409
                         Ok
```

The first program shows that 413 bytes of memory were required to set aside space for the potential 101 values to be assigned to the subscripts of the array variable. The second program set aside 4 fewer bytes since no space was reserved for a value of A(0).

5.   ```
10 A(5) = 56
20 OPTION BASE 1
RUN
Duplicate definition in 20
Ok
```

Line 10 is equivalent to **10 DIM A(10): A(5) = 56** and, hence, **OPTION BASE 1** followed the DIMensioning of an array variable.

6.   ```
10 OPTION BASE 1
20 DIM A(25)
30 ERASE A
40 OPTION BASE 0
Duplicate Definition in 40
Ok
```

Once we have decided to begin subscripts with 1, we can't reconsider unless we first CLEAR all variables.

APPLICATIONS

Some programmers like to number subscripts beginning with 1. If a particular program uses multi-subscripted array variables, then substantial memory space can be conserved by using the OPTION BASE statement. For instance, if an undimensioned double-subscripted array does not make use of the subscript 0, then invoking OPTION BASE 1 saves the space of 21 variables.

322

OUT

The micro-processor receives data from and sends data to the various components of the computer through mechanisms known as ports. For instance, there are ports associated with the keyboard, the disk drives, the speaker, and the screen. A piece of data consists of a byte (corresponding to an integer from 0 to 255), and each port has a number assigned to it. The statement

```
OUT n,m
```

sends the byte m to port n.

EXAMPLE

Port 952 is used to communicate with the Monochrome Display. The byte 1 turns off the screen and the byte 255 turns it back on. The byte 15 stops the blinking of characters.

```
10 COLOR 7,0
20 PRINT "Hello"
30 A$ = INPUT$(1)
40 OUT 952,1
50 A$ = INPUT$(1)
60 OUT 952,255
70 COLOR 23,0
80 PRINT "Goodbye"
90 A$ = INPUT$(1)
100 OUT 952,15
110 A$ = INPUT$(1)
120 OUT 952,255: COLOR 7,0: CLS
RUN
Hello
Goodbye
Ok
```

The statement appearing in lines 30, 50, 90 and 110 causes the execution of the program to pause until a key is pressed. Initially, the word "Hello" is displayed. After any key is hit, the screen goes blank and stays blank until a key is hit. Then the blinking word "Goodbye" is displayed. The blinking continues until a key is hit. Hitting a key once more returns the situation to its normal state and clears the screen.

COMMENTS

1. The value of n must be in the range 0 to 65535.

2. The function INP is used to *receive* data from various ports.

OUT

APPLICATIONS

1. The OUT statement is used to obtain direct control of a device. For instance, **OUT 97,204** turns off the keyboard and **OUT 97,76** turns it back on.

2. In high-resolution graphics, **OUT 985,c** changes the foreground color to c.

3. The OUT statement can be used to turn off the speaker. In the following program, press any key to stop the music.

```
10 PLAY "MB CDEFGAB>C"
20 WHILE INKEY$="":WEND
30 OUT 97,INP(97) AND 252
```

4. In text mode with a color monitor, you normally have access to only 8 background colors. If you are willing to give up blinking, all 16 colors can be available. Just execute the statement **OUT 984,8** in 40-column width or the statement **OUT 984,9** in 80-column width.

5. In medium-resolution graphics, to obtain background color c and a high-intensity version of palette p, execute **OUT 985,c+16+32*p**. Therefore, four different palettes are available.

6. (PC AT only) When a key is held down for more than one-half second (the default delay time), it repeats ten times per second (the default typematic rate). To change the delay rate to d quarter-seconds (d = 1, 2, 3 or 4) and the typematic rate to approximately r repetitions per second (r between 2 and 30), execute **OUT 96,243: OUT 96,n** where $n = (d-1)*32 + CINT(11.5*LOG(29/r))$.

PAINT

The graphics statements LINE, CIRCLE, DRAW, and PSET provide the means to draw figures on the screen. The PAINT statement allows us to color closed figures. We assume that the reader is familiar with the way that coordinates of points are specified in graphics modes. (See Appendix C for details.)

This discussion deals primarily with the medium-resolution graphics mode. (See Comment 4 for the use of the PAINT statement in high-resolution graphics mode.) Medium-resolution graphics mode with color enabled is invoked with the statement **SCREEN 1,0**. A statement of the form **COLOR b,p** is used to select one of 16 background colors, b, and one of 2 palettes, p. Each palette consists of 4 colors: numbered 0, 1, 2, and 3, where 0 is the same as the background color.

Suppose that a closed figure has a boundary of color c (that is, c is one of the 4 colors of the selected palette). If the point (x,y) is in the interior of the figure, then the statement

PAINT (x,y),n,c

fills the interior of the figure with the color n. Here, n is also one of the 4 colors of the selected palette. In the event that color n is not specified, it will be color 3. If both are omitted, they will both be taken as 3.

EXAMPLES

1. Suppose that the screen contains 3 concentric circles. The inner circle is color 1, the middle circle is color 2, and the outer circle is color 3. The diagrams in Figure 1 show the effects of 3 different PAINT statements.

2. Suppose that the screen contains two rectangles as shown on the left of Figure 2, where the smaller rectangle is color 1 and the larger rectangle is color 2. Then the statement

PAINT (160,100),3,2

produces the coloring on the right.

3. The following program shows the general idea behind forming a pie graph. Lines 30-50 draw a circle in color 1 that is partitioned into three sectors. Lines 60-80 fill these sectors with 3 different colors. (See Figure 3.)

```
10 CLS: KEY OFF
20 SCREEN 1,0: COLOR 0,1
30 CIRCLE (160,100),90,1,-1,-3.2
40 CIRCLE (160,100),90,1,-3.2,-5.3
50 CIRCLE (160,100),90,1,-5.3,-1
60 PAINT (170,100),1,1
70 PAINT (160,90),2,1
80 PAINT (160,110),3,1
```

PAINT

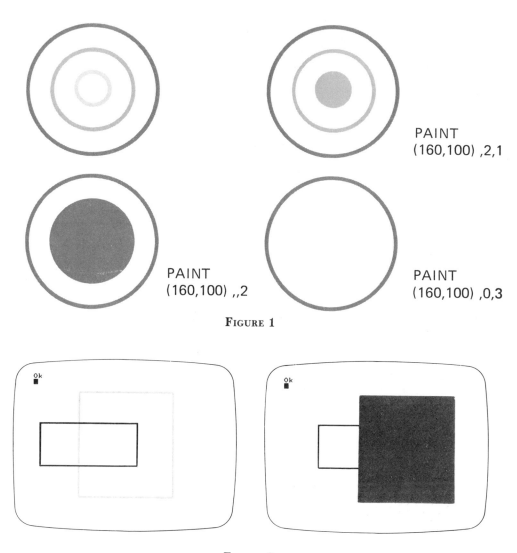

PAINT
(160,100) ,2,1

PAINT
(160,100) ,,2

PAINT
(160,100) ,0,3

FIGURE 1

FIGURE 2

COMMENTS

1. The PAINT statement can only be used with Advanced BASIC. That is, the command BASICA must have been given when BASIC was invoked.

2. As with all graphics statements, the PAINT statement requires a graphics monitor.

3. The coordinates of the point (x,y) can be given in relative form (that is, as STEP (r,s)).

326

PAINT

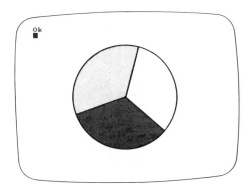

FIGURE 3

4. High-resolution graphics mode is invoked by the statement **SCREEN 2**. There are only two colors—the background color, 0, and the foreground color, 1. Therefore, the values of n and c are restricted to 0 and 1. If the color n is omitted, it will default to the color c.

5. In versions of BASIC prior to BASIC 2.0, the PAINT statement makes use of BASIC's stack. If the region being painted has a complicated boundary, we might overflow the stack and receive the message "Out of memory." The stack can be enlarged by a statement of the form **CLEAR,,m**. (See the discussion of CLEAR for further details.)

FURTHER DISCUSSION

BASIC 2.0 and subsequent versions allow a closed region to be PAINTed with a tiled pattern specified by the user. Some samples are shown in Figure 4. The procedure for designing the pattern is different for high-resolution graphics than for medium-resolution graphics and so we consider each case separately.

In high-resolution graphics, each tile is 8 pixels horizontally and from 1 to 64 pixels vertically. We specify a tile by identifying each pixel as on or off. Each row of the tile can be associated with an 8-tuple of 0s and 1s, where the 1s correspond to the pixels to be turned on and the 0s correspond to the pixels to be turned off. Each of the 8-tuples is the binary representation of a decimal integer from 0 to 255. Figure 5 shows the tiling used in Figure 4a, along with the binary 8-tuples and integers associated with each row.

The tile in Figure 5 is specified by the string

$$T\$ = CHR\$(0) + CHR\$(63) + CHR\$(48) + CHR\$(48) + CHR\$(60) +$$
$$CHR\$(48) + CHR\$(48) + CHR\$(48) + CHR\$(0)$$

In medium-resolution graphics, each tile is 4 pixels horizontally and from 1 to 64 pixels vertically. We specify a tile by giving the color (0, 1, 2, or 3) of

327

PAINT

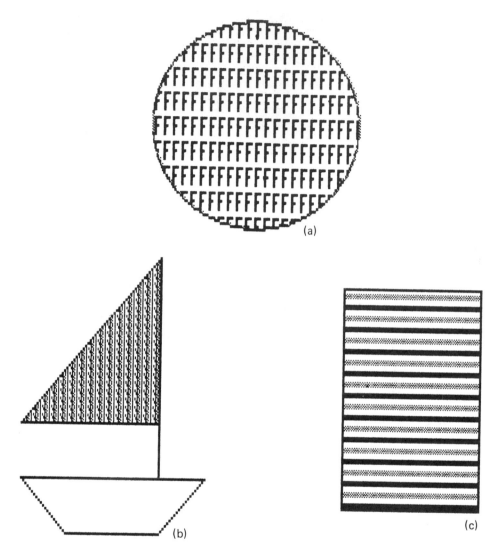

FIGURE 4

each pixel. Then we translate each of the four numbers into binary notation (0 is 00, 1 is 01, 2 is 10, and 3 is 11). Each row of the tile can be associated with an 8-tuple of 0s and 1s, by stringing together the 4 binary numbers in the row. Each of the 8-tuples is the binary representation of a decimal integer from 0 to 255. Figure 6 shows the tiling used in Figure 4b, along with the binary 8-tuples and integers associated with each row.

The tile in Figure 6 is specified by the string

$$T\$ = CHR\$(70) + CHR\$(85) + CHR\$(78)$$

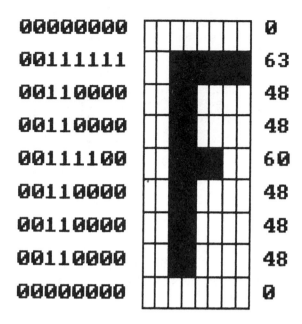

00000000	0
00111111	63
00110000	48
00110000	48
00111100	60
00110000	48
00110000	48
00110000	48
00000000	0

Figure 5

01000110	1	0	1	2	70
01010101	1	1	1	1	85
01001110	1	0	3	2	78

Figure 6

In either high- or medium-resolution graphics, suppose that a tile has r rows with associated integers $n_1, n_2, \ldots, n_r$. Then the string

$$T\$ = CHR\$(n_1) + CHR\$(n_2) + \ldots + CHR\$(n_r)$$

specifies the tile. If a closed region has a boundary of color c and contains the point (x,y) in its interior, then the statement

```
PAINT (x,y),T$,c
```

fills in the region by tiling it with the tile T$.

In medium-resolution graphics, the above PAINT statement will not produce the desired result if there are two or more adjacent single-color rows whose pixels are all the same color as the background. If there are at most two

329

PAINT

adjacent rows of this type, then an additional parameter can be appended to the PAINT statement to remedy the situation. If the number associated with these rows is n, then the statement

```
PAINT (x,y),T$,c,CHR$(n)
```

will produce the desired tiling.

FURTHER EXAMPLES

4. The following program uses the tile in Figure 5 to obtain the tiling shown in Figure 4a.

```
10 CLS: SCREEN 2
20 CIRCLE (100,75),90
30 T$ = CHR$(0) + CHR$(63) + CHR$(48) + CHR$(48) + CHR$(60)
   + CHR$(48) + CHR$(48) + CHR$(48) +CHR$(0)
40 PAINT (100,75),T$
```

5. The following program uses the tile in Figure 6 to obtain the tiling shown in Figure 4b.

```
10 CLS: SCREEN 1,0
20 DRAW "L60 E60 D80 L60 F20 R40 E20 L20"
30 T$ = CHR$(70) + CHR$(85) + CHR$(78)
40 PAINT (150,90),T$
```

6. The following program draws the striped rectangle shown in Figure 4c. Each stripe is made up of a pair of adjacent single-color rows. Since there are adjacent pairs of single-color rows in the background color 0, the additional parameter CHR$(0) must be appended to the PAINT statement.

```
10 CLS: SCREEN 1,0
20 LINE (10,10) - (50,90),,B
30 T$ = CHR$(255) + CHR$(255) + CHR$(0) + CHR$(0) +
   CHR$(170) + CHR$(170) + CHR$(0) + CHR$(0)
40 PAINT (30,50),T$,,CHR$(0)
```

FURTHER COMMENTS

6. When a region is tiled, the tiles are placed in such a way that, if the pattern were continued over the entire screen, the upper left-hand corner of the screen would contain the upper left-hand pixel of the tile. Hence, if two intersecting regions are tiled with the same tile, they will blend perfectly where they overlap.

7. Appendix K, which gives the binary representations of the numbers from 0 to 255, is helpful in designing tiles.

8. The following demonstration program shows the tiles (in high-resolution graphics) associated with various sequences of at most 11 integers. Each time that the user enters an integer from 0 to 255, the program draws the row of pixels associated with that number. To terminate the program, enter the number 256.

```
10 SCREEN 1,0:CLS:KEY OFF
20 WINDOW SCREEN (-80,0)-(208,90)
30 M=7:X=0
40 LOCATE 2*X+1,20:INPUT " ",A
50 WHILE (A<=255) AND (X<=10)
60    LINE (0,M*X)-(8*M,M+M*X),,B
70    FOR Y=1 TO 7
80      LINE (Y*M,M*X)-(Y*M,M+M*X)
90    NEXT Y
100   FOR I= 1 TO 8
110     IF (A MOD 2) = 1 THEN PAINT ((8-I)*M+1,M*X+1),3,3
120       A=A\2
130   NEXT I
140   X=X+1
150   LOCATE 2*X+1,20:INPUT " ",A
160 WEND
170 LOCATE 2*X+1,20:PRINT "        ";
180 LOCATE 22,1:END
```

9. The tile specifier, T$, is just a string. Hence, any string of length at most 64 can be used for T$. The following program will tile the entire screen in a pattern determined by the string supplied by the user.

```
10 CLS: KEY OFF
20 INPUT "Type in any string of characters: ",T$
30 PAINT (5,5),T$
RUN
Type in any string of characters: FUN
```

(The pattern produced is the same one that appears in the sailboat in Figure 4b.)

APPLICATIONS

1. The PAINT statement is invaluable when creating scenes on the screen.

2. The LINE statement allows us to draw rectangles that are filled in with their boundary color. However, the PAINT statement provides the capability of filling them with other colors.

PAINT

3. Up to 4 sectors of a pie chart can be colored with different colors. With BASIC 2.0 and subsequent versions, many more sectors can be differentiated from each other by tiling them with different patterns.

PEEK

This discussion assumes an understanding of how memory locations are specified. (See the discussion of DEF SEG.) Each memory location contains a block of 8 binary bits that corresponds to a number from 0 to 255 in binary notation. We say that the location contains that number. After a DEF SEG statement has specified a segment of memory, the value of

```
PEEK(n)
```

will be the number contained in the memory location with offset n.

COMMENT

1.   The statement POKE is complementary to PEEK. It is used to *place* numbers into memory locations.

EXAMPLE

The BASIC error messages can be found beginning with the memory location with offset 181 in segment 63024. The following program PEEKs into memory to retrieve the first three messages.

```
10 DEF SEG = 63024
20 FOR N = 0 TO 21
30    A = PEEK(181+N)
40      PRINT A;
50 NEXT N
60 PRINT
70 FOR N = 0 TO 50
80      PRINT CHR$(PEEK(181+N));
90 NEXT N
RUN
 78  69  88  84  32  119  105  116  104  111  117  116  32
 70  79  82  0  83  121  110  116  97
NEXT without FOR Syntax error RETURN without GOSUB
Ok
```

APPLICATIONS

1.   PEEK is used extensively when working with machine language programs.

2.   See Appendix H for several applications of PEEK.

PEN

The PEN statement requires a graphics monitor.

Light pens are about the same size and shape as the small flashlights that doctors use to look at throats. A cord extends from one end of the pen to a connector, which is screwed into the back of the computer. This connector also makes contact with the graphics adapter. There are two types of light pens. (See Figure 1.) The "touch-ring" model is activated by pointing the tip of the pen at the screen (from a distance of a few inches) and pressing the metal clip. It is deactivated by releasing the metal clip. The "push-tip" model is activated by pressing the tip of the pen against the screen. It is deactivated by relaxing the pressure. In our discussion, we use the terminology that applys to touch-ring pens.

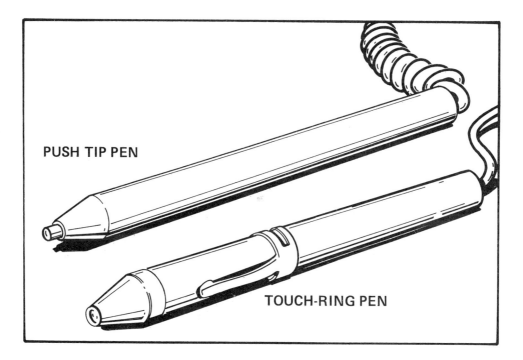

PUSH TIP PEN

TOUCH-RING PEN

FIGURE 1

For purposes of displaying text characters, the screen is subdivided into 25 rows (numbered 1 to 25) and 40 or 80 columns (numbered 1 to 40 or 1 to 80). We assume that the reader is familiar with the way that the positions of characters are specified. (See the discussion of the LOCATE statement.) When a light pen is pointed at a specific location on the screen, it is able to identify the row number and column number of that location. As we shall see in the subsequent examples, this capability allows us to interact with the screen directly (that is, without using the keyboard).

334

The statement

```
PEN ON
```

causes the computer to check the pen after the execution of each BASIC statement to see if the pen is active. Suppose that the pen is pointed at the screen and that the clip is pressed and held down for a few seconds. (The pen can be held still or moved around the screen.) Each time the computer checks the pen, it records the answers to 4 questions:

1. Has the pen just been activated?
2. Is the pen currently activated?
3. At what character location of the screen was the pen pointing when it was most recently activated?
4. If the pen is currently active, at what character location is it now pointing?

Question 1 will have the answer "yes" at the first check after the clip is pressed and will have the answer "no" at subsequent checks. The function

```
PEN(0)
```

has the value -1 when the answer is "yes" and the value 0 when the answer is "no." Question 2 will have the answer "yes" at each check as long as the clip remains pressed. The function

```
PEN(3)
```

has the value -1 when the answer is "yes" and the value 0 when the answer is "no." Question 3 is answered by the functions

```
PEN(6)  and PEN(7)
```

that have as their values the row and column numbers of the location at which the pen was aimed when the clip was pressed. Question 4 is answered by the functions

```
PEN(8)  and PEN(9)
```

that have as their values the row and column numbers of the location at which the pen is currently pointed. These values change when the pen is moved around the screen. The statement

```
PEN OFF
```

tells the computer to stop checking the light pen.

PEN

EXAMPLES

1. ```
10 SCREEN 0,1: COLOR 15,1: KEY OFF: CLS
20 PEN ON
30 FOR I = 1 TO 286
40   PRINT PEN(0);
50 NEXT I
```

After entering RUN, activate and deactivate the light pen a few times. The screen will be filled mostly with zeros. However, a minus one will appear each time the metal clip is pressed.

2. ```
10 SCREEN 0,1: COLOR 15,1: KEY OFF: CLS
20 PEN ON
30 LOCATE 12,20
40 PRINT PEN(3);
50 GOTO 30
```

After you enter RUN, the number zero will appear on the screen. If the light pen is activated, the number will change to minus one until the light pen is deactivated. To terminate this program, press Ctrl-Break.

3. ```
10 SCREEN 0,1: COLOR 15,1: KEY OFF: CLS
20 PEN ON
30 IF PEN(0)=0 THEN 30
40 LOCATE 12,12
50 PRINT "ROW"; PEN(6);
60 PRINT "COLUMN"; PEN(7) " "
70 GOTO 40
```

After you enter RUN, aim the light pen at the screen and activate the light pen. The location of that place will appear on row 12. Now release the metal clip, aim the light pen at another place, and again activate the light pen. The numbers in row 12 will change to give the location of the new place. Continue this process as long as you like. To terminate the program, press Ctrl-Break.

4. Alter the program of Example 3 by changing the 6 in line 50 to an 8 and the 7 in line 60 to a 9. After the program is RUNning, hold down the metal clip and move the light pen around the screen. The numbers in row 12 will change regularly to give the location of the current position of the light pen.

5. The following program shows how the light pen can be used for computer assisted instruction. (See Figure 2.)

```
10 SCREEN 0,1: COLOR 15,1: WIDTH 40
20 CLS: KEY OFF
30 PRINT "Approximately how many post"
40 PRINT "offices are there in the"
50 PRINT "entire United States?"
60 LOCATE 8,13: PRINT CHR$(219) 1200
70 LOCATE 12,13: PRINT CHR$(219) 30000
```
```

```
80 LOCATE 16,13: PRINT CHR$(219) 100000
90 PEN ON
100 IF PEN(0)=0 THEN GOTO 100
110 A=PEN(6)
120 IF A<11 OR A>13 THEN PRINT "Try Again": GOTO 100
130 PRINT "Correct, 30000"
```

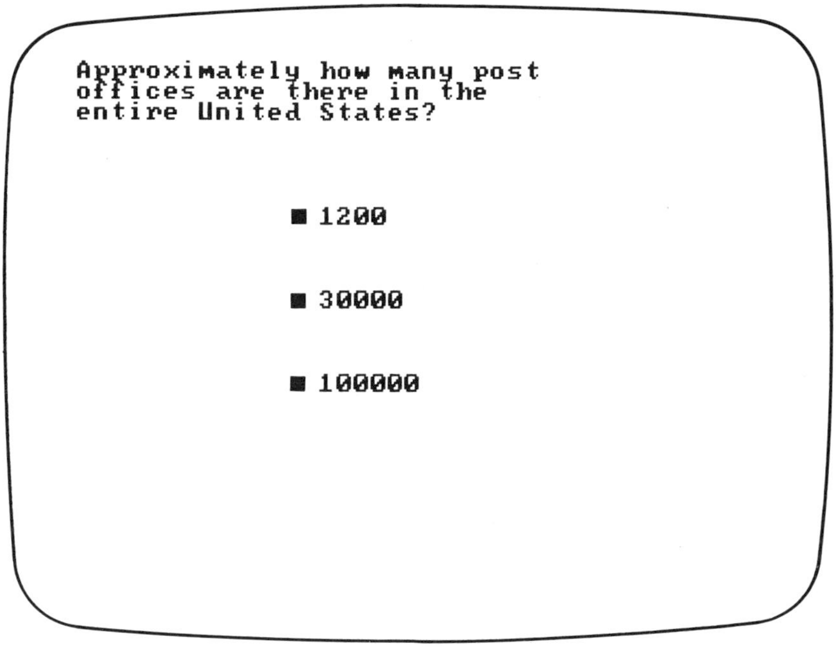

FIGURE 2

Now touch the light pen to one of the rectangles and press the metal clip. If you guessed incorrectly, release the metal clip and try again.

6. The following program allows two people to play tick-tack-toe on the screen. To make a move, just touch the light pen to one of the 9 regions and press the metal clip. Successive activations produce alternating Xs and Os in the desired regions.

```
10 CLS: SCREEN 1,0: COLOR 1,1: KEY OFF
20 LINE (0,66)-(319,66)
30 LINE (0,133)-(319,133)
40 LINE (108,0)-(108,199)
50 LINE (216,0)-(216,199)
60 PEN ON
70 IF PEN(0)=0 GOTO 70
80 IF A$ = "X" THEN A$ = "O": GOTO 100
```

PEN

```
90 A$ = "X"
100 R = PEN(6): C = PEN(7)
110 IF C<13 THEN B = 6: GOTO 130
120 IF C<26 THEN B = 21 ELSE B=33
130 IF R<9 THEN A = 5: GOTO 150
140 IF R<17 THEN A = 13 ELSE A = 21
150 LOCATE A,B: PRINT A$
160 GOTO 70
```

COMMENTS

1.   We found that our light pen worked better with certain color combinations than with others. In the above programs we set the color to a blue background and a white foreground.

2.   Programs 1 through 5 use text mode. However, these programs also will run in graphics modes. Just change **SCREEN 0,1** to **SCREEN 1,0** or **SCREEN 2**, and change the COLOR statement accordingly. In Example 5, lines 60 through 80 must be altered since CHR$(219) cannot be displayed in graphics mode.

3.   In Examples 5 and 6, we gave the user some leeway in aiming the light pen. This is usually a good idea. For instance, if line 120 in Example 5 had been

```
120 IF A = 12 THEN PRINT "Try Again": GOTO 100
```

the program might have malfunctioned.

FURTHER DISCUSSION

With the two graphics modes, the screen is subdivided into either 64,000 or 128,000 small rectangles, referred to as points. See Appendix C for a discussion of specifying coordinates of points in the graphics modes. To the best of our knowledge, no light pens currently available can identify all of these points. They can distinguish 40 different positions in the x direction and 100 different positions in the y direction. The different positions in the y direction are identified as 0, 2, 4, 6, . . . , 198 and the positions in the x direction are identified by 0, 8, 16, 24, . . . , 312 in medium-resolution graphics mode and 0, 16, 32, 48, . . . , 624 in high-resolution graphics mode. Using these numbering systems, the pen identifies each point with a number that is close to its actual coordinates.

Suppose that the pen is pointed at the screen in graphics mode and that the clip is pressed and held down for a few seconds. The pen can be held still or moved around the screen. Then the functions

PEN(1) and **PEN(2)**

have as their values the approximate x and y coordinates of the point at which the pen was aimed when the clip was pressed. The functions

```
PEN(4) and PEN(5)
```

have as their values the approximate x and y coordinates of the point at which the pen is currently aimed. The values change as the pen is moved around the screen. PEN(2) and PEN(5) assume even-numbered values from 0 to 198. In medium-resolution graphics, PEN(1) and PEN(4) assume the numbers from 0 to 312 that are divisible by 8. In high-resolution graphics, PEN(1) and PEN(4) assume the numbers from 0 to 624 that are divisible by 16.

FURTHER EXAMPLES

7.
```
10 SCREEN 1,0: COLOR 1,1: KEY OFF: CLS
20 PEN ON
30 IF PEN(0)=0 THEN GOTO 30
40 LOCATE 12,3
50 PRINT "x-coordinate" PEN(1);
60 PRINT " y-coordinate" PEN(2) " "
70 GOTO 40
```

After you enter RUN, aim the light pen at any point on the screen and activate the light pen. The approximate coordinates of that point will appear on row 12. Now release the metal clip, aim the light pen at another point, and reactivate the light pen. The numbers in row 12 will change to give the approximate coordinates of the new point. Continue this process as long as you like. To terminate the program press Ctrl-Break.

8. Alter the program of Example 7 by changing the 1 in line 50 to 4 and the 2 in line 60 to 5. After the program is RUNning, hold down the metal clip and move the light pen around. The numbers in row 12 will change to give the approximate coordinates of the current position of the light pen.

9. The following program turns the screen into a drawing pad. Activate the pen and, while holding down the metal clip, pretend that you are writing or sketching with the light pen. (To terminate the program press Ctrl-Break.) The output shown in Figure 3 was formed by writing the letters "Ok" in script.

```
10 CLS: SCREEN 1,0: COLOR 1,1: KEY OFF
20 PEN ON
30 IF PEN(0) = -1 THEN PSET (PEN(1),PEN(2)) ELSE GOTO 30
40 LINE -(PEN(4),PEN(5))
50 GOTO 40
```

PEN

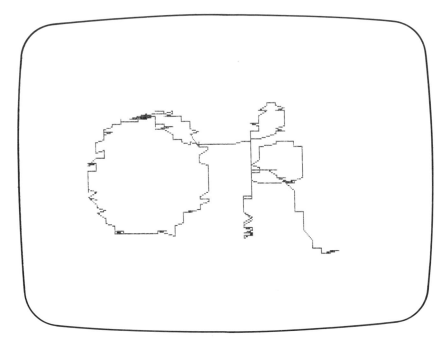

FIGURE 3

FURTHER COMMENTS

4.   It is important to execute the statement **PEN ON** before any of the PEN functions are used. Otherwise, the error message "Illegal function call" results. However, when the PEN functions are no longer needed, it is a good idea to disable the light pen with the statement **PEN OFF**.

5.   The statement **PEN STOP** is used in conjunction with the statement ON PEN GOSUB. (See the discussion of ON PEN for further details.)

6.   The light pen is reset to off by the commands CHAIN, CHAIN MERGE, CLEAR, LOAD, MERGE, NEW, and RUN, or by the deletion or entering of a program line.

APPLICATIONS

1.   Light pens allow the user to interact with the computer without having to use the keyboard. Light pens can be used for creating color graphics, menu selection, interaction with graphs, and computer-assisted instruction.

340

The computer can play musical compositions via the PLAY statement. The programmer designates the notes, length of play, and the tempo of the composition. (The PLAY statement can only be used with Advanced BASIC. That is, the command BASICA must have been given when BASIC was invoked.)

PART I PITCH OF NOTES

The piano keyboard consists of 88 keys. Eighty-four of these keys can be played on the computer. In Figure 1, these 84 keys are grouped into 7 octaves labeled 0 to 6.

FIGURE 1

The following demonstration program plays all of the 'natural' notes in this range. (*Note:* If you are using an early version of BASIC replace line 220 by `220 FOR J=1 to 550: NEXT: RETURN`.)

```
10 CLS: SCREEN 0
20 S$ = "CDEFGAB"
30 FOR I = 0 TO 6
40     PLAY "MB O=I; XS$; "
50     PRINT "OCTAVE "; I,"C  ";: GOSUB 210
60     PRINT "D  ";: GOSUB 210
70     PRINT "E  ";: GOSUB 210
80     PRINT "F  ";: GOSUB 210
90     PRINT "G  ";: GOSUB 210
100    PRINT "A  ";: GOSUB 210
110    PRINT "B  " : GOSUB 210
120 NEXT
130 COLOR 31: LOCATE 4,15: PRINT "C"
140 LOCATE 10,1: PRINT "middle C"
150 FOR K = 1 TO 8000: NEXT
160 COLOR 15,0
170 LOCATE 4,15: PRINT "C"
180 LOCATE 5,37: PRINT STRING$(4,17)
190 LOCATE 10,1: PRINT SPC(25)+"default octave"
200 COLOR 7,0: END
210 T=TIMER
220 IF TIMER-T<.45 THEN 220 ELSE RETURN
```

341

PLAY

Each note is identified by its octave (0 to 6) and letter (A to G). Sharps and flats are denoted by trailing the letter with "#" or "+" for a sharp and "-" for a flat. PLAY statements contain the word **PLAY** followed by a string containing information about the notes to be played. A typical statement is

```
PLAY "O3 C"
```

which results in middle C being played. The statement

```
PLAY "O2 DE O4 E+B-"
```

results in 4 notes being played in succession, the first 2 being from octave 2 and the second 2 from octave 4. In general, the letter O followed by one of the numbers 0 to 6 mandates that all subsequent notes will be from the designated octave, until another octave is specified. Even subsequent PLAY statements will be effected by the designated octave. If no octave is specified before the first note is PLAYed, the note will be taken from octave 4.

Octaves also can be specified by statements of the form

```
PLAY "O = var; notes"
```

where var is a numeric variable. For instance, the statement

```
K=3: PLAY "O = K; C"
```

produces middle C.

A sequence of notes can be defined as a substring, and then the entire substring can be called by the PLAY statement. Within the PLAY statement, the substring must be preceded by the letter X and followed by a semicolon. See Examples 1 and 3.

EXAMPLES

1.  ```
    10 PLAY "EF+"
    20 PLAY "O1 CD-E"
    30 PLAY "EF#"
    ```

Since no octave is specified in line 10, the first 2 notes (E and F sharp) will be from octave 4, the default octave. The remaining 5 notes (C, D flat, E, E, and F sharp) are all from octave 1. The octave designation O1 continues to affect future PLAY statements until another octave designation is made. This program also could have been written as

```
PLAY "EF+ O1 CD-EEF#"
```

or as

```
S$ = "EF+": PLAY "XS$; O1 CD-E XS$;"
```

342
```

2.
```
10 PRINT "Scale of D Minor"
20 PLAY "D E F G A B- O5 C+ D"
```

3.
```
10 SCREEN 0,1
20 PRINT "Fr" + CHR$(138) + "re Jacques"
30 F$ = "CDEC"
40 PLAY "O3 XF$; XF$; EFG"
```

4. The following program plays the beginning of Frère Jacques in the octave designated by the user.

```
10 F$ = "CDEC"
20 INPUT "Octave (0-6)"; n
30 PLAY "O=n; XF$; XF$; EFG"
```

PART II   BACKGROUND VERSUS FOREGROUND

In the Music Foreground (MF) mode, whenever a PLAY statement is encountered during the running of a program, the designated notes are played before the next statement of the program is executed. In the Music Background (MB) mode, the computer stores up to 32 notes and pauses in a buffer and plays them while continuing to execute the program. These modes are invoked with the statements **PLAY "MF"** and **PLAY "MB"**. The default mode is Music Background in BASIC 2.1, and Music Foreground in all other versions of BASIC. The default mode results when one of the commands CHAIN, CHAIN MERGE, CLEAR, LOAD, MERGE, NEW, or RUN is executed, or when a program line is entered or deleted.

FURTHER EXAMPLE

5. When the following program is run, the words appear as soon as the tune begins playing. If the MB in line 10 was replaced by MF, the words would not appear until the tune finished playing.

```
10 PLAY "MB"
20 PLAY "CCDCFE"
30 PRINT "Happy Birthday to You"
```

PART III   LENGTH OF NOTES

The standard musical notes are whole notes (1/1), half notes (1/2), quarter notes (1/4), eighth notes (1/8), 16th notes (1/16), 32nd notes (1/32), and 64th notes (1/64). The computer not only can produce all of these lengths but can produce 1/nth notes for any n from 1 to 64. The following demonstration program plays middle C in 64 different lengths:

PLAY

```
10 CLS
20 LOCATE 12,1
30 PRINT "This is a  whole  note."
40 PLAY "MF O3 C1"
50 FOR I = 2 TO 64
60    LOCATE 12,11
70    PRINT " 1 /"; I
80    PLAY "L=I; O3 C"
90 NEXT I
```

When one of the letters A to G in a PLAY statement is trailed by the number n, that note will have the length of a 1/nth note. For instance, the statement

PLAY "C2 C1 C25"

results in the key of C (above middle C) being played 3 times, first as a half note, then as a whole note, and finally as a 25th note.

Lengths of notes also can be specified by the letter L trailed by a number from 1 to 64, which mandates that (until another length is specified) all subsequent notes that don't carry their own trailing length designation will have that length. Even subsequent PLAY statements will be affected by the specified length. If no length is specified before the first note is PLAYed, notes will be played as quarter notes until otherwise specified. For instance, the statement

PLAY "CC8 L16 CCC L1 CCC2"

results in the key of C being played 8 times, first as a quarter note, then as an eighth note, 3 times as a 16th note, twice as a whole note, and finally as a half note.

Lengths also can be specified by statements in the form

PLAY "L = var; notes"

where var is a numeric variable. For instance, the statement

K=8: PLAY "L = K; C"

plays C as an eighth note.

The letter P trailed by a number n from 1 to 64 produces a pause (or rest) of duration 1/n. For instance, the statement

PLAY "C P2 C P16 C"

plays the key C three times separated by half and 16th note pauses. Pauses can be also specified by statements of the form PLAY "P = var; notes"

344

where var is a numeric variable. For instance, the statement **K=8: PLAY "C P = K; C"** plays C twice, separated by an eighth note pause.

In standard musical notation, a small dot after a note or rest means it is to last half as long again (one and a half times) its normal length. Trailing a note or pause in a PLAY statement with a period produces the same effect. For instance, the statement

```
PLAY "C C. C8. C.. L15 P4. C2. C."
```

plays C six times with lengths 1/4, 3/8, 3/16, 9/16, 3/4, and 1/10. There is a pause of length 3/8 between the fourth and fifth notes.

In standard musical notation, a small dot over or under a note means that the note should be short and sharp with a pause between each note and the next one. This is called *staccato*. A curved line over or under several notes means that they should be played smoothly with no pause between each note and the next. This is called *legato*. Staccato and legato are induced within PLAY statements by the pairs of letters MS and ML. The pair MN refers to *normal* music. The pair of letters MS within a PLAY statement mandates that all subsequent notes be played staccato until one of the pair of letters MN or ML is encountered. Similar considerations apply to ML.

FURTHER EXAMPLES

6.
```
10 PRINT "Jingle bells, Jingle bells"
20 PLAY "MF O3 L8 EE E4 EE E4"
30 PRINT "Jingle all the way"
40 PLAY "EG C. D16 E4 P4"
50 PRINT "Oh what fun it is to ride in a"
60 PLAY "FF F. F16 F EE L16 EE"
70 PRINT "One horse open"
80 PLAY "L4 GGFD"
90 PRINT "Sleigh"
100 PLAY "C1"
```

7. The following program plays the first part of Happy Birthday with staccato notes, then normally, and finally in legato. Notice that in the legato mode, the first two Cs blend into a single long note.

```
10 B$ = "CCDCFE"
20 PLAY "MS XB$;"
30 PLAY "MN XB$;"
40 PLAY "ML XB$;"
```

8. This program plays the beginning of Frère Jacques using the length of notes designated by the user.

PLAY

```
10 F$ = "CDEC"
20 INPUT "Length of notes (1-64)"; n
30 PLAY "L = n; XF$; XF$; EFG"
```

PART IV TEMPO

The speed or tempo of music is usually given in Italian. Some common tempos are:

Tempo	Translation	Approx. number of 1/4 notes per minute
Largo	Very slow	50
Adagio	Slow	70
Andante	Slow and flowing	90
Moderato	Medium	110
Allegro	Fast	130
Vivace	Lively	150
Presto	Very fast	170

The following demonstration program plays the scale of C major at each of the tempos listed above.

```
10 CLS
20 PLAY "MF"
30 FOR I = 50 TO 170 STEP 20
40    PRINT I; "quarter notes per minute"
50    PLAY "T=I; O3 CDEFGAB O4 C"
60 NEXT I
```

The tempo of a composition can be specified by the letter T trailed by a number n from 32 to 255, which mandates that all subsequent notes will be played at the speed of n quarter notes per minute until another tempo is specified. If no tempo is specified before the first note is PLAYed, the tempo will be 120 quarter notes per minute until otherwise altered. For instance, the statement

```
PLAY "C T60 C"
```

plays C twice, first for 1/2 second and then for 1 second.

Tempo can also be specified by statements of the form

```
PLAY "T = var; notes"
```

where var is a numeric variable. For instance, the statement

346

```
K=150: PLAY "T = K; CCDCFE"
```

plays the beginning of Happy Birthday in vivace.

PART V   DESIGNATING KEYS BY NUMBERS

The 84 keys discussed in Part I were identified by a combination of octave (0 to 6) and letter (A to G with possible + or −). These keys can also be identified by the letter N trailed by one of the numbers from 1 to 84 as follows:

Octave 0 Key No.	Octave 1 Key No.	Octave 2 Key No.	Octave 3 Key No.	Octave 4 Key No.	Octave 5 Key No.	Octave 6 Key No.
C 1	C 13	C 25	C 37	C 49	C 61	C 73
C+ 2	C+ 14	C+ 26	C+ 38	C+ 50	C+ 62	C+ 74
D 3	D 15	D 27	D 39	D 51	D 63	D 75
D+ 4	D+ 16	D+ 28	D+ 40	D+ 52	D+ 64	D+ 76
E 5	E 17	E 29	E 41	E 53	E 65	E 77
F 6	F 18	F 30	F 42	F 54	F 66	F 78
F+ 7	F+ 19	F+ 31	F+ 43	F+ 55	F+ 67	F+ 79
G 8	G 20	G 32	G 44	G 56	G 68	G 80
G+ 9	G+ 21	G+ 33	G+ 45	G+ 57	G+ 69	G+ 81
A 10	A 22	A 34	A 46	A 58	A 70	A 82
A+ 11	A+ 23	A+ 35	A+ 47	A+ 59	A+ 71	A+ 83
B 12	B 24	B 36	B 48	B 60	B 72	B 84

The combination N0 is used to identify a pause. For instance, the statement

```
PLAY "N37 N0 N38"
```

plays middle C, a pause, and then C#.
Notes also can be specified by statements of the form

```
PLAY "N = var;"
```

where var is a numeric variable. For instance, the statement

```
K=37: PLAY "N = K;"
```

plays middle C.

FURTHER EXAMPLES

```
9. 10 PRINT "Jingle bells, Jingle bells"
   20 PLAY "MF L8 N41 N41 L4 N41 L8 N41 N41 L4 N41"
   30 PRINT "Jingle all the way"
```

PLAY

```
40 PLAY "L8 N41 N44 N37. L16 N39 L4 N41 NO"
50 PRINT "Oh what fun it is to ride in a"
60 PLAY "L8 N42 N42 N42. L16 N42 L8 N42 N41 N41 L16 N41 N41"
70 PRINT "One horse open"
80 PLAY "L4 N44 N44 N42 N39"
90 PRINT "Sleigh"
100 PLAY "L1 N37"
```

10. The following program plays all 84 notes.

```
10 PLAY "MF"
20 FOR I = 1 TO 84
30     PRINT I;
40     PLAY "T255 N = I;"
50 NEXT I
```

PART VI   ENHANCEMENTS BEGINNING WITH BASIC 2.0

Suppose that an octave has been set by default, as octave 4, or by the letter O followed by a number. Then the character

> >

inserted in the string causes the specified octave number to be increased by 1. If the current octave is 6, then the > character has no effect. Similarily, the character

> <

decreases the octave number by 1. See Example 11.

The hassles resulting from working with the buffer used with the Music Background option have been lessened by the addition of two statements in BASIC 2.0 and subsequent versions. The statement PLAY(n) reads the number of notes remaining in the buffer. The statement ON PLAY(n) induces a branching to a subroutine when the number of notes in the buffer reaches a certain level. See the discussions of these statements for details.

FURTHER EXAMPLE

11. The following program, which requires BASIC 2.0 or subsequent versions, plays a double scale, up and back.

```
10 A$ = "CDEFGAB": B$ = "BAGFEDC"
20 PLAY "O2 XA$; > XA$; > C"
30 PLAY "< XB$; < XB$;"
```

COMMENTS

1. We have consistently used uppercase letters in PLAY statements and have included spaces to improve readability. Neither of these conventions is necessary. For instance, line 20 of Example 6 could have been written

```
20 PLAY "mfo3l8eee4eee4"
```

2. Semicolons are essential following inserted substrings (see Examples 3, 4, and 7) and designations such as O = n (see Examples 4 and 10).

3. The notes produced by the PLAY statement also can be produced by the SOUND statement. However, PLAY is preferable for musical compositions, SOUND for sound effects.

4. The major drawback in playing music on the computer is the inability to vary loudness. Every note is played with the same intensity.

5. Programs that will be compiled should not use the command "XA$;" or any of the other commands involving variables and semicolons. An alternative is provided by the statement VARPTR$. See the discussion of VARPTR$ for details.

PLAY(n)

The statement PLAY(n) is not available with versions of BASIC preceding BASIC 2.0. This discussion assumes a familiarity with the PLAY statement; in particular, the Music Background (MB) mode.

The MB command of the PLAY statement sets up a buffer to store notes so that the execution of the program can continue while the music is being played. At any time, the value of the function

```
PLAY(0)
```

is the number of notes currently in the Music Background buffer.

EXAMPLES

1. The following program places 15 notes in the music background buffer and keeps a running count of the number of notes yet to be played.

```
10 CLS
20 LOCATE 12,1
30 PRINT "There are    notes currently "
40 PRINT "in the music background buffer."
50 A$="CDEFGAB"
60 PLAY "MB 01  XA$; > XA$; > C"
70 FOR I = 1 TO 600
80 LOCATE 12,10: PRINT PLAY(0)
90 NEXT I
```

2. The following program uses the PLAY(n) function to display a message at the appropriate time.

```
10 A$="CDEFGAB"
20 PLAY " MB 01  XA$; > C P4 XA$; > C"
30 PRINT "This is the scale of C major."
40 IF PLAY(0) = 7 THEN 60
50 GOTO 40
60 PRINT "Here is the scale played one octave higher."
```

COMMENTS

1. The value of PLAY(0) is always 0 when the program is running in the Music Foreground mode.

2. The value of PLAY(0) is the same as the value of PLAY(n), where n is any numeric constant. For instance, line 80 of Example 1 could have been written 80 `LOCATE 12,10: PRINT PLAY(2.7)`.

3. The Music Background buffer can hold up to 32 notes provided that the notes are played legato (ML). Otherwise, the buffer can hold at most 16 notes at any one time.

350

The graphics function PMAP is not available with versions of BASIC before BASIC 2.0. This discussion assumes a familiarity with the ways that coordinates are specified in graphics modes. For a discussion of the standard coordinate system, also known as the *physical* coordinate system, see Appendix C. User-defined coordinates, known as *world* coordinates, are explained in the discussion of the statement WINDOW.

Suppose that a WINDOW statement has been used to specify a world coordinate system, and that (WX,WY) are the world coordinates of a point. Then the value of

```
PMAP(WX,0)
```

is the first physical coordinate of that point, and the value of

```
PMAP(WY,1)
```

is the second physical coordinate of that point. If (PX,PY) are the physical coordinates of a point, then the value of

```
PMAP(PX,2)
```

is the first world coordinate of the point, and the value of

```
PMAP(PY,3)
```

is the second world coordinate of the point.

EXAMPLES

Suppose that the screen is set in high-resolution graphics mode, and the statement WINDOW (3,5)-(9,10) is used to define a world coordinate system. Figure 1 shows the world coordinates along with the corresponding physical coordinates of several points. The world coordinates have been written above the physical coordinates.

```
1.  10 SCREEN 2
    20 WINDOW (3,5)-(9,10)
    30 INPUT "World coordinates: ", WX,WY
    40 PRINT "The physical coordinates are ";
    50 PRINT PMAP(WX,0); ","; PMAP(WY,1)
    RUN
    World coordinates: 7,3
    The physical coordinates are  426 , 279
    Ok
```

As shown here, the functions are even defined for points off the screen.

PMAP

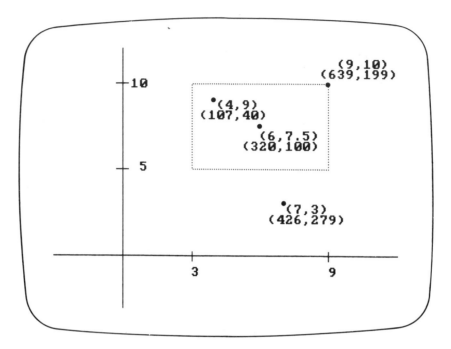

FIGURE 1

2.  ```
    10 SCREEN 2
    20 WINDOW (3,5)-(9,10)
    30 INPUT "Physical coordinates: ", PX,PY
    40 PRINT "The world coordinates are ";
    50 PRINT PMAP(PX,2); ","; PMAP(PY,3)
    RUN
    Physical coordinates: 320,100
    The world coordinates are  6.004695 , 7.487457
    Ok
    ```

Notice that when calculating world coordinates, PMAP gives single-precision results, whereas, when calculating physical coordinates, PMAP gives integer values.

COMMENTS

1. The function PMAP can only be used with Advanced BASIC. That is, the command BASICA must have been given when BASIC was invoked.

2. The definitions of the four PMAP functions can be abbreviated to

    ```
    (PX,PY) = (PMAP(WX,0),PMAP(WY,1))
    (WX,WY) = (PMAP(PX,2),PMAP(PY,3))
    ```
    ```

APPLICATIONS

1.   Suppose that we decide to use the DRAW statement to draw a figure beginning at a point whose world coordinates are known. Since the DRAW statement does not recognize world coordinates, we must first use the PMAP function to obtain the physical coordinates of the point.

2.   The WINDOW and VIEW statements are often used together to project graphics into a viewport. However, the parameters used in the VIEW statement are the physical coordinates of two corners of the viewport. If the world coordinates of the corners are (X1,Y1) and (X2,Y2), then the statement

```
VIEW (PMAP(X1,0),PMAP(Y1,1))-(PMAP(X2,0),PMAP(Y2,1))
```

will activate the proper viewport.

POINT

With the two graphics modes, the screen is subdivided into either 64,000 or 128,000 small rectangles or points. (See Appendix C for a discussion of specifying coordinates of points in graphics mode.)

In the high-resolution graphics mode, which is invoked by the statement **SCREEN 2**, there are only two colors, black and white. These colors are referred to by the numbers 0 and 1.

In the medium-resolution graphics mode with color enabled, which is invoked by the statement **SCREEN 1,0**, there are 16 choices for background color and 2 choices of palette. The COLOR statement is used to specify the background color and the palette. (See the discussion of the COLOR statement for further details.) Each palette consists of 4 colors, referred to as 0, 1, 2, and 3, where 0 is the same as the background color.

In either of the two graphics modes, the value of

```
POINT (x,y)
```

is the number of the color of the point with coordinates (x,y).

EXAMPLES

1. Each letter of text that is displayed on the screen in high-resolution graphics mode occupies an 8 by 8 rectangle of points. The following program shows us the points that are turned on to form the letters A through G.

```
10 SCREEN 2: CLS: KEY OFF
20 PRINT "ABCDEFG"
30 FOR I = 0 TO 7
40     LOCATE 2+I,1
50     FOR J = 0 TO 55
60         IF POINT(J,I)=0 THEN PRINT " "; ELSE PRINT "*";
70     NEXT J
80     PRINT
90 NEXT I
RUN
ABCDEFG
    **      ******      ****    *****       *******   *******    ****
   ****     **   **   **    **  **  **      **     *   **     *  **    **
  **   **   **   **  **   **     **       **   *   **   *   **
  **   **   *****    **          **       **   ****    ****     **
  ******    **   **  **          **       **   *   **   *   **      ***
  **   **   **   **  **    **    **  **    **     *   **         **    **
  **   **   ******    ****    *****       *******   ****        *****

Ok
```

2. A variation of the above program displays letters vertically on the screen.

```
10 SCREEN 1,0: CLS
20 PRINT "ABCDEFG"
30 FOR J = 0 TO 55
40 FOR I = 0 TO 7
50 IF POINT(J,I)=3 THEN PSET (163-I,J)
60 NEXT I,J
```

3.
```
10 SCREEN 1,0: CLS
20 COLOR 9,0
30 PSET(160,100),2
40 PRINT POINT(160,100); POINT(160,101)
RUN
  2  0
Ok
```

The background color is light blue and the tiny point in the center of the screen is red.

4. The POINT function is used in computer animation to determine if two objects are about to collide. In the following program a barrier of random length appears and a ball moves across the screen. See Figure 1. The POINT function detects objects in the path of the ball and tells whether the direction of the ball should be reversed. Lines 30-40 draw the rectangular barrier, and line 50 draws the ball. Line 60 takes a picture of the ball, and line 110 moves that picture across the screen. Lines 70 to 100 direct the motion.

```
10 DIM B(4)
20 SCREEN 1: CLS: KEY OFF
30 RANDOMIZE VAL(RIGHT$(TIME$,2))
40 LINE (200,0)-(220,199*RND),,BF
50 CIRCLE (3,100),2: PAINT (3,100)
60 GET (0,97)-(6,103),B
70 BX = 3: DX = 1
80 IF POINT(BX+4,99) THEN DX = -1
90 IF (BX<4 AND DX=-1) OR BX>315 GOTO 20
100 BX = BX+DX
110 PUT (BX-3,97),B,PSET: GOTO 80
```

COMMENT

1. If the coordinates x and y are not integers, they will be rounded to integers. If y is not between 0 and 199 or if x is not between 0 and 319 (in medium-resolution graphics) or 0 and 639 (in high-resolution graphics), then the value of POINT(x,y) will be -1.

POINT

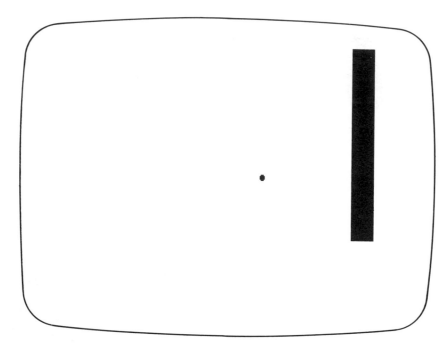

FIGURE 1

FURTHER DISCUSSION

BASIC 2.0 and subsequent versions provide a second form of the POINT function. After any graphics statement is executed, there is a special point, known as the *last point referenced*, remembered by the computer. This point is often used as a reference point by subsequent graphics statements. At any time, the value of the function

```
POINT(0)
```

is the first coordinate of the last point referenced, and the value of the function

```
POINT(1)
```

is the second coordinate of the last point referenced.

FURTHER EXAMPLE

5.   The following program requires Advanced BASIC 2.0 (or later versions). The output of the program is shown in Figure 2.

```
10 SCREEN 1,0
20 PSET (200,100)
```

```
30 LOCATE 13,26: PRINT POINT(0); POINT(1)
40 LINE -(60,50)
50 LOCATE 6,1: PRINT POINT(0); POINT(1)
60 CIRCLE (70,140),67
70 LOCATE 18,8 : PRINT POINT(0); POINT(1)
80 PSET (1000,300)
90 LOCATE 1,30 : PRINT POINT(0); POINT(1)
```

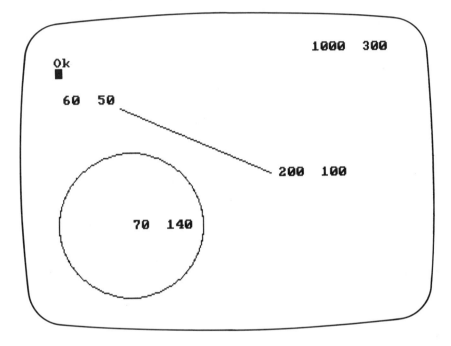

FIGURE 2

FURTHER COMMENTS

2. BASIC 2.0 and subsequent versions provide the capability of specifying user-defined coordinate systems, known as world coordinate systems. (See the discussion of the WINDOW statement for details.) After a world coordinate system has been specified by a WINDOW statement, the values of the functions POINT(2) and POINT(3) will be the first and second world coordinates, respectively, of the last point referenced. If no WINDOW statement is currently active, the values of these functions will be the ordinary, or physical, coordinates of the last point referenced.

APPLICATIONS

1. The POINT function is used extensively in computer animation to detect collosions, as in Example 4.

POINT

2. The POINT function can be used, by employing the ideas of Examples 1 and 2, to create banners on the printer.

3. When working with BASIC 2.0 and subsequent versions, the second form of the POINT function is useful when combining an image that is specified in world coordinates with an image specified in physical coordinates.

This discussion assumes an understanding of the way memory locations are specified. (See the discussion of DEF SEG.) Each memory location contains a block of 8 binary bits that corresponds to a number m, where m ranges from 0 to 255. The location is said to contain the number m. After a DEF SEG statement has specified a segment of memory, the statement

```
POKE n,m
```

places the value m in the memory location with offset n.

EXAMPLES

1. Normally, the cursor can wander anywhere on the screen except the 25th line. The cursor can actually be restricted to any rectangular region of the screen provided that the left side of the region is also the left side of the screen. If so, only the characters inside this rectangle will scroll. If the top of the rectangle is row T, the bottom is row B, and the right side is column R, then the three numbers T, B, and R describe the confining rectangle. These numbers are stored in BASIC's Data Segment in the memory locations with offsets 91, 92, and 41. The following program sets these numbers to their standard values, labels lines 1 to 22, and then restricts the cursor to the rectangle with T=5, B=16, and R=30. After running the program, use the cursor control keys and the Home key to move the cursor around the rectangle. Then LIST the program and notice that only the characters in the rectangle scroll. To return to the normal situation, add the program line **45 END** and rerun the program.

```
10 DEF SEG: CLS: KEY OFF: WIDTH 80
20 POKE 91,1: 'Top
30 POKE 92,24: 'Bottom
40 POKE 41,80: 'Right
50 FOR I = 1 TO 22
60     LOCATE I,37: PRINT I
70 NEXT I
80 POKE 91,5: 'Top
90 POKE 92,16: 'Bottom
100 POKE 41,30: 'Right
```

2. There are certain characters that can not be displayed on the screen with the PRINT statement. These characters and their associated numbers are shown in Figure 1. If N is one of the associated numbers, then the statement **PRINT CHR$(N)** produces a special effect such as "carriage return" or "cursor down." However, when these numbers are POKEd into appropriate memory locations, the associated characters are displayed on the screen.

POKE

FIGURE 1

When using a graphics monitor, the contents of the screen are stored in Segment &HB800. In width-80 text mode, the memory locations with offsets 0, 2, 4, . . . ,158 store the contents of the top row of the screen. The following program allows the user to select a number from 0 to 255 and then displays the associated character. If the number is not one of the numbers in Figure 1, then the character with the ASCII value of the selected number is displayed.

```
10 SCREEN 0,0,0: CLS
20 DEF SEG = &HB800
30 INPUT C
40 POKE 16,C
RUN
? 97      a
Ok
RUN
? 14      ♫
Ok
RUN
? 13      ♪
Ok
```

3.   The memory location having offset 1047 in segment 0 contains the status of the keys Ins, Caps Lock, Num Lock, Scroll Lock, Alt, Ctrl, Left Shift, and Right Shift. The byte in this memory location is an 8-tuple of 0s and 1s. Each bit gives the status of one of the above-mentioned keys, as follows:

Ins	Caps Lock	Num Lock	Scroll Lock	Alt	Ctrl	Left Shift	Right Shift

A particular bit is 1 if the corresponding key is active (i.e., on or pressed) and is 0 if the corresponding key is inactive. For instance, if the byte is 01100000, then the Caps Lock key and the Num Lock key are active and all of the other keys are inactive. (So, pressing letter keys will produce upper case letters and pressing keys on the numeric keypad will produce digits.) To set the keyboard status, write down the 8-tuple of 0s and 1s that describes the desired status, look up the corresponding decimal or hexadecimal number in Appendix K, and POKE this number into the memory location with absolute memory location 1047.

After the following program was run, the leftmost white key from each row of keys was pressed. (To return to the standard situation, press the Caps Lock and right shift keys.)

```
10 DEF SEG = 0
20 POKE 1047,65: '65 corresponds to 01000001
RUN
Ok
!qa
```

COMMENTS

1.   The statement POKE is complementary to PEEK, which is used to *read* the contents of memory locations. It is perfectly safe to PEEK anywhere in memory; no harm can possibly be done. However, care must be exercised in deciding where to POKE. For instance, if we POKE into the memory locations that contain the current BASIC program, the program will be changed.

2.   ROM (Read Only Memory) is located beginning in segment 62464 (or &HF000). POKEing into ROM has no effect.

APPLICATIONS

1.   The computer contains switches that record the hardware configuration. When the computer is turned on, the state of these switches is recorded in specified memory locations. Hence, if we change the hardware configuration, we can POKE the appropriate memory location instead of opening up the computer and adjusting a switch. This is commonly done when changing back and forth from the Monochrome Display to a color monitor.

2.   POKE is used to place machine language programs into unused parts of memory. These programs can then be used as subroutines by BASIC. See USR and CALL for details.

3.   See Appendix H for further applications of POKE.

POS

The screen can display 80 characters of text per line. The positions of these characters are numbered from 1 to 80 (beginning at the left side of the screen). At any time, the value of

```
POS(0)
```

will be the number of the column position of the cursor.

EXAMPLES

```
1.  10 PRINT "E";: A = POS(0)
    20 PRINT " PLURIBUS";: B = POS(0)
    30 PRINT " UNUM";: C = POS(0)
    40 PRINT A; B; C
    RUN
    E PLURIBUS UNUM 2  11  16
    Ok
```

2.   In the following program, POS is used to assure that each line of the display will be, at most, 30 characters long.

```
10 FOR I = 1 TO 27
20    READ A$
30    IF LEN(A$)>31-POS(0) THEN PRINT
40    PRINT A$+" ";
50 NEXT I
60 DATA ABS, ASC, ATN, AUTO, BEEP, BLOAD, BSAVE, CALL, CDBL,
CHAIN, CHR$, CINT, CIRCLE, CLEAR, CLOSE, CLS, COLOR, COM(n),
COMMON, CONT, COS, CSNG, CSRLIN, CVI, CVS, CVD, DATA
RUN
ABS ASC ATN AUTO BEEP BLOAD
BSAVE CALL CDBL CHAIN CHR$
CINT CIRCLE CLEAR CLOSE CLS
COLOR COM(n) COMMON CONT COS
CSNG CSRLIN CVI CVS CVD DATA
Ok
```

COMMENTS

1.   The argument of the POS function is a dummy argument. Any number, not just 0, can be used with the same result. For instance, we can write POS(1), POS(2), and so on.

2.   POS often is used in conjunction with the CSRLIN function, which gives the number of the cursor's row.

362

APPLICATIONS

1.   POS, in conjunction with CSRLIN and LOCATE, gives the programmer the capability to wander all over the screen and return to a location specified relative to the starting point.

2.   Certain programs request input from the user but require that the information be placed in a certain rectangular portion of the screen. POS can be used to guarantee that the user will not be able to place information outside that region.

PRINT

The PRINT statement may be the single most common BASIC statement. It tells the computer to display information on the screen. Our discussion is presented in three parts: printing strings, printing numbers, and the use of commas and semicolons.

PART I   PRINTING STRINGS

There are 256 different characters that can be used in a string. These characters and their ASCII values are listed in Appendix A. Certain characters in the list, such as "beep" and "cursor down," can't be readily displayed on the screen. The undisplayable characters are those numbered 7, 9 through 13, and 28 through 31. Only 94 of the characters appear on the white keys in the center of the keyboard. The others are invoked by the CHR$ function. For instance, the string "Bell"+CHR$(7) consists of 5 characters, with "beep" as the last character.

If A$ is a string, then the statement

```
PRINT A$
```

causes all of the displayable characters in the string to be displayed on the screen and all other characters to be executed.

EXAMPLES

1. `PRINT "Song:":PRINT "Fr"+CHR$(138)+"re":PRINT "Jacques"`
   ```
   Song:
   Frère
    Jacques
   Ok
   ```

2. `PRINT "": PRINT: PRINT CHR$(31);`


   ```
   Ok
   ```
   "" is the null (or empty) string and CHR$(31) is the character "cursor down." Each statement had the same effect.

3. `A$ = "Bell"+CHR$(7): PRINT A$`
   ```
   Bell    (also the speaker beeped)
   Ok
   ```

PART II   PRINTING NUMBERS

If N is a number, then the statement

```
PRINT N
```

causes the number to be displayed on the screen. If N is a numeric variable or a mathematical expression involving numeric constants or variables, then the value of N will be displayed. The PRINT statement automatically inserts a space following the displayed number. Also, a space is inserted preceding positive numbers and zero. Negative numbers are preceded by "$-$".

FURTHER EXAMPLES

4.  ```
    PRINT 123: PRINT -3.2: PRINT 12345679*9: PRINT SQR(9)
     123
    -3.2
     111111111
     3
    Ok
    ```

5.  ```
    10 A = 2: B = 10: C = 5+B: D = 3*4
    20 PRINT A+B: PRINT D-7: PRINT C: PRINT -1*SQR(A)
    RUN
     12
     5
     15
    -1.414214
    Ok
    ```

PART III   COMMAS AND SEMICOLONS IN PRINT STATEMENTS

In BASIC 1.1, the 80-character line is divided into 6 print zones (5 of width 14 and 1 of width 10). The first zone consists of positions 1 to 14, the second zone consists of positions 15 to 28, and so on. In later versions of BASIC, the 80-character line is divided into 5 print zones (4 of width 14 and 1 of width 24). The 40-character line is divided into 2 print zones (the first of width 14 and the second of width 26).

Normally, PRINT statements execute a carriage return and line feed after displaying characters on the screen, which causes the next PRINT statement to display on the next line. However, if a PRINT statement is followed by a comma, the carriage return and line feed are suppressed, and the next PRINT statement displays its characters beginning with the next unused print zone. If a PRINT statement is followed by a semicolon, the carriage return and line feed are suppressed, and the next PRINT statement displays its characters immediately following the first set of characters.

Commas and semicolons can be used to condense several PRINT statements into one multiple PRINT statement. A multiple PRINT statement consists of several expressions separated by commas or semicolons. For instance, the line

PRINT

```
PRINT A$,: PRINT B;: PRINT C;: PRINT D$,
```

can be written as

```
PRINT A$, B; C; D$,
```

Further Examples

6.
```
10 PRINT "ten",
20 PRINT "doll";
30 PRINT "ars"
RUN
ten           dollars
Ok
```

7.
```
PRINT 1,: PRINT 2;: PRINT 3
 1                2 3
Ok
```

The number 1 is displayed in location 2, the number 2 in location 16, and the number 3 in location 19. Positive numbers are preceded and followed by spaces.

8.
```
10 G$ = "gee": N = 6
20 PRINT "A"; "B", "C", "D"; "E"; N; G$, "H"
RUN
AB             C              DE 6 gee       H
Ok
```

9.
```
PRINT "SONG", SONG
SONG            0
Ok
```

The first item is a string and the second is a numeric variable, which has value 0 until assigned another value.

Comments

1. A semicolon separating two items in a multiple PRINT statement can often be omitted. It may be omitted if the first item is a string constant, string variable, BASIC or user-defined function, or a numeric constant with a type declaration tag. In addition, the semicolon may be omitted if the second item is a string constant or if the first item is a numeric constant that is not followed by another numeric constant.

```
PRINT 3% 2 CHR$(49) 0 "Blastoff"
 3  2 1 0 Blastoff
Ok
```

```
10 A$="Chateau"
```

```
20 PRINT "An"1806A$" Lafite"" claret"
RUN
An 1806 Chateau Lafite claret
Ok
```

2.   PRINT statements often display numbers in a different form from that originally typed. The displayed form is the one most appropriate to the precision of the number. Some examples are:

Original form	Displayed form
3.20	3.2
2E+4	20000
87654321!	8.765432E+07
1.4D+10	14000000000
14E+9	1.4E+10

3.   PRINT statements try to keep each item displayed all on one line. If the item is too long to be placed in its intended location, the entire value will be displayed on the next line. For instance, if A$, B$, and C$ are each strings of 30 characters the statement **PRINT A$; B$; C$** causes A$ and B$ to be placed on one line and C$ to be placed on the next line. Strings of length greater than 80 must be split between two lines.

4.   When a comma separates two items in a multiple PRINT statement, there will always be at least one space separating the displayed items. Thus, if the first item ends in the last column of a zone, the next print zone will be skipped, and the second item printed in the following zone.

```
10 WIDTH 80
20 PRINT "Thomas Woodrow", "Wilson"
RUN
Thomas Woodrow           Wilson
Ok
```

5.   There are subtleties involved in the way BASIC 1.1 handles the sixth print zone in an 80-character line. Consider the statement

```
PRINT "one", "two", "three", "four", "five", M$, N$, R$
```

where the values of M$ and N$ are strings of length m and n. The words "one" through "five" will be placed at the beginnings of the first five print zones of a line.

   If $m > 10$, M$ will be placed in the first print zone of the next line.

   If $m < 10$, M$ will be placed in the sixth print zone. Further,

      if $n < 10$, N$ will be placed beginning in location 5 of the next line

PRINT

and R\$ will be placed at the beginning of the second zone of that line (that is, starting at location 15)

or,

if n>=10, N\$ will be placed beginning in location 5 of the next line and R\$ will be placed at the beginning of the third zone of that line.

If m=10, M\$ will be placed on the next line in locations 5 to 14 and N\$ will be placed at the beginning of the third print zone of that line.

6. The statement `PRINT CHR$(34)` should be used to display a quotation mark. The statement `PRINT """"` just skips a line.

7. A PRINT statement with no list of items will simply produce a carriage return and line feed. Thus, such PRINT statements can be used to generate blank lines. Note that PRINT by itself need not always produce a blank line. If the previously executed PRINT statement ended with a comma or semicolon, then PRINT by itself will simply supply the carriage return and line feed which had been suppressed. The statement PRINT "", which prints the empty string, has the same effect as PRINT by itself.

8. A question mark can be used in place of the word PRINT. For instance, the statement `PRINT 123` can be written `? 123`. If used in a program, no memory is saved. When LISTed, a statement entered using ''?'' for PRINT will show PRINT.

9. The statement `PRINT CHR$(n)`, where n>127, will only display the intended characters in text mode. See Comment 5 in discussion of CHR\$.

10. The word PRINT can be displayed by pressing Alt-P.

Further Examples

10. In the following program, PRINT is used to draw the ace of hearts. (The LOCATE statements move the cursor to specified positions, and the STRING\$ statements form strings consisting of a specified number of repetitions of a single specified character.)

```
10 SCREEN 0
20 CLS: LOCATE 7,9: PRINT CHR$(218);STRING$(9,196);CHR$(191)
30 FOR I=8 TO 13
40   LOCATE I,9: PRINT CHR$(179); STRING$(9,32); CHR$(179)
50 NEXT I
60 PRINT CHR$(192); STRING$(9,196); CHR$(217)
70 LOCATE 8,10: PRINT "A"+CHR$(3)
80 LOCATE 13,17: PRINT "A"+CHR$(3)
```

11. In the following program, PRINT is used to produce motion. A flying object approaches a space ship until the space ship dissolves it with a laser ray.

```
10 CLS: LOCATE 15,1
20 PRINT ">==>"
```

```
30 FOR I=1 TO 20
40   LOCATE 15,40-I: PRINT CHR$(17)+" "
50   FOR J=1 TO 200
60 NEXT J,I
70 LOCATE 15,5: PRINT STRING$(16,45)
80 FOR K=1 TO 200: NEXT K
90 LOCATE 15,5: PRINT STRING$(16,32)
```

APPLICATIONS

1. The PRINT statement is clearly of value for providing output from a program.

2. PRINT is a useful debugging tool. After a part of a program has been run, intermediate results can be displayed.

PRINT USING

The PRINT USING statement permits us to display information in specified formats. Our discussion is presented in five parts: numbers, dollar signs and asterisks, strings, literals, and multiple statements.

PART I DISPLAYING NUMBERS

Consider the number 1234. Some possible ways to display this number are:

with leading and trailing spaces	1234
with no leading or trailing spaces	1234
with two leading spaces	1234
with a comma	1,234
with a trailing decimal point	1234.
in standard scientific notation	1.234E+03
in other exponential forms	.1234E+04
with a leading plus sign	+1234
with a trailing plus sign	1234+

Consider the number -.567. Some possible ways to display this number are:

with a leading zero	−0.567
rounded to two places	−.57
with four decimal places	−.5670
with a trailing minus sign	.567−
rounded to an integer	−1

All of the above formats can be specified by the PRINT USING statement. The specifying is done by a string made up of the formatting characters #, -, +, ∧, comma, and period.

If N is a whole number and A$ is a string of n #s, then the statement

```
PRINT USING A$; N
```

reserves a block of length n in which to display the number. The units digit will be placed in the rightmost place in the block. The 10's digit will be placed just to the left of it, and so on. If a decimal point is placed at the end of the string A$, and the number N has integer precision, then N will be displayed with a trailing decimal point. If any of the # signs, other than the leftmost, are replaced by commas, then commas will be placed after every third digit. (See Examples 1 to 3).

If the leftmost # is replaced with a plus sign, then the number will be preceded by a plus sign if it is positive, and by a negative sign if it is negative. If a plus sign is placed at the end of the string A$, then the number will be displayed with a trailing plus or minus sign. If a minus sign is placed at the end of the string A$, then the number will be displayed with a trailing minus sign if it is negative and with a space otherwise. (See Examples 4 to 7.)

Next, consider the case in which N is a number (not necessarily a whole number), and A$ has a decimal point with n #s to the left and m #s to the right of the decimal point. The statement **PRINT USING A$; N** reserves n spaces to the left of the decimal point for the whole number part of N and displays m decimal places. The decimal portion of the number is rounded or padded with zeros as necessary to fit into the m places. If ΛΛΛΛ is placed at the end of the string A$, then the number will be displayed in exponential notation with a leading space or minus sign, n–1 digits to the left of the decimal point, and m digits to the right. (See Examples 8 to 12.)

EXAMPLES

1. `PRINT USING "#####"; 123`
    ```
    123
    ```
    Ok

2. `PRINT USING "####."; -12`
    ```
    -12.
    ```
    Ok

3. `PRINT USING "#####,##"; 1234567`
    ```
    %1,234,567
    ```
    Ok

The % symbol resulted because a block of length 8 was reserved and the formatted number had 9 characters.

4. `PRINT USING "+####"; 123`
    ```
    +123
    ```
    Ok

5. `PRINT USING "####+"; 45`
    ```
    45+
    ```
    Ok

6. `PRINT USING "######-"; -78`
    ```
    78-
    ```
    Ok

7. `A$ = "#######,.+": PRINT USING A$; -2345`
    ```
    2,345.-
    ```
    Ok

8. `PRINT USING "####.###"; 12.34567`
    ```
    12.346
    ```
    Ok

9. `PRINT USING "###.##"; 3.2`
    ```
    3.20
    ```
    Ok

10. `PRINT USING "##.##"; .055`
    ```
    0.06
    ```
    Ok

PRINT USING

Notice that the presence of #s to the left of the decimal point guarantees that something will be displayed there.

11. `PRINT USING "###.###^^^^"; 1234567`
       `12.346E+05`
       `Ok`

12. `PRINT USING "##.##^^^^"; -.0123`
       `-1.23E-02`
       `Ok`

PART II   DISPLAYING DOLLAR SIGNS AND ASTERISKS

Some possible ways to display numbers with preceding dollar signs and asterisks are:

dollar sign adjacent to number	$ 12.34
dollar sign a fixed distance from decimal point	$ 12.34
asterisks preceding a number	****** 12.34
asterisks preceding a dollar sign	*****$ 12.34
dollar sign preceding asterisks	$***** 12.34
asterisk a fixed distance from decimal point	* 12.34

These displays result from the following statements:

          PRINT USING   "$$######.##";   12.34
          PRINT USING   "$#######.##";   12.34
          PRINT USING   "**######.##";   12.34
          PRINT USING   "**$#####.##";   12.34
          PRINT USING   "$**#####.##";   12.34
          PRINT USING   "*#######.##";   12.34

Notice that each string and each display contains 11 characters including spaces.

Earlier, we considered the statement **PRINT USING A\$; N**, in which A$ contained n #s to the left of the decimal point and m #s to the right. When some of the leftmost #s are replaced by dollar signs or asterisks, the number will be displayed as before (that is, flush right in a reserved block of $m+n+1$ positions). However, some of the leading blank spaces will be replaced as follows:

Leftmost three entries of A$	Effect
$$#	$ in space just to left of number
$##	$ displayed in leftmost position
**#	* displayed in all blank spaces
**$	$ to left of number, * in other spaces
$**	$ at left, * in other blank spaces
*##	* displayed in leftmost position

In each case, the length of the display will be the same as the length of the formatting string A$.

PART III   DISPLAYING STRINGS

Consider the string constant "Massachusetts". Some possible ways of displaying this string are:

Display entire string	Massachusetts
Display the first letter	M
Display the first four letters	Mass

These displays result from the following statements:

PRINT USING "&"; "Massachusetts"
PRINT USING "!"; "Massachusetts"
PRINT USING "\   \"; "Massachusetts"

These displays also can be obtained from the PRINT statement and the LEFT$ function. The value of obtaining them with PRINT USING will become apparent in Part IV.

If B$ is a string, then the statement **PRINT USING "&"; B$** displays the string B$, and the statement **PRINT USING "!"; B$** displays the first character of B$. These statements have the same effect as **PRINT B$** and **PRINT LEFT$(B$,1)**. If A$ is a string of length n consisting of two \ signs separated by n-2 spaces, then the statement **PRINT USING A$; B$** displays the first n characters of B$. It has the same effect as **PRINT LEFT$(B$,n)** when B$ has at least n characters. When B$ has less than n characters, the n-character string consisting of B$ followed by spaces is displayed.

PART IV   LITERALS

In PARTS I, II, and III, we considered PRINT USING statements for various types of format strings A$. If L$ and R$ are ordinary strings, then the string L$+A$+R$ also can be used as a format string in a PRINT USING statement. This new string is just one of the standard format strings with extra characters tacked onto the beginning and end. It results in L$ being displayed as usual and then followed immediately by the result of PRINT USING with A$ as format string, which in turn is followed immediately by R$. The final result is the same as if the entire string L$+A$+R$ were displayed, and then A$ replaced by the display of a standard PRINT USING statement. Since the characters in L$ and R$ have no real formatting effect, they are referred to as *literals*.

Complications can arise if we try to use symbols such as $ or # as literal characters. To guarantee that such characters are treated as literals, they must be preceded by the underscore character "_". (We must use "__" to display an underscore. The pairs "_$", "_#", and "__" result in only one character being displayed.)

PRINT USING

FURTHER EXAMPLES

13.   PRINT USING "The sum of **######,.## dollars."; 12345
     The sum of ***12,345.00 dollars.
     Ok

Here L$ is "The sum of " and R$ is " dollars."

14.   10 A$ = "en&ment"
     20 FOR I = 1 TO 4
     30   READ B$
     40   PRINT USING A$; B$
     50 NEXT I
     60 DATA act, joy, circle, viron
     RUN
     enactment
     enjoyment
     encirclement
     environment
     Ok

15.   PRINT USING "We're _###."; 1
     We're # 1.
     Ok

PART V   MULTIPLE PRINT USING STATEMENTS

In general, format strings of PRINT USING statements can consist of several of the standard format strings discussed in PARTS I, II, and III strung together and interspersed with literals. The PRINT USING statement will consist of such a format string followed by a semicolon and then a sequence of numbers and strings separated by commas. The items in the sequence are considered one at a time. The first item is formatted by the first standard format string, the second item by the second standard format string, and so on. If all the standard format strings are used, the standard format strings are recycled, and the next item will be formatted by the first standard format string. Meanwhile, all literals are displayed as soon as the standard format string preceding them is used.

FURTHER EXAMPLES

16.   10 A$ = "Pay to the order of & the sum of $**#######,_."
     20 PRINT USING A$; "France", 27267622
     RUN
     Pay to the order of France the sum of $27,267,622.
     Ok

17.   10 PRINT "Month   Quantity Sold   Profit"
     20 A$ = "\ \   ############, $$#######,."

```
30 PRINT USING A$; "January", 34567, 172835
40 PRINT USING A$; "February", 9876, 49380
RUN
Month        Quantity Sold          Profit
Jan               34,567        $172,835
Feb                9,876         $49,380
Ok
```

18.
```
10 PRINT " N   "; "  TAN(N)   "
20 FOR N = 1 TO 4
30    PRINT USING "##      ##.###" ;N, TAN(N);
40    PRINT ,, TAN(N)
50 NEXT N
RUN
 N     TAN(N)
 1     1.557                1.557408
 2    -2.185               -2.18504
 3    -0.143               -.1425466
 4     1.158                1.157821
Ok
```

The right-hand column shows the same column of values when displayed with an ordinary PRINT statement.

19.
```
10 A$ = "##th Pres.: !. &    "
20 PRINT USING A$;10,"JOHN","TYLER",11,"JAMES","POLK"
RUN
10th Pres.: J. TYLER   11th Pres.: J. POLK
Ok
```

COMMENTS

1. When using format strings not containing &, the length of the display resulting from each complete application of the format string is the same as the length of the format string.

2. If a number has more digits than the characters in its associated format string allow, the number will be printed preceded by a percent sign. For instance, the statement **PRINT USING "##"; 123** results in %123 being displayed. Also, the desired spacing might be thrown off.

3. As we observed in Example 19, if there are more items than standard format strings, the standard format strings are recycled. No recycling of items takes place if there are more standard format strings than items. As soon as a standard format string for which there is no corresponding item is reached, nothing further is displayed.

4. The items of a PRINT USING statement can be separated by semicolons instead of commas with the same result. However, unlike those in PRINT statements, the items cannot be separated just by spaces.

PRINT USING

5.   When a comma or a semicolon is placed at the end of a PRINT USING statement, the result is the same as when a semicolon is placed at the end of a PRINT statement; the cursor does not move, and the next item to be displayed will begin at the next position.

6.   At most 24 #s can be used together in a PRINT USING statement.

7.   A good way to get comfortable with the effect of the various USING patterns on numbers is to run the following program and experiment.

```
10 LINE INPUT "specify USING pattern: ", U$
20 INPUT "Specify numeric value: ", N
30 PRINT USING U$; N
40 GOTO 10
```

APPLICATIONS

1.   PRINT USING statements are used to organize displayed data as in Example 17.

2.   Mathematical tables are easiest to read when formatted with PRINT USING statements, since the decimal points will be lined up and the numbers uniformly rounded. See Example 18.

3.   PRINT USING statements are used to fill in numbers on checks. The format string ** prevents checks from being altered.

PRINT# and PRINT# USING

A sequential file is a sequence of pieces of information that reside on a disk. The pieces of information can only be read from the file from beginning to end. They are entered initially into the file in order, beginning with the first entry. After that, additional pieces of information can only be added to the end of the file. These are entered into the file with the statements WRITE#, PRINT#, and PRINT# USING.

A sequential file is created initially with a statement of the form **OPEN filespec FOR OUTPUT AS #n**. (See Appendix F and the discussion of OPEN for further details.) If A$ is a string, then the statement

    PRINT #n, A$

enters the string A$ into file number n. If A is a number, then the statement

    PRINT #n, A

enters A with a trailing space (and also a leading space if the number is positive or zero) into file number n.

The PRINT# statement places information into the file in in much the same way that the PRINT statement displays information on the screen. In particular, if the PRINT# statement lists two items separated by a semicolon, the items will be recorded into the file with no space between them. If the two items are separated by a comma, the second item will be placed in the next available print zone. (Each print zone on the disk consists of 14 locations. Also, if necessary, a print zone will be skipped to provide at least one space between the two items.)

If a PRINT# statement does not end with a semicolon or a comma, the newly entered pieces of information are trailed by 2 special characters. We denote these by CR (carriage return) and LF (line feed). When the file is CLOSEd, the special character that we donote by AR (arrow indicating end of file) is automatically inserted following the last character of the file. The character AR is used by the EOF function to alert us that there is no further information in the file. When the statement ends with a comma, enough spaces are added to fill the current print zone.

If A$ is a format string, then a statement of the form

    PRINT #n, USING A$; list of expressions

places information into the file in the same manner that PRINT USING displays information on the screen. (See the discussion of PRINT USING for further details.)

EXAMPLES

1. `10 OPEN "STATES" FOR OUTPUT AS #1`

PRINT# and PRINT# USING

```
20 INPUT "State,Capital,Area,Pop.(000)"; S$, C$, A, P
30 IF S$ = "end" THEN 60
40 PRINT #1, S$; C$; A; P
50 GOTO 20
60 CLOSE #1
RUN
State,Capital,Area,Pop.(000)? Alabama,Montgomery,51705, 3917
State,Capital,Area,Pop.(000)? Alaska, Juneau, 591004, 412
State,Capital,Area,Pop.(000)? Arizona, Phoenix, 114000, 2794
State,Capital,Area,Pop.(000)? end,1,2,3
Ok
```

If we could look at the file on the disk, we would see the following characters recorded there:

```
AlabamaMontgomery 51705  3917 <CR/LF>AlaskaJuneau 591004
    412 <CR/LF>ArizonaPhoenix 114000  2794 <CR/LF/AR>
```

The notation <CR/LF> represents the two characters CR and LF.

2. If line 40 of the program in Example 1 is replaced by

```
40 PRINT #1, S$, C$, A, P
```

the file will appear as follows:

```
Alabama         Montgomery      51705           3917 <CR/LF>Alaska
        Juneau          591004          412 <CR/LF>Arizona
    Phoenix         114000         2794 <CR/LF/AR>
```

3. If line 40 of the program in Example 1 is replaced by

```
40 PRINT #1, USING "& &  ###,###  ##,###"; S$, C$, A, P
```

the file will appear as follows:

```
Alabama  Montgomery   51,705   3,917<CR/LF>Alaska   Juneau
591,004      412<CR/LF>Arizona  Phoenix  114,000   2,794<CR/
LF/AR>
```

COMMENTS

1. When information is entered into a sequential file with a PRINT# statement, it usually is intended to be read from the file with a LINE INPUT# statement. (See the discussion of LINE INPUT# for further details.) For instance, the following program would display the entire contents of the file created in Example 2.

378

PRINT# and PRINT# USING

```
10 OPEN "STATES" FOR INPUT AS #1
20 FOR I = 1 TO 3
30    LINE INPUT #1, A$
40    PRINT A$
50 NEXT I
60 CLOSE #1
RUN
Alabama        Montgomery     51705      3917
Alaska         Juneau         591004     412
Arizona        Phoenix        114000     2794
Ok
```

2. The statement WRITE# also is used to enter information into a sequential file. WRITE# places the information on the disk in much the same way that WRITE displays information on the screen. For example, if line 40 of Example 1 were changed to

```
40 WRITE #1, S$, C$, A, P
```

the file would appear as follows.

```
"Alabama","Montgomery",51705,3917<CR/LF>"Alaska","Juneau",
591004,412<CR/LF>"Arizona","Phoenix",114000,2794<CR/LF/AR>
```

When information is entered into a sequential file with a WRITE# statement, it usually is intended to be read from the file with INPUT# statements.

3. In the event that information is entered into a sequential file using a PRINT# statement with the intent of being read by an INPUT# statement, quotation marks and commas must be inserted. For instance, if line 40 of Example 1 were changed to

```
40 PRINT #1, CHR$(34); S$; CHR$(34); CHR$(44);
    CHR$(34); C$; CHR$(34); CHR$(44); A; CHR$(44); P
```

the file would look almost like the one in Comment 2. (*Note:* CHR$(34) is a quotation mark and CHR$(44) is a comma.) The only difference is that the numbers would be preceded and followed by spaces.

4. You will not always hear the whirling sound of the disk drive as soon as a PRINT# statement is executed. The computer stores the pieces of information in a portion of memory set aside as a buffer for the file, then physically records them onto the disk when the buffer is full. CLOSE statements cause all information remaining in the buffer to be recorded.

5. The # sign in PRINT# statements can be written following the word PRINT with or without an intervening space. For instance, line 40 of Example 1 also could have been written **40 PRINT#1, S$; C$; A; P.**

PRINT# and PRINT# USING

6. PRINT# also is used in writing communications files. In this case, the statement

```
PRINT #n, A$
```

sends the string A$ to the communications file buffer. When using PRINT# with communications files, you often will want to use the semicolon option after the variable in order to suppress unwanted carriage returns from your transmission. The format shown above appends a carriage return to the transmitted variable.

7. Be careful that a file was OPENed FOR OUTPUT or APPEND before you enter information with PRINT#. In the event that the file was inadvertently OPENed for INPUT, executing PRINT# will not produce an error message. However, no information will be entered into the file.

APPLICATIONS

Sequential files provide a compact storage device for data. This data can then be accessed and used by other programs. The PRINT# statement can be used to construct sequential files.

PSET and PRESET

With the two graphics modes, the screen is subdivided into either 64,000 or 128,000 small rectangles, referred to as points. Any of these points can be turned on or off by the PSET and PRESET statements, and in medium-resolution graphics mode with color enabled, can be turned on in color. See Appendix C for a discussion of coordinates of points in graphics mode.

PART I HIGH-RESOLUTION GRAPHICS

In the high-resolution graphics mode, which is invoked by the statement SCREEN 2, there are only two colors, black and white. The statement

```
PSET (x,y)
```

turns on the point (x,y) in the color white. The statement

```
PRESET (x,y)
```

turns off the point (x,y), resulting in black. The coordinates can be given either in relative form with respect to the last point referenced or in absolute form.

EXAMPLES

1. ```
   10 SCREEN 2: CLS: KEY OFF
   20 PSET (32,10)
   30 PSET STEP (110,70)
   RUN (See Figure 1)
   ```

2. ```
   10 SCREEN 2: CLS: KEY OFF
   20 PSET STEP (-50,10)
   30 PSET (600,180)
   RUN (See Figure 2)
   ```

In line 20, the center of the screen was taken as the last point referenced.

3. The following program draws a solid square with its center point deleted.

   ```
   10 SCREEN 2: CLS: KEY OFF
   20 LINE (296,91)-(343,110),,BF
   30 PRESET (320,100)
   ```

4. The following program draws the graph of the function designated in line 10. (See Figure 3.) The x-axis is scaled from -6 to 6 and the y-axis from -40 to 40. Different scales can be selected by changing the values of R and S in line 20. Other functions can be graphed by changing the expression to the right of the equal sign in line 10.

PSET and PRESET

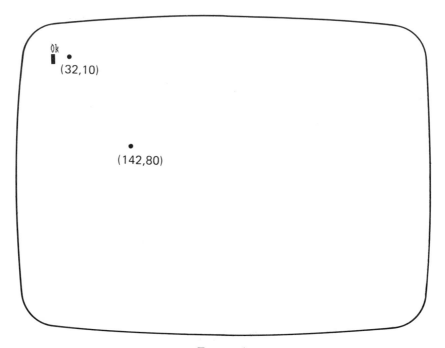

FIGURE 1

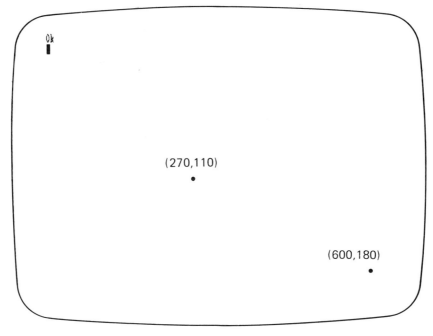

FIGURE 2

PSET and PRESET

```
10 DEF FNA(X) = 30*SIN(X)
20 R=6: S=40
30 SCREEN 2: CLS: KEY OFF
40 LINE (0,100)-(639,100): LINE (320,0)-(320,199)
50 LOCATE 7,34: PRINT S/2
60 LOCATE 14,60: PRINT R/2
70 LINE (480,95)-(480,105)
80 LINE (310,50)-(330,50)
90 FOR I = 0 TO 639
100    J = 100-(100/S)*FNA(R*(I-320)/319)
110    PSET (I,J)
120 NEXT I
```

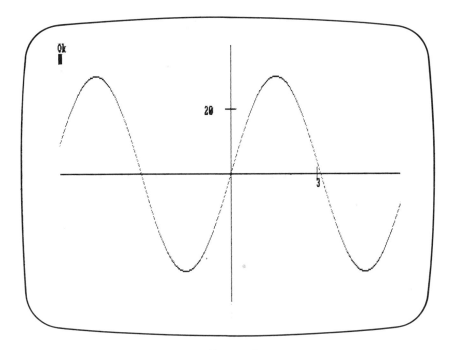

FIGURE 3

PART II   MEDIUM-RESOLUTION GRAPHICS

In medium-resolution graphics mode with color enabled, which is invoked by the statement **SCREEN 1,0**, there are 16 choices for background color and 2 choices of palette. Each palette consists of 4 colors, referred to as 0, 1, 2, and 3, where 0 is the same as the background color. (See the discussion of the COLOR statement for further details.) After a background color and palette have been selected, the statement

PSET and PRESET

```
PSET (x,y), n
```

colors the point (x,y) in color n of the palette. If the parameter n is omitted, the point will be colored in color 3. The statement

```
PRESET (x,y), n
```

does the same thing, except that omitting parameter n results in the point having color 0, the background color. The coordinates can be given either in relative form with respect to the last point referenced or in absolute form.

FURTHER EXAMPLE

5.   The following program sets a white background and colors 900 randomly chosen points with colors alternating from green to red to brown. Then, after a short pause, the points are changed to white one at a time (that is, they disappear into the background).

```
10 SCREEN 1,0: CLS: KEY OFF
20 X=RND(-1): COLOR 7,0
30 FOR I = 1 TO 900
40    PSET (319*RND,199*RND), (I MOD 3) + 1
50 NEXT I
60 FOR J=1 TO 2000: NEXT J
70 X=RND(-1)
80 FOR K = 1 TO 900
90    PRESET (319*RND,199*RND)
100 NEXT K
110 COLOR 0,1
```

The statement X=RND(-1) in lines 20 and 70 guarantees that the same sequence of numbers will be generated for use in lines 40 and 90.

COMMENTS

1.   In high-resolution graphics, the parameter n also can be used. If it is used, the values 0 and 2 result in the point being white, and the values 1 and 3 result in its being black.

2.   If the coordinates of the specified point in a PSET or PRESET statement are not integers, they are rounded to the nearest integer. If either (rounded) coordinate is outside of the range -32768 to 32767, the error message "Overflow" results. If the coordinates are in this range, but do not correspond to any point on the screen, no visual effect will take place on the screen. However, the coordinates become the coordinates of the last point referenced.

PSET and PRESET

Applications

1. PSET is used to draw graphs of functions, as in Example 4.

2. If (x,y) are the coordinates of a point on the screen, then the statement `PSET (x,y),POINT(x,y)` will specify (x,y) as the last point referenced.

3. Theoretically, any graphics display can be produced with PSET and PRESET. However, we usually try to incorporate other graphics statements, such as CIRCLE, DRAW, and LINE.

PUT (Files)

A random file can be thought of as consisting of an ordered set of records numbered 1, 2, 3, and so on. Random files are accessed by statements of the form **OPEN filespec AS #n LEN=g**. (See Appendix F and Part II of the discussion of OPEN for further details.) When a file is OPENed, a portion of memory referred to as a buffer is set aside to serve as an intermediary between the keyboard and the file. Information is placed into the buffer by LSET and RSET statements. Then the statement

```
PUT #n,r
```

copies the information into the file as record number r. If the number r is omitted, the record number will be the one following the number most recently used in a PUT or GET statement.

EXAMPLES

Note: These examples require an understanding of the FIELD, LSET, and RSET statements.

1.
```
10 OPEN "B:PRES" AS #1 LEN=22
20 FIELD #1, 20 AS NF$, 2 AS SF$
30 LSET NF$ = "George Washington"
40 LSET SF$ = "VA"
50 PUT #1,1
60 LSET NF$ = "James Monroe"
70 LSET SF$ = "VA"
80 PUT #1,5
90 LSET NF$ = "John Adams"
100 LSET SF$ = "MA"
110 PUT #1,2
120 LSET NF$ = "Thomas Jefferson"
130 LSET SF$ = "VA"
140 PUT #1
150 CLOSE #1
```

Records do not have to be assigned numbers in order. The first piece of information was assigned to record 1, the second to record 5, and the third to record 2. Since line 140 contains no record number, and since the most recent PUT statement assigned information to record 2, the information about "Thomas Jefferson" will be assigned to record 3.

2. The following program illustrates the fact that PUT does not erase the contents of the file buffer, but merely copies the contents of the buffer onto the disk.

```
10 OPEN "Test" AS #1 LEN = 10
20 FIELD #1, 5 AS AF$, 5 AS BF$
```

```
30 LSET AF$ = "abc"
40 RSET BF$ = "def"
50 PUT #1,1
60 LSET BF$ = "123"
70 PUT #1,2
80 FIELD #1, 10 AS TF$
90 PRINT TF$
100 CLOSE #1
RUN
abc    123
Ok
```

COMMENTS

1.   The # sign appearing in a PUT statement can be omitted. For instance, line 70 of Example 2 also can be written: **70 PUT 1,2.**

2.   Consider the program in Example 1. Line 80 not only assigned the data on "James Monroe" as record 5, but it also reserved a space of 66 characters for records 2, 3, and 4. Lines 110 and 140 filled in some of this space with records 2 and 3. However, space still remained for missing record 4. If we could look at the sector of the disk containing the file, it would appear something like this (where spaces have been denoted by asterisks):

George Washington***VAJohn Adams**********MAThomas Jefferson****
VA********************James Monroe********VA

3.   In versions of BASIC prior to BASIC 2.0, record numbers can have any value from 1 to 32767. Beginning with BASIC 2.0, record numbers can range from 1 to 16777215.

4.   You will not necessarily hear a disk drive whirl each time a PUT statement is executed. The computer waits until there is a substantial amount of data to be recorded onto the disk before actually completing the physical transfer.

5.   The GET statement is used to *retrieve* a record from the disk and place it into the buffer.

6.   The PUT statement may also be used with certain types of sophisticated communications files normally associated with a network. The statement **PUT #n,m** writes m bytes of the n file buffer to the communications adapter that has been associated with n in an OPEN COM statement. When the communications buffer is filled using LSET or RSET instructions, its contents are not transmitted until a PUT statement is given. PUT takes the first m characters of the buffer and transmits them. You may omit the parameter m, in which case PUT transmits the entire buffer. If you rewrite only a portion of the buffer, then any old information that has not been overwritten is still in the buffer and may be retransmitted.

PUT (Graphics)

The graphics PUT statement usually is used in conjunction with the graphics GET statement. (The reader should skim the discussion of the GET statement before proceeding.) Suppose that a rectangular portion of the screen has been recorded into an array by a GET statement. Then the statement

```
PUT (x,y), arrayname, PSET
```

will place an exact image of the rectangular region on the screen, positioned with its upper left-hand corner at the point (x,y).

EXAMPLES

1. In the following program, the letter B is displayed in a position that cannot be addressed with the LOCATE statement. See Figure 1.

```
10 SCREEN 1: CLS
20 LOCATE 1,1: PRINT "B"
30 DIM C%(9)
40 GET (0,0)-(7,7),C%
50 PUT (12,4), C%, PSET
60 LOCATE 3
```

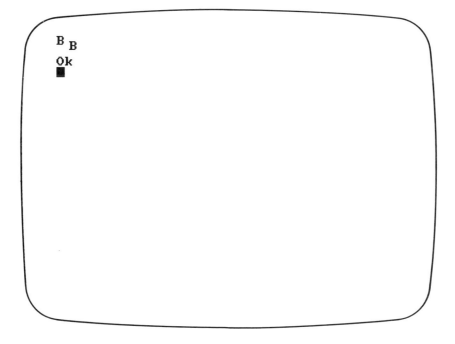

FIGURE 1

388

2.   The following program draws a truck and then moves it across the screen. See Figure 2.

```
10 CLS: SCREEN 1
20 CIRCLE (105,60),10: PAINT (105,60),3
30 CIRCLE (35,60),10: PAINT (35,60),3
40 LINE (21,21)-(101,40),,BF
50 LINE (21,40)-(119,60),,BF
60 DIM T(314): GET (20,21)-(119,70),T: CLS
70 FOR I = 1 TO 200
80    PUT (I,100),T,PSET
90 NEXT I
```

Lines 20-50 draw the truck, line 60 records its picture, and lines 70-90 move the truck across the screen. The rectangle chosen in line 60 was a little bigger than is necessary to contain the truck. It had a slight blank border on the left. This border erased the overhanging part of the previous truck each time a new picture of the truck was placed on the screen.

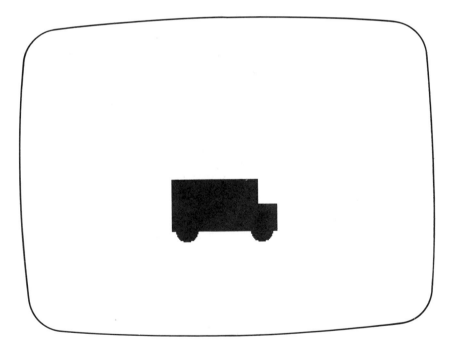

FIGURE 2

FURTHER DISCUSSION

The word PSET, which appears at the end of the above PUT statements, is referred to as the *action* of the statement. There are four other possible actions:

389

PUT (Graphics)

PRESET, AND, OR, and XOR. First consider the effects of these actions for high-resolution graphics mode.

PART I   ACTIONS IN HIGH-RESOLUTION GRAPHICS MODE

In high-resolution graphics mode, which is set by the statement SCREEN 2, each point is colored either black or white. Suppose that a rectangular portion of the screen has been recorded into an array by a GET statement. Then each of the actions effect the rectangular region having the point (x,y) as its upper left-hand corner and having the same size as the original rectangle.

The statement

```
PUT (x,y), arrayname, PRESET
```

displays a reversed image of the original rectangular region. Every point that was originally white will be black and vice versa.

The remaining three actions interact with whatever images are already in the rectangular part of the plane that is to be PUT upon. The action AND results in a point being white if it is already white and is also white in the image being transferred. The action OR results in a point being white if it is already white or if it is white in the image being transferred. The action XOR results in a point being white if it is either already white or if it is white in the image being transferred, but not both. If no action is specified in a PUT statement, then XOR is automatically invoked.

FURTHER EXAMPLES

3.   The following program draws a circle and GETs a large rectangle containing the circle. Figure 3 shows the original circle and the rectangle used in the GET statement. Figures 4 through 8 show the results obtained from adding an additional line that PUTs down a copy of the rectangle shifted to the left. Each of the five different actions is used.

```
10 SCREEN 2: CLS
20 DIM C(1543)
30 CIRCLE (360,100),120
40 PAINT (360,100)
50 GET (160,40)-(560,160),C
60 FOR T=1 TO 1200: NEXT T
```

4.   Line 80 of Example 2 can be modified by replacing PSET by PRESET, AND, OR, or XOR. Can you predict the visual effect of each of these changes? Give it some thought, then make the changes and run the program.

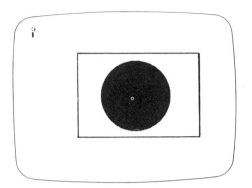

FIGURE 3
Original Circle

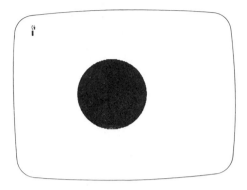

FIGURE 4
70 PUT (80,40),C,PSET

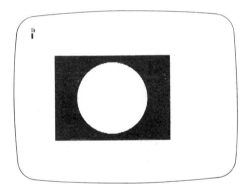

FIGURE 5
70 PUT (80,40),C,PRESET

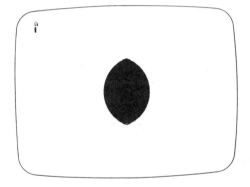

FIGURE 6
70 PUT (80,40),C,AND

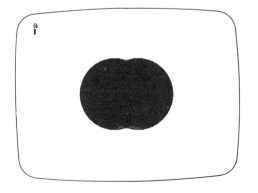

FIGURE 7
70 PUT (80,40),C,OR

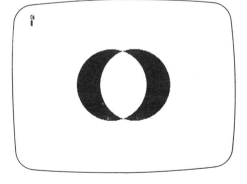

FIGURE 8
70 PUT (80,40),C,XOR

PUT (Graphics)

5. XOR is commonly used in animation. PUTting an image on top of itself with XOR has the effect of erasing the image and restoring the original background. The following program results in a ball bouncing around the screen. Press Ctrl-Break to terminate the program.

```
10 DIM B(5)
20 SCREEN 2: CLS: KEY OFF
30 CIRCLE (20,20),4: PAINT (20,20)
40 GET (16,16)-(24,24),B
50 BX = 20: BY = 20: DX = 1: DY = 1
60 IF BY>191 OR BY<5 THEN DY=-1*DY
70 IF BX>631 OR BX<5 THEN DX=-1*DX
80 OBX=BX:OBY=BY
90 BX=BX+DX: BY=BY+DY
100 PUT (OBX-4,OBY-4),B,XOR
110 PUT (BX-4,BY-4),B,XOR
120 GOTO 60
```

It happens that this bouncing ball will pass through every point of the screen. To convince yourself that this does indeed occur, delete line 100 and then run the program.

6. As a variation of Example 5, alter the above program by adding

```
25 LINE (320,0)-(410,199),,BF
```

A solid vertical rectangle will be drawn in the middle of the screen. After the ball passes through the rectangle, the rectangle will still be intact.

PART II   ACTIONS IN MEDIUM-RESOLUTION GRAPHICS MODE

In medium-resolution graphics mode with color enabled, which is invoked by the statement **SCREEN 1,0**, there are 16 choices of background color and two choices of palette. The COLOR statement is used to specify the background color and the palette. (See the discussion of the COLOR statement for further details.) Each palette consists of 4 colors, 0, 1, 2, and 3, where 0 is the background color.

Suppose that a rectangular portion of the screen has been recorded into an array by a GET statement. Then each of the actions affect the rectangular region having the point (x,y) as its upper left-hand corner, and having the same size as the original rectangle.

The action PSET causes an exact copy of the original rectangle to be displayed. The action PRESET displays a reverse image. Points of color 3 are changed to color 0 and vice versa. Similarly, colors 1 and 2 are interchanged.

PUT (Graphics)

The remaining three actions interact with the colors that are already in the rectangular part of the plane that is to be PUT upon. The color of each point is determined by its existing color on the screen, the color of the corresponding point in the original rectangle, and the action. The resulting colors are given by the following tables.

Original Color

		0 1 2 3	0 1 2 3	0 1 2 3
Screen	0	0 0 0 0	0 1 2 3	0 1 2 3
Color	1	0 1 0 1	1 1 3 3	1 0 3 2
	2	0 0 2 2	2 3 2 3	2 3 0 1
	3	0 1 2 3	3 3 3 3	3 2 1 0
		AND	OR	XOR

The resulting colors can also be obtained from a knowlege of logical operators and the binary representation of numbers. (See Appendix G.) For instance, to determine the result of colors 2 and 3 with respect to the action AND, write the two numbers in binary notation and apply the logical operator AND componentwise. Since 2 is 10 in binary notation, and 3 is 11, 10 AND 11 is 10 or 2.

COMMENTS

1.   The PUT statement requires Advanced BASIC. That is, the command BASICA must have been given when BASIC was invoked.

2.   If no action is specified in a PUT statement, then XOR is automatically invoked.

3.   If the original rectangle has dimensions h by v, then the coordinates (x,y) used in the PUT statement must be chosen such that y is between 0 and 199-v, and x is between 0 and 319-h in medium-resolution mode, and between 0 and 639-h in high-resolution mode.

APPLICATIONS

1.   The PUT statement is used extensively in animation, as illustrated in Examples 2 and 5.

2.   The PUT statement allows us to place characters anywhere we choose on the screen. We are not limited to the range of the LOCATE command. For instance, it can be used to label axes with considerable accuracy.

3.   We can use PSET to design a character set that is half the size of the standard character set. Then, using GET and PUT, we can display twice as many characters across the screen as normally possible. This is especially useful when designing small labels to use with graphs.

RANDOMIZE

A RANDOMIZE statement is only used preceding an RND function. An RND function randomly selects a number between 0 and .9999999. (See the discussion of the RND function for further details.) Consider the following program:

```
10 PRINT RND;RND;RND
RUN
 .2734893  .7892671  .4198236
Ok
RUN
 .2734893  .7892671  .4198236
Ok
```

Each time this program runs, it will produce the same sequence of three numbers. Think of the computer as having a long list of numbers in the range 0 to .9999999. For each RUN of a program, the computer assigns the first number of the list to the first RND that it encounters, the second number of the list to the next RND, and so on. The RANDOMIZE statement is used to change the list. Selecting a new list is referred to as *reseeding* the random number generator.

When the statement

```
RANDOMIZE
```

is encountered during the RUNning of a program, the computer suspends execution and displays

```
Random Number Seed (-32768 to 32767)?
```

The user then types a number in the specified range to reseed the random number generator.

EXAMPLE

1.
```
10 RANDOMIZE
20 PRINT RND;RND;RND
RUN
RANDOM NUMBER SEED (-32768 TO 32767)? 56
 .6244104  .7637128  .6741136
OK
RUN
RANDOM NUMBER SEED (-32768 TO 32767)? -12.34
 .3847559  .5764265  .9547228
OK
RUN
```

```
RANDOM NUMBER SEED (-32768 TO 32767)? 56
  .6244104  .7637128  .6741136
OK
```

Notice that responding with the same seed number produced the same sequence of random numbers.

FURTHER DISCUSSION

A variation of the RANDOMIZE statement allows for reseeding of the random number generator without interrupting the running of the program. The statement

```
RANDOMIZE n
```

where n is a number from -32768 to 32767 has the same effect as using the RANDOMIZE statement and responding with the number n after the question is posed. For instance, the program in Example 1 can be altered as follows:

```
10 RANDOMIZE 56
20 PRINT RND;RND;RND
RUN
  .6244104  .7637128  .6741136
Ok
```

COMMENTS

1. In BASIC 1.1, if the response to the seed question is not a whole number, it will be rounded to a whole number. Hence, two responses that round to the same value have the same effect when used to reseed the random number generator. (Such is not the case in BASIC 2.0 and later versions.) If the (rounded) value is not in the proper range, an "Overflow" error message results.

2. The RANDOMIZE statement can be followed with an expression instead of a numeric constant. For instance, we can have **RANDOMIZE A+2*B**.

3. The RND function can also be reseeded by means of the RND(x) variation. If a RANDOMIZE statement precedes an RND(x) function, the RND(x) function dominates.

4. Example 2 makes use of the function TIME\$ to reseed the random number generator. BASIC version 2.0 added a new function, TIMER, that simplifies this task considerably. The value of the function TIMER is the number of seconds from time 0 (midnight or system reset) to the current time. The statement

```
RANDOMIZE TIMER
```

RANDOMIZE

automatically uses the computer's clock to reseed the random number generator. See Example 3.

FURTHER EXAMPLES

2.
```
10 N =(1+VAL(RIGHT$(TIME$,2)))*(1+VAL(MID$(TIME$,4,2)))
20 PRINT N
30 RANDOMIZE N
40 PRINT RND, RND, RND
RUN
 161
 .1503198       .2172346       .2197985
Ok
RUN
 1978
 .700857        .3156232       .6746325
Ok
```

The number N was [1+(seconds)] times [1+(minutes)]. The 1s were added to keep the value of N from being zero too often.

3. The following program, which requires BASIC version 2.0 or later, is an improvement over Example 2.

```
10 PRINT TIMER
20 RANDOMIZE TIMER
30 PRINT RND, RND, RND
RUN
 696.18
 .6451318       .1390485       .2590441
Ok
RUN
 705.57
 .4862573       .9281721       .9541734
Ok
```

READ statements are only used in conjunction with DATA statements. DATA statements store a list of constants, and READ statements assign successive values from the list to variables.

Suppose that a program has just one DATA statement consisting of, say, several string constants, and the first READ statement to be encountered is the statement

```
READ A$
```

This statement results in the variable A$ being assigned the first constant in the DATA statement. The statement **READ A$** is like a LET statement. It's as if we said "LET A$ = the first constant in the list specified by the DATA statement." If the next READ statement encountered is **READ B$** then the variable B$ will be assigned the second constant in the DATA statement as its value. Successive READ statements assign successive constants to variables.

EXAMPLE

```
1. 10 DATA RED, WHITE, BLUE, "JULY 4,1776"
   20 READ A$
   30 READ B$
   40 READ C$
   50 READ D$
   60 PRINT A$, B$, C$, D$
   RUN
   RED            WHITE          BLUE          JULY 4,1776
   Ok
```

DISCUSSION

A single READ statement can assign values to several variables at once. For instance, lines 20-50 of Example 1 can be replaced by the single line

```
20 READ A$, B$, C$, D$
```

In general, a program might have several DATA statements appearing at various places in the program. READ statements treat the constants as if they were combined into one long DATA statement, with the constants from the lowest numbered DATA statement coming first, the constants from the next higher numbered DATA statement coming next, and so on.

Up to now, we have focused on DATA statements consisting only of string constants. However, DATA statements also can consist of numeric constants or a mixture of numeric and string constants. The important point to keep in mind is that the constants appearing in DATA statements should be of the same types as the variables to which they are assigned. Otherwise, the error message "Syntax error" or an unintended assignment might result. (See Examples 6 and 7.)

READ

COMMENTS

1.   See the discussion of the DATA statement for some useful comments about the two types of constants.

2.   If the DATA statements contain fewer constants than are called for by the READ statements, the error message "Out of DATA" results.

3.   The RESTORE statement can be used in a program to cause subsequent READ statements to go to any DATA statement for the next constant to be assigned. See the discussion of RESTORE for further details.

4.   There are three kinds of numeric constants and variables: integer, single-, and double-precision. Numeric variables occurring in READ statements can be assigned numeric constants having different precisions. However, if they differ, the numeric constant will be converted to the precision of the variable whenever possible.

FURTHER EXAMPLES

2.
```
10 DATA JAN, FEB, MAR
20 DATA 23, 17, 34
30 READ A$, B$, C$
40 PRINT A$, B$, C$
50 READ A, B, C
60 PRINT A, B, C
RUN
JAN             FEB             MAR
 23              17              34
Ok
```

3.
```
10 READ A, B$
20 DATA 123.45
30 READ C$, D
40 DATA SIX, SEVEN, 8, 9
50 PRINT A, B$, C$, D
RUN
 123.45         SIX             SEVEN           8
Ok
```

Consider line 10. After assigning the value 123.45 to variable A, all the values in line 20 were used. Hence, the next DATA statement (line 40) was entered to find the next value. Also notice that the value 9 in line 40 was never assigned to a variable. There can be an excess of constants, but not an excess of variables.

4.
```
10 FOR I = 1 TO 4
20    READ A
30    PRINT A;
40 NEXT I
50 DATA 6, 7, 8
```

```
RUN
 6  7  8
Out of DATA in 20
Ok
```

Note that the line number given in the error message is that of the READ statement, not the DATA statement.

```
5.  10 GOTO 30
    20 DATA Twenty
    30 READ A$
    40 DATA Forty
    50 PRINT A$
    RUN
    Twenty
    Ok
```

The program seems to skip line 20 and take no notice of it. However, the READ statement does not care that line 20 was skipped. It searches through the entire program and finds the lowest numbered DATA statement, no matter where the statement occurs.

```
6.  10 DATA Ten
    20 READ A
    30 PRINT A
    RUN
    Syntax error in 10
    Ok
    10 DATA Ten
```

```
7.  10 DATA 10
    20 READ A$
    30 PRINT A$
    RUN
    10
    Ok
```

Did you expect this program to produce an error statement? The READ statement treated 10 as a string constant and assigned it to the string variable A$. Had line 30 been **30 PRINT A$ + 5**, the result would not be 15 but rather the message "Type mismatch in 30."

```
8.  10 DATA 1.6
    20 READ A%
    30 PRINT A%
    RUN
     2
    Ok
```

The single-precision constant 1.6 was rounded to 2 when converted to an integer constant. (See the discussion of CINT.)

REM

It is a good idea to make notes about a program to remind you of the purposes of its various parts. A statement of the form

```
REM remark
```

allows the programmer to enter a remark as a line of a program. The remark is displayed whenever the program is LISTed, but is overlooked when the program is executed.

EXAMPLES

1.
```
10 REM Compound Interest Program
20 INPUT "Amount Deposited"; A
30 INPUT "Interest rate per period";I
40 INPUT "Number of periods"; N
50 B = A*(1+I)^N : REM Formula for Compound Interest
60 PRINT USING "Balance:$$######,.##";B
RUN
Amount Deposited? 1000
Interest rate per period? .02
Number of periods? 16
Balance:    $1,372.78
Ok
```

When this program is LISTed, it appears exactly as above. When the program was run, the computer took no action when it encountered the REM statements, and proceeded to the next line of the program. In the above illustration, it computed the balance after four years on a deposit of one thousand dollars at an interest rate of 8% compounded quarterly.

2.
```
10 REM     ******************************************
20 REM     *                                        *
30 REM     *        THIS PROGRAM WRITTEN BY          *
40 REM     *                                        *
50 REM     *            JOHN SMITH                   *
60 REM     *                                        *
70 REM     ******************************************
80
 .
 .
```

COMMENTS

1. An apostrophe can be used as a substitute for the word REM. For instance, in Example 1, lines 10 and 50 could have been written:

400

```
10 'Compound Interest Program

50 B = A*(1+I)^N : 'Formula for Compound Interest
```

2. Usually, when a remark is placed at the end of a line using an apostrophe, as in line 50 of Comment 1, the colon isn't necessary. That is, line 50 could also have been written

```
50 B = A*(1+I)^N    'Formula for Compound Interest
```

The colon is only necessary at the end of DATA statements.

```
10 DATA Ryan 'pitcher
20 DATA 100.9 'fastest pitch (mph)
30 READ A$: PRINT A$
40 READ B: PRINT B
RUN
Ryan 'pitcher
Syntax error in 20
Ok
20 DATA 100.9 'fastest pitch (mph)
```

3. Whenever a REM statement is used as one of several statements on a single line, the REM statement must be last. Otherwise, the statements following it will be overlooked by the computer. For instance,

```
10 PRINT "ONE": REM Counting Program: PRINT "TWO"
RUN
ONE
Ok
```

Since the REM statement preceded the statement PRINT "TWO", the statement PRINT "TWO" was not executed.

4. REM statements slow execution of the program slightly. Hence, it is not a good idea to include them in a loop that will be executed many times. Some programmers maintain two copies of a program, one with REM statements and one without. That way they have a well-documented program and also a version that runs quickly and uses up less memory space. Utility programs are available that will remove all REM statements from a program.

5. A GOTO or GOSUB statement may branch to a REM statement. If so, the computer will just execute the next line after the REM statement. However, this is not regarded as good programming practice. If the REM statement is later removed, so that the program will take up less space and execute faster, the GOTO or GOSUB will have no destination.

REM

APPLICATIONS

1. Most long programs consist of several parts. Some programmers like to have space separating these parts on the printout of the program. This can be accomplished by preceding each part with a few lines consisting of just line numbers followed by apostrophes.

2. A subroutine is a subprogram that is called several times during execution of the program to perform some specific task. It is good programming practice to precede each subroutine with a REM statement stating the task performed by the subroutine. This is helpful if you go back to the program after a considerable time or if another person tries to understand the program.

3. When debugging a program you might want to remove a line from the program and put it back later. Instead of deleting it and later retyping it, just put an apostrophe after the line number. The line will be treated as a REM statement and will not be executed. Later, all you have to do is remove the apostrophe.

RENUM

When writing a program, we usually number the lines with a regular increment. Most of the programs in this book have 10 as the first line number and also use 10 as the increment between successive line numbers. However, before a program runs correctly, we often have to insert additional lines between the original lines. We can return to the more esthetically pleasing regular incrementation of lines by invoking the command RENUM. Specifically, the command

    RENUM

will change the line numbers of the program currently in memory so that the first line number is 10 and successive line numbers increase by 10.

A variation of the RENUM command allows us to select any numbers we like for the first line and the increment. The command

    RENUM m, ,n

will change the line numbers so that the first line number is m and successive line numbers increase by n. If either m or n is not specified, it assumes the default value 10.

We also have the option of changing only line numbers from some point on, instead of beginning with the lowest line number. The command

    RENUM m,r,n

begins the renumbering with line number r. The new number of line r will be m, and successive line numbers will increase by n. Care must be exercised when using this variation of the RENUM command. The number m must be greater than the number of every line preceding line r.

COMMENTS

1. The RENUM command cannot be invoked if so doing would result in a line receiving a number greater than the largest allowable line number, 65529. For instance, if a program has 7000 lines, then the command **RENUM** results in an "Illegal function call" message. However, the command **RENUM ,,5** is valid.

2. The RENUM command automatically changes the line numbers referred to in GOTO, GOSUB, THEN, ELSE, ON . . . GOTO, ON . . . GOSUB, and ERL statements.

3. Suppose that the original program was incorrect in that it contained a line such as **100 GOTO 200** but the program did not have a line numbered 200. A RENUM command would result in the error message "Undefined line number 200 in 100". The number 200 would not be changed, but the number 100

RENUM

would be changed. Analogous results hold for errors involving the other statements mentioned in Comment 2.

EXAMPLES

```
1.  1 PRINT "ONE"
    2 PRINT "TWO" : GOTO 4
    3 PRINT "THREE"
    4 PRINT "FOUR"
    RENUM
    Ok
    LIST
    10 PRINT "ONE"
    20 PRINT "TWO" : GOTO 40
    30 PRINT "THREE"
    40 PRINT "FOUR"
    Ok
    RENUM 80,20,5
    Ok
    LIST
    10 PRINT "ONE"
    80 PRINT "TWO" : GOTO 90
    85 PRINT "THREE"
    90 PRINT "FOUR"
    Ok
```

2. The RENUM command cannot be used to interchange the order of two lines.

```
    25 PRINT "TWO"
    30 PRINT "ONE"
    RENUM 15,30,5
    Illegal function call
    Ok
```

3. A well-structured program contains numerous subroutines. The following technique can be used to keep track of the line numbers of the subroutines, even when the lines are RENUMbered. Suppose that Subroutine One occupies lines 200-300, Subroutine Two occupies lines 400-600, and Subroutine Three occupies lines 800-850. To obtain the locations of all of the subroutines, execute `F=1:GOTO 10`.

```
    10 IF F=0 THEN 60
    20 LIST 30-50
    30 LIST 200-300: 'Subroutine One
    40 LIST 400-600: 'Subroutine Two
```

```
50 LIST 800-850: 'Subroutine Three
60 REM Beginning of Program
```

APPLICATIONS

1. The RENUM command can be used to spread out line numbers if we haven't left enough room to insert new lines. On the other hand, the command can be used to tighten up a program for which the higher line numbers run the risk of exceeding 65529.

2. The RENUM command can be used to take a subroutine from one program and insert it into another program. For instance, suppose you want to take the 20 lines of program A with numbers ranging from 100 to 190 and put these lines into program B with numbers ranging from 800 to 990. The steps would be

> LOAD program A
> DELETE all lines except 100-190
> execute the command **RENUM 800**
> SAVE this program in ASCII format
> LOAD program B
> MERGE the program saved in the 4th step.

3. The statement **RENUM 65529,65529** is useful in debugging a program. It will not change any line numbers but will point out all incorrect line references.

```
10 GOTO 20
RENUM 65529,65529
Undefined line 20 in 10
Ok
```

∥RESET

Data files are created on disks and accessed by OPEN statements. In addition, OPEN statements can be used to access the screen, printer, and keyboard. When a file or a device is OPENed, it is assigned a number and referred to by this number when written to or read from. (See the discussion of OPEN for further details.) Also, each number has a corresponding reserved portion of memory, called its buffer, that temporarily holds information until it is processed. After one or more files or devices have been OPENed, the statement

    RESET

sends all of the information currently in the buffers to the appropriate places and severs all associations between numbers and files or devices.

COMMENTS

1. RESET can only be used with Advanced BASIC. That is, the command BASICA must have been given when BASIC was invoked.

2. The statement RESET has almost the same effect as the CLOSE statement with no file numbers specified.

EXAMPLE

```
10 OPEN "SCRN:" FOR OUTPUT AS #1
20 PRINT #1, "Joan Benoit"
30 RESET
40 PRINT #1, "Greg Meyer"
RUN
Joan Benoit
Bad file number in 40
Ok
```

RESTORE

The RESTORE statement is used only in conjunction with DATA and READ statements. DATA statements store a list of constants, and READ statements assign successive values from the list to variables. (See the discussions of the DATA and READ statements.) Suppose that the statement

```
RESTORE
```

is encountered during the execution of a program. Nothing happens until the next READ statement is encountered. That READ statement then acts as if it were the first READ statement encountered during the execution of the program. It assigns values beginning with the first constant of the lowest numbered DATA statement.

Here is another way to think of the RESTORE statement. Imagine that at any time there is an arrow pointing at the next DATA constant to be accessed by a READ statement. Each time a READ statement assigns a value to a variable, the arrow moves to the next DATA constant. When the RESTORE statement is encountered, the arrow is set back to the first constant of the lowest numbered DATA statement.

We also may wish to read items beginning with a DATA statement other than the first one, or read items beginning with a DATA statement specified by the user in response to an INPUT statement. The statement

```
RESTORE n
```

resets the arrow to point to the first constant of the DATA statement in line n. If line n is not a DATA statement, then the arrow will point to the first constant of the first DATA statement that occurs after line n.

EXAMPLES

1.  ```
    10 DATA One, Two, Three
    20 READ A$, B$
    30 RESTORE
    40 READ C$
    50 PRINT A$, B$, C$
    RUN
    One            Two            One
    Ok
    ```

2.  ```
    10 READ A, B, C, D
    20 PRINT A; B; C; D
    30 RESTORE 70
    40 READ A, B
    50 PRINT A; B
    60 DATA 1, 2
    ```

RESTORE

```
70 DATA 3, 4
RUN
 1  2  3  4
 3  4
Ok
```

COMMENT

The commands CLEAR, MERGE, RUN, and CHAIN MERGE automatically perform a RESTOREation of data items. This happens even with CHAIN MERGE statements using the ALL option. Also, deleting or entering a program line causes data to be RESTOREd.

```
10 DATA 1,2
20 READ A: PRINT A
30 CLEAR
40 READ B: PRINT A; B
RUN
 1
 0  1
Ok
```

APPLICATIONS

1. The RESTORE statement can be used to access a directory. The following program looks up phone numbers in a simplified telephone directory.

```
10 INPUT "NAME";N$
20 IF N$="*" THEN END
30 READ A$, B$
40 IF A$ <> N$ GOTO 30
50 PRINT B$
60 RESTORE
70 GOTO 10
80 DATA AL, 123-4567, TOM, 987-6543
90 DATA JANE, 202-765-4321,BILL, 666-6666
RUN
NAME? TOM
987-6543
NAME? JANE
202-765-4321
NAME? *
Ok
```

If a name not in the directory is given in response to the question, an "Out of DATA in 20" message results. A friendlier way to handle a name not in the

408

directory is to report it with a PRINT statement, rather than having the program terminate due to an error. To achieve a friendly response when a name is not found, add a trailer value to the directory; for instance **100 DATA ZZZZZ,000-0000**. Then add **35 IF A$="ZZZZZ" THEN PRINT "Name not found.":GOTO 60**

2. The RESTORE statement can be used to display words vertically on the screen. Consider the following program:

```
10 DATA ONE, TWO, THREE, FOUR, FIVE, SIX
20 FOR I = 1 TO 5
30    FOR J = 1 TO 6
40      READ C$
50      D$=MID$(C$,I,1)
60      PRINT TAB(5*J) D$;
70    NEXT J
80    PRINT
90    RESTORE
100 NEXT I
RUN
      O    T    T    F    F    S
      N    W    H    O    I    I
      E    O    R    U    V    X
                E    R    E
                E
Ok
```

‖RESUME

Appendix E lists the error messages that can result when running a program. An error handling subroutine can be written to take corrective measures instead of having an error message displayed and the program terminated. Suppose that the error handling subroutine begins on line n. After the statement **ON ERROR GOTO** n is encountered, any error (other than "Division by zero") will cause the program to branch to line n (the first line of the routine). This process is referred to as *error trapping*. RESUME statements are located at the end of the error handling subroutine to branch to other parts of the program. The statement

RESUME

causes the program to branch back to the statement at which the error occurred. The error handling subroutine, we hope, took care of whatever problem triggered the error. The statement

RESUME NEXT

causes the program to branch to the statement following the statement at which the error occurred. The statement

RESUME m

causes the program to branch to line m.

EXAMPLES

1.
```
10 ON ERROR GOTO 60
20 INPUT "Type a positive number: ", N
30 R = SQR(N)
40 PRINT "The square root of"; N; "is"; R
50 END
60 N=(-1)*N
70 RESUME
RUN
Type a positive number: 64
The square root of 64 is 8
Ok
RUN
Type a positive number: -2
The square root of 2 is 1.414214
Ok
```

This program assumes that if the user types a negative number, the negative sign was not intended. In the second run, the lines were executed in the following order: 10,20,30,60,70,30,40,50.

410

2.   See the discussion of ON ERROR for examples using RESUME NEXT and RESUME m.

COMMENTS

1.   Error handling subroutines should be preceded by an END or STOP statement to protect them from being entered unintentionally. For instance, in Example 1, if line 50 was deleted, the RESUME statement would have been encountered without an error having occurred. This would have resulted in an infinite loop involving lines 60 and 70.

2.   Suppose that an error has been trapped, but that a RESUME statement has not yet been encountered. If one of the commands CHAIN MERGE, CLEAR, MERGE, or RUN is executed, or if a program line is entered or deleted, then the computer will forget that it is executing an error trapping routine. When RESUME is reached, the message ''RESUME without error'' will be displayed.

3.   When an error occurs, an error-condition flag is set. The RESUME statement turns off this flag to show that the error handling routine has been completed. If another error occurs while the flag is still set, the program will terminate and an error message will be displayed.

4.   The statement **RESUME** can also be written **RESUME 0**.

RETURN

A RETURN statement is always preceded by a GOSUB statement. The combination provides a variation of a GOTO statement. When the statement GOSUB n is encountered, the program branches to line n; that is, line n will be the next line executed. However, the computer remembers where it branched from and, as soon as it encounters the statement

    RETURN

it branches back to the statement after the GOSUB statement. If several GOSUB statements are executed before a RETURN is encountered, the program branches to the statement after the most recently encountered GOSUB.

As a model of the way the computer keeps track of GOSUB statements, think of the location of each GOSUB statement as being written on a sheet of paper. When the first GOSUB is encountered, its sheet of paper is placed on a table. When the second GOSUB is encountered, its sheet of paper is placed on top of the first one. As each GOSUB is encountered, its sheet is placed on top of the pile. When a RETURN statement is encountered, the piece of paper that is currently on the top of the pile is used to determine where to branch back to, and then this piece of paper is discarded. (This is called a "LIFO," Last In First Out, or "pushdown" stack.)

A variation of the RETURN statement allows us to discard the top piece of paper from the pile without branching to the statement following its GOSUB statement. Instead, we can branch anywhere we choose. The statement

    RETURN t

discards the top piece of paper from the pile and branches to line t.

COMMENTS

1. Consider the pile of sheets of paper discussed above. In the event that a RETURN statement is encountered and the pile is empty, the error message "RETURN without GOSUB" results. This can happen if a RETURN statement is encountered before any GOSUB has been executed, if more RETURN statements have been encountered than GOSUB statements, or if the pending GOSUB statements have been forgotten due to the execution of one of the commands, CHAIN MERGE, CLEAR, LOAD, MERGE, or RUN, or forgotten due to the entering or deletion of a program line.

2. In order to use the RETURN t variation, the computer must be operating with Advanced BASIC. That is, we must have typed BASICA when invoking BASIC.

3. RETURN t can actually be used to discard the top piece of paper from the pile without really branching anywhere. Just make sure that RETURN t is the last statement on its line and take t to be the number of the next line.

412

4. If more GOSUB statements than RETURN statements are encountered during the execution of a program, no error message will result. Those GOSUB statements for which no matching RETURN statement is found will appear to act like GOTO statements. However, if a program ends with some GOSUB statements unmatched, and the RETURN statement is encountered in direct mode, the program will resume execution with the statement after the most recently executed and unmatched GOSUB statement. Note, however, that the computer will forget any unmatched GOSUB statements if one of the commands CLEAR, CHAIN MERGE, MERGE, or RUN is executed, or if a program line is entered or deleted.

EXAMPLES

See the discussion of the GOSUB and RETURN statements for three standard examples. The following examples make use of the RETURN t variation.

1.
```
10 PRINT "One ";
20 GOSUB 100
30 PRINT "Thirty"
40 PRINT "Three ";
90 END
100 PRINT "Two ";
110 RETURN 40
RUN
One Two Three
Ok
```

2.
```
10 PRINT "One ";
20 GOSUB 100
30 PRINT "Four"
90 END
100 PRINT "Two ";
110 GOSUB 200
120 PRINT "One twenty"
130 RETURN
200 PRINT "Three ";
210 RETURN 220
220 RETURN
RUN
One Two Three Four
Ok
```

At first, it looks like we might be in trouble, since the program contains more RETURN statements than GOSUB statements. However, line 210 discards the piece of paper corresponding to the GOSUB in line 110, and so the RETURN in line 130 is never encountered. The sequence in which the lines are executed is 10, 20, 100, 110, 200, 210, 220, 30, 90.

RETURN

APPLICATIONS

A subroutine is a subprogram that resides inside a larger program. The subroutine performs some specific task that may have to be repeated many times during the running of the main program. Subroutines usually contain RETURN statements and are entered by GOSUB statements branching to their first lines.

RIGHT$

If A$ is a string and n is a positive whole number, then

```
RIGHT$(A$,n)
```

is the string consisting of the rightmost n characters of A$.

COMMENTS

1.   There are 256 different characters that can be used in a string. These characters and their ASCII values are listed in Appendix A. All of these characters are counted when they appear in a string, even the undisplayable characters, such as "carriage return," "beep," and "cursor down." All spaces are counted, even leading and trailing spaces.

2.   Although the RIGHT$ function is defined only for strings, it can be used indirectly to extract a specified number of digits from a number. For instance, if A is a whole number (not expressed in floating-point form), then the n least significant digits of A are VAL(RIGHT$(STR$(A),n)).

3.   The functions LEFT$ and MID$ are similar to RIGHT$.

4.   The value of n in RIGHT$(A$,n) can be any number between 0 and 255.4999. If n is not a whole number, it will be rounded to the nearest whole number. If the (rounded) value is 0, RIGHT$ will return the empty string, "". If the value is greater than the number of characters in A$, then RIGHT$ will return the entire string A$.

EXAMPLES

1.   PRINT RIGHT$("Truman, Harry S.",9),VAL(RIGHT$(STR$(1234),2))
```
    Harry S.     34
   Ok
```

2.   ```
10 C$ = "A Very Merry"+CHR$(31)+"Xmas"
20 PRINT RIGHT$(C$,11)
RUN
 Merry
       Xmas
Ok
```

(*Note:* CHR$(31) is the undisplayable character "cursor down.")

3.   The following program sets up a timer for a specified number (up to 59) of seconds.

```
10 INPUT "Number of seconds"; S%
20 TIME$ ="00:00:00": CLS
30 S$ = RIGHT$(TIME$,2)
40 LOCATE 12,20: PRINT S$
```
```

RIGHT$

```
50 IF VAL(S$) = S% THEN BEEP: END
60 GOTO 30
```

4. The following program isolates a person's last name from her full name.

```
10 INPUT "Full name (f/m/l)"; N$
20 FOR I = 1 TO LEN(N$)
30 A$ = RIGHT$(N$,I)
40 IF ASC(A$) = 32 THEN 70
50 NEXT I
60 A$ = " "+N$
70 PRINT "Your last name is"; A$; "."
RUN
Full name (f/m/l)? Elizabeth Frances Gandyra
Your last name is Gandyra.
Ok
```

APPLICATIONS

The RIGHT$ function is used to manipulate strings, as shown in Example 4.

The command RMDIR is not available in versions of BASIC before BASIC 2.0.

Versions of BASIC beginning with 2.0 support a hierarchial directory structure in which files and directories are specified by paths through the structure. See Appendix D for a detailed discussion of directories and paths. Directories are created with the command MKDIR. Any file can be removed with the command KILL. Directories can be removed only if they contain no files or sub-directories. If so, then the removal is carried out by the command

```
RMDIR A$
```

where A$ is a path from the current directory to the directory to be removed.

EXAMPLES

The following examples refer to the tree diagram presented in Appendix D.

1. Suppose that the disk is in drive C. The following sequence of commands will remove the directory NOVEL.

```
KILL "C:\ANN\NOVEL\CH1"
KILL "C:\ANN\NOVEL\CH2"
KILL "C:\ANN\NOVEL\CH3"
RMDIR "C:\ANN\NOVEL"
```

If drive C is the default drive, then C: may be omitted from each of these commands. Also, if the root directory is the current directory, it would not be necessary to precede the name ANN with a back-slash.

2. Suppose that the disk is in the default drive, and that the current directory for that drive is ANN. Then the last command in Example 1 can be replaced by

```
RMDIR "NOVEL"
```

COMMENTS

1. The string expression for the path must not be longer than 63 characters.

2. The entries " . <Dir> " and " .. <Dir> ", which are placed by BASIC into every directory, cannot be killed. These are the only two entries which are allowed in a directory being removed by RMDIR.

RND

The true capabilities of the computer are revealed as we explore the various applications of the RND function. This function is pivotal in simulation, whether it be the simulation of a game of chance or of a complex business operation.

The RND function should be thought of as randomly selecting a number between 0 and .9999999. However, when used in conjunction with other functions, it can select a number at random from any collection of numbers.

Consider the spinner pictured in Figure 1. Think of the circumference of the circle as having length one, and every point on the circumference as being labeled with its clockwise distance from the top of the circle. Suppose that the spinner is well balanced and that the numbers can be read to 7 significant digits. Each time the pointer is flicked, it will give a number from 0 to .9999999. The spinner selects a number at *random* from 0 to .9999999. Whenever we use the RND function in an application, we can think of it as such a spinner.

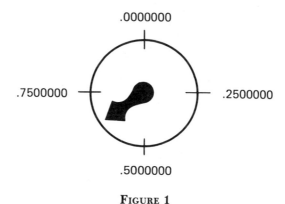

.0000000

.7500000 .2500000

.5000000

FIGURE 1

EXAMPLES

1.  ```
    PRINT RND; RND; RND; RND+7
     .6291626   .1948297   .6305799   7.862575
    Ok
    ```

2.  ```
    10 A = RND: B = 5*RND
    20 PRINT A;B;B+2
    RUN
     .6291626   .9741485   2.974149
    Ok
    ```

(*Note:* You will get different results than those shown above.)

FURTHER DISCUSSION

The RND function is not truly random, but calculates its way through the same list of ''random'' numbers every time a program is executed. Consider the following program.

```
10 FOR I = 1 TO 3
20    PRINT RND;
30 NEXT I
RUN
 .6291626   .1948297   .6305799
Ok
RUN
 .6291626   .1948297   .6305799
Ok
```

This program will produce the same three numbers every time it is run. In general, whenever a program is run, RND produces the same sequence of numbers. This can be quite useful for debugging purposes, however, we usually do not want a sequence of random numbers to be so predictable. Variations of the RND function allow us to change the sequence of numbers that will be generated.

Let x be any negative number. Then insertion of any statement of the form

```
A = RND(x)
```

results in a specific sequence being generated. The sequence depends on x, and different values of x result in different sequences. (However, multiplying x by any power of two produces the same sequence as x.)

Selecting a new sequence is referred to as *reseeding* the random number generator. The random number generator also can be reseeded via the RANDOMIZE statement. (See the discussion of RANDOMIZE for details.)

The use of RND(x), where x is positive, has the same effect as RND. It just generates the next random number. Invoking RND(0) results in the previous value of RND being repeated.

The sequences of numbers that are generated are called *pseudo*random because they appear to be random, and satisfy many tests of random numbers, but are in fact generated by a simple algorithm which gives the same result each time.

FURTHER EXAMPLES

3.
```
10 FOR I = 1 TO 5
20      PRINT RND;
30 NEXT I
RUN
```

RND

```
    .6291626   .1948297   .6305799   .8625749   .736353
Ok
NEW
10 INPUT B
20 A = RND(B)
30 FOR I = 1 TO 3
40   PRINT RND;
50 NEXT I
RUN
? 0
    .6291626   .1948297   .6305799
Ok
PRINT RND(7)
    .8625749
Ok
RUN
? -5
    .5568615   .7943624   .4965937
Ok
PRINT RND(7)
    .833198
Ok
RUN
? -56.78
    .4585411   .5263355   .4896391
Ok
RUN
? -5
    .5568615   .7943624   .4965937
Ok
RUN
? -20
    .5568615   .7943624   .4965937
Ok
PRINT RND(0)
    .4965937
Ok
```

4. The following program uses the function TIME$ to reseed the random number generator.

```
10 INPUT "Ask a question:",Q$
20 A = RND(-VAL(RIGHT$(TIME$,2)))
30 IF A<.5 THEN PRINT "Yes" ELSE PRINT "No"
RUN
Ask a question: Should I play bridge tonight?
```

420

```
Yes
Ok
```

Applications

1.   It is possible to simulate the outcome of rolling a pair of dice. Each die will show a whole number from 1 to 6. If A is a number between 0 and .9999999, then 6*A will be between 0 and 5.999999. If we throw away the decimal portion of the number by using the function FIX, we will have a whole number from 0 to 5. Hence, the result of

```
FIX(6*RND)+1
```

will be a whole number from 1 to 6 with each number just as likely to occur as any other number. This is the same outcome that results from rolling a well balanced die.

The following program prints the outcomes from rolling a pair of dice 5 times.

```
10 FOR I = 1 TO 5
20    PRINT FIX(6*RND)+1;FIX(6*RND)+1;"      ";
30 NEXT I
  6  4     6  4     4  5     6  6     3  2
Ok
```

2.   As a generalization of Application 1, the result of

```
M*RND+N
```

is a number between N and N+M, including N. If M and N are whole numbers, the result of

```
FIX(M*RND)+N
```

is a whole number between N and N+M-1 inclusive. Here, M is positive, but N can be positive, negative, or zero.

The outcome of the spin of a roulette wheel can be simulated as the result of

```
FIX(38*RND)-1
```

where "-1" is interpreted as "00".

3.   Airlines simulate their operations in order to determine the best allocation of personnel and equipment. There are many unknowns, such as volume of business, failure of equipment, and weather conditions. Statisticians analyze these uncertainties to determine patterns and make predictions. Let's examine one pattern.

RND

Suppose that the air conditioning system for each plane in a certain fleet of airplanes breaks down after an average of 100 hours of use. The time between successive breakdowns is unpredictable. It might be as short as 1 hour or as long as 500 hours. When simulating the total operation of the airline, statisticians use the RND function to come up with a plausible sequence of times between breakdowns. Statisticians have determined that the best function to use is

```
-100*LOG(1-RND)
```

Consider the following program.

```
10 FOR I = 1 TO 10
20   PRINT -100*LOG(1-RND);
30 NEXT I
RUN
 241.2541  80.78954  460.0669  73.15242  94.50838
 132.3711  192.1372  351.1367  47.91446  36.52531
Ok
```

This program simulates breakdowns of the air conditioning system of a particular airplane to occur after 241.25 hours, then after another 80.79 hours, etc. This result, when used in conjunction with simulations of all of the other demands on the maintenance crew of the airline, enables the airline to determine how many people to allocate to maintenance. Such calculations are called *Monte Carlo* calculations because of their use of random numbers.

4.   For Statisticians: In Application 3, the times between successive breakdowns of the air conditioning system of an airplane was an exponential random variable with mean 100. The general procedure for obtaining a sample from an arbitrary continuous random variable is as follows:

Let $F(x)$ be the cumulative distribution function for the random variable. Let $G(y)$ be the inverse of $F(x)$. That is, $G(y)$ is obtained by solving $y=F(x)$ for x in terms of y. Then the number $G(RND)$ will be a random number from the given distribution.

For instance, an exponential random variable with expected value m has the cumulative distribution function

$$F(x) = 1 - EXP(-x/m)$$

Solving $y = F(x)$ for x, we obtain

$$x = -m*LOG(1-y)$$

$$\text{or } G(y) = -m*LOG(1-y)$$

The result of running the program

```
10 INPUT "m= "; m
20 FOR I = 1 TO 10
30   PRINT -m*LOG(1-RND)
40 NEXT I
```

will be a sample of 10 observations from the random variable.

(*Note:* The exponential distribution is valid for numerous observations, including lifetimes of electrical components, durations of phone calls, interarrival times, and time intervals between successive emissions of particles by radioactive material.)

RUN

After a BASIC program has been written, the computer will be in direct mode, and the program will be in memory. The command

RUN

will then execute the program.

A variation of the RUN command causes the execution of the program to begin at a designated line instead of at the lowest numbered line. The command

RUN n

causes the program to begin execution at line n.

If you want to execute a program that is on a disk drive, the command

RUN filespec

will replace the current program with the specified program and execute the new program.

COMMENTS

1.   The RUN command clears all variables from memory, removes all information that has been set with DEF FN or DEFtype statements, RESTOREs all data, causes all DIMensioned arrays to become undimensioned, closes all open files, and disables event trapping that has been set with statements such as ON ERROR, ON KEY(n), ON PEN, ON STRIG(n), ON PLAY(n), and ON TIMER. In graphics modes, the "last point referenced" is set to the center of the screen and the effects of previously executed WINDOW and VIEW statements are voided. OPTION BASE 1 is reset to OPTION BASE 0, the speaker is turned off, and lightpens and joystick buttons are deactivated. In BASIC 2.1, Music Foreground is reset to Music Background. In all other versions of BASIC, Music Background is reset to Music Foreground. When RUN is executed inside a subroutine, the computer forgets that a GOSUB has occurred, and when it is executed inside a FOR . . . NEXT or WHILE . . . WEND loop, forgets that the loop is active. However, RUN does not reset printer specifications, such as line spacing and doublestrike.

2.   When RUNning a program that resides on a disk drive, the R option allows open data files to remain open. The format of the command is

RUN filespec,R

3.   Pressing the F2 function key displays and enters the RUN command.

424

4. When used in program mode, the **RUN filespec** variation passes control to another program and is similar to the CHAIN command.

5. If the name of a program to be executed has the extension BAS, it is not necessary to use the extension when specifying the program.

6. An attempt to RUN a data file results in the error message "File not found."

EXAMPLES

1. ```
   10 A$ = "COMPUTER"
   20 PRINT A$
   RUN
   COMPUTER
   Ok
   ```

2. ```
   A$ = "COMPUTER"
   Ok
   10 PRINT A$
   RUN
   
   Ok
   ```

Nothing was displayed, since the RUN command cleared all variables from memory before executing the program. The string variable A$ took its unspecified form, the null string.

3. Suppose that the program given in Example 1 resides on drive B and has the name PROG.BAS.

   ```
   RUN "B:PROG"
   COMPUTER
   Ok
   ```

4. Suppose that the program given in Example 1 resides on drive B and has the name PROG.BAS.

   ```
   10 PRINT "MY ";
   20 RUN "B:PROG"
   RUN
   MY COMPUTER
   Ok
   ```

5. The following lines might be placed at the end of a game program.

   ```
   970 PRINT "Would you like to try again ";
   980 INPUT "(Y or N)"; A$
   990 IF A$="Y" THEN RUN
   1000 END
   ```

RUN

6.  ```
    10 A = 10
    20 PRINT A
    RUN
     10
    Ok
    RUN 20
     0
    Ok
    ```

7.  ```
    10 PRINT "This disk contains:"
    20 PRINT
    30 PRINT "Attack        Stars"
    40 PRINT "Cards         Maze"
    50 PRINT: PRINT
    60 PRINT "What game would you"
    70 INPUT "like to play"; GAME$
    80 RUN GAME$
    ```

APPLICATIONS

1. The RUN command can be used to work with two different programs in memory at the same time. Suppose the first program has line numbers 10-90. Type the second program using line numbers from 110 on, and put the command END in line 100. Then use the command **RUN** to execute the first program, and use the command **RUN 110** to execute the second program.

2. RUN n is frequently used to enable the testing of a part of a large program without executing the entire program.

After writing a BASIC program, you can store a copy as a file on a disk with the SAVE command. You can then recall the program at a later time to execute or edit it. In order to SAVE a program, you must specify certain pieces of information—the drive containing the disk, the name to be given to the program, and possibly the directory to contain the file. This information comprises the "filespec," a string beginning with the letter of the drive and a colon, and ending with the filename. The filespec might also contain a path to designate the directory to hold the file. The command

```
SAVE filespec
```

stores the program in the specified place with the specified name.

COMMENTS

1. BASIC was invoked from DOS by typing the word BASIC or BASICA following A>, B>, C>, or D>. The combination used identifies the "default drive." For instance, had the screen read **B> BASIC** when BASIC was invoked, then drive B would be the default drive.

When using the SAVE command, you have the option of not specifying the drive. If so, the program will be stored on the disk in the default drive. For instance, if A is the default drive, then the command **SAVE "SALES.MAY"** will store the program on the disk in drive A and give it the name SALES.MAY.

2. Filenames consist of two parts—a name of at most 8 characters followed by an optional extension consisting of a period and at most 3 characters. If you use no more than 8 letters for the name of a BASIC program and omit an extension, then the extension ".BAS" will be automatically added to the name. For instance, if you SAVE a BASIC program with the command **SAVE "SALES"** and then use the FILES command to obtain the name of the file, the program will appear as

```
SALES    .BAS
```

(*Note:* You will be able to LOAD or RUN the above program by just referring to its name without the extension. However, you must also use the extension when reNAMEing or KILLing the program.)

3. If the name given to a program by the SAVE command is the same as the name of a file that already exists in the specified place, that file will be overwritten and lost.

4. The SAVE command stores the entire current program on the disk. If you want to store just a portion of the program, use a command of the form **LIST m-n, filespec**. (See the discussion of the LIST command for further details.)

SAVE

5. When a program is SAVEd, there are three different formats in which it can be recorded on the disk. The commands discussed so far record the information in what is known as compressed binary (or tokenized) format. The other two possibilities are called ASCII format and encoded binary (or protected) format.

To store a program in ASCII format, follow the standard SAVE command with a comma and the letter A. The command

```
SAVE filespec, A
```

records the current program in ASCII format. ASCII format should be used in the following situations:

    (a) The program is to be MERGEd with another program. (See the discussions of the MERGE command and the CHAIN statement for further details.)

    (b) You will be using a text editor or other word processing software and might want to insert the program into a document.

    (c) You want to edit the program in DOS. With ASCII format the program can be read by EDLIN.

    (d) You want to be able to order the program in DOS using the TYPE command.

    (e) You want to transmit the program over phone lines.

To store a program in encoded binary (or protected format), follow the standard SAVE command with a comma and the letter P. The command

```
SAVE filespec, P
```

records the current program in protected format. This format protects the program in the sense that after it is LOADed from the disk, it cannot be directly LISTed or EDITed.

6. If a program has been SAVEd in protected format (say, with the name "PROG"), it can be converted to one of the other formats by applying the following procedure in direct mode:

    (a) Execute `DEF SEG:NEW`

    (b) Execute `BSAVE "UN.PRO",1124,1`

    (c) Execute `LOAD "PROG"`

    (d) Execute `BLOAD "UN.PRO"`

Now the program can be LISTed or EDITed, and reSAVEd in any of the three formats.

7. Programs SAVEd in one of the two binary formats require about 20% less space on the disk and LOAD faster than programs SAVEd in ASCII format.

8. After SAVEing a program, the program remains in memory. Hence, you can continue to edit the program. However, if you change the program and then SAVE it on the same disk directory using the same name as before, the previous version will be erased. In order to retain both of them, you must give the new version a different name from the previous version.

9. It is a good idea to save your programs frequently during development and editing. That way a recent copy is always available on disk. Some programmers make it a practice to execute a SAVE command after writing twenty lines of a program. In some cases, they begin a program with a SAVE command. This is usually done with a program that passes control to another program during its execution. (After the program has been completed and debugged, the SAVE command line can be deleted.)

10. Many programmers use a personal naming convention for suffixes to keep track of the different types of files. For instance, files SAVEd in ASCII format might be given a name having the extension "TXT" and binary files would be given the extension "BAS". This way, just by looking at the extension they can tell which type of format a file has.

11. Suggestion: Always make the first line of a program

    1 'SAVE "progname"

(*Note:* The apostrophe is equivalent to the statement REM.) This line serves as a title and identifies a hard copy listing. When SAVEing the program, instead of typing the SAVE command, just execute **EDIT 1**, press the Del key thrice, and then press Enter. This method avoids misspelling errors. Also, if you are modifying several programs, it prevents you from accidentally SAVEing the current program under the name of a recently SAVEd program and wiping out that program.

12. The word SAVE" can be displayed by pressing the F4 key.

EXAMPLES

1. The following command takes the program currently in memory, records it on the disk in drive B, and gives it the name SALES.

    SAVE "B:SALES"

2. The following command takes the program currently in memory, records it on the default drive in ASCII format, and gives it the name REVENUE.

    SAVE "REVENUE",A

SCREEN (Function)

The SCREEN function identifies the text character displayed in a specified location of the screen and identifies its color.

PRELIMINARIES

1. The screen can display 25 lines of text, with each line consisting of 80 characters. We think of the screen as being subdivided into 25 rows (numbered from 1 to 25 starting at the top of the screen) and 80 columns (numbered from 1 to 80 starting at the left side of the screen). The character in the rth row, cth column is obtained by starting at the upper left-hand corner of the screen and counting r units down and c units to the right.

2. There are 256 different characters recognized by the computer. These characters and their ASCII values are listed in Appendix A. Two hundred and forty-six of these characters can be displayed on the screen with PRINT statements. The ASCII values of the displayable characters are 0 through 6, 8, 14 through 27, and 32 through 255.

3. The COLOR statement is used to create special effects (e.g., blinking) and to generate colors. The 16 colors at our disposal are identified by numbers. The colors and their numbers are:

0 Black	4 Red	8 Grey	12 Light Red
1 Blue	5 Magenta	9 Light Blue	13 Light Magenta
2 Green	6 Brown	10 Light Green	14 Yellow
3 Cyan	7 White	11 Light Cyan	15 High Intensity White

In text mode, each character is displayed with a foreground and a background. The pair of numbers f,b describes the color of the character, where f is the number of the foreground color and b is the number of the background color. With color monitors, 16 colors can be used as the foreground color and the first eight colors can be used as the background color. The IBM Monochrome Display is only capable of using colors 0, 7, and 15 as foreground and 0 and 7 as background. Also, in both situations the foreground color can blink. (See the discussion of the COLOR statement for further details.)

FURTHER DISCUSSION

If r and c are numbers, then

```
SCREEN(r,c)
```

will be the ASCII value of the character displayed in the rth row, cth column of the screen. If the color of the character is described by f,b, then

```
SCREEN(r,c,1)
```

430

will be the number 16*b+f, if the foreground is not blinking, or 112 plus that number, if the foreground is blinking.

EXAMPLES

1. The following program requires a color monitor or color TV screen.

```
10 SCREEN 0,1: CLS: COLOR 14,1
20 PRINT "Hello"
30 PRINT SCREEN(1,2); SCREEN(1,2,1)
RUN
Hello   (on top line with yellow foreground, blue background)
 101   30
Ok
```

2. The following program will run on the Monochrome Display.

```
10 SCREEN 0: CLS: COLOR 31,0
20 PRINT CHR$(34): COLOR 7,0
30 PRINT SCREEN(1,1); SCREEN(1,1,1)
RUN
"   (on top line blinking with high intensity white
 34   143                    foreground, black background)
Ok
```

Here, f is 15, b is 0, and (16*0+31)+112 is 143.

3. The following program assigns to the string variable A$ the string consisting of the first 10 characters in the second row of the screen.

```
10 CLS: PRINT "Santa: Is there a state just south of MD?"
20 PRINT "Yes, Santa Claus, there is a Virginia."
30 FOR I = 1 TO 10
40    A$ = A$ + CHR$(SCREEN(2,I))
50 NEXT I
60 PRINT A$
RUN
Santa: Is there a state just south of MD?   (on top line)
Yes, Santa Claus, there is a Virginia.
Yes, Santa
Ok
```

COMMENTS

1. If the value of SCREEN(r,c,1) is less than 128, the numbers f and b can be found by dividing 16 into the value using long division. The quotient will be b and the remainder will be f. Otherwise, subtract 128, proceed as before,

SCREEN (Function)

and add 16 to the value determined for f. The following program produces the numbers f and b when the value is less than 128:

```
10 INPUT "value:", V
20 F=V MOD 16: B=V\16
30 PRINT "foreground color"; F
40 PRINT "background color"; B
```

2. The number 1 in SCREEN(r,c,1) can be replaced with any nonzero number or numeric variable. The function SCREEN(r,c,0) is identical to the function SCREEN(r,c).

3. The number r must be in the range 1 to 25, and the number c must be in the range 1 to 80 (for a WIDTH 80 screen) or 1 to 40 (for a WIDTH 40 screen). Otherwise the error message ''Illegal function call'' results.

4. The word SCREEN can be displayed by pressing Alt-S.

5. The SCREEN function can be used to identify text that appears in graphics mode. However, SCREEN(r,c) will have the value zero if there is any graphic (such as a point or a line segment) displayed in any part of the specified location.

APPLICATIONS

Consider a program that asks the user to write his name, enter it, and then write his address. The standard way to access these two pieces of data is via INPUT statements. Suppose the user notices, after typing in his address, that he misspelled his name. There is no way to make the correction. However, instead of using INPUT statements, the user can be asked to type his name at a certain location and then type his address at another specified location. He can be allowed to make as many changes as he likes. After he indicates that the data is correct, SCREEN functions can be used to read the characters and put them into strings.

SCREEN (Statement)

This discussion applies only to computers using a graphics monitor. There are three available display modes: text mode and medium- and high-resolution graphics modes. Although text can be displayed with any of the three modes, only the last two modes accept graphics (points, lines, and circles). Color is available only with the first two modes.

Each of the modes accepts 25 rows of text. In high-resolution graphics mode, each row displays 80 text characters. In medium-resolution graphics mode, each row displays 40 text characters. In text mode, we have the choice of specifying the number of text characters per row at either 40 or 80. This choice is made via the WIDTH statement. For graphics purposes, medium-resolution mode partitions the screen into 200 rows of 320 pixels each and high-resolution mode partitions the screen into 200 rows of 640 pixels each.

There are three different types of graphics monitors that can be attached to graphics adapters: TV sets, composite monitors, and RGB monitors.

The following statements are used to specify the mode and, when using non-RGB monitors, to enable or disable color.

SCREEN 0,1	text mode, color enabled on non-RGB monitors
SCREEN 0,0	text mode, color disabled on non-RGB monitors
SCREEN 1,0	medium-resolution graphics mode, color enabled on non-RGB monitors
SCREEN 1,1	medium-resolution graphics mode, color disabled on non-RGB monitors
SCREEN 2	high-resolution graphics mode

COMMENTS

1. When BASIC is first invoked, the display mode is automatically set to **SCREEN 0,0**.

2. Either of the two parameters can be omitted. If this is done, the first parameter assumes its most recent value and the second becomes zero.

3. A SCREEN statement can have any number as its second parameter. Nonzero numbers have the same effect as 1.

4. The parameters can consist of numeric expressions (such as $A + 2$, or $SQR(A)$).

5. The word SCREEN can be displayed by pressing Alt-S.

EXAMPLE

1. Assume that BASIC has just been invoked.

```
10 SCREEN ,1        (text mode, color)
20 SCREEN 2         (high-resolution)
30 SCREEN 1         (medium-resolution, color enabled)
```

SCREEN (Statement)

FURTHER DISCUSSION

Initially, let's assume that we are working with a WIDTH 40 display in text mode. Pretend that we can attach 8 screens to the computer and display text characters on whatever screen we choose. If the screens are numbered from 0 to 7 and if "a" is one of these numbers, then the statement

```
SCREEN ,,a
```

can be used to designate the chosen screen. Now pretend that we can only see one screen at a time (again of our choosing). If v is a number, the statement

```
SCREEN ,,,v
```

could be used to designate the screen to be seen.

Well, even though we can't actually hook up eight screens to the computer, the SCREEN statement allows us to work with eight screens at the same time. We refer to the screens as *pages*, numbered from 0 to 7, and use the statement

```
SCREEN ,,a,v
```

to designate page number "a" as the page to be written on (the active page) and page number v as the page to be displayed (the visual page). In general, a statement of the form

```
SCREEN m,n,a,v
```

sets the mode, enables or disables color, and selects both the active and visual pages.

FURTHER COMMENTS

6. When working with a WIDTH 80 text mode screen, we are limited to 4 pages, numbered 0 to 3.

7. When BASIC is first invoked, the values of a and v are both 0.

8. Whenever the "a" parameter is specified and the v parameter is not, the v parameter is given the same value as the "a" parameter. Otherwise, if either parameter is unspecified, it assumes its most recent value.

9. The statement CLS, which erases the screen, and the functions CSRLIN and POS, which record the location of the cursor, refer to the active page.

10. To clear all of the pages, just toggle the second parameter of the SCREEN statement. For instance, the statements **SCREEN 0,1: SCREEN 0,0** will clear all pages.

11. When using the multiple page option, we often will be writing on a screen that we can't see. Also, when we return to write on a page we wrote on

previously, the cursor might be in a different location from where it was when we left that page. We can use the CSRLIN and POS functions to keep track of its location.

12. In text mode, do not execute the command SYSTEM unless page 0 is both the active and visual page.

13. The statement SCREEN 0,0,0, which is the same as SCREEN 0,0,0,0, can be displayed by pressing the function key F10.

FURTHER EXAMPLE

2. The following program writes information on page 2 while we are still looking at page 0. We are then shown page 2.

```
10 SCREEN 0,0,0: CLS
20 PRINT "This is page 0."
30 PRINT "We are PRINTing on page 2."
40 PRINT "In a second we will see "
50 PRINT "what is on page 2."
40 SCREEN 0,0,2,0
50 FOR I = 1 TO 66
60    PRINT "This is page 2.",
70 NEXT I
80 SCREEN 0,0,2,2
90 FOR T = 1 TO 3000: NEXT T
100 SCREEN 0,0,0
110 LOCATE 12,1
120 PRINT "We have returned to page 0."
```

APPLICATIONS

1. Multiple pages allow us to print data on a page that is out of view and then produce a complete display at once.

2. Multiple pages are useful when writing a program that will incorporate subroutines from other existing programs. The first subroutine is LISTed onto page 1 and then RENUM and NEW commands are executed. The same procedure is used to obtain a copy of each of the other subroutines on the other pages. The main program is written on page 0. To incorporate one of the subroutines, the page is changed and each of the lines on the page are entered, possibly with some alterations, into the program.

SGN

The function SGN tells whether a given number is positive, zero, or negative. Specifically:

$$\text{SGN}(x) = \begin{cases} 1 & \text{if } x > 0 \\ 0 & \text{if } x = 0 \\ -1 & \text{if } x < 0 \end{cases}$$

EXAMPLES

1. ```
PRINT SGN(3.40); SGN(0); SGN(-35)
 1 0 -1
Ok
```

2. ```
10 A# = 45D+12: B = -1^3
20 PRINT SGN(A#); SGN(B); SGN(1+B)
RUN
 1 -1  0
Ok
```

APPLICATIONS

1. The SGN function is useful whenever we want to choose a course of action that depends on whether a certain number is below, equal to, or above another number. The following program tests a person's knowledge of the earliest all-electronic digital computer.

```
10 INPUT "In what year was the ENIAC computer completed";A
20 ON 2+SGN(A-1946) GOTO 30,40,50
30 PRINT "Not that long ago, try again.": GOTO 10
40 PRINT "Correct.": END
50 PRINT "Earlier than that, try again.":GOTO 10
RUN
In what year was the ENIAC computer completed? 1940
Not that long ago, try again.
In what year was the ENIAC computer completed? 1946
Correct.
Ok
```

2. The SGN function can be used in conjunction with the FIX function to round numbers. The following program rounds numbers to 3 decimal places.

```
10 INPUT A#
20 PRINT FIX(1000*A#+.5*SGN(A#))/1000
```

To round numbers to r decimal places, replace 1000 with "1" followed by r zeros.

436

3. The statement `FOR I=A TO B STEP SGN(B-A)` will run through all whole numbers from the whole number A to the whole number B, no matter which of the two numbers is the larger.

SHELL

The SHELL statement, which allows you to execute DOS commands and programs from within a BASIC program, is not valid for BASIC releases earlier than 3.0.

When the computer is turned on with the DOS diskette in one of the drives, a copy of the program COMMAND.COM is loaded into memory. (COMMAND.COM is a program file that contains all of the internal commands of DOS.) After BASIC is invoked, there are two programs in memory, COMMAND.COM and BASIC.COM. Executing the statement

```
SHELL
```

places a third program (another copy of COMMAND.COM) in memory, and passes control to this program. At this point, the user can issue almost any command or run almost any program that can normally be run from DOS. Then, executing the command EXIT in DOS removes the second copy of COMMAND.COM from memory and returns to BASIC. Any BASIC program that had been in memory, any user-defined functions that had been specified, and all variables that had been assigned values before SHELL was executed, will still be in memory. If A$ is a string containing the name of a command or program that can be executed from DOS, then executing the statement

```
SHELL A$
```

loads a second copy of COMMAND.COM into memory, passes control to this copy of DOS, runs the program or executes the command specified by A$, removes the second copy of COMMAND.COM from memory, and returns to BASIC. As before, BASIC programs, variables, and user-defined functions are left intact in memory.

EXAMPLES

1.  ```
    10 A = 123
    20 DEF FNF(X) = X*X
    RUN
    Ok
    PRINT A; FNF(4)
     123  16
    Ok
    SHELL

    The IBM Personal Computer DOS
    Version 3.00 (C)Copyright IBM Corp 1981, 1982, 1983, 1984
    ```
    ```

```
A>chkdsk

   362496 bytes total disk space
    37888 bytes in 2 hidden files
    29696 bytes in 22 user files
   294912 bytes available on disk

   262144 bytes total memory
   225120 bytes free

A>CLS
A>EXIT

Ok
PRINT A; FNF(4)
 123   16
Ok
LIST
10 A = 123
20 DEF FNF(X) = X*X
Ok
```

2.  ```
    10 SHELL "FORMAT B:"
    20 CLS
    30 PRINT "We have returned to BASIC."
    RUN

    Insert new diskette for drive B:
    and strike ENTER when ready

    Formatting...Format complete

       362496 bytes total disk space
       362496 bytes available on disk

    Format another (Y/N)?N
    We have returned to BASIC.
    Ok
    ```

COMMENTS

1. The SHELL statement should only be used with computers having at least 128K of RAM.

2. Programs that stay resident in memory, such as GRAPHICS.COM should not be executed with SHELL. If so, the message "Can't continue after SHELL" is produced and BASIC exits to the initial DOS.
    ```

SHELL

3. Executing the statement **SHELL "BASIC"** produces the message "You cannot SHELL to Basic" and returns control to BASIC. Executing the statement **SHELL** and then attempting to invoke BASIC gives the same message and returns control to the second DOS.

4. If the statement **SHELL A$** is executed and A$ is a batch file, then the last command in the batch file should be EXIT. Otherwise, control will not be passed back to BASIC.

5. Immediately after the SHELL statement, you should also issue a SCREEN statement followed by a CLS statement in order to restore the screen.

6. Before executing SHELL, close all files that will be used by a DOS command or program. The files can be reopened when control is passed back to BASIC.

7. SHELL is a reserved word in BASIC 2.0 and 2.1. However, the statement is not documented in either version. The SHELL statement can be used in these versions of BASIC, but is not guaranteed to be free of bugs.

SIN is the trigonometric function sine. For an acute angle in a right triangle, the sine of the angle is the ratio:

$$\frac{\text{length of the side opposite the angle}}{\text{length of hypotenuse}}$$

See Appendix M for the definition of the sine function for arbitrary angles and a discussion of radian measure. For any number x, the value of the function

```
SIN(x)
```

is the sine of the angle of x radians.

COMMENTS

1. Although x can be any number, SIN(x) will always be between -1 and 1. Figure 1 contains the graph of y = SIN(x).

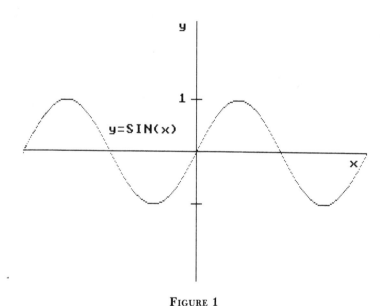

FIGURE 1

2. In BASIC 1.1 (and earlier versions) the value of SIN(x) is always a single-precision number. BASIC 2.0 and later versions provide the option of computing SIN(x) as a double-precision number. To obtain this option, invoke BASIC from DOS with the command **BASIC /D**. Then, whenever x is a double-precision number, the value of SIN(x) will be computed as a double-precision number.

SIN

3.   The inverse of the sine function is the arcsine function. This function is not available directly as a BASIC function. However, it can be defined in terms of ATN and SQR, which are BASIC functions:

Arcsin(x) = ATN(x/SQR(1-x^2))

Arcsin(x) is the angle between -1.570796 and 1.570796 (i.e., between -π/2 and π/2) whose sine is x.

EXAMPLES

(Examples 1 through 4 result from using BASIC 2.0 (or subsequent versions) without the /D option, or from using an earlier version of BASIC. Example 5 assumes BASIC 2.0 (or subsequent versions) with the /D option.)

1.   ```
     PRINT SIN(1); SIN(-5.678); SIN(2E+8)
      .841471   .5689143 -.6770875
     Ok
     ```

2.   ```
     PRINT SIN(2*3+4); SIN(1.23456789)
      -.5440213   .9440058
     Ok
     ```

3.   ```
     10 A = 2: C# = .6435011#: D# = SIN(C#)
     20 PRINT SIN(A); SIN(C#); D#
     RUN
      .9092974   .6   .6000000238418579
     Ok
     ```

Note the difference between the results obtained for SIN(C#) and D#, which is assigned the value SIN(C#). SIN(C#) was computed as the single-precision number .6. The statement D# = SIN(C#) had the effect of converting .6 to double-precision; that is, D# is actually CDBL(.6). (See the discussion of CDBL for an explanation of the conversion.)

4.   ```
     10 DEF FNARCSIN(x) = ATN(x/SQR(1-x^2))
     20 A = SIN(1): B = FNARCSIN(A)
     30 C = FNARCSIN(.5): D = SIN(C)
     40 PRINT A; B; C; D
     RUN
      .841471   1   .5235988   .5
     Ok
     ```

In general, for any number x between -π/2 and π/2, ARCSIN(SIN(x)) = x, and for any number x between -1 and 1, SIN(ARCSIN(x)) = x.

5.   ```
     PRINT SIN(1%); SIN(1); SIN(1#)
      .841471   .841471   .8414709848078965
     Ok
     ```
     ```

APPLICATIONS

1. The sine function appears in many formulas found in physics, mathematics, and engineering. For instance, if a projectile is fired at an initial velocity of v feet per second at an angle A radians with the ground, then (in the absence of air resistance) the projectile will be in flight for v*SIN(A)/16 seconds.

SOUND

The pitch of a regular sound is measured in hertz, abbreviated Hz. Technically, the number of hertz is the number of cycles per second of the causitive vibration. The normal human ear can perceive sounds from about 20 to 20,000 Hz. Sounds of more than 20,000 Hz are ultrasonic. The lowest key on the piano produces a frequency of 55 and the highest key a frequency of 8372 Hz.

The SOUND statement produces a sound of specified pitch and duration. Pitch is measured in hertz, and duration is measured in units of about .055 seconds. A duration of 1 second corresponds to 18.2 units. The statement

    SOUND f,d

results in a sound of pitch f Hz with a duration of d units.

COMMENTS

1. The table on the left gives the frequencies for the notes in the octave beginning with middle C, and the table on the right gives some common durations:

Note	Frequency	Time (seconds)	Duration
C	523.25	1/200	.091
D	587.33	1/100	.182
E	659.26	1/50	.364
F	698.46	1/25	.728
G	783.99	1/2	9.1
A	880	1	18.2
B	987.77	1.5	27.3
C	1046.5	3600	65535

2. In SOUND statements, frequency can range from 37 to 32767 and duration from 0 to 65535. A statement of the form SOUND 32767, d results in silence for the specified duration. An ultrasonic tone, inaudible to humans, is being generated. Such a statement is used to create a pause between sounds. See Example 3.

3. Although we illustrate the SOUND statement with musical notes, the PLAY statement is more appropriate to use when composing music.

4. The discussion of the PLAY statement describes the two modes Music Foreground and Music Background. These modes are also relevant for the SOUND statement. (Music Background is the default mode for BASIC 2.1 and Music Foreground is the default mode for all other versions of BASIC.) In the Music Foreground mode, when a SOUND statement is followed by other statements of different types, these statements will be executed while the tone is still being generated. See Example 4. However, as soon as another

SOUND statement is encountered, execution pauses until the first tone has been terminated. Upon termination, the second SOUND statement is executed (and subsequent statements as before.).

In the Music Background mode, when SOUND statements are encountered the program continues and stores the tones to be produced in a buffer to be executed in turn. This allows tones to be produced in the background while material is being displayed on the screen. Up to 32 tones can be stored in the buffer. See Examples 6 and 7.

There is an exception to the above rules: Whenever a SOUND statement of duration 0 is encountered, the current tone and all pending tones are immediately terminated. See Examples 5 and 7.

5. The computer can not alter the loudness of the tone.

EXAMPLES

1. The following statement produces the tone middle C for 1 second.

```
SOUND 523.25, 18.2
```

2. The following program displays a wide range of frequencies. Each tone is held for a duration of about 1/4 second. (*Note:* The use of the PLAY statement mandates that we operate with Advanced BASIC.)

```
10 CLS: PLAY "MF"
20 LOCATE 12,1
30 PRINT "This sound has frequency"
40 FOR I = 37 TO 9000 STEP 100
50    LOCATE 12,26
60    PRINT I
70    SOUND I,5: SOUND 32767,1
80 NEXT I
```

3. The following program plays middle C for 1 second, pauses for 2 seconds, and then plays middle C again for 1 second.

```
10 SOUND 523.25, 18.2
20 SOUND 32767, 36.4
30 SOUND 523.25, 18.2
```

4. The following program creates the sound effect of an ambulance siren. A number is displayed after every other tone. Comment 4 explains why the numbers appear when they do.

```
10 PLAY "MF"
20 FOR I=1 TO 5
30    SOUND 700, 9
40    SOUND 500, 9
```

SOUND

```
50    PRINT I
60 NEXT I
70 SOUND 100, .1
80 PRINT "Ambulance Siren Over"
```

5.   The duration of 0 in line 20 causes the following program to produce silence. If line 20 were omitted, middle C would be produced for 1 second.

```
10 SOUND 523.25, 18.2
20 SOUND 400, 0
```

6.   The following program produces the tones associated with the 8 C keys of the piano. Line 10 causes the sentence "The 8 Cs of the piano" to be displayed as soon as the program begins running. If this line were **10 PLAY "MF"**, the sentence would appear while the last C was SOUNDing.

```
10 PLAY "MB"
20 FOR N= 0 TO 7
30    SOUND 65.4*2^N, 9
40 NEXT N
50 PRINT "The 8 Cs of the piano"
```

7.   The following program produces the tone of A below middle C. The tone will continue to sound until the letter S is typed and entered. If line 10 were **PLAY "MF"**, the tone would continue for 1 hour before line 40 would be executed.

```
10 PLAY "MB"
20 SOUND 440, 65535
30 SOUND 440, 65535
40 INPUT "Enter S to stop the sound! ", A$
50 IF A$="S" THEN SOUND 100,0: PRINT "Thank you": END
60 GOTO 40
```

APPLICATIONS

1.   The SOUND statement is used in game programs to produce sound effects.

2.   The SOUND statement is used to jazz up programs that require a response from the user. For instance, computer-assisted instruction programs often ask questions. One sound effect can be issued after a correct answer and another after an incorrect answer.

3.   The SOUND statement can be used to produce a delay of specified duration. The statements

```
PLAY "MF": SOUND 32767,18.2*T: SOUND 32767,1
```

cause the program to pause for exactly T seconds.

If L is a positive number, then

    SPACE$(L)

is a string consisting of L spaces.

COMMENTS

1. SPACE$(L) is the same as STRING$(L," ").

2. The number L can have any value from 0 to 255.4999. If L is not a whole number, it is rounded to the nearest whole number. SPACE$(0) is the null string, " ".

3. SPACE$ can be evaluated for any numeric expression. For instance, SPACE$(2*3) is valid. So is the statement H=5: PRINT SPACE$(H).

4. The SPC function inserts spaces among items being displayed on the screen and can serve some of the same functions as SPACE$.

EXAMPLES

1. PRINT SPACE$(5) + "Personal" + SPACE$(3) + "Computer"
         Personal   Computer
    Ok

2. 10 A = 2: B$ = SPACE$(4): C$ = SPACE$(3*A-1): D$ = SPACE$(0)
    20 PRINT B$ + "U." + D$ + "S." + C$ + "Presidents"
    RUN
        U.S.   Presidents
    Ok

3. The following program moves a message across the screen.

    ```
    10 A$ = SPACE$(80)+"IBM PERSONAL COMPUTER"+" ": CLS
    20 FOR I = 1 TO 102
    30    LOCATE 15: PRINT MID$(A$,I,80)
    40    FOR J = 1 TO 100
    50 NEXT J,I
    ```

APPLICATIONS

1. The SPACE$ function can be used to obtain strings of uniform length. This is valuable for printing purposes and for inserting information into data files.

SPACE$

2. The SPACE$ function can be used to erase a specific portion of the screen by just PRINTing over it with a string of spaces. (See, for instance, Application 3 in the discusion of LOCATE.)

3. SPACE$ is useful in forming format strings for PRINT USING statements.

The SPC function is used in conjunction with the PRINT statement to insert spaces among the items being displayed. Since the PRINT statement has so many subtleties, considerable care is required to describe accurately the effects of the SPC function. We recommend that the discussion of PRINT be read before proceeding.

Suppose we are displaying items on an 80 character per line screen. If n is a whole number from 0 to 79 and

    SPC(n)

is placed in a PRINT statement, then n spaces will be displayed at that point. If the current line does not have n positions remaining, then those spaces which will not fit on the current line will be displayed at the beginning of the next line. If SPC(n) is the last item in a PRINT statement, it will suppress the terminating carriage return and line feed that PRINT would normally perform.

EXAMPLES

1. PRINT SPC(3); "left"; SPC(5); "right"
       left   right
    Ok

2. PRINT SPC(75); "Computer", SPC(7); "Terminal"

    Computer   Terminal
    Ok

The word "Computer" is placed at the beginning of the second line, since it cannot fit on the first line after SPC(75). The comma after the word "Computer" results in the next item, the seven spaces of SPC(7), starting in print zone 2. The word "Terminal" starts in column 22, immediately after these seven spaces.

3. In the following statement, spaces are denoted by asterisks.

```
PRINT STRING$(73,"X"); "LINE1"; SPC(5); "LINE2"
XXXXXXXXXXXXXXXXXXXXXXXXXXXXXXXXXXXXXX ... XXXXXXXXXXLINE1**
***LINE2
Ok
```

4. In the following example, the first PRINT statement has the same result as if it had ended with a semicolon.

```
PRINT "Merry" SPC(1): PRINT "Christmas"
Merry Christmas
Ok
```

SPC

5. The following program uses SPC to right-justify a list of names:

```
10 FOR I = 1 TO 4
20    READ A$
30    PRINT  SPC(10-LEN(A$));A$
40 NEXT I
50 DATA WASHINGTON, ADAMS, JEFFERSON, MADISON
RUN
WASHINGTON
     ADAMS
  JEFFERSON
    MADISON
Ok
```

6. The following program centers a string in the middle of an 80-character line.

```
10 WIDTH 80
20 INPUT A$
30 PRINT SPC(40-LEN(A$)/2); A$
```

COMMENTS

1. SPC can be used with LPRINT and PRINT# in exactly the same way that it is used with PRINT. SPC *must* be used in conjunction with one of these three statements.

2. The value of n in SPC(n) may be any number from -32768.49 to 32767.49. If n is not a whole number, it will be rounded. If the (rounded) value of n is negative, then SPC(n) is interpreted as SPC(0). If n's value is not less than the current line WIDTH, n is replaced by "n MOD WIDTH." For example, if our line width is 80, then **SPC(80)** is the same as **SPC(0)**, **SPC(83.2)** is the same as **SPC(3)**, and **SPC(175.8)** is the same as **SPC(16)**. If we are using the printer and have specified **WIDTH 60**, then **SPC(75)** is the same as **SPC(15)**.

3. If SPC(n) is used with PRINT# to enter data into a sequential file and n is larger than 255, then n is replaced by n MOD 256.

4. SPC differs from the function SPACE$ in two important ways. First, SPACE$ forms a string of up to 255 spaces, which the PRINT statement will not split across two lines (unless the length of SPACE$ is more than the WIDTH of a line). On the other hand, the number of spaces which SPC will insert in a line is limited by the value of the WIDTH, but, if necessary, SPC will split up the spaces over two lines. Second, **A$ = SPACE$(3)** and **MID$(SPACE$(4)+"IBM",2,3)** are valid statements using SPACE$, but their counterparts using SPC are not.

450

5. Be careful that you do not leave a space between the C and the parenthesis in SPC(n). Otherwise, it will be interpreted as an array.

Applications

The SPC function is used to display information in an orderly fashion. For instance, in the above examples, we used SPC to right-justify a list of names and to center a word on a line.

SQR is the square root function. For any nonnegative number x, the value of

    SQR(x)

is the nonnegative number whose square is x. The graph of y=SQR(x) is shown in Figure 1.

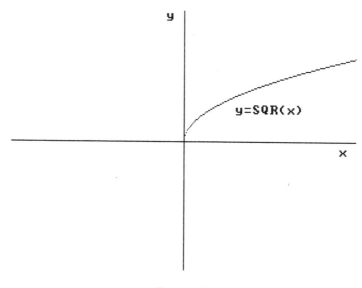

FIGURE 1

COMMENTS

1. The value of x can range from 0 to 1.701411E+38. For greater values of x, SQR(x) results in an "Overflow" error message and the number 1.304382E+19, which is the square root of machine infinity.

2. The use of SQR(x) for negative values of x results in an "Illegal function call" error message.

3. SQR(x) is the same as x∧.5 . However, SQR(x) is calculated faster by BASIC.

4. In versions of BASIC preceding BASIC 2.0, the value of SQR(x) is always a single-precision number. BASIC 2.0 and subsequent versions provide the option of computing SQR(x) as a double-precision number. To exercise this option, invoke BASIC with the command BASIC/D or BASICA/D. Then, whenever x is a double-precision number, the value of SQR(x) will be computed as a double-precision number.

5. When using BASIC 2.0 (or subsequent versions) without the /D option, or earlier versions of BASIC, entering high numbers in double-precision notation causes the computer to freeze. Specifically, the statement **PRINT SQR(1.701412D+38)** results in the computer being totally unresponsive. Even pressing Ctrl-Alt-Del has no effect. The only recourse is to turn the computer off and start over.

EXAMPLES

Examples 1 and 2 result from using BASIC 2.0 (or a later version) without the /D option or from using an earlier version of BASIC.

1. PRINT SQR(9); SQR(3.14); SQR(2E+30); SQR(123456789)
      3 1.772005 1.414214E+15 11111.11
    Ok

2. 10 A = .5:B = 8*A:C# = .2#
    20 PRINT SQR(A);SQR(A+1);SQR(B);SQR(C#)
    RUN
      .7071068 1.224745 2 .4472136
    Ok

The value of SQR(C#) is a single-precision number even though C# is a double-precision number.

3. The following example was executed using BASIC 2.0 with the /D option.

    PRINT SQR(2%); SQR(2); SQR(2#)
     1.414214 1.414214 1.414213562373095
    Ok

APPLICATIONS

The SQR function is involved in many mathematical and statistical formulas. For instance, the length of the hypotenuse of a right triangle is the square root of the sum of the squares of the other two sides. In statistics, the standard deviation of a collection of data is the square root of the result obtained by dividing the sum of the squares of the distances of each of the pieces of data from the mean by the number of pieces of data.

STICK

The STICK function requires a special board called the Game Control Adapter, and a joystick, which is connected to the Game Control Adapter.

The joystick shown in Figure 1 has two buttons and a lever that can be pushed in any direction. This discussion deals solely with the lever. (See the discussions of STRIG, STRIG(n), and ON STRIG for information about the buttons.)

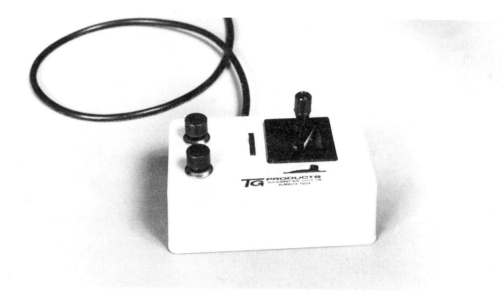

FIGURE 1

The position of the lever is described by a pair of numbers called the x- and y-coordinates of the lever. The range of values of these coordinates varies for different joysticks and can be adjusted with certain joysticks. Hence, the numbers that we will use for illustrative purposes will not correspond exactly to the ones for your joystick. However, the programs presented should run with any joystick.

Each coordinate ranges from 1 to 200. When the lever is at rest, its coordinates both have value 100. When the lever is moved horizontally, its y-coordinate stays constant and its x-coordinate varies from 1 (at the leftmost position) to 200 (at the rightmost position). When the lever is moved vertically, its x-coordinate stays constant and its y-coordinate varies from 1 (at the top) to 200 (at the bottom).

The following demonstration program displays the coordinates of the different lever positions. While the program is running, move the lever to different positions and watch the values of the coordinates change. Press Ctrl-Break to terminate the program.

```
10 SCREEN 0: CLS
20 LOCATE 12,15
30 PRINT "x-coordinate" STICK(0)
40 LOCATE 14,15
50 PRINT "y-coordinate" STICK(1)
60 GOTO 20
```

The function

```
STICK(0)
```

has as its value at any time the current x-coordinate of the lever, and the function

```
STICK(1)
```

has as its value at any time the current y-coordinate of the lever. For instance, when the lever is at rest, the statement **PRINT STICK(0); STICK(1)** displays **100 100**.

EXAMPLES

The programs in Examples 3, 4, and 5 require a graphics monitor. Examples 2, 4, and 5 require Advanced BASIC.

1. The following program allows the user to move an airplane around the screen by moving the lever. Press Ctrl-Break to terminate the program.

```
10 CLS: SCREEN 0: WIDTH 80
20 A$ = ">==>"
30 X = 1: Y = 1
40 X1 = X: Y1 = Y
50 X = STICK(0)/4: Y = 1+STICK(1)/11
60 LOCATE Y1,X1: PRINT "     "
70 LOCATE Y,X: PRINT A$
80 FOR I =1 TO 95: NEXT
90 GOTO 40
```

The values of the STICK functions were adjusted to meet the requirements of the LOCATE statement.

2. The following program, which requires Advanced BASIC, produces musical notes that change with the position of the lever. The x-coordinate of the lever determines the pitch of the notes and the y-coordinate determines their duration. Press Ctrl-Break to terminate the program.

```
10 A = STICK(0)/3
20 B = .8*STICK(1) + 30
```

STICK

```
30 PLAY "MF T=B; N=A;"
40 GOTO 10
```

3. The following program turns the screen into a drawing pad. Moving the lever causes a moving dot to trace a figure. Press Ctrl-Break to terminate the program.

```
10 SCREEN 1,0: COLOR 1,1: CLS: KEY OFF
20 PSET(STICK(0),STICK(1))
30 X = STICK(0)
40 Y = STICK(1)
50 LINE  -(X,Y)
60 GOTO 30
```

4. One of the earliest video games used joysticks to move paddles and play a simple game of tennis. The following program shows how the joystick can be used to move a paddle. This program uses the graphics function GET to store a picture of the paddle and the graphics function PUT to place the paddle in the position specified by the lever. Press Ctrl-Break to terminate the program.

```
10 SCREEN 1,0: COLOR 1,1: CLS: KEY OFF
20 LINE (170,100)-(175,115),3,BF
30 DIM P(100)
40 GET (170,75)-(175,140),P
50 CLS
60 X = STICK(0):Y = STICK(1)
70 IF Y>130 THEN Y = 130
80 PUT(170,Y),P,PSET
90 GOTO 60
```

(For further insights into the tennis videogame, see Example 3 in the discussion of the POINT function. That example shows how to determine if a ball is about to strike a paddle.)

5. The following program uses the lever to move a ball around the screen. Again, the program requires the GET and PUT graphics statements. Press Ctrl-Break to terminate the program.

```
10 SCREEN 1,0: COLOR 1,1: CLS: KEY OFF
20 CIRCLE(2,2),2: PAINT (2,2),3
30 DIM B(10)
40 GET (0,0)-(4,4),B
50 PUT (0,0),B
60 X = STICK(0): Y = STICK(1)
70 PUT(X,Y),B,PSET
80 X1 = X: Y1 = Y
```

```
90 X = STICK(0): Y = STICK(1)
100 IF Y>195 THEN Y = 195
110 PUT (X,Y),B: PUT (X1,Y1),B
120 GOTO 80
```

COMMENTS

1. Two joysticks can be connected to the computer. This feature is not available with BASIC 1.00 or BASIC 1.05. If two joysticks are connected, the coordinates of the lever of the first joystick will be given by the functions STICK(0) and STICK(1), and the coordinates of the second joystick will be given by the functions STICK(2) and STICK(3).

2. The function STICK(0) actually observes the values of all four STICK functions and must be invoked before any of the other three functions can be used. For instance, notice that in line 60 of Example 4, we recorded the x-coordinate of the lever, even though the y-coordinate was the only one needed to position the paddle. If the statement X = STICK(0) had been omitted, we would not have received the correct values of STICK(1).

APPLICATIONS

Joysticks are used primarily for games. The players can control the positions of objects on the screen as in Examples 1, 4, and 5.

STOP

While running a program, you can press Ctrl-Break to stop the execution of the program. You cannot predict in advance exactly where the program will stop. As an alternative, including the statement

```
STOP
```

in a line of the program guarantees that the program will stop execution at that line. The computer will display **Break in n** where n is the number of the line containing the STOP statement. The computer will then be in direct mode. The command CONT entered while in direct mode causes the program to continue execution at the statement following the STOP statement.

COMMENTS

1.   After STOPing a program, there are further options for proceeding other than by using CONT. The command RUN will rerun the program from the beginning. The statements **RUN m, GOTO m** and **GOSUB m** will continue execution of the program beginning with line number m. However, RUN and **RUN m** cause the variables to lose their values.

2.   After a program has been STOPped and the computer is in direct mode, you can display and change values of variables and make calculations. However, if you enter or delete a line of the program or execute one of the statements CLEAR, MERGE, or CHAIN MERGE, then you cannot use CONT to resume running the program. You can, however, continue execution by using a RUN, GOTO, or GOSUB statement.

3.   The END statement is similar to the STOP statement. Both cause the program to stop execution and can be followed by CONT, GOTO, GOSUB, or RUN to resume execution. There are two primary differences. END closes all open files, whereas STOP leaves them open. Also, END does not cause a ''Break in n'' message to be displayed.

EXAMPLES

1.   The following program displays the balance after each month (for 120 months) when $1000 is deposited at 12% interest compounded monthly. Upon running the program, you will see the balances for the first 12 months followed by the message ''Break in 60''. If you then type CONT, the next 12 months will be displayed. Without the STOP statement, the first 108 months would have flickered by too fast to be read, and only the last 12 months would be clearly displayed.

```
10 FOR I = 1 TO 109 STEP 12
20    CLS
30    FOR J = 0 TO 11
```

```
40        PRINT I+J,1000*(1.01)^(I+J)
50     NEXT J
60     STOP
70 NEXT I
```

```
2.  10 A = 30
    20 PRINT 20
    30 PRINT A
    40 STOP
    50 PRINT 50
    RUN
     20
     30
    Break in 40
    Ok
    A = 40
    Ok
    GOTO 30
     40
    Break in 40
    Ok
    CONT
     50
    Ok
    RUN
     20
     30
    Break in 40
    Ok
    30 PRINT A+100
    CONT
    Can't continue
    Ok
```

APPLICATIONS

1. STOP is used when debugging a program. The programmer inserts the STOP statement at a crucial point in the program and then, while in direct mode, checks the values of certain variables to make sure that everything is in order. After the programmer is convinced that the program is functioning properly, he deletes the STOP statement.

2. Sometimes programmers insert a STOP statement before a subroutine to guarantee that the subroutine will only be executed as the result of a GOSUB statement.

STR$

Each number has a standard representation that is appropriate to its precision and magnitude. Some examples follow:

Number	Standard Representation
2.50	2.5
3E+2	300
.00000003	3E-08
&H10	16
12345678	12345678
-56	-56

If n is a number, then

    STR$(n)

is the string consisting of the characters in the standard representation of n.

COMMENTS

1.   When n is a negative number, the first character of STR$(n) is a minus sign. Otherwise, the first character is a space.

2.   The VAL function undoes the STR$ function in the sense that, for any number n, VAL(STR$(n)) is equal to n.

3.   The STR$ function can be applied to numeric expressions. See Example 1.

4.   Most numbers take up much more space in memory when stored as strings rather than as numeric constants.

EXAMPLES

1.   ```
     PRINT STR$(2.50); STR$(2+3); STR$(1D-8); LEN(STR$(25))
      2.5 5 .00000001  3
     Ok
     ```

2.   ```
     10 A = 23.45: B = &H11: C = 87654321
     20 PRINT STR$(A); STR$(B);
     30 PRINT STR$(C); STR$(87654321)
     RUN
      23.45 17 8.765432E+07 87654321
     Ok
     ```

In line 10, since C is a single-precision variable, the number 87654321 was converted to a single-precision number.

3.   Often, house addresses are used as strings but sorted by street number. The STR$ function allows us to have it both ways.

```
10 INPUT "House number"; N
20 INPUT "Street name"; S$
30 PRINT "The address is";STR$(N)+" "+S$
RUN
House number? 1600
Street name? Pennsylvania Avenue
The address is 1600 Pennsylvania Avenue
Ok
```

4.   When displaying a number, we must be aware of the blank characters that may be added before or after the number itself.

```
10 A$="3.14159"
20 A=VAL(A$)
30 T$="to five decimal places"
40 PRINT "pi="; A$; T$
50 PRINT "pi="; A; T$
60 PRINT "pi="; STR$(A); T$
RUN
pi=3.14159to five decimal places
pi= 3.14159 to five decimal places
pi= 3.14159to five decimal places
Ok
```

APPLICATIONS

1.   In order to make programs user-friendly, we often work with numbers as strings and use the functions STR$ and VAL to go back and forth.

2.   The STR$ function is essential in programs doing symbolic manipulation of numbers. One example is a program that will express the sum of two fractions as a fraction.

‖STRIG

The STRIG statement and function requires a special board, called the Game Control Adapter, and a joystick, which is connected to the Game Control Adapter.

The joystick shown in Figure 1 has two buttons and a lever that can be pushed in any direction. This discussion deals only with the buttons. (See the discussion of the STICK function for information about the lever.)

FIGURE 1

The statement

    STRIG ON

causes the computer to check the joystick after execution of each BASIC statement to see if any buttons are being pressed. The function

    STRIG(1)

assumes the value -1, if the lower button is currently pressed, and the value 0 otherwise. The function

    STRIG(5)

assumes the value -1, if the upper button is currently pressed, and the value 0 otherwise. The function

    STRIG(0)

has value 0 until the lower button is pressed, and then has value -1. It holds this value (even if the button is released) until after the value of the function is requested, at which time the value reverts to 0. In other words, this function tells if the lower button has been pressed since the program began execution or since the last time the value of the function was requested. The function

```
STRIG(4)
```

which provides information about the upper button, is analogous to the function STRIG(0).

EXAMPLES

1. The following program presents the values of the 4 functions every 5 seconds. A beeping sound precedes each presentation of function values.

```
10 CLS: STRIG ON
20 LOCATE 10,15: PRINT "STRIG(0) =" STRIG(0)
30 LOCATE 12,15: PRINT "STRIG(1) =" STRIG(1)
40 LOCATE 14,15: PRINT "STRIG(4) =" STRIG(4)
50 LOCATE 16,15: PRINT "STRIG(5) =" STRIG(5)
60 FOR I = 1 TO 3000: NEXT I
70 BEEP: GOTO 20
```

Try different combinations of button pressing. For instance, press a button, but release it before the beeping sound. Or hold a button down for awhile. Press Ctrl-Break to terminate the program.

2. The following program produces a spaceship and an attacking missile. Press the lower button to shoot down the missile. After shooting down the missile, press the upper button within four seconds to produce another missile.

```
10 CLS: LOCATE 15,1
20 PRINT ">==>"
30 STRIG ON
40 FOR I=1 TO 39
50    LOCATE 15,40-I: PRINT CHR$(17)+" "
60    FOR J=1 TO 200: NEXT J
70    IF STRIG(1) = 0 THEN 140
80    LOCATE 15,5: PRINT STRING$(36-I,45)
90    FOR K=1 TO 200: NEXT K
100   LOCATE 15,5: PRINT STRING$(36-I,32)
110   FOR K=1 TO 3000: NEXT K
120   IF STRIG(4) = -1 THEN 40
130   END
140 NEXT I
```

STRIG

COMMENTS

1. Advanced BASIC is required in order to use both buttons. That is, the command BASICA must have been given when BASIC was invoked. With DISK BASIC, only the lower button can be used.

2. Actually, two joysticks can be connected to the computer. If this is done, the functions STICK(2), STICK(3), STICK(6), and STICK(7) produce information about the second joystick analogous to the functions STICK(0), STICK(1), STICK(4), and STICK(5). (*Note:* BASIC 1.00 and BASIC 1.05 allow only one joystick.)

3. It is important that the statement **STRIG ON** be executed before any of the joystick button functions are used. Otherwise the error message "Illegal function call" results. However, when the button functions are no longer needed, it is a good idea to disable the buttons with the statement **STRIG OFF**.

4. Two other statements that are important for working with joystick buttons are ON STRIG and STRIG(n).

5. The command **CLEAR** resets the buttons to off, as would a **STRIG OFF** statement.

APPLICATIONS

Joysticks are used primarily for games. The players use the levers to move objects around on the screen and use the buttons to initiate certain actions, as in Example 2.

STRIG(n)

A typical joystick consists of a lever and two buttons. The STICK function is used to read the position of the lever, and the STRIG function is used to determine which buttons have been pressed. (See the discussions of either of these functions for a picture of a joystick.)

The computer has the capability of responding to the pressing of a button by branching to a subroutine. This process is referred to as "trapping" a joystick button. The statement

```
STRIG(0) ON
```

is used in conjunction with the statement **ON STRIG(0) GOSUB m** to trap the lower button. The statement **STRIG(0) ON** causes the computer to constantly check the status of the lower button for possible trapping, and the statement **ON STRIG(0) GOSUB m** instructs the computer to respond to the pressing of the lower button by branching to line m. We say that STRIG(0) ON enables trapping of the lower button. The statement

```
STRIG(0) OFF
```

disables trapping of the lower button. The statements **STRIG(4) ON** and **STRIG(4) OFF** enable and disable trapping of the upper button. (See the discussion of the statement ON STRIG(n) for further details.)

The statement

```
STRIG(0) STOP
```

enables a delayed trapping of the lower button. The combination of this statement and **ON STRIG(0) GOSUB m** results in the computer remembering if the lower button has been pressed, but delaying branching until the statement **STRIG(0) ON** is executed. The statement **STRIG(4) STOP** enables a delayed trapping of the upper button. See Example 2.

EXAMPLES

```
1.   10 STRIG(0) ON
     20 ON STRIG(0) GOSUB 90
     30 PRINT "Press the lower joystick button"
     40 IF A=0 THEN 40
     50 STRIG(0) OFF
     60 PRINT "Press it again"
     70 FOR I = 1 TO 4000: NEXT I
     80 END
     90 BEEP
     100 A=1
     110 RETURN
```

STRIG(n)

Line 40 will be executed repeatedly until the lower button of the joystick is pressed. Then the speaker will beep and lines 40, 50, and 60 will be executed once. Line 70 produces a delay of 5 seconds to allow you to press the lower button again. However, this time no beeping sound is heard, since trapping was disabled in line 50.

2.
```
10 CLS: KEY OFF
20 ON STRIG(4) GOSUB 90
30 LOCATE 12,9: PRINT "The time is"
40 STRIG(4) STOP
50 LOCATE 12,21
60 PRINT TIME$
70 STRIG(4) ON
80 GOTO 40
90 T=T+1: LOCATE 1,1
100 PRINT "The upper button has been pressed" T "times"
110 RETURN
```

This program turns the computer into a clock. Also, the first row of the screen keeps a running count of the number of times that the upper button of the joystick has been pressed. This count is updated by the subroutine in lines 90 through 110, which is entered every time the upper button is pressed. Line 40 guarantees that the subroutine will not be entered right after line 50. If this were to happen, the computer would PRINT the button data on row one and then RETURN to line 60 and PRINT the current time on row 2. To see this occur, change line 80 to **80 GOTO 50** and press the upper button repeatedly.

COMMENTS

1. The statements discussed here can only be used with Advanced BASIC. That is, the command BASICA must have been given when BASIC was invoked. Also, use of a joystick requires the Game Control Adapter.

2. When two joysticks are connected to the computer, the buttons on the second joystick are controlled with statements containing STRIG(2) and STRIG(6). This feature is not available with BASIC 1.00 and BASIC 1.05.

3. The trapping of all buttons is disabled if one of the commands CHAIN, CHAIN MERGE, CLEAR, LOAD, MERGE, or RUN is executed, or if a program line is entered or deleted.

APPLICATIONS

Joysticks are used primarily for games. The players use the levers to move objects and use the buttons to initiate certain actions. (See Example 2 in the discussion of ON STRIG(n).)

STRING$

Appendix A lists 256 different characters and their ASCII values. If c is one of these characters (say, with ASCII value m) and L is a number, then a string of L c's will result from each of the following functions:

```
STRING$(L,"c")
```

```
STRING$(L,m)
```

```
STRING$(L,C$)
```

where C$ is any string whose first character is c.

EXAMPLES

1.  ```
    PRINT STRING$(5,"+"); STRING$(3,60); STRING$(4,"Ron")
    +++++<<<RRRR
    Ok
    ```

The ASCII value of " < " is 60.

2.  ```
    10 A$ = STRING$(5,"*"): B$ = "blue": C = 4
    20 PRINT A$+STRING$(3,B$); A$; STRING$(C,B$)
    RUN
    *****bbb*****bbbb
    Ok
    ```

3.  ```
    PRINT "Merry" + STRING$(2,31) + "Xmas"
    Merry

         Xmas
    Ok
    ```

The ASCII value of "cursor down" is 31.

4. The following program draws a bar chart from sales data.

    ```
    10 FOR I = 1 TO 3
    20    READ M$, S
    30    PRINT M$ + " " + STRING$(S,"="); S
    40 NEXT I
    50 DATA Jan, 25, Feb, 21, Mar, 32
    RUN
    Jan   ========================= 25
    Feb   ===================== 21
    Mar   ================================ 32
    Ok
    ```
    ```

STRING$

5. The following program centers a word in a field of underline characters in a width 40 screen.

```
10 WIDTH 40: INPUT X$
20 L = (40-LEN(X$))\2
30 PRINT STRING$(L,"_")+X$+STRING$(L,"_"
)+STRING$(LEN(X$) MOD 2,"_");
RUN
? APPENDIX
_____APPENDIX_____
Ok
```

COMMENTS

1. STRING$(L," ") produces the same result as SPACE$(L).

2. STRING$(L,"c") is not valid if c is the quotation mark.

3. If L is not an integer it will be rounded to an integer. If the (rounded) value of L is negative or greater than 256, the error message "Illegal function call" results.

APPLICATIONS

1. The STRING$ function is used in conjunction with LPRINT to embellish printouts. For instance, a portion of a page can be separated from the rest of the page by a row of asterisks, *.

2. The STRING$ function can be used with the nondisplayable characters (such as carriage return and those which move the cursor) to gain flexibility in the placement of displayable characters.

The SWAP statement is used to switch the values of two variables. For instance, if A and B are variables of the same type that have been assigned values, then the statement

```
SWAP A, B
```

assigns B's value to A, and A's value to B.

Comments

1. The variables can both be string variables or both numeric variables. If they are numeric variables, they must both have the same precision (that is, integer, single-, or double-precision). If the variables are not of the same type, a "Type mismatch" error results.

2. The variables can also be array variables; again, provided that they are the same type. However, the SWAP statement cannot be used to switch all of the values of two arrays at once. For instance, suppose that A and B are one-dimensional arrays with subscripts ranging from 0 to 10. Then, the routine

```
110 FOR I = 0 TO 10
120    SWAP A(I), B(I)
130 NEXT I
```

will interchange corresponding values of the two arrays. However, this same result cannot be accomplished with the single statement SWAP A, B.

Examples

1.
```
10 A$ = "COMPUTER"
20 B$ = "MY"
30 SWAP A$, B$
40 PRINT A$; " "; B$
RUN
MY COMPUTER
Ok
```

2. This program alphabetizes two words. It can be expanded to a program that will alphabetize any list of words. (See the bubble sort program in the discussion of FOR . . . NEXT.)

```
10 INPUT "First Word";A$(1)
20 INPUT "Second Word";B$(1)
30 IF A$(1)>B$(1) THEN SWAP A$(1), B$(1)
40 PRINT A$(1), B$(1)
RUN
```

SWAP

```
First Word? MAT
Second Word? CAT
CAT            MAT
Ok
```

3. ```
   10 A = 5: B$ = "FIVE"
   20 SWAP A, B$
   RUN
   Type mismatch in 20
   Ok
   ```

4. ```
   10 A% = 5: B = 6
   20 SWAP A%, B
   RUN
   Type mismatch in 20
   Ok
   ```

Although the two variables are both numeric variables, A% is an integer numeric variable and B is a single-precision numeric variable.

5. ```
   10 A = 5%: B = 6
   20 SWAP A, B
   RUN
   Ok
   ```

The statement **A = 5%** had the effect of converting the integer constant 5 to the single-precision constant 5. (See the discussion of CSNG for elaboration.) Since A and B were both single-precision variables, the switch was allowed.
   ```

Many operations cannot be easily performed with BASIC. Some examples are:

1. copying a disk
2. checking how much space remains on a disk
3. formatting a disk
4. running certain software packages

In order to perform one of these operations, we should first return to the Disk Operating System (DOS). This is accomplished by the command

```
SYSTEM
```

COMMENTS

1. The DOS diskette does not have to be in one of the disk drives before giving the SYSTEM command. However, the DOS diskette must be inserted before certain DOS commands (referred to in the DOS Reference Manual as "external") are invoked.

2. The SYSTEM command causes any BASIC program currently in memory to be lost. Hence, important programs should be SAVEd on a disk before invoking the SYSTEM command.

3. The SYSTEM command automatically closes all data files that might have been left open.

4. BASIC was initially invoked from DOS by typing the word BASIC or BASICA following A>, B>, C>, or D>, which identifies the "default drive." For instance, had the screen read **B> BASIC** when BASIC was invoked, then drive B would be the default drive. When DOS starts up, it automatically makes drive A the default drive. When we give the command SYSTEM, the letter of the default drive (followed by >) appears on the screen.

5. In BASIC 3.0 (and later versions), DOS can be invoked by the SHELL command. The user is then able to return to BASIC with the original BASIC program intact.

EXAMPLES

1. Suppose that drive B is the default drive and that we are operating in BASIC.

```
Ok
SYSTEM
B>
```

SYSTEM

2. Suppose that we are currently operating in BASIC, have the DOS diskette in drive A (the default drive), and would would like to know how much space remains on a diskette in drive B.

```
Ok
SYSTEM
A>CHKDSK B:
        30 disk files
    160256 bytes total disk space
     79360 bytes remain available

     65536 bytes total memory
     53360 bytes free
```

In this example we typed the words SYSTEM and CHKDSK B:.

The screen is capable of displaying 80 characters per line (referred to as a WIDTH 80 screen) or 40 characters per line (referred to as a WIDTH 40 screen). We will assume a WIDTH 80 screen in this discussion. The modifications for the WIDTH 40 screen will be clear. The positions on the line are named Position 1, Position 2, . . . , Position 80.

The TAB function is used in conjunction with the PRINT statement to display items at specified positions on the screen. If n is a positive whole number and A$ is a string, where the sum of n and the length of A$ is at most 81, then the statement

```
PRINT TAB(n) A$
```

will display the value of A$ beginning at position n. A similar result holds for numeric variables or constants; however, we must take into account the trailing (and sometimes leading) spaces displayed with numbers. The TAB function also can be used in multiple PRINT statements to position the items.

EXAMPLES

1. ```
   PRINT TAB(3) "Boca Raton":PRINT TAB(3) 1:PRINT TAB(3) -5
     Boca Raton
       1
      -5
   Ok
   ```

2. ```
   10 FOR I = 1 TO 5
   20     READ A$, B$, C$
   30     PRINT A$ TAB(8) B$ TAB(29) C$
   40 NEXT I
   50 DATA YEAR, BEST PICTURE, DIRECTOR
   60 DATA 1960, The Apartment, Wilder
   70 DATA 1961, West Side Story, Wise
   80 DATA 1962, Lawrence of Arabia, Lean
   90 DATA 1963, Tom Jones, Richardson
   RUN
   YEAR    BEST PICTURE         DIRECTOR
   1960    The Apartment        Wilder
   1961    West Side Story      Wise
   1962    Lawrence of Arabia   Lean
   1963    Tom Jones            Richardson
   Ok
   ```

COMMENTS

1. The TAB function respects all of the subtleties of the PRINT statement. For instance, if there is not enough room on the line to display an item in the

TAB

position specified by TAB, the item will be placed at the beginning of the next line. If the TAB function is followed by a comma, then the next item will be displayed not at the TAB location, but at the beginning of the next print zone after the TAB location.

2.   The TAB function will not cause the cursor to backspace. If the number n specifies a position that is to the left of the current cursor position, the next item will be placed on the next line beginning at position n.

3.   The argument n in TAB(n) can be any number from -32768.49 to 32767.49. If n is not a whole number it will be rounded to a whole number. If n is less than 1, then TAB(n) is interpreted as TAB(1). If the (rounded) value of n is greater than 80, then TAB(n) is interpreted as TAB(r) where r is the remainder resulting from dividing the (rounded) value of n by 80. For a WIDTH 40 screen, if n is greater than 40 then r is the remainder resulting from dividing the (rounded) value of n by 40.

4.   If the line to contain the displayed items already has some characters displayed in it, TAB will convert everything in its path to spaces. In this respect, the two statements **LOCATE 1,1: PRINT TAB(9) "*"** and **LOCATE 1,9: PRINT "*"** have different results. The first statement is the same as **LOCATE 1,1: PRINT SPACE$(8)+"*"**. The second statement will preserve all of the characters already displayed in the first 8 positions.

5.   TAB can be used with LPRINT and PRINT# in exactly the same way that it is used with PRINT. A WIDTH statement can be used to specify the line width for the printer. This number should be used in place of 80 in the above discussion. When TAB(n) is used with PRINT# to send items to a sequential file, integer values of n greater than 255 will be replaced by their remainder when n is divided by 256 and will induce a carriage return and line feed pair if one was not placed at the end of the previous data.

6.   The argument of TAB can be any numeric expression, such as $2+3$ or $X*4$.

7.   If TAB(n) is the last item in a PRINT statement, then, after advancing to column n, TAB will also suppress the carriage return and line feed which PRINT would normally perform. Therefore, the next PRINT statement will continue displaying on the same line. (See Example 7.)

FURTHER EXAMPLES

3.   **PRINT TAB(75) "Grand Hotel"**

```
Grand Hotel
Ok
```

4.   **PRINT TAB(5), "The Broadway Melody"**

```
                        The Broadway Melody
Ok
```

474

5. PRINT TAB(30) "Cavalcade" TAB(5) "It Happened One Night"
                               Cavalcade
       It Happened One Night
   OK

6. PRINT TAB(84) "Mutiny on the Bounty"
       Mutiny on the Bounty
   Ok

7. PRINT "Mysterious Island" TAB(25): PRINT "Centennial"
   Mysterious Island   Centennial
   Ok

Notice that the first PRINT statement had the same result as if it had ended with a semicolon.

8. The following program draws a simple graph of the equation $Y = (X - 7)\wedge2 + 1$. See Figure 1. Tilt your head to the right when viewing the graph. The lowest point on the graph has coordinates (7,1).

```
10 FOR X = 0 TO 14
20 PRINT TAB((X-7)^2 + 1) "*"
30 NEXT
RUN
```

Ok

FIGURE 1

475

TAB

APPLICATIONS

1. The TAB function is used to organize data into columns, as in Example 2.

2. TAB can be used to draw rudimentary graphs of functions. The printer allows us to plot these graphs using a large number of values of x.

3. TAB can be used to right-justify data. For instance, the statement **PRINT TAB(30-LEN(A\$)) A\$** will display A$ with its last character at position 30.

TAN is the trigonometric function tangent. For an acute angle in a right tri-angle, the tangent of the angle is the ratio:

$$\frac{\text{length of the side opposite the angle}}{\text{length of the side adjacent to the angle}}$$

The definition of the tangent function for arbitrary angles and a discussion of radian measure are presented in Appendix M. For any number x, except as noted in Comment 1 below, the value of the function

TAN(x)

is the tangent of the angle of x radians.

COMMENTS

1.   The tangent function is defined for all x except for x = $\pi/2$, $-\pi/2$, $3*\pi/2$, $-3*\pi/2$, etc. Figure 1 contains the graph of y = TAN(x).

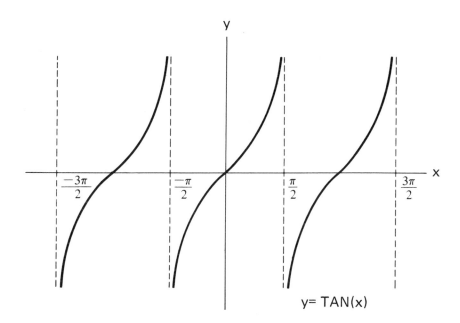

y= TAN(x)

FIGURE 1

2.   In versions of BASIC preceding BASIC 2.0, the value of TAN(x) is always a single-precision number. Versions beginning with BASIC 2.0 pro-vide the option of computing TAN(x) as a double-precision number. To exer-cise this option, invoke BASIC with the command BASIC/D or BASICA/D.

TAN

Then, whenever x is a double-precision number, the value of TAN(x) will be computed as a double-precision number.

3. The inverse of the tangent function is the function arctangent. This function is the BASIC function ATN. ATN(x) is the angle between between $-\pi/2$ and $\pi/2$ whose tangent is x.

EXAMPLES

Examples 1 through 3 are appropriate for BASIC 2.0 (or a later version) without the /D option or for earlier versions of BASIC.

1.  ```
    PRINT TAN(1); TAN(-5.678); TAN(2E+8); TAN(1.23456789)
     1.557408  .6917763  .9200778  2.861238
    Ok
    ```

2.  ```
    10 A = 2: B = 7*A: C# = .7328151#: D# = TAN(C#)
    20 PRINT TAN(A); TAN(B); TAN(C#); D#
    RUN
    -2.18504  7.244607  .9  .8999999761581421
    Ok
    ```

Note the difference between the results obtained for TAN(C#) and D# (which has been assigned the value TAN(C#)). TAN(C#) was computed as the single-precision number, .9. The statement D# = TAN(C#) had the effect of converting .9 to double-precision; that is, D# is actually CDBL(TAN(C#)). (See the discussion of CDBL for an explanation of the conversion.)

3.  ```
    10 A = TAN(1): B = ATN(A): C = ATN(.5): D = TAN(C)
    20 PRINT A; B; C; D
    RUN
     1.557408  1  .4636476  .5
    Ok
    ```

In general, for any number x between $-\pi/2$ and $\pi/2$, ATN(TAN(x)) = x, and for any number x, TAN(ATN(x)) = x.

4. This example used BASIC 2.1 with the /D option.

    ```
    PRINT TAN(2%); TAN(2); TAN(2#)
    -2.18504 -2.18504 -2.185039863261519
    Ok
    ```

APPLICATIONS

Surveyors use the tangent function to measure the distance across a river. In Figure 2, the angle A is determined by using a transit and sighting a tree on the opposite side of the river. The width of the river is computed to be L*TAN(A).
    ```

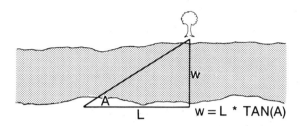

$w = L * \text{TAN}(A)$

FIGURE 2

‖TIME$

The computer has an internal clock that can be accessed by BASIC. TIME$ can be used as a statement to set the clock or as a variable to read the clock.

PART I   TIME$ AS A STATEMENT

If T$ is an appropriate string stating the time (see Comment 1) then the statement

```
TIME$ = T$
```

sets the clock to the stated time.

COMMENT

1.   The string T$ must be a sequence of 1, 2, or 3 whole numbers separated by colons or periods. The first number, which gives the hour, must be between 0 and 23. Midnight is 0 o'clock and 11 PM is 23 o'clock. The second number, if included, gives the minutes and must be between 0 and 59. The third number, if included, gives the seconds and also must be between 0 and 59. Some possibilities and their corresponding times are:

T$	Corresponding Time
3:21:51	21 minutes and 51 seconds past 3 AM
14:5	2:05 PM
0	midnight
23:59:59	1 second before midnight
12.01	1 minute past noon

PART II   TIME$ AS A VARIABLE

The variable

```
TIME$
```

always has as its value a string of 8 characters giving the current time on the clock.

FURTHER COMMENTS

2.   The value of TIME$ will always have the form hh:mm:ss, where each number consists of 2 digits (with the first digit possibly zero).

3. When the computer is first turned on, DOS requests a value for TIME$. If no value is specified, the value of TIME$ is set to ''00:00:00.'' The clock then keeps time starting at this value.

EXAMPLES

1.  ```
    TIME$ = "1:2:3": B$ = TIME$: PRINT B$
    01:02:03
    Ok
    ```

2.  ```
    A$ = "0:12": TIME$ = A$: PRINT TIME$
    00:12:00
    Ok
    ```

3. The following program turns the computer into a stopwatch. The variable INKEY$ takes its value from a pressed key. Hence, it has the value '''' until a key is pressed.

```
10 PRINT "Press any key to start stopwatch"
20 IF INKEY$="" GOTO 20
30 CLS: BEEP
40 PRINT "Press any key to stop": PRINT
50 TIME$="0"
60 PRINT "Elapsed time is ";
70 LOCATE 3,17
80 PRINT TIME$
90 IF INKEY$="" GOTO 70
RUN
Press any key to start stopwatch
```
(key pressed)
```
Press any key to stop

Elapsed time is 00:02:10
```

The time stated in the last sentence will change until a key is pressed.

4. The following sequence of lines, which produce a pause of 7 seconds, can be modified to produce a pause of up to 59 seconds.

```
10 TIME$ = "0"
20 WHILE VAL(RIGHT$(TIME$,2)) < 7
30 WEND
Ok
```

TIME$

APPLICATIONS

1. TIME$ can be used to determine the running time of a program by setting the time to zero in the first line of the program and having the time displayed by the last line of the program.

2. The computer can be turned into an alarm clock via TIME$.

3. TIME$ is often used to reseed the random number generator. (See the discussion of RANDOMIZE for further details.)

The function TIMER is not available in versions of BASIC prior to BASIC 2.0.

When the computer is first turned on, its internal clock is set to 00:00:00 (i.e., midnight). The time of day can be reset in DOS by responding to the request "Enter new time:" or can be reset in BASIC by using the TIME$ statement.

There are 86400 seconds in a day. At any time, the value of the function

```
TIMER
```

is the number of seconds from 00:00:00 to the current time on the clock.

EXAMPLES

1. Suppose that the computer was turned on about 2 minutes ago and that the time was not reset.

```
PRINT TIMER
 120.45
Ok
```

The computer has been operating for 120 and 45/100 seconds.

2. In the following example, line 10 sets the time to one minute past midnight.

```
10 TIME$ = "0:01:00"
20 FOR I = 1 TO 8
30    PRINT TIMER;
40 NEXT I
RUN
 59.97  60.08  60.08  60.14  60.19  60.25  60.25  60.3
Ok
```

So, who's perfect?

3. In the following speed quiz, the response time is reported.

```
10 T = TIMER
20 INPUT "What is the square root of 5 times the square root
of 20"; A
30 IF A <> 10 THEN PRINT "Wrong": GOTO 20
40 PRINT "Correct. ";
50 PRINT "You answered the question in"; TIMER-T; "seconds."
RUN
What is the square root of 5 times the square root of 20? 8
```

483

TIMER

```
Wrong
What is the square root of 5 times the square root of 20? 10
Correct. You answered the question in 19.66003 seconds.
Ok
```

4.   The following sequence of lines, which produces a pause of 7 seconds, can be modified to produce a pause of up to 24 hours.

```
10 TIME$ = "0"
20 WHILE TIMER < 7
30 WEND
```

COMMENTS

1.   The value of TIMER is a single-precision numeric constant between 0 and 86400.

2.   Although the function TIME$ is related to TIMER, it is important to remember that the value of TIME$ is a string, whereas the value of TIMER is a number.

The command TRON is used to debug a program. Suppose that you have just written a program and would like to analyze it by tracing the sequence of lines executed when RUNning the program. The command

```
TRON
```

causes the line number of each line to be displayed as it is executed, along with all information that would have otherwise been displayed. We can disable the tracing of successive line numbers by executing the command

```
TROFF
```

EXAMPLE

1.
```
10 INPUT N
20 S = 0
30 FOR I = 1 TO N
40    S = S + I
50 NEXT I
60 PRINT "THE SUM OF THE FIRST";N;"NUMBERS IS";S
70 GOTO 10
TRON
Ok
RUN
[10]? 2
[20][30][40][50][40][50][60]THE SUM OF THE FIRST 2
NUMBERS IS 3
[70][10]? _
Break in 10
Ok
TROFF
Ok
RUN
? 5
THE SUM OF THE FIRST 5 NUMBERS IS 15
? _
```

COMMENTS

1. After invoking the TRON command, tracing will continue with every execution of the program even after the program has been edited and lines have been added and deleted. Tracing will continue until either TROFF has been invoked or until the program has been removed from memory with a NEW, LOAD, or CHAIN command.

TRON and TROFF

2.   The function keys F7 and F8 enter the TRON and TROFF commands, respectively.

3.   Often, the use of TRON results in so much information appearing on the screen that scrolling takes place. Scrolling (and the execution of the program) can be halted by pressing Ctrl-Num Lock and then resumed by pressing any key (other than the shift keys).

4.   TRON and TROFF also can be used in program lines to analyze just a portion of the program.

Problems exist that we would like the computer to solve, yet writing a BASIC program to do the job can prove extremely awkward, or a program, when written, can prove to be very slow in executing. This is especially true for programs that manipulate individual bits or bytes of memory, or programs that execute a set of instructions a large number of times. In these cases it is often useful to solve part of the problem using a machine language subroutine. The function

```
USRn (var)
```

allows a BASIC program to transfer control to a machine language subroutine. Here, n is one of the digits 0 through 9, which, together with USR, names a machine language subroutine which has been placed in memory. A single argument, var, is allowed for passing data to a USR function. For example, if user-defined subroutine 5 is to make use of B$, then the appropriate call statement is **USR5(B$)**.

You should think of USR as a user-defined function specified by a machine language subroutine. Just as with any user-defined function, you must precede its first use with a DEF statement which defines it. In the case of a USR function, the appropriate DEF statement is of the form

```
DEF USRn = L
```

where L is the offset into the current memory segment of the first byte of the machine language subroutine. (See DEF USR for further details.)

COMMENTS

1. A machine language subroutine called by USR may have only one piece of data passed to it.

2. You may not pass arrays with USR.

3. In a USR call, you may omit the n, in which case, USR0 is assumed.

4. USR functions are not erased by commands such as RUN, NEW, and CLEAR. The offset associated with USRn can be changed only by a new DEF USRn statement.

5. Both the USR functions and CALL statements allow BASIC programs to pass control to machine language subroutines. The CALL statement can pass more than one argument, and is therefore more versatile.

VAL

If the leading characters of the string A$ correspond to a number, then

    VAL(A$)

will be the number represented by these characters. Otherwise, VAL(A$) will be zero.

EXAMPLES

1.  ```
    PRINT VAL("123"); VAL("8.5 percent"); VAL("$123.45")
      123  8.5  0
    Ok
    ```

2.  ```
    10 A$="-67.00": B$="two": C$="2E+3": D=VAL("1,234")
    20 PRINT VAL(A$); VAL(B$); VAL(C$); D
    RUN
    -67  0  2000  1
    Ok
    ```

COMMENTS

1. The VAL function undoes the STR$ function in the sense that for any number n, VAL(STR$(n)) is equal to n.

2. The VAL function produces a double-precision numeric constant. See Example 4.

3. The VAL function recognizes numbers even when they are written in hexadecimal or octal notation.

4. The VAL function ignores all spaces. See Example 5.

5. The VAL function will not accept a string containing a percent symbol (%) unless it is preceded at some point by a character which is not a blank or digit. For instance, the expressions VAL("23%"), VAL("%5"), and "VAL ("5 %") all result in the message "Syntax error." However, VAL ("A%") and VAL("23-%") are acceptable.

6. Pressing ALT-V displays the word VAL.

7. VAL("") is 0.

FURTHER EXAMPLES

3.  ```
    A$ = STR$(14.50): PRINT VAL(A$)
      14.5
    Ok
    ```

4.  ```
    PRINT 123E+09; VAL("123E+09")
     1.23E+11  123000000000
    Ok
    ```

5. PRINT VAL("&H10"); VAL("&10"); VAL("1   2p")
      16 8 12
    Ok

6. The following program provides a way to interact with the computer while dealing with numeric input.

```
10 INPUT "Type a number (Enter E to Exit): ", N$
20 IF N$="E" THEN END
30 N = VAL(N$)
40 PRINT "The square of ";N$; " is"; N*N
50 GOTO 10
RUN
Type a number (Enter E to Exit): 15
The square of 15 is 225
Type a number (Enter E to Exit): E
Ok
```

Had we used a numeric variable in line 10, we would not have had such a convenient way to exit the program.

7. PRINT VAL("123 E 2nd Ave.")
      12300
    Ok

In this example, the combination "E 2" was an acceptable form of scientific notation.

APPLICATIONS

The VAL function is valuable in making programs user-friendly. Numeric data is input as a string and then converted back to a number after being altered as necessary. (See Application 2 in the discussion of LEN.)

VARPTR

A part of memory, referred to as BASIC's Data Segment, is set aside as a workspace for BASIC. In particular, the values of all variables are stored in BASIC's Data Segment. The statement DEF SEG specifies BASIC's Data Segment as the current segment. Throughout this discussion, we assume that the current segment is BASIC's Data Segment.

PART I   NUMERIC VARIABLES

Numeric variables are of three types: integer, single-, and double-precision. (See the discussion of DEFtype statements.) Integer variables are stored in 2 bytes of memory, single-precision variables in 4, and double-precision variables in 8. If numvar is one of these numeric variables, then the value of the function

```
VARPTR(numvar)
```

is the offset into BASIC's Data Segment of the first byte in the sequence of bytes storing the value of the variable.

COMMENTS

1.   If n is an integer from 0 to 32767, then n can be written in the form

$$n = r + 256*q$$

where r is less than 256 and q is less than 128. To determine q and r, perform long division. Dividing 256 into n produces a quotient q and a remainder r. The integer n is stored in 2 bytes, with r as the value of the first byte and q as the value of the second byte.

2.   Single- and double-precision numbers are stored using a floating point binary format. (See Appendix B for a discussion of the binary representation of numbers.) We will present one illustration of how this format works. The single-precision constant 57.625 has the binary representation 111001.101, which also can be written as

.11100110100000000000000 T6

where T6 stands for $2\wedge 6$. The bytes contain the following pieces of information:

```
. 1 1 1 0 0 1 1 0    1 0 0 0 0 0 0 0    0 0 0 0 0 0 0
  \ rt part of  /    \   2nd byte  /    \   1st byte  /
    3rd byte
```

The first binary digit of the third byte is a 0 since the number is positive. Hence, the binary representation of the third byte is 01100110. The fourth

490

byte has the value 128 + 6, where +6 is the power of 2, recorded above as T6. Hence, the 4 bytes are 0, 128, 102, and 134.

EXAMPLES

1.   The following program makes use of the PEEK function. PEEK(L) identifies the byte that is in location L.

```
10 DEF SEG
20 N% = 773
30 L = VARPTR(N%)
40 PRINT PEEK(L); PEEK(L+1)
RUN
 5  3
Ok
```

$$\begin{array}{r} 3 \\ 256 \overline{\smash{\big)}\ 773} \\ 768 \\ \hline 5 \end{array}$$

Note: Hence, $773 = 5 + 256*3$

2.
```
10 DEF SEG
20 A = 57.62500
30 L = VARPTR(A)
40 FOR I = 0 TO 3
50   PRINT PEEK(L+I);
60 NEXT I
RUN
 0   128   102   134
Ok
```

PART II   STRING VARIABLES

After a string constant has been assigned to a string variable, a 3-byte descriptor is associated with the string variable. The first byte gives the length of the string constant and the other two bytes give the location of the initial byte of the sequence of bytes storing the constant. If these two bytes have values a and b, then the offset in BASIC's Data Segment of the initial byte is a+256*b. If strvar is a string variable to which a string constant has been assigned, then the value of the function

```
VARPTR(strvar)
```

is the offset into BASIC's Data Segment of the first of the three bytes in the descriptor.

VARPTR

3.
```
10 DEF SEG
20 A$ = "abcd"
30 M = VARPTR(A$)
40 N = PEEK(M+1) + 256*PEEK(M+2)
50 FOR I = 0 TO PEEK(M)-1
60    PRINT PEEK(N+I);
70 NEXT I
RUN
 97  98  99  100
Ok
```

Note: The ASCII value for "a" is 97.

4. Add the following lines to the program in Example 3, and after RUNning the entire program, LIST line 20. (*Note:* The statement **POKE n,m** places the number m in memory location having offset n.)

```
80 POKE N,3: POKE N+1,4: POKE N+2,5: POKE N+3,6
90 PRINT: PRINT A$
RUN
 97  98  99  100
♥ ♦ ♣ ♠
Ok
LIST 20
20 A$ = "♥ ♦ ♣ ♠"
Ok
```

PART III   ARRAYS

If var is the name of a numeric or string array, then the value of

```
VARPTR(var(n))
```

is the offset into BASIC's Data Segment of the initial byte of the sequence of bytes containing var(n) or its descriptor.

FURTHER EXAMPLES

5.
```
10 DEF SEG
20 K=0
30 DIM A(2)
40 A(0)=57.62501: A(1)=0: A(2)=1
50 L = VARPTR(A(0))
60 FOR K = 0 TO 11
70    PRINT PEEK(L+K);
```

492

```
80 NEXT K
RUN
 2  128  102  134  0  0  0  0  0  0  0  129
Ok
```

6.
```
10 DEF SEG
20 K = 0
30 DIM AB$(3)
40 AB$(0)="Four": AB$(1)="score"
50 AB$(2)="and": AB$(3)="seven"
60 L = VARPTR(AB$(0))
70 FOR K = 0 TO 11
80    PRINT PEEK(L+K);
90 NEXT K
RUN
 4  102  16  5  117  16  3  136  16  5  150  16
Ok
FOR T = 0 TO 3:PRINT CHR$(PEEK(102 + 256*16 + T));:NEXT T
Four
Ok
```

The numbers 102, 16, 117, 16, 136, 16, 150, and 16, which correspond to memory locations, might differ from those you obtain.

FURTHER COMMENT

3.   Care must be taken when working with VARTPR for arrays. Initializing ordinary variables moves the location of the data for arrays. Hence, ordinary variables should be initialized before VARPTR is called. For instance, in Example 6 the variable K was initialized in line 20. Had line 20 been omitted, initializing K in line 70 would have moved each of the bytes of the array into memory locations of offsets eight higher than originally.

PART IV   FILES

If a file has been OPENed AS #n, then the value of the function

```
VARPTR(#n)
```

is the offset into BASIC's Data Segment of the starting address of the file control block for the specified file.

APPLICATIONS

VARPTR is used to obtain the address of a variable or array so that it may be passed to an assembly language subroutine by the CALL statement. The following program prints the contents of a text screen. The three-byte pro-

VARPTR

gram is stored in the first three bytes of the single-precision variable H. See Example 1 in the discussion of CALL for another example.

```
10 H=0: DEF SEG
20 PRSC=VARPTR(H)
30 FOR I%=0 TO 2
40   READ A%
50   POKE PRSC+I%,A%
60 NEXT I%
70 CALL PRSC
80 DATA &HCD,&H5,&HCB
```

VARPTR$

This discussion assumes a familiarity with the functions ASC and VARPTR. Suppose that a variable, var, has been assigned a value, val. Information about the type of var: integer numeric, single-precision numeric, double-precision numeric, or string, and the location in memory of val, is returned by the function

    VARPTR$(var)

in the form of a string of 3 characters. The first character is determined by the type of the variable, var. For an integer numeric variable, the first character will be a reverse-image smiling face; that is, the character with ASCII value 2. For a single-precision numeric variable, the first character will be a diamond; the character with ASCII value 4. For a double-precision numeric variable, the first character will be a reverse-image cross; the character with ASCII value 8. For a string variable, the first character will be a heart; the character with ASCII value 3.

For a numeric variable, the ASCII values of the last two characters give the offset into BASIC's Data Segment of the memory location containing the first byte of the variable. For a string variable, the ASCII values of the last two characters give the offset into BASIC's Data Segment of the memory location of the first byte of the three byte descriptor associated with the string. Specifically, in either case the memory location will have offset ASC (2nd character) + 256*ASC (3rd character).

EXAMPLES

BASIC 1.1 was used to execute these programs.

1.
```
10 DEF SEG
20 A% = 123
30 S$ = VARPTR$(A%)
40 PRINT S$
50 FOR I = 1 TO 3
60   PRINT ASC(MID$(S$,I,1));
70 NEXT I
RUN
☻↓ ♫
 2  25  14
Ok
```

Since 25 + 256*14 = 3609, the variable is stored in the two bytes beginning with the byte having offset 3609 into BASIC's Data Segment.

2.
```
10 A = 1234567
20 S$ = VARPTR$(A)
30 PRINT S$
40 FOR I = 1 TO 3
```

```
50   PRINT ASC(MID$(S$,I,1));
60 NEXT I
RUN
♦ → ♫
 4  26  14
Ok
```

3.
```
10 DEF SEG
20 A# = 1234.56789
30 S$ = VARPTR$(A#)
40 PRINT " " + S$
50 FOR I = 1 TO 3
60   PRINT ASC(MID$(S$,I,1));
70 NEXT I
RUN
■ $ ♫
 8  36  14
Ok
```

4.
```
10 DEF SEG
20 A$ = "computer"
30 S$ = VARPTR$(A$)
40 PRINT S$
50 FOR I = 1 TO 3
60   PRINT ASC(MID$(S$,I,1));
70 NEXT I
RUN
♥ ! ♫
 3  33  14
Ok
```

Since $33 + 256*14 = 3617$, the statement DEF SEG: PRINT PEEK(3617) displays the number 8, the length of the string. The number PEEK(3618)+256*PEEK(3619) is the offset of the memory location containing the first character of the string.

FURTHER DISCUSSION

The PLAY statement has the provision that octaves, tempos, and lengths can be set within a string via expressions of the form

"Y = var;"

where Y is one of the letters O, T, or L. Such expressions can be replaced by expressions of the form

"Y =" + VARPTR$(var)

Also, substrings can be inserted within a string (to be PLAYed) via expressions of the form

"XS$;"

where S$ is a string. These expressions can be replaced by expressions of the form

"X" + VARPTR$(S$)

(See the discussion of PLAY for further details.)

FURTHER EXAMPLES

The following programs require Advanced BASIC.

5. `K=3: PLAY "O = K; C"`

and

`    K=3: PLAY "O =" + VARPTR$(K) + "C"`

both produce middle C.

6. `K=150: PLAY "T = K; CCDCFE"`

and

`    K=150: PLAY "T =" + VARPTR$(K) + "CCDCFE"`

both play the beginning of Happy Birthday with a vivace tempo.

7. `K=8: PLAY "L = K; C"`

and

`    K=8: PLAY "L =" + VARPTR$(K) + "C"`

both play C as an eighth note.

8. In the following program, lines 20 and 30 have the exact same effect. They both play a few bars of Happy Birthday.

```
10 S$ = "CCDC"
20 PLAY "XS$; FE XS$; GF"
30 PLAY "X"+VARPTR$(S$)+"FE"+"X"+VARPTR$(S$)+"GF"
```

COMMENT

VARPTR$ can be used with the statement DRAW in much the same way that it is used with PLAY.

APPLICATIONS

The expressions "Y = var;" and "XS$;" discussed above cannot be used with PLAY statements if the resulting program is to be compiled. In this case the alternate forms involving VARPTR$ must be used. Similar considerations apply to DRAW statements.

VIEW

The graphics statement VIEW is not available with versions of BASIC preceding BASIC 2.0. This discussion assumes a familiarity with the statements WINDOW, PSET, PRESET, LINE, and CIRCLE.

The effect of VIEW is to define a rectangular region of the graphics screen as *active*. After a VIEW statement has been executed, graphics will be displayed only in the active region.

Consider the rectangular portion of the medium-resolution graphics screen having (x1,y1) as its upper left-hand corner and (x2,y2) as its lower right-hand corner. Then, after the two statements

```
WINDOW SCREEN (0,0)-(319,199)

VIEW  (x1,y1)-(x2,y2)
```

have been executed, all graphics specified by PSET, PRESET, LINE, and CIRCLE will be scaled and displayed inside the specified rectangular region. The rectangular region is referred to as a *viewport*. If color has been enabled, and the palette and background color have been selected, then the viewport will have color p of the palette, and the boundary will have color b of the palette, if the second statement is expanded to

```
VIEW (x1,y1)-(x2,y2),p,b
```

If either p or b is omitted, the viewport assumes the background color. Analogous results hold for the high-resolution screen. In this case, the coordinates (319,199) must be replaced by the coordinates (639,199).

EXAMPLE

1.   The following program produced Figure 1. Line 20 drew a circle in the standard manner. Lines 30 and 40 specified that future drawings be projected into the upper-right quarter of the screen. The number 3 appearing in line 40 caused a boundary, in color 3 of the current palette, to appear surrounding the viewport. The circle drawn by line 50 was scaled to fit into the viewport in the same proportions as the original circle fit into the entire screen.

```
10 CLS: KEY OFF: SCREEN 1,0
20 CIRCLE (80,100),40
30 WINDOW SCREEN (0,0)-(319,199)
40 VIEW (160,1)-(318,100),,3
50 CIRCLE (80,100),40
```

FURTHER DISCUSSION

The WINDOW SCREEN statement used above can be replaced by a more general WINDOW statement specifying world coordinates. If so, then the

498

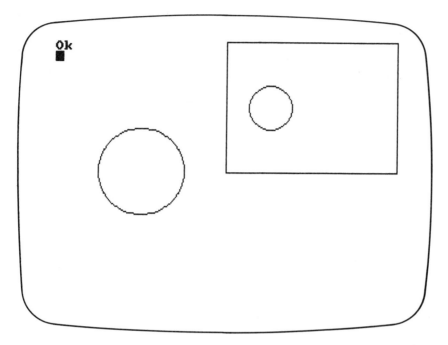

FIGURE 1

graphics projected into the viewport will be a scaled version of the graphics that would have been drawn (using world coordinates) onto the entire screen in the absence of the VIEW statement. Note, however, that the world coordinates established by the WINDOW or WINDOW SCREEN statement do not affect the creation of the viewport by the VIEW statement. The coordinates appearing in the VIEW statement are always interpreted as physical coordinates. See Example 2.

If a WINDOW statement is not active at the time that the VIEW statement is executed, then no scaling takes place. However, points specified to be drawn by graphics statements will be translated x1 points to the right and y1 points down, and will be drawn only if the new location is within the viewport. (Think of the viewport as taking a picture of the upper left-hand part of the screen.) See Example 4.

If the statement **VIEW (x1,y1)-(x2,y2),p,b** is replaced by the statement

VIEW SCREEN (x1,y1)-(x2,y2),p,b

then no scaling or relocation occurs. Instead, when a figure is drawn, only the portion of the figure inside the viewport will be visible. See Example 3.

VIEW

FURTHER EXAMPLES

2. When a VIEW statement is followed by another VIEW statement, only the second viewport will be active. That is, subsequent graphics statements address themselves to the second viewport. The following program uses the VIEW statement, in conjunction with the WINDOW statement, to vary the size of a graph. See Figure 2.

```
10 CLS: KEY OFF: SCREEN 1,0
20 WINDOW (-6.3,-2)-(6.3,2)
30 VIEW (1,1)-(159,99),,3
40 GOSUB 140
50 VIEW (161,101)-(240,149),,1
60 GOSUB 140
70 VIEW (242,151)-(282,176),,2
80 GOSUB 140
90 VIEW (284,178)-(304,190),,3
100 GOSUB 140
110 LOCATE 22,1:END
120 '=========================
130 'DRAW GRAPH OF SIN FUNCTION
140 LINE (-6.3,0)-(6.3,0)
150 LINE (0,2)-(0,-2)
160 FOR X=-6.28 TO 6.28 STEP .1
170 PSET(X,SIN(X))
180 NEXT X
190 RETURN
```

3. Consider the sailboat drawn in Example 4 of the discussion of DRAW. The following program draws a portion of the sailboat by executing a VIEW SCREEN statement before drawing. See Figure 3.

```
10 CLS: KEY OFF: SCREEN 1
20 VIEW SCREEN  (140,80)-(200,150),,3
30 DRAW "L60 E60 D80 L60 F20 R40 E20 L20"
```

4. If we delete line 30 in Example 1, the result will be the portion of the circle shown in Figure 4.

COMMENTS

1. The statement VIEW can only be used with Advanced BASIC. That is, the command BASICA must have been given when BASIC was invoked.

2. VIEW does not affect the scale of a LINE ''style,'' a PAINT ''tile,'' or a figure drawn with DRAW statements.

500

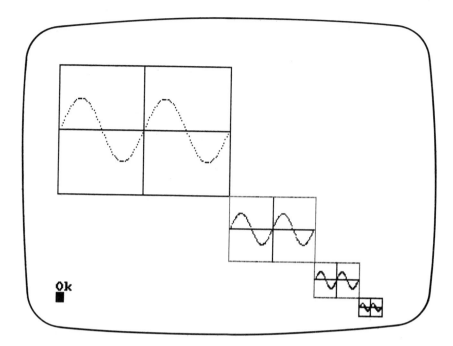

FIGURE 2

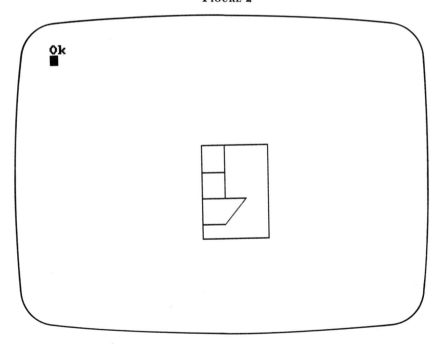

FIGURE 3

VIEW

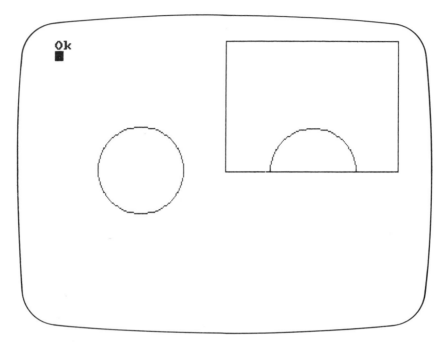

FIGURE 4

3. The size and location of text characters that have been PRINTed on the screen are not affected by VIEW statements.

4. If a CLS statement is executed while a VIEW statement is active, only the contents of the viewport will be cleared. This applies to text as well as to graphics. To clear the entire screen without altering active WINDOW and VIEW statements, use the key combination Ctrl-Home, or the statement **PRINT CHR$(12)**. To clear the entire screen and also deactivate the viewport, use the statement **VIEW:CLS**.

5. The viewport is deactivated if one of the commands CHAIN, CHAIN MERGE, CLEAR, LOAD, MERGE, or RUN is executed, or if a program line is entered or deleted.

6. The x coordinates appearing in a VIEW statement can be interchanged without affecting the result. The same situation holds for the y coordinates. For example, the following statements specify the same viewport.

```
VIEW (10,20)-(30,40)
VIEW (30,20)-(10,40)
VIEW (10,40)-(30,20)
VIEW (30,40)-(10,20)
```

APPLICATIONS

The VIEW statement makes it easy to enlarge or contract rectangular portions of the screen and place the new picture wherever we choose.

WAIT

The micro-processor receives data from and sends data to the various parts of the computer through mechanisms known as ports. For instance, there are ports associated with the keyboard, the disk drives, the speaker, and the screen. A piece of data consists of a byte (corresponding to an integer from 0 to 255), and each port has a number assigned to it.

A byte is an eight-tuple of zeros and ones, consisting of the binary representation of its corresponding number. The rightmost bit is said to occupy position 0, the next bit is said to occupy position 1, . . . , and the leftmost bit is said to occupy position 7. For instance, the byte corresponding to the number 34 has ones in its first and fifth positions, and zeros elsewhere.

If n is a whole number from 0 to 255, then the statement

```
WAIT p,n
```

causes the execution of the program to be suspended until the byte pending at the port p has the bit 1 in one or more of the positions where the binary representation of n has a 1.

EXAMPLES

1.   The statement **WAIT 1018,34** causes the execution of the program to be suspended until the byte pending at the communications port 1018 has a 1 in either its first or fifth positions. Hence, for instance, the byte 131 (i.e., 10000011) causes execution to proceed and the byte 132 (i.e., 10000100) continues to suspend execution.

2.   Port 97 communicates with the speaker. The following program requires Advanced BASIC.

```
10 PLAY "MB CDEFGAB O5 C"
20 PRINT INP(97)
30 WAIT 97,1
40 PRINT INP(97)
RUN
 79
 79
Ok
```

Line 10 plays a scale as background music. That is, the program continues to execute while the scale is being played. The value of INP(97) while the speaker was active, in this case the number 79 (or 01001111), will vary with different versions of BASIC. When this program was executed, the two numbers and the Ok appeared before the PLAYing stopped.

FURTHER DISCUSSION

If n is a whole number from 0 to 255, then the statement

```
WAIT p,n,255
```

causes the execution of the program to be suspended until the byte pending at the port p has the bit 0 in one or more of the same positions where the binary representation of n has a 1. Now suppose that m is any whole number from 0 to 255. The statement

```
WAIT p,n,m
```

causes the execution of the program to be suspended until the byte pending at port p has the bit 0 at one of the positions for which both n and m have ones, or has the bit 1 at one of the positions for which n has a 1 and m has a zero.

FURTHER EXAMPLES

3. The statement **WAIT 1018,34,32** causes the execution of the program to be suspended until the byte pending at the communications port 1018 has either a 1 in its first position or a 0 in its fifth position. Hence, for instance, the byte 131 (i.e., 10000011) causes execution to proceed and the byte 172 (i.e., 10101101) continues to suspend execution.

4. The following program requires Advanced BASIC. Since the number 79 does not have a 0 in position 0, line 30 caused execution to pause until the scale was finished playing.

```
10 PLAY "MB CDEFGAB O5 C"
20 PRINT INP(97)
30 WAIT 97,1,1
40 PRINT INP(97)
RUN
 79
 76 (appeared after playing stopped)
Ok
```

COMMENTS

1. The statement **WAIT p,n,m** causes the execution of the program to pause until the value of ((b XOR m) AND n) is nonzero. Here, b is the byte pending at port p. See Appendix G for a discussion of logical operators.

2. WAIT statements can easily cause infinite loops. The key combination Ctrl-Break can be used to terminate loops.

WAIT

APPLICATIONS

The WAIT function is used in communications software to monitor the status of communications ports and pause until certain patterns appear.

WHILE and WEND

The pair of statements, WHILE and WEND, combine the capabilities of an IF statement and a FOR . . . NEXT loop. A configuration of program lines of the form:

```
     .
     .
     .
50 WHILE condition
     .
     .
     .
90 WEND
     .
     .
     .
```

(known as a WHILE . . . WEND loop) cause the sequence of lines between lines 50 and 90 to be executed repeatedly, as long as the condition is true. (The numbers 50 and 90 were selected solely for illustrative purposes.)

Some common types of conditions involve the following relationships between numbers or strings:

Relationship	Numbers	Strings
=	is equal to	is identical to
<	is less than	precedes alphabetically
>	is greater than	follows alphabetically
< >	is not equal to	is not identical to
< =	is less than or equal to	precedes alphabetically or is identical to
> =	is greater than or equal to	follows alphabetically or is identical to

(When strings are alphabetized, ASCII values are used to determine the order of each pair of characters.)

EXAMPLES

1. The following program searches a list of data items for the name given and then supplies the requested information.

```
10 INPUT "Name: ", N$
20 WHILE J$<>N$
```

WHILE and WEND

```
30     READ J$, Y$
40 WEND
60 PRINT "Justice "; J$; " was appointed in "; Y$
70 DATA Brennan, 1956, White, 1962, Marshall, 1967
80 DATA Burger, 1969, Blackmun, 1970, Powell, 1972
90 DATA Rehnquist, 1972, Stevens, 1975, O'Connor, 1981
RUN
Name: Stevens
Justice Stevens was appointed in 1975
Ok
```

2.   The following program computes third powers of numbers until a certain point.

```
10 A=1
20 WHILE A*A*A<100
30     PRINT A;A*A*A,
40     A=A+1
50 WEND
RUN
 1  1           2  8           3  27          4  64
Ok
```

(*Note:* Since the third power of 5 is 125, which is not less than 100, the loop terminated when the value of A reached 5.)

COMMENTS

1.   Within a single WHILE . . . WEND loop, there should be only one WEND statement. For instance, the following program results in the error message "WEND without WHILE in 60". Line 40 should read **40 IF X=5 THEN 60.**

```
10 INPUT "Select a positive number: ", X
20 WHILE X>=0
30     X=X-1
40     IF X=5 THEN WEND
50     PRINT 1/(5-X)
60 WEND
```

2.   Conditions consisting of expressions involving numeric constants and variables often can be written without using any relationships (such as = and < >). When used in a WHILE statement, such conditions are considered to be false if the number obtained from evaluating the expression is zero, and are considered to be true otherwise. The statement **WHILE A** has the exact meaning as the statement **WHILE A<>0.** They both result in the loop being repeated as long as the value of A is not 0.

508

3. Complex conditions can be constructed from simple conditions by using logical operators, such as AND, OR, and NOT. (Appendix G contains a detailed discussion of logical operators.) Just like arithmetic operators ($+$, $-$, $/$, $*$, $\wedge$), logical operators are performed in a specific order. NOT is performed first, then AND, finally OR. Also, arithmetic operators are evaluated before relationships, and both take precedence over logical operators. Some possibilities and their interpretations are:

$$\text{NOT cond 1 AND cond 2 OR cond 3}$$
((NOT cond 1) AND cond 2) OR cond 3

$$\text{cond 1 OR NOT cond 2 AND cond 3}$$
cond 1 OR ((NOT cond 2) AND cond 3)

$$\text{C<A+B AND A-5}$$
$(C < (A+B))$ AND $(A\text{-}5)$

4. A WHILE . . . WEND loop can contain another WHILE . . . WEND loop itside it. Schematically,

```
        ⎧ WHILE condition 1
        ⎪ .
  first ⎪     WHILE condition 2 ⎫ second
  loop  ⎨ .                     ⎬ loop
        ⎪     WEND              ⎭
        ⎪ .
        ⎩ WEND
```

The first WEND in the program is related to **WHILE condition 2**.

5. Every routine that uses FOR . . . NEXT statements can be rewritten with WHILE . . . WEND instead. This is usually not a good idea, since FOR . . . NEXT loops execute faster. However, there is one limitation of FOR . . . NEXT loops that can be handled by WHILE . . . WEND loops, namely, the situation in which the index is a double-precision variable. See Example 4.

6. When doing arithmetic calculations, rounding errors can sometimes prevent WHILE . . . WEND statements from giving the desired result. In certain situations, conditions like $A<>B$ should be replaced by something like $ABS(A\text{-}B)>.005$. See Example 5.

7. Any routine using WHILE . . . WEND can be rewritten using IF and GOTO statements. However, many programmers prefer WHILE . . . WEND statements because they are closer to the way people think.

8. The computer will forget that it is executing a WHILE . . . WEND loop if one of the commands CHAIN MERGE, CLEAR, MERGE, or RUN is executed, or if a program line is entered or deleted.

WHILE and WEND

FURTHER EXAMPLES

3.
```
10 A = 0: B = 0
20 WHILE A<2
30     PRINT A;: A=A+1
40     WHILE B
50         PRINT A+B;:B=B+1
60     WEND
70 WEND
RUN
  0  1  2  3  1
Ok
```

(*Note:* The inner loop was encountered twice. On the first encounter, B started at 0; on the second, B started at 3.)

4. Compare these two programs:

```
10 FOR I#=12345678# TO 12345680#
20     PRINT I#,
30 NEXT I#
RUN
Type mismatch in 10
Ok
```

```
10 I#=12345678#
20 WHILE I#<=12345680#
30     PRINT I#,: I#=I#+1#
40 WEND
RUN
 12345678       12345679       12345680
Ok
```

5. The following program will compute the square root of any number to much greater precision than the SQR function can with BASIC 1.1. The mathematical technique used is known as the Newton-Raphson algorithm.

```
10 DEFDBL A,B
20 B=10#
30 INPUT A
40 WHILE ABS(B*B-A)>A*.0000000000000001#
50     B=B-((B*B-A)/(2#*B))
60 WEND
70 PRINT B
RUN
? 2#
 1.414213562373095
Ok
```

510

6.  ```
    10 PRINT "Press any letter to continue"
    20 WHILE INKEY$="": WEND
    30 BEEP
    ```

The INKEY$ variable assumes the value of whatever key has just been pressed. Line 20, above, seems more natural than the equivalent statement using IF, `20 IF INKEY$="" GOTO 20.`

7.  ```
    10 A = 1
    20 WHILE A<5
    30 PRINT A;: A = A + 1
    40 CLEAR
    50 WEND
    RUN
     1
    WEND without WHILE in 50
    Ok
    ```

8. The following program will display the contents of any sequential file:

    ```
    10 INPUT "File to read"; F$
    20 OPEN F$ FOR INPUT AS #1
    30 WHILE NOT EOF(1)
    40     LINE INPUT #1, A$
    50     PRINT A$
    60 WEND
    ```

APPLICATIONS

WHILE . . . WEND loops have all of the applications of FOR . . . NEXT loops and many of the applications of IF statements. See the discussions of these statements.

WIDTH

The WIDTH statement is used to set the number of text characters that will be displayed on each line of the screen or printed on each line by the printer.

PART I   SCREEN

The WIDTH statement functions differently with the IBM Monochrome Display than with a graphics monitor. This discussion applies exclusively to graphics monitors.

The SCREEN statement is used to select one of three different modes for the screen: text (SCREEN 0), medium-resolution graphics (SCREEN 1), or high-resolution graphics (SCREEN 2). Text can be displayed in any of the three modes. In high-resolution graphics mode, 80 characters will be displayed on each line, and in medium-resolution graphics mode, 40 characters will be displayed on each line. The characters will be twice as wide in medium-resolution graphics mode. In text mode we have the choice of specifying either 80 or 40 characters per line. Suppose that the statement SCREEN 0 has been executed. Then the statement

    WIDTH 80

guarantees that all text will appear 80 characters per line and the statement

    WIDTH 40

guarantees that all text will appear 40 characters per line.

COMMENTS

1.   If the current screen mode is medium-resolution graphics, the statement WIDTH 80 will change the mode to high-resolution graphics. If the current screen mode is high-resolution graphics, the statement WIDTH 40 will change the mode to medium-resolution graphics.

2.   When a WIDTH statement actually changes the number of characters per line, it also clears the screen.

3.   When the computer is first turned on, the words LIST, RUN, LOAD'', etc., are displayed on the 25th line of the screen. In WIDTH 80 mode, 10 words are displayed, whereas in WIDTH 40 mode, only the first 5 of these words are displayed.

4.   The IBM Monochrome Display is only capable of displaying one size of text character—the size corresponding to WIDTH 80. The statement SCREEN 0: WIDTH 40 causes characters to be displayed only on the left half of the screen, thereby creating a pseudo WIDTH 40 screen.

5. The WIDTH statement can be invoked in two other formats. The statement **WIDTH "SCRN:",w** where w is 40 or 80, has the same effect as the statement **WIDTH w.**

EXAMPLE

1.
```
10 A$ = "One must carve one's life out of the wood one has."
20 SCREEN 0: WIDTH 80
30 PRINT A$
40 FOR I=1 to 2000: NEXT
50 WIDTH 40
60 PRINT A$
70 FOR I=1 to 2000: NEXT
80 WIDTH 80
90 PRINT A$
RUN
One must carve one's life out of the wood one has.
```
<screen cleared>
```
One must carve one's life out of the woo
d one has.
```
<screen cleared>
```
One must carve one's life out of the wood one has.
Ok
```

PART II   PRINTER

Normally, the printer will print 80 characters per line. However, the statement

   WIDTH "LPT1:", w

causes the printer to print w characters per line.

FURTHER COMMENTS

6. The maximum number of characters per line varies with the printer. The maximum number is 132 for the IBM 80 CPS Matrix Printer and the EPSON MX-80.

7. The printer can be made to suppress a line feed and just do a carriage return after PRINTing. This is accomplished by OPENing the printer as a random file with a statement of the form **OPEN "LPT1:" AS #n** and then executing the statement **WIDTH #n, 255.** See Example 3.

8. The printer can be OPENed as a sequential file with a statement of the form **OPEN "LPT1:" FOR OUTPUT AS #n.** Then the width can be set with a statement of the form **WIDTH #n, w.**

WIDTH

FURTHER EXAMPLES

The output of the following programs will appear on the printer.

2.
```
10 A$ = "To be great is to be misunderstood. - Emerson"
20 WIDTH "lpt1:", 80
30 LPRINT A$
40 WIDTH "lpt1:", 25
50 LPRINT A$
RUN
To be great is to be misunderstood. - Emerson
To be great is to be misu
nderstood. - Emerson
```

3.
```
10 OPEN "lpt1:" AS #1
20 WIDTH #1, 255
30 PRINT #1, "Diligence is the mother of good fortune."
40 PRINT #1, STRING$(39,"_")
50 LPRINT
60 PRINT #1,"Cervantes"
70 CLOSE #1
RUN
Diligence is the mother of good fortune.
Cervantes
```

There was a carriage return but no line feed after line 30. Hence, line 40 caused the 39 underlined characters to be printed on the same line as the quotation. Line 50 then caused both a carriage return and a line feed. Without it, ''Cervantes'' would have been printed on top of the quotation.

The graphics statement WINDOW is not available with versions of BASIC preceding BASIC 2.0.

Figure 1 shows two types of coordinate systems, known as left-hand (Figure 1a) and right-hand (Figure 1b) coordinate systems.

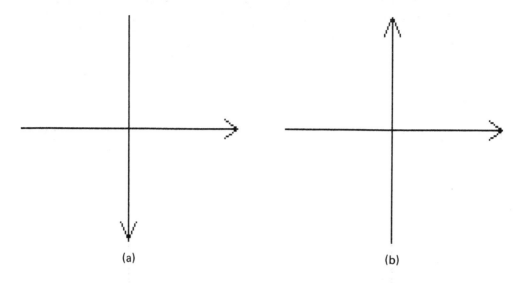

(a)   (b)

FIGURE 1

The two graphics screens can be thought of as being embedded in left-hand coordinate systems. See Figure 2. The coordinates of points on the screen are determined by the two coordinate systems. See Appendix C for further details.

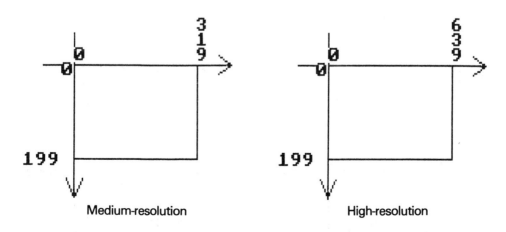

Medium-resolution   High-resolution

FIGURE 2

515

WINDOW

The statement WINDOW allows us to embed the graphics screens into *any* left-hand or right-hand coordinate system and thereby specify the coordinates of points on the screen as we choose. Two possible embeddings, along with the resulting coordinates of several points, are shown in Figure 3. In Figure 3a the x coordinates range from 1 to 5 and the y coordinates range from 20 to 60. In Figure 3b, the x coordinates range from -10 to 10 and the y coordinates range from -2 to 4.

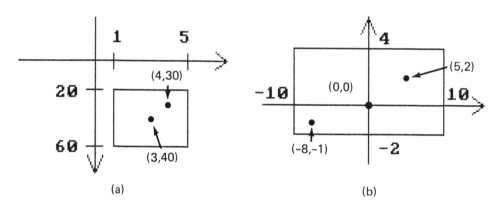

FIGURE 3

In general, if the x coordinates are to range from x1 to x2, and the y coordinates are to range from y1 to y2, then this can be set by the statement

```
WINDOW SCREEN (x1,y1)-(x2,y2)
```

which embeds the screen in a left-hand coordinate system as shown in Figure 4a, and the statement

```
WINDOW (x1,y1)-(x2,y2)
```

which embeds the screen in a right-hand coordinate system as shown in Figure 4b. After either of these statements has been executed, the graphics statements PSET, PRESET, CIRCLE, and LINE will use the new coordinate system.

EXAMPLES

1. To obtain a left-hand coordinate system in which the x coordinates range from -3 to 3 and the y coordinates range from 0 to 10, execute the statement

```
WINDOW SCREEN (-3,0)-(3,10)
```

Figure 5a shows the resulting coordinates for several points. The center of the screen will have coordinates (0,5).

516

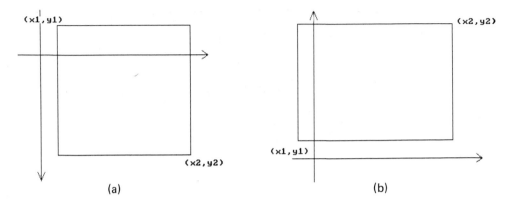

FIGURE 4

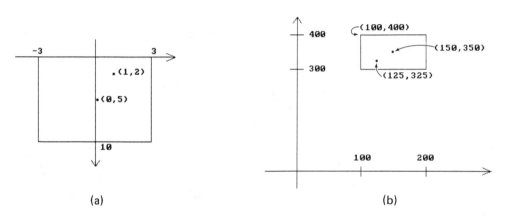

FIGURE 5

2. To obtain a right-hand coordinate system in which the x coordinates range from 100 to 200 and the y coordinates range from 300 to 400, execute the statement

```
WINDOW (100,300)-(200,400)
```

Figure 5b shows the resulting coordinates for several points. The center of the screen has coordinates (150,350).

3. The following program produced Figure 6.

```
10 CLS: KEY OFF
20 WINDOW SCREEN (0,0)-(30,30)
30 LINE (1,3)-(7,25)
40 PSET (10,10)
50 CIRCLE (20,15),7
```

517

WINDOW

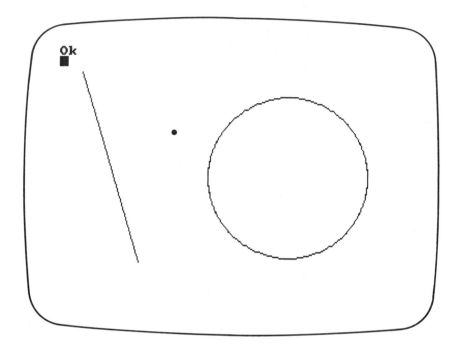

FIGURE 6

COMMENTS

1. The statement WINDOW can only be used with Advanced BASIC. That is, the command BASICA must have been given when BASIC was invoked.

2. The standard graphics coordinates of points; that is, those discussed in Appendix C, are known as the *physical coordinates* of the points. The new coordinates, as determined by a WINDOW or WINDOW SCREEN statement are called the *world coordinates* of the points. Whereas physical coordinates always have nonnegative integer values, world coordinates can have any values.

3. After having specified world coordinates with a WINDOW statement, we can return to standard coordinates by executing a WINDOW statement without the word SCREEN and with no coordinates specified. We will also return to standard coordinates if we change the screen mode, execute one of the commands CHAIN, CHAIN MERGE, CLEAR, LOAD, MERGE, NEW, or RUN, or enter or delete a program line.

FURTHER EXAMPLES

4. The following program produces the results shown in Figure 7. The point (4,3.5) is the center of the screen. The point (12,4) is not on the screen. However, the computer imagines where this point is located in the world coordinate system and draws a portion of the line from (2,2) to this point. This tech-

518

nique for dealing with points off the screen is known as *line clipping*. See the discussion of LINE for further details.

```
10 CLS: KEY OFF
20 WINDOW (1,2)-(7,5)
30 PSET (4,3.5)
40 LINE (2,2)-(12,4)
50 WINDOW
60 CIRCLE (60,60),10
```

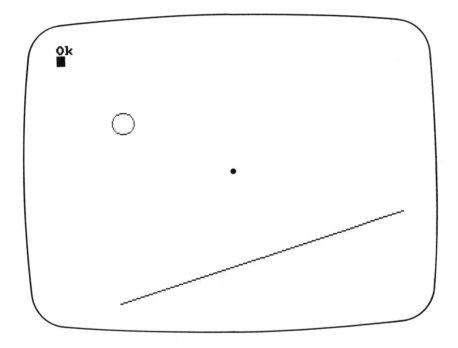

FIGURE 7

5. The standard normal curve of statistics has positive y values that are always less than .4 and that are negligible for values of x having absolute value greater than 3. The following program, which draws the graph of the standard normal curve shown in Figure 8, specifies that x range from -3 to 3 and that y range from -.5 to .5. The program can be executed in either medium- or high-resolution graphics.

```
10 CLS: KEY OFF
20 WINDOW (-3,-.5)-(3,.5)
30 LINE (-3,0)-(3,0)
40 LINE (1,.05)-(1,-.05)
50 LINE (0,-.5)-(0,.5)
```

WINDOW

```
60 LINE (-.2,.1)-(.2,.1)
70 FOR X = -3 TO 3 STEP .01
80 PSET (X,.3989423*EXP(-.5*X*X))
90 NEXT X
```

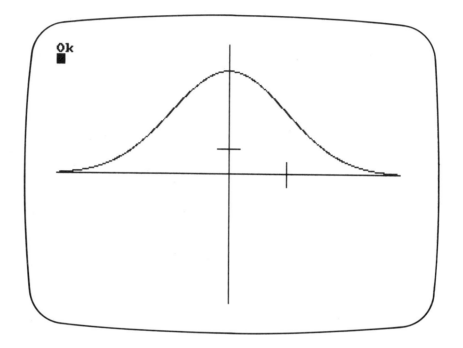

FIGURE 8

6. Each time a world coordinate system is specified in a program, the coordinate system determines how points will be placed until another WINDOW statement is executed. By varying the coordinate system, figures can be enlarged, shrunk, and moved to different parts of the screen. The following program produced Figure 9.

```
10 CLS: KEY OFF
20 GOSUB 100
30 WINDOW SCREEN (0,0)-(900,600)
40 GOSUB 100
50 WINDOW SCREEN (-50,50)-(190,190)
60 GOSUB 100
70 END
80 '=============================
90 'DRAW FIGURE
100 CIRCLE (160,80),20
110 PAINT (160,80),2,3
```

```
120 LINE (160,97)-(160,150)
130 LINE (160,120)-(190,110)
140 LINE (160,120)-(130,110)
150 LINE (160,150)-(190,180)
160 LINE (160,150)-(130,180)
170 RETURN
```

FIGURE 9

FURTHER COMMENTS

4.   The x coordinates appearing in a WINDOW statement can be interchanged without affecting the result. The same holds for the y coordinates. For example, the following statements specify the same coordinate system.

```
WINDOW (1,2)-(3,4)
WINDOW (3,2)-(1,4)
WINDOW (1,4)-(3,2)
WINDOW (3,4)-(1,2)
```

5.   The PMAP function can be used to convert from physical coordinates to world coordinates and vice versa. See the discussion of PMAP for details.

6.   The size and location of text characters that have been PRINTed on the graphics screen, are not altered by WINDOW statements.

521

WINDOW

7. DRAW statements are not affected by WINDOW statements. Also, WINDOW statements do not alter the scale of a LINE "style" or a PAINT "tile."

8. The WINDOW statement sets the "last point referenced" to the center of the screen.

9. After a WINDOW statement has been executed, BASIC 2.0 does not properly interpret the relative form of specifying coordinates.

APPLICATIONS

1. The WINDOW statement simplifies the drawing of graphs. Compare Example 5 with Example 4 in the discussion of PSET and PRESET to appreciate the hassles that are avoided when using a custom made coordinate system. Similarly, the programs which produced a bar graph and a line graph in Examples 6 and 7 of the discussion of LINE could have been simplified considerably with WINDOW.

2. Programs written using WINDOW statements will produce the same scale figures whether run with medium- or high-resolution graphics.

The WRITE statement is used to display data on the screen and, in a sense, is a specialized PRINT statement. If A$ is a string, then the statement

```
WRITE A$
```

causes the value of A$ to be displayed on the screen enclosed in quotation marks, even if A$ was input without quotation marks. If A is a number, then the statement

```
WRITE A
```

causes the value of A to be displayed on the screen without any trailing or leading spaces.

EXAMPLES

1.  ```
    WRITE "AB":WRITE 23:A$="CDE":A=456:WRITE A$:WRITE A
    "AB"
    23
    "CDE"
    456
    Ok
    ```

2.  ```
    10 INPUT A$
    20 WRITE A$
    30 WRITE A$+"ment"
    RUN
    ? enjoy
    "enjoy"
    "enjoyment"
    Ok
    ```

COMMENTS

1. Multiple WRITE statements consist of the word WRITE followed by several items separated by commas or semicolons. The commas and semicolons serve only to separate items and do not have the same effect as they do in multiple PRINT statements. The items will be displayed one after another separated by commas.

2. Semicolons or commas may *not* be used at the end of WRITE statements. If they are, the error message "Missing operand" results.

3. Spaces may not be used in place of semicolons to separate strings. If they are, the message "Syntax error" results.

4. Spaces separating numbers are ignored. See Example 4.

WRITE

5. Unlike the PRINT statement, WRITE uses all of the positions on a line before going on to the next line, even if it means splitting up strings or numbers. For instance, the statement **WRITE STRING$(73,"*"),123456789** displays a quotation mark followed by 73 asterisks, a quotation mark, a comma, the characters 1234 on one line, and the characters 56789 on the next line.

6. There are 256 different characters that can be used in a string. These characters and their ASCII values are listed in Appendix A. Certain characters in the list, such as "beep" and "carriage return," with ASCII values 7 and 13, are referred to as *undisplayable characters*. The undisplayable characters are those numbered 7, 9 through 13, and 28 through 31. Only 94 of the characters appear on the white keys in the center of the keyboard. The others are invoked by the CHR$ function. For instance, the string "Bell"+CHR$(7) consists of 5 characters, with "beep" as the fifth character. If A$ is a string, then the statement **WRITE A$** causes all of the displayable characters in the string to be displayed on the screen and all of the other characters to be executed. Even if a string consists of just one undisplayable character, the quotation marks, with nothing between them, still appear.

FURTHER EXAMPLES

3. ```
WRITE 12, 34, "five"; " six", 7
12,34,"five"," six",7
Ok
```

4. ```
10 X = 3: Y = 12: N$ = "Jessie": M$ = " Owens"
20 WRITE X*Y, N$+M$, 2    3
RUN
36,"Jessie Owens",23
Ok
```

5. ```
WRITE 1, CHR$(7), 2, CHR$(13), 3
1,"",2,"   (also, the speaker beeped)
",3
Ok
```
```

A sequential data file is a sequence of pieces of information that reside on a disk. The pieces of information can only be read from the file from beginning to end. They are entered into the file in order, beginning with the first entry. Additional pieces of information can only be added to the end of the file. They are entered into the file with the two statements PRINT# and WRITE#.

A sequential file is created with a statement of the form **OPEN filespec FOR OUTPUT AS #n.** (See the discussion of OPEN for further details.) If A$ is a string, then the statement

    WRITE #n, A$

enters the string A$ surrounded by quotation marks into file number n. If A is a number, then the statement

    WRITE #n, A

enters the number A, without any leading or trailing spaces, into file number n. The statement

    WRITE #n, A$, A

enters A$ and A as before, but with a comma separating them. Similarly, if the statement WRITE #n is followed by a list of several strings and/or numbers separated by commas and semicolons, all of the strings and numbers will appear as before, separated by commas.

After each WRITE# statement, the newly entered pieces of information are automatically trailed by 2 special characters. We denote these characters by CR (carriage return) and LF (line feed). When the file is closed, the character that we denote by AR (arrow indicating end of file) is placed after the last character.

EXAMPLES

1.  ```
    10 OPEN "RIVERS" FOR OUTPUT AS #1
    20 WRITE #1, "Nile", 4160
    30 WRITE #1, "Amazon", 4080
    40 CLOSE #1
    ```

If we could look at the disk, we would see the following characters in the file named RIVERS:

    "Nile",4160<CR/LF>"Amazon",4080<CR/LF/AR>

The notation <CR/LF> represents the pair of characters CR and LF.

2.  ```
    10 OPEN "RIVERS" FOR APPEND AS #1
    ```

WRITE#

```
20 R$ = "Yangtze"
30 L = 3720
40 WRITE #1, R$, L
50 CLOSE #1
```

The file RIVERS will now appear as follows:

```
"Nile",4160<CR/LF>"Amazon",4080<CR/LF>"Yangtze",3720<CR/LF/AR>
```

```
3.  10 OPEN "ADDRESS" FOR OUTPUT AS #3
    20 INPUT "Name"; N$
    30 INPUT "Street"; S$
    40 INPUT "City"; C$
    50 WRITE #3, N$, S$, C$
    60 CLOSE #3
    RUN
    Name? Ron Reagan
    Street? 1600 Penn. Ave.
    City? "Washington, D.C."
```

The file ADDRESS will appear on the disk as follows:

```
"Ron Reagan","1600 Penn. Avenue","Washington, D.C."<CR/LF/AR>
```

Notice that when INPUTting "Washington, D.C.", the quotation marks are necessary due to the comma that occurs inside the string.

COMMENTS

1. When pieces of information are entered into a sequential file with WRITE# statements, they usually are intended to be read from the file with INPUT# statements. (See the discussion of INPUT# for further details.)

2. The statement PRINT# is also used to enter information into a sequential file. However, PRINT# places the information on the disk in much the same way that PRINT displays information on the screen. For example, if the WRITE# statements in lines 20 and 30 of Example 1 are changed to PRINT# statements, the file RIVERS will appear as follows:

```
Nile          4160 <CR/LF>Amazon        4080 <CR/LF/AR>
```

When pieces of information are entered into a sequential file with PRINT# statements, they usually are intended to be read from the file with LINE INPUT# statements.

3. You will not always hear the whirling sound of the disk drive as soon as a WRITE# statement is executed. The computer stores the pieces of information in memory and then records them onto the disk when the buffer is full. However, CLOSE statements cause all stored information to be recorded.

526

4. The # sign in WRITE# statements can be written following the word WRITE with or without an intervening space. For instance, line 50 of Example 3 also could have been written **50 WRITE#3, N$, S$, C$.**

5. WRITE# may be used with communications files, in which case it writes to the communications buffer exactly as if it were a disk file buffer. However, WRITE# is rarely used in communications, since it automatically inserts quotation marks around strings, which would be undesirable in most applications.

APPLICATIONS

1. Sequential files provide a compact storage device for data. This data can then be accessed and used by other programs. The WRITE# statement is used extensively to construct sequential files.

2. Be careful that a file was OPENed FOR OUTPUT or APPEND before you enter information with WRITE#. In the event that the file was inadvertently OPENed for INPUT, executing WRITE# will not produce an error message. However, no information will be entered into the file.

APPENDIX A

ASCII Value	Character	ASCII Value	Character	ASCII Value	Character
000	(null)	041	)	082	R
001	☺	042	*	083	S
002	☻	043	+	084	T
003	♥	044	,	085	U
004	♦	045	—	086	V
005	♣	046	.	087	W
006	♠	047	/	088	X
007	(beep)	048	0	089	Y
008	◘	049	1	090	Z
009	(tab)	050	2	091	[
010	(line feed)	051	3	092	\
011	(home)	052	4	093	]
012	(form feed)	053	5	094	^
013	(carriage return)	054	6	095	—
014	♫	055	7	096	`
015	☼	056	8	097	a
016	►	057	9	098	b
017	◄	058	:	099	c
018	↕	059	;	100	d
019	‼	060	<	101	e
020	¶	061	=	102	f
021	§	062	>	103	g
022	▬	063	?	104	h
023	↨	064	@	105	i
024	↑	065	A	106	j
025	↓	066	B	107	k
026	→	067	C	108	l
027	←	068	D	109	m
028	(cursor right)	069	E	110	n
029	(cursor left)	070	F	111	o
030	(cursor up)	071	G	112	p
031	(cursor down)	072	H	113	q
032	(space)	073	I	114	r
033	!	074	J	115	s
034	"	075	K	116	t
035	#	076	L	117	u
036	$	077	M	118	v
037	%	078	N	119	w
038	&	079	O	120	x
039	'	080	P	121	y
040	(	081	Q	122	z

528

ASCII Value	Character	ASCII Value	Character	ASCII Value	Character	ASCII Value	Character
123	{	164	ñ	205	=	246	÷
124	¦	165	Ñ	206	⫟	247	≈
125	}	166	ª	207	⫞	248	°
126	~	167	º	208	⊥	249	·
127	⌂	168	¿	209	⊤	250	·
128	Ç	169	⌐	210	⫟	251	√
129	ü	170	¬	211	⊔	252	ⁿ
130	é	171	½	212	⊢	253	²
131	â	172	¼	213	⊢	254	■
132	ä	173	¡	214	⊓	255	(blank 'FF')
133	à	174	«	215	⫟		
134	å	175	»	216	⫟		
135	ç	176	░	217	┘		
136	ê	177	▓	218	┌		
137	ë	178	▓	219	█		
138	è	179	│	220	▄		
139	ï	180	┤	221	▌		
140	î	181	╡	222	▐		
141	ì	182	╢	223	▀		
142	Ä	183	╖	224	α		
143	Å	184	╕	225	β		
144	É	185	╣	226	Γ		
145	æ	186	║	227	π		
146	Æ	187	╗	228	Σ		
147	ô	188	╝	229	σ		
148	ö	189	╜	230	μ		
149	ò	190	╛	231	τ		
150	û	191	┐	232	Φ		
151	ù	192	└	233	Θ		
152	ÿ	193	┴	234	Ω		
153	Ö	194	┬	235	δ		
154	Ü	195	├	236	∞		
155	¢	196	—	237	ø		
156	£	197	+	238	ε		
157	¥	198	╞	239	∩		
158	₧	199	╟	240	≡		
159	ƒ	200	╚	241	±		
160	á	201	╔	242	≥		
161	í	202	╩	243	≤		
162	ó	203	╦	244	⌠		
163	ú	204	╠	245	⌡		

APPENDIX B

Binary Representation of Numbers

Normally we write numbers in decimal (i.e., base 10) notation. For instance, if a, b, c, d, e are digits from 0 to 9, then

abc.de

represents the number

a*100 + b*10 + c*1 + d*(1/10) + e*(1/100)

or $a*10^2 + b*10^1 + c + d*(1/10)^1 + e*(1/10)^2$

The number also can be written in floating-point form as

.abcde*10^3

or   .abcdeE+3

In general, E+n means 10 raised to the nth power and E-n means 1/10 raised to the nth power.

When representing numbers in *binary* notation, the number 2 plays the role of 10, and the only digits used are 0 and 1. For instance if a, b, c, d, e are each 0 or 1, then in binary notation

abc.de

represents the number

$a*2^2 + b*2^1 + c + d*(1/2) + e*(1/2)^2$

or   a*4 + b*2 + c*1 + d*(1/2) + e*(1/4)

The number also can be written in floating-point form as

.abcde*2^3

or   .abcdeT+3

We will use T+n or T n to mean 2 raised to the nth power and T-n to mean 1/2 raised to the nth power. Multiplying a binary number by 2 raised to the nth power has the effect of moving the binary point (it isn't a decimal point now) n places to the right. Multiplying a binary number by 1/2 raised to the nth power has the effect of moving the binary point n places to the left.

Examples

1.   Let's convert the binary number .1101101T+4 to decimal form. This number is written in floating-point form. The notation T+4 tells us to move the decimal point 4 places to the right. We obtain

1101.101

Each digit to the left of the decimal point will be multiplied by a power of 2 and each digit to the right of the decimal point will be multiplied by a power of 1/2. We obtain

$1*(2)^3 + 1*(2)^2 + 0*(2)^1 + 1 + 1*(1/2)^1 + 0*(1/2)^2 + 1*(1/2)^3$

or $1*(8) + 1*(4) + 0*(2) + 1 + 1*(1/2) + 0*(1/4) + 1*(1/8)$
or   13 5/8   or   13.625

2.   Let's convert the binary number 1000.01T-2 to decimal form. The notation T-2 tells us to move the decimal point two places to the left. We obtain

   10.0001

The corresponding decimal representation is

   $1*(2)^1 + 0 + 0*(1/2)^1 + 0*(1/2)^2 + 0*(1/2)^3 + 1*(1/2)^4$
or $1*(2) + 0 + 0*(1/2) + 0*(1/4) + 0*(1/8) + 1*(1/16)$
or   2 1/16   or   2.0625

3.   Converting from decimal to binary form is more difficult. The following demonstration program converts any number to its binary representation. The output will be in floating-point form with 56 significant digits (the 56th digit is somewhat suspect) followed by T+n for 2 raised to the nth power and T-n for 1/2 raised to the nth power.

```
10 PRINT "THIS PROGRAM CONVERTS ANY NUMBER TO ITS BINARY
REPRESENTATION."
20 PRINT "THE NUMBER CAN BE GIVEN IN DECIMAL, HEXADECIMAL,
OR OCTAL FORM."
30 DEF SEG: INPUT "NUMBER";A#
40 X = VARPTR(A#): E% = PEEK(X+7)-128
50 IF SGN(E%) = -1 THEN E$ = STR$(E%): GOTO 70
60 E$ = "+"+RIGHT$(STR$(E%),2)
70 D% = PEEK(X+6): GOSUB 160
80 BL$(1) = RIGHT$(DCB$,7)
90 IF B(1) = 0 THEN S$ = "" ELSE S$"-"
100 FOR K = 2 TO 7
110    D% = PEEK(X+7-K): GOSUB 160
120 BL$(K) = DCB$: NEXT K
130 BL$ = BL$(1): FOR L = 2 TO 7
140 BL$ = BL$+BL$(L): NEXT L
150 PRINT S$+"."+"1"+BL$+"T"+E$: END
160 FOR I = 8 TO 1 STEP -1
170 B(I) = D% MOD 2
180 B$(I) = RIGHT$(STR$(B(I)),1)
190 D% = D%\2 :NEXT I
200 DCB$ = B$(1): FOR J = 2 TO 8
210 DCB$ = DCB$+B$(J): NEXT J
220 RETURN
```

A sample run is

```
RUN
THIS PROGRAM CONVERTS ANY NUMBER TO ITS BINARY REPRESENTATION.
```

APPENDIX B

```
THE NUMBER CAN BE GIVEN IN DECIMAL,HEXADECIMAL,OR OCTAL FORM.
NUMBER? 123.45
.11110110111001100110011001100110011001100110011001101000T+7
0k
```

The representation obtained by this program is the same representation that the computer uses when doing double-precision arithmetic. To find the single-precision representation, round the binary number to 24 significant digits.

SPECIFYING COORDINATES IN GRAPHICS MODES

For graphics purposes, each point of the screen is specified by a pair of numbers, called coordinates. The point with coordinates (x,y) can be reached by starting at the upper left-hand point of the screen and moving x points to the right and then y points down. (See Figure 1a.) This convention for labeling points arises from a mathematical coordinate system with the positive y axis pointing downward. (See Figure 1b.) The convention for specifying graphics points differs from the convention for locating text. See the discussion of LOCATE for a description of how locations are identified for displaying text.

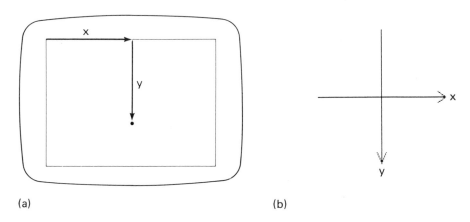

(a)   (b)

FIGURE 1

The values of y range from 0 to 199. The values of x range from 0 to 319 in medium-resolution graphics mode and from 0 to 639 in high-resolution graphics mode. The center of the screen has coordinates (160,100) in medium-resolution and (320,100) in high-resolution graphics mode. Figure 2 shows the coordinates of several points. The coordinates discussed above are known as the *absolute coordinates* of the point. A point also can be identified by giving its position relative to another point, referred to as the reference point. If R is some reference point on the screen, then the coordinates

     STEP (s,t)

(known as *relative coordinates*) specify the point that is obtained by starting at R, moving s units in the x direction (that is, to the right if s is positive and to the left if s is negative), and then moving t units in the y direction (that is, down if t is positive and up if t is negative). In other words, if the absolute coordinates of R are (x,y), then the absolute coordinates of the new point are (x+s,y+t).

APPENDIX C

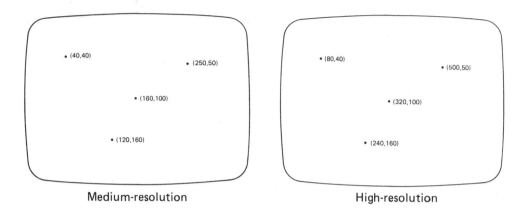

Medium-resolution   High-resolution

FIGURE 2

Figure 3 shows the relative coordinates of several points, with the center of the screen taken as the reference point.

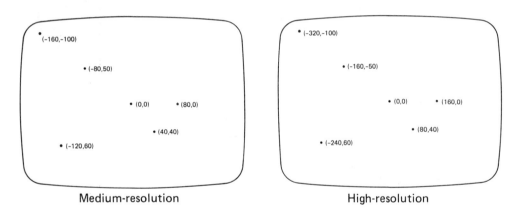

Medium-resolution   High-resolution

FIGURE 3

The graphics statements LINE, CIRCLE, DRAW, PSET, and PRESET draw points on the screen. After each of these is executed, there is a special point, known as the *last point referenced,* that the computer remembers. For the CIRCLE statement, it is the center of the circle. For the other statements, it is the last point drawn or referred to by the statement. This point is usually taken as the reference point when specifying the relative coordinates of the next point to be mentioned. The center of the screen is set as the last point referenced when the screen mode is changed, when one of the commands CHAIN, CHAIN MERGE, CLEAR, CLS, LOAD, MERGE, NEW, or RUN is executed, or when a program line is entered or deleted.

APPENDIX D

DIRECTORIES AND PATHS

When a disk is formatted, a directory is created to keep track of the different items located on that disk. In versions of BASIC preceding BASIC 2.0, the entries in the directory had to be the names of files. With BASIC 2.0 and subsequent versions, there is another type of entry; the name of another directory, called a *sub-directory*. Sub-directories function just like the original directory. They can contain both the names of files and other sub-directories. In this manner, a hierarchical directory structure is obtained.

Let's consider a concrete example of a hierarchical directory structure. Suppose that a computer is used at home by Ann and Bob, and that they keep all of their files on a single disk, a hard disk being the best choice. The main directory, referred to as the *root directory,* contains 3 entries: SPACE-MAN.BAS, ANN, and BOB. SPACEMAN.BAS is a BASIC program that they both enjoy and share in common. ANN is a sub-directory that has been set aside for Ann's use, and BOB is a sub-directory to be used by Bob. We might write

    root dir = { SPACEMAN.BAS, ANN, BOB }

Now, Ann analyzes the family's stock portfolio with a BASIC program called STOCKS.BAS and keeps the addresses of their friends in a data file called ADDRESS.DAT. Also, Ann is writing two books: a mathematics text and a novel. Bob travels for business purposes and has a BASIC program called TRAVELEX.BAS that he uses to itemize travel expenses. Also, he is an avid baseball fan and keeps a data file on each of his favorite teams. The contents of their directories are as follows:

    ANN = { STOCKS.BAS, ADDRESS.DAT, MATH, NOVEL }
    BOB = { TRAVELEX.BAS, BASEBALL}

Here, MATH and NOVEL are sub-directories of the directory ANN, and BASEBALL is a sub-directory of the directory BOB. The entries of these new directories are as follows:

    MATH = { CH1, CH2, CH3, CH4, CH5 }
    NOVEL = { CH1, CH2, CH3 }
    BASEBALL = { ORIOLES, YANKEES, ANGELS }

All of the entries in these directories are data files.

Each file and directory is given, as its full name, a moniker that identifies its lineage. Let's suppose that the disk is in drive C. Then the complete name of the file containing the first chapter of the mathematics book is

    C:\ANN\MATH\CH1

and the full name of the directory containing the baseball teams is

    C:\BOB\BASEBALL

These names can be used with the BASIC statements that deal with files. For instance, we can execute `LOAD "C:\BOB\TRAVELEX.BAS"` or `OPEN "C:\ANN\ADDRESS.DAT" FOR APPEND AS #1`.

APPENDIX D

Diagrams, called tree diagrams, can be drawn to help remember the hierarchical structure of the directories. The tree for the household above is shown in Figure 1.

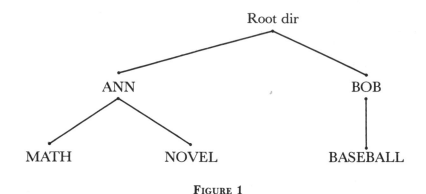

FIGURE 1

Each directory can be arrived at by tracing a path through this diagram. Formally, a *path* is a string specifing a directory. An example of a path is "\ANN\MATH".

Program files are created by SAVEing a program, and data files are created by OPENing a sequential file for OUTPUT or OPENing a random file. Directories are created with the BASIC command MKDIR.

Whereas program and data files can be KILLed, directories can only be removed with the command RMDIR. However, in order for a directory to be removed, it must contain no files or sub-directories. (Each directory, except the root directory, contains the entries ". <Dir>" and ".. <Dir>" which are used by BASIC. These entries need not, in fact cannot, be killed.)

The concept of default drive simplifies working with several disk drives at once. To simplify working with trees of directories, BASIC keeps track of a *current directory* for each drive. Initially, the current directory for each drive is the root directory of the disk in that drive. However, the current directory can be changed by executing a CHDIR command. BASIC statements that do not contain complete names refer to the current directory. For instance, if BOB is the current directory on disk C:, then the command `RUN "C:TRAVELEX.BAS"` would execute Bob's travel expenses program.

There are some conventions that facilitate working with directories. The string "..\" tells us to start the path by going from the current directory to the preceding directory. For instance, if "C:\ANN\MATH" is the current directory, then the command `CHDIR "C:..\NOVEL"` will change the current directory on drive C: to "C:\ANN\NOVEL". The back-slash character by itself refers to the root directory. For example, the command `CHDIR "C:\"` changes the current directory on disk drive C to the root directory.

In summary, we specify a directory by giving a path to it from the current directory. We specify a file by giving the path to the directory containing the file, followed by the name of the file.

ERROR MESSAGES

Message	Number
Advanced feature	73
Bad file mode	54
Bad file name	64
Bad file number	52
Bad record number	63
Can't continue	17
**Can't continue after SHELL	-
Communication buffer overflow	69
Device Fault	25
Device I/O Error	57
Device Timeout	24
Device Unavailable	68
Direct statement in file	66
Disk full	61
Disk Media Error	72
Disk not Ready	71
Disk Write Protected	70
Division by zero	11
Duplicate Definition	10
FIELD overflow	50
File already exists	58
File already open	55
File not found	53
FOR Without NEXT	26
Illegal direct	12
Illegal function call	5
**Incorrect DOS version	-
Input past end	62
Internal error	51
Line buffer overflow	23
Missing operand	22
NEXT without FOR	1
No RESUME	19
Out of DATA	4
Out of memory	7
Out of paper	27
Out of string space	14
Overflow	6
*Path/file access error	75
*Path not found	76

APPENDIX E

Note: Single (double) asterisks denote messages not contained in versions of BASIC before BASIC 2.0 (3.0).

SEQUENTIAL AND RANDOM FILES

Data processing is one of the primary uses for computers. Data can be stored as files on disks in two formats: sequential and random files.

PART I SEQUENTIAL FILES

As a model for a sequential file, consider a roll of adding machine tape. Suppose that we recorded the names and phone numbers of friends on this tape with indelible ink and just entered them one after another with no blank lines between entries and no attempt to alphabetize. Our list of data might look something like this:

> Leonard Slye, 123-4567
> Henry McCarty, 987-6543
> Ehrich Weiss, 345-9876
> Claude Dukenfield, 832-3287

In order to search for a name we would have to begin reading from the top of the list. We could not delete or change any entry in the list unless we recopied the entire list and made the correction when we came to it. However, we could add additional names and phone numbers to the end of the list.

Our telephone directory could be placed into a sequential file on a disk. The names and phone numbers would not be listed in a column on the disk, but would be arranged linearly. One possible arrangement follows:

```
"Leonard Slye","123-4567"<CR/LF>"Henry McCarty","987-6543"...
```

Here the computer is using quotation marks to identify strings, and using commas and the carriage return and line feed to separate data items. In this case, the commas and the pair of characters <CR/LF> are referred to as delimiters.

When reading a sequential file, the computer always begins with the first item and reads the pieces of information in order, one at a time, until it finds the item being searched for. The computer cannot delete or change any piece of information in the file unless the entire file is recopied. However, additional items of information can be added to the end of the file.

Sequential files are created with statements in the form **OPEN filespec FOR OUTPUT AS #n,** where filespec specifies the drive containing the disk and gives a name to the file, and n is a number (usually 1, 2, or 3) that will temporarily identify the file. Information is entered into the file with the statements WRITE#, PRINT#, and PRINT# USING. After we have finished placing information into the file, we execute the statement **CLOSE #n.** For instance, the following program will place the first three names and phone numbers into a file.

APPENDIX F

```
10 OPEN "B:PHONE" FOR OUTPUT AS #3
20 WRITE #3, "Leonard Slye", "123-4567"
30 WRITE #3, "Henry McCarty", "987-6543"
40 WRITE #3, "Ehrich Weiss", "345-9876"
50 CLOSE #3
```

Here the disk is placed in drive B:, the file is named "PHONE", and is temporarily referred to as file #3.

In order to read a sequential file we first must gain access to it with a statement in the form **OPEN filespec FOR INPUT AS #n.** Then we can copy information from the file with the statements INPUT#, LINE INPUT#, and INPUT$. INPUT# is usually used to retrieve items that have been entered with WRITE#, and LINE INPUT# is usually used to retrieve items that have been entered with PRINT#. INPUT# reads the next available item (or items) from the file and assigns it to a variable (or variables). LINE INPUT# reads everything up to the next CR/LF pair and assigns it to a string variable. INPUT$ reads a specified number of characters from the file and assigns the string containing them to a string variable. The following program can be used to search the file PHONE for a telephone number.

```
10 INPUT "Name"; N$
20 OPEN "B:PHONE" FOR INPUT AS #1
30 INPUT #1, A$, B$
40 IF A$ = N$ THEN 60
50 GOTO 30
60 PRINT B$
70 CLOSE #1
RUN
Name? Henry McCarty
987-6543
Ok
```

In order to add information to the end of a sequential file, we first gain access to the file with a statement in the form **OPEN filespec FOR APPEND AS #n,** and then record additional items of data, just as we did initially. The following program will add one more name to the file PHONE.

```
10 OPEN "B:PHONE" FOR APPEND AS #2
20 WRITE #2, "Claude Dukenfield", "832-3287"
30 CLOSE #2
```

While using a file, we can obtain information about the file with the statements EOF, LOC, and LOF, which tell whether the end of the file has been reached, the approximate number of blocks (of 128 characters) which have been processed in the file, and the length of the file.

The following demonstration program will read the first 2000 characters of a sequential file and display them on the Monochrome Display. Carriage returns appear as single musical notes and line feeds appear as reverse-image circles. The end-of-file character appears as an arrow pointing to the right. Press any key to clear the screen.

```
10 INPUT "FILE TO READ"; A$
20 DEF SEG = &HB000: SCREEN 0
30 OPEN A$ FOR INPUT AS #1
40 I=0: CLS: KEY OFF: WIDTH 80
50 WHILE NOT EOF(1)
60    IF I>1999 THEN 100
70    B$=INPUT$(1,1)
80    POKE 2*I,ASC(B$)
90    I=I+1
100 WEND
110 POKE 2*I,26
120 CLOSE #1
130 W$=INPUT$(1): CLS
```

In order to run the above program when using a graphics screen, change line 20 to 20 DEF SEG = &HB800:SCREEN 0,0,0.

PART II   RANDOM FILES

As a model of a random file, consider a box of index cards where each card has a numbered tab. The numbers include every integer from one to the number of index cards in the box. Each index card has been laid out into special regions where information can be printed. Each of these regions consists of a sequence of spaces, each capable of holding a single character. Each of the regions is called a field, and the number of spaces in a particular field is called the width of the field. Figure 1 shows a possible layout for index cards to contain information about colleges in the USA. Each card is organized into four fields of widths 23, 2, 14, and 16.

Name _

State located _ _

Town located _ _ _ _ _ _ _ _ _ _ _ _ _ _

President _ _ _ _ _ _ _ _ _ _ _ _ _ _ _ _

FIGURE 1

This format allows for the name of a college to consist of 23 or fewer characters. If the name is longer than that it must be abbreviated. The second field contains exactly enough space to hold its information, but the third and fourth fields might require abbreviations. Figures 2 and 3 show examples of the way data can be entered.

APPENDIX F

Name _ _ _ _ _ _ _ _ O B E R L I N _ C O L L E G E
State located O H
Town located O B E R L I N _ _ _ _ _ _ _ _
President S T A R R _ _ _ _ _ _ _ _ _ _ _

FIGURE 2

Name _ _ _ M A S S . _ I N S T . _ O F _ T E C H .
State located M A
Town located C A M B R I D G E _ _ _ _ _ _
President G R A Y _ _ _ _ _ _ _ _ _ _ _ _ _

FIGURE 3

Notice that the name of each college has been written in the rightmost part of its field, whereas the other entries have been written in the leftmost part. We say that the colleges have been right-justified and the other data left-justified.

In order to read one of the index cards, all we have to do is ask for it by number and pull it out of the box. We can change the information by replacing the index card by another card containing the new information. (The new card should have the same number on its tab as the original card). We can delete a card from the file by replacing it by a blank card with the same number on its tab. We can add a completely new card either by putting it at the end of the file box and giving it a number that is higher than the highest card in the box, or using it to replace a blank card.

Our college directory can be placed into a random file on a disk. A block of fifty-five spaces would be reserved for the contents of each index card. We refer to this block as a record, and say that the record length is 55. Fields follow one after another linearly within a record. Records follow one after the other on the disk. For instance, the contents of the record corresponding to the index card in Figure 2 would appear as in Figure 4.

_ _ _ _ _ _ _ _ O B E R L I N C O L L E G E O H O B E R
L I N _ _ _ _ _ _ _ _ S T A R R _ _ _ _ _ _ _ _ _ _ _ _

FIGURE 4

Notice that no delimiters appear on the disk. The computer is told that each record has length 55 and, therefore, knows exactly where each record ends.

Random files are created with statements in the form **OPEN filespec AS #n LEN = g,** where filespec specifies the drive containing the disk and gives a name to the file, n is a number (usually 1, 2, or 3) that will temporarily identify the file, and g is the record length. A FIELD statement is then used to give each field a name and specify its width. Information is entered into the file via a two-step procedure. A portion of memory, referred to as a buffer, is automatically set aside for the file. The information for a single record is placed into the buffer one field at a time. This is accomplished with the statements LSET and RSET, depending on whether the items are to be left- or right-justified. Then the total record is copied into the file as record number r by the statement PUT #n, r. Records also are read from random files with a two-step procedure. The statement GET #n, r places a copy of record number r into the buffer. Individual fields are then accessed by referring to them by their names. After we have finished working with the file, we execute the statement CLOSE #n.

The following program creates a random file named "COLLEGES" and enters the two records shown in Figures 2 and 3. It then reads certain information from the first record.

```
10 OPEN "A:COLLEGES" AS #3 LEN = 55
20 FIELD #3, 23 AS CF$, 2 AS SF$, 14 AS TF$, 16 AS PF$
30 RSET CF$ = "OBERLIN COLLEGE"
40 LSET SF$ = "OH"
50 LSET TF$ = "OBERLIN"
60 LSET PF$ = "STARR"
70 PUT #3, 1
80 RSET CF$ = "MASS. INST. OF TECH."
90 LSET SF$ = "MA"
100 LSET TF$ = "CAMBRIDGE"
110 LSET PF$ = "GRAY"
120 PUT #3, 2
130 GET #3, 1
140 PRINT CF$; "  "; PF$
150 GET #3, 2
160 PRINT CF$; "  "; PF$
170 CLOSE #3
RUN
        OBERLIN COLLEGE STARR
    MASS. INST. OF TECH. GRAY
Ok
```

Numeric data must be converted to string data before being placed in a random file. The functions MKI$, MKS$, and MKD$ are used to convert numbers to strings, and the functions CVI, CVS, and CVD are used to convert these strings back to numbers. Also, the functions LOC and LOF are used to determine the current position within the file and the approximate number of records in the file.

APPENDIX G

LOGICAL OPERATORS

The six logical operators, NOT, AND, OR, XOR, EQV, and IMP, are used primarily in two ways. In Part I we explore their role in building compound conditions for IF statements, and in Part II we show how they operate on integers.

PART I CONDITIONS FOR IF STATEMENTS

Some common types of conditions involve the following relationships between numbers or strings.

Relationship	Numbers	Strings
=	is equal to	is identical to
<	is less than	precedes alphabetically
>	is greater than	follows alphabetically
< >	is not equal to	is not identical to
< =	is less than or equal to	precedes alphabetically or is identical to
> =	is greater than or equal to	follows alphabetically or is identical to

Note: Non-alphabetical characters are ordered according to their ASCII values.

Conditions involving relationships between numbers or strings are either true (T) or false (F). Some examples of simple conditions, along with their truth values, are

Condition	Truth value	Condition	Truth value
2 < 3	T	"Y" > "X"	T
2∧3 = 3∧2	F	"A" > = "B"	F

Compound conditions can be formed by negating and/or combining simple conditions with logical operators. The truth value of a compound condition can be determined by the truth values of the component simple conditions and the logical operators used. In the following table, the conditions cond1 and cond2 are used to form compound conditions. For each of these compound conditions, the table specifies when the compound condition will have the truth value T.

Compound Condition	Requirements for a Truth Value of T
NOT cond1	True only if cond1 is False
cond1 AND cond2	True if both cond1 and cond2 are True

cond1 OR cond2	True if one or both of cond1 and cond2 are True
cond1 XOR cond2	True if exactly one of cond1 or cond2 is True
cond1 EQV cond2	True if *both* cond1 and cond2 are True, or if *both* are False
cond1 IMP cond2	True if cond1 and cond2 are both True, or if cond1 is False

The meanings of NOT, AND, and OR are obvious. XOR means eXclusive OR. The terms "EQuiValent" and "IMPlies" have different meanings in the field of logic than they do in everyday usage. Formally, two statements are said to be logically equivalent if they have the same truth values. Hence, any two true statements are equivalent. Formally, one statement is said to logically imply another statement if, whenever the first statement is true, then so is the second. In the event that the first statement is false, then the compound statement "statement1 implies statement2" can be thought of as being vacuously true.

Some examples of compound conditions, along with their truth values, follow:

NOT ("A" $>=$ "B")	T
2 < 3 AND 2∧3 = 3∧2	F
2 < 3 OR 2∧3 = 3∧2	T
2 < 3 XOR 2∧3 = 3∧2	T
("A" $>=$ "B") EQV ("Y" $<>$ "y")	F
("A" $>=$ "B") IMP ("Y" $<>$ "y")	T

Compound conditions can involve more than one logical operator. If so, the order in which the operations are executed is first NOT, then AND, then OR, then XOR, then EQV, and finally IMP. For instance, the condition NOT ("A"$>=$"B") OR (2<3) is the same as the condition (NOT ("A"$>=$"B")) OR (2<3), and hence has the truth value T.

BASIC assigns the number -1 to true conditions and the number 0 to false conditions. The following examples illustrate this feature.

EXAMPLES

1.
```
PRINT 2<3, "B"<"A"
 -1              0
Ok
```

2.
```
10 DEFDBL A,B,M
20 DEF FNMAX(A,B) = -(A>B)*A-(B>A)*B
30 INPUT "Type two numbers: ", A, B
40 IF A=B THEN PRINT "The numbers are equal.": END
50 PRINT "The maximum number is "; FNMAX(A,B)
RUN
Type two numbers: 4,7
The maximum number is 7
Ok
```

APPENDIX G

PART II OPERATIONS ON INTEGERS

We restrict our discussion to operations on the integers from 0 to 255, involving the logical operators AND, OR and XOR. We assume that the reader is familiar with the binary representation of integers. (See Appendix B for details.)

For the moment, let's consider just the two integers 0 and 1. The following tables give the definitions of the logical operations AND, OR and XOR for these two values.

AND	0	1		OR	0	1		XOR	0	1
0	0	0		0	0	1		0	0	1
1	0	1		1	1	1		1	1	0

These definitions make sense if we think of 0 as false and 1 as true.

The logical operators above can be extended to eight-tuples of zeros and ones by operating on corresponding entries of the eight-tuples individually. For instance, 01000111 OR 10010011 is 11010111 and 01101010 XOR 11010100 is 10111110.

Let m and n be any two integers between 0 and 255. To apply logical operators to m and n, first represent each of them in binary notation as an eight-tuple of zeros and ones. (After obtaining the binary representation of the numbers, just append some zeros to the left, if necessary, to obtain eight-tuples.) Then apply the logical operators to the eight-tuples and convert the resulting eight-tuple back to an integer.

FURTHER EXAMPLES

3. `PRINT 135 AND 11`
       3
    Ok

The numbers 135 and 11 correspond to the binary eight-tuples 10000111 and 00001011. Now, 10000111 AND 00001011 is 00000011 which is the binary representation of 3.

4. The following demonstration program combines numbers that are specified by the user.

```
10 CLS: DEFINT A-Z
20 INPUT "first number (between 0 and 255)";F
30 INPUT "second number (between 0 and 255)";S
40 INPUT "logical operator: AND, OR, XOR";L$
50 D = F: GOSUB 170
60 PRINT F,,DCB$
70 D = S: GOSUB 170
80 PRINT S,,DCB$
90 IF (L$="AND") OR (L$="and") THEN D = F AND S
```

```
100 IF (L$="OR") OR (L$="or") THEN D = F OR S
110 IF (L$="XOR") OR (L$="xor") THEN D = F XOR S
140 P = D: GOSUB 170
150 PRINT F; L$; S; "is"; P, DCB$
160 END
170 REM Convert D to binary eight-tuple
180 FOR I = 8 TO 1 STEP -1
190    B(I) = D MOD 2: D = D\2
200    B$(I) = RIGHT$(STR$(B(I)),1)
220 NEXT I
230 DCB$ = B$(1)
240 FOR J = 2 TO 8: DCB$ = DCB$ + B$(J): NEXT J
270 RETURN
```

5. The byte in absolute memory location 1047 gives the status of the four toggle keys (Insert, Caps Lock, Num Lock, and Scroll Lock). In particular, the second bit from the left will be a 1 if the Caps Lock key is active, and a 0 otherwise. The following program determines whether or not the Caps Lock key is active.

```
10 DEF SEG = 0
20 A = PEEK (1047)
30 IF (A AND 64)=64 THEN 60
40 PRINT "The Caps Lock key is not active.
50 END
60 PRINT "The Caps Lock key is active."
```

APPENDIX H

SOME USES OF PEEK AND POKE

PART I   DEF SEG = 0

The computer reserves certain low-order memory locations to hold information such as the status of various keyboard keys, the current screen mode, and the types of devices attached to the computer. BASIC programs can use the function PEEK to read these memory locations, and the function POKE to alter them. The statements in Part I should be preceeded by **DEF SEG = 0**.

1.   The following statements set and determine the status of the keyboard toggle keys.

CAPS LOCK KEY

PEEK(1047) AND 64 has value 0 if keyboard in lowercase and value 64 if in uppercase mode.
To specify lowercase state: POKE 1047, PEEK(1047) AND 191
To specify uppercase state: POKE 1047, PEEK(1047) OR 64
To toggle state: POKE 1047, PEEK(1047) XOR 64
PEEK(1048) AND 64 has value 64 if key pressed, 0 otherwise.

NUM LOCK KEY

PEEK(1047) AND 32 has value 0 for cursor control state and value 32 for numeric keypad state.
To specify cursor control state: POKE 1047,PEEK(1047) AND 223
To specify numeric keypad state: POKE 1047,PEEK(1047) OR 32
To toggle state: POKE 1047, PEEK(1047) XOR 32
PEEK(1048) AND 32 has value 32 if key pressed, 0 otherwise.

INS KEY

PEEK(1047) AND 128 has value 128 for insert state, 0 otherwise.
To specify insert state: POKE 1047,PEEK(1047) OR 128
To specify non-insert state: POKE 1047,PEEK(1047) AND 127
To toggle state: POKE 1047, PEEK(1047) XOR 128
PEEK(1048) AND 128 has value 128 if key pressed, 0 otherwise.

SCROLL LOCK KEY

PEEK(1047) AND 16 has value 16 for scroll lock state, 0 otherwise.
To specify scroll lock state: POKE 1047,PEEK(1047) OR 16
To specify alternate state: POKE 1047,PEEK(1047) AND 239
To toggle state: POKE 1047, PEEK(1047) XOR 16
PEEK(1048) AND 16 has value 16 if key pressed, 0 otherwise.

2.   The following statements test the status of some special keys.

PEEK(1047) AND 8 has value 8 if Alt key pressed, 0 otherwise.
PEEK(1047) AND 4 has value 4 if Ctrl key pressed, 0 otherwise.
PEEK(1047) AND 2 has value 2 if left shift key pressed, 0 otherwise.
PEEK(1047) AND 1 has value 1 if right shift key pressed, 0 otherwise.
PEEK(1047) AND 3 has value 0 if neither shift key pressed.
(PC AT only) **PEEK(1048) AND 4** has value 4 if Sys Req key pressed, 0 otherwise.

3.   To check screen mode:

PEEK(1097)   = 0 text mode, WIDTH 40, color disabled
= 1 text mode, WIDTH 40, color enabled
= 2 text mode, WIDTH 80, color disabled
= 3 text mode, WIDTH 80, color enabled
= 4 medium-res. graphics, color enabled
= 5 medium-res. graphics, color disabled
= 6 high-resolution graphics
= 7 Monochrome display

PEEK(1098)+256*PEEK(1099) gives the width in columns.

4.   To check display type:

PEEK(1040) AND 48   =   0 no monitors !
= 16 40 x 25 color/graphics monitor
= 32 80 x 25 color/graphics monitor
= 48 Monochrome display

5.   To select display type:

Monochrome   **POKE 1040,PEEK(1040) OR 48**
Graphics   **POKE 1040,(PEEK(1040) AND 207) OR 16**

6.   The keyboard buffer is physically placed somewhere in locations 1054-1085. It begins at location **PEEK(1050)+1024** and ends (after possibly cycling back to location 1054), at location **PEEK(1052)+1023**. Ordinary characters use every other location. Extended characters use two locations, with the first location containing the null character. The statement **POKE 1050,PEEK(1052)** clears the keyboard buffer.

7.   The internal clock ticks approximately 18.2 times per second. The number of ticks that have occurred since midnight is given by

PEEK(1132) + 256*PEEK(1133) + 65536*PEEK(1134)

8.   Size of RAM in KB: **PEEK(1043) + 256*PEEK(1044)**

9.   Number of diskette drives:

(PEEK(1040) AND 1)*(PEEK(1040) AND 193) =   0 no drives
=   1 one drive
=   65 two drives
= 129 three drives
= 193 four drives

APPENDIX H

10. Number of printer adapters: **(PEEK(1041) AND 192)/64**

11. Number of game adapters: **(PEEK(1041) AND 16)/16**

12. Number of RS232 cards attached: **(PEEK(1041) AND 14)/2**

13. The shape of the cursor can be set with a statement of the form LOCATE ,,,I,J. (See the discussion of the LOCATE statement for details.) **PEEK(1121) AND 31** has value I and **PEEK(1120) AND 31** has value J.

14. When using text mode with a graphics monitor, there are several "pages" at our disposal. The cursor locations for the various pages are given as follows: Let CR(n) and CC(n) be the Cursor Row and Cursor Column for page n. Then **PEEK(1105+2*n)** has value CR(n)-1, and **PEEK(1104+2*n)** has value CC(n)-1.

15. Visual page (i.e. page currently displayed): **PEEK(1122)**

16. Subscripts and superscripts can be displayed in the top half of the graphics screens. The following programs place the string B$ as a subscript of the string A$. The value of R must be between 1 and 12, and the value of C must be at most one more than the width of the screen minus the sum of the lengths of the two strings. In order to display B$ as a superscript of A$, replace the R in line 40 by R-1.

```
10 SCREEN 1: CLS              10 SCREEN 2: CLS
20 LOCATE R,C: PRINT A$;      20 LOCATE R,C: PRINT A$;
30 POKE 1098,20               30 POKE 1098,40
40 LOCATE 2*R: PRINT B$       40 LOCATE 2*R: PRINT B$
50 POKE 1098,40               50 POKE 1098,80
```

17. Segment number of BASIC's data segment:

```
PEEK(1296) + 256*PEEK(1297)
```

18. In graphics mode, the statement PRINT CHR$(n), where n is a number from 128 to 254, causes the computer to display an 8 by 8 rectangle of pixels that form the character stored in a sequence of 127 blocks of eight bytes each. These 1016 bytes begin at the memory location of offset **PEEK(124) + 256*PEEK(125)** in segment **PEEK(126) + 256*PEEK(127)**. To create a character set for ASCII values 128-254:

    a. Select the portion of memory to hold the bytes describing the characters.

    b. Poke the pattern for character 128 into the first eight memory locations, the pattern for character 129 into the next eight locations, and so on.

    c. Poke the offset and segment of the first byte into locations 124 to 127.

19. In medium-resolution graphics, background color and palette are selected by the statement COLOR b,p. **PEEK(1126) AND 15** will have the

value b and (PEEK(1126) AND 32)/32 will have the value p. In text mode with a color monitor, the value of PEEK(1126) MOD 32 will be the border color.

PART II   DEF SEG

BASIC's Data Segment is specified as the current segment by the statement DEF SEG. This segment contains, among other things, the current BASIC program and the values of variables. The statements in Part II should be preceded by DEF SEG.

1.   Normally, the first 24 lines of the screen scroll as the screen fills. However, the scrolling portion of the screen can consist of any rectangular portion beginning on the left side of the screen. The following statements specify that the scrolling portion of the screen consists of the first c positions of lines a through b. In addition, the cursor will be confined to this region.

```
POKE 41,c: POKE 91,a: POKE 92,b
```

2.   In direct mode, pressing Ctrl-PrtSc causes the printer to print all output as it appears on the screen. This is referred to as an *echo* to the printer. Pressing Ctrl-PrtSc again turns off echoing to the printer. In program (or direct) mode, the statement POKE N,255 turns on echoing and the statement POKE N,0 turns off echoing, where N = 1880, 1883, 1887 or 1889 in BASIC Versions 2.0, 2.1, 3.0, or 3.1 respectively.

3.   Current BASIC line number: PEEK(46) + 256*PEEK(47)

4.   Line number of last BASIC error: PEEK(839) + 256*PEEK(840)

5.   Medium-resolution text color: PEEK(78) AND 3

6.   To set text color in medium-resolution graphics mode to color c of the current palette (c = 1, 2, or 3): POKE 78,c

7.   Byte containing beginning of text of current BASIC program:
PEEK(48) + 256*PEEK(49)

8.   Byte containing start of BASIC variables:
PEEK(856) + 256*PEEK(857)

9.   Byte containing start of BASIC array variables:
PEEK(858) + 256*PEEK(859)

10.   The row number of the cursor is given by PEEK(86) and the column number is given by PEEK(87).

PART III   DEF SEG = 64206 (OR &HFACE)

The following memory locations are part of ROM, Read Only Memory.

1.   The strings that are assigned to the function keys when BASIC is first

APPENDIX H

invoked are stored in ROM in the 71 memory locations beginning with the location of offset 13. A null character appears at the end of each string.

2. In graphics mode, each character is displayed in an 8 by 8 array of pixels that can be stored as a sequence of eight bytes. The bytes for the characters having ASCII values 0 to 127 are stored in the memory locations having offsets from 19854 to 20877.

3. To obtain the version date of ROM:

```
FOR I=21269 TO 21276: PRINT CHR$(PEEK(I));: NEXT I
```

4. To determine computer being used:

```
PEEK(21278)     = 255 PC
                = 254 PC XT or Portable PC
                = 253 PCjr
                = 252 PC AT
```

RESERVED WORDS

ABS	*ENVIRON$	LOC	RENUM
AND	EOF	LOCATE	RESET
ASC	EQV	LOF	RESTORE
ATN	ERASE	LOG	RESUME
AUTO	*ERDEV	LPOS	RETURN
BEEP	*ERDEV$	LPRINT	RIGHT$
BLOAD	ERL	LSET	*RMDIR
BSAVE	ERR	MERGE	RND
CALL	ERROR	MID$	RSET
CDBL	EXP	*MKDIR	RUN
CHAIN	FIELD	MKD$	SAVE
*CHDIR	FILES	MKI$	SCREEN
CHR$	FIX	MKS$	SGN
CINT	FNxxxxxx	MOD	*SHELL
CIRCLE	FOR	MOTOR	SIN
CLEAR	FRE	NAME	SOUND
CLOSE	GET	NEW	SPACE$
CLS	GOSUB	NEXT	SPC(
COLOR	GOTO	NOT	SQR
COM	HEX$	OCT$	STEP
COMMON	IF	OFF	STICK
CONT	IMP	ON	STOP
COS	INKEY$	OPEN	STR$
CSNG	INP	OPTION	STRIG
CSRLIN	INPUT	OR	STRING$
CVD	INPUT#	OUT	SWAP
CVI	INPUT$	PAINT	SYSTEM
CVS	INSTR	PEEK	TAB(
DATA	INT	PEN	TAN
DATE$	*INTER$	PLAY	THEN
DEF	*IOCTL	*PMAP	TIME$
DEFDBL	*IOCTL$	POINT	*TIMER
DEFINT	KEY	POKE	TO
DEFSNG	*KEY$	POS	TROFF
DEFSTR	KILL	PRESET	TRON
DELETE	LEFT$	PRINT	USING
DIM	LEN	PRINT#	USR
DRAW	LET	PSET	VAL
EDIT	LINE	PUT	VARPTR
ELSE	LIST	RANDOMIZE	VARPTR$
END	LLIST	READ	*VIEW
*ENVIRON	LOAD	REM	WAIT

APPENDIX I

WEND	WIDTH	WRITE	XOR
WHILE	WINDOW	WRITE#	

An asterisk preceding a word indicates that it is a reserved word in BASIC 2.0 and later versions, but *not* a reserved word in earlier versions of BASIC.

APPENDIX J

SCAN CODES

Key	Code (Dec)	(Hex)	Key	Code (Dec)	(Hex)
Esc	1	01	: / ;	39	27
! / 1	2	02	" / '	40	28
@ / 2	3	03	~ / `	41	29
# / 3	4	04	L. Shift	42	2A
$ / 4	5	05		/ \	43	2B
% / 5	6	06	Z	44	2C
^ / 6	7	07	X	45	2D
& / 7	8	08	C	46	2E
* / 8	9	09	V	47	2F
(/ 9	10	0A	B	48	30
) / 0	11	0B	N	49	31
_ / -	12	0C	M	50	32
+ / =	13	0D	< / ,	51	33
Bks	14	0F	> / .	52	34
Tab	15	0F	? / /	53	35
Q	16	10	Right Shift	54	36
W	17	11	PrtSc / *	55	37
E	18	12	Alt	56	38
R	19	13	Space	57	39
T	20	14	Caps Lock	58	3A
Y	21	15	F1	59	3B
U	22	16	F2	60	3C
I	23	17	F3	61	3D
O	24	18	F4	62	3E
P	25	19	F5	63	3F
{ / [	26	1A	F6	64	40
} /]	27	1B	F7	65	41
Return	28	1C	F8	66	42
Ctrl	29	1D	F9	67	43
A	30	1E	F10	68	44
S	31	1F	Num Lock	69	45
D	32	20	Scroll Lock	70	46
F	33	21	7 / Home	71	47
G	34	22	8 / Up	72	48
H	35	23	9 / PgUp	73	49
J	36	24	-	74	4A
K	37	25	4 / Left	75	4B
L	38	26	5	76	4C

APPENDIX J

Key	Code (Dec)	(Hex)	Key	Code (Dec)	(Hex)
6 / Rt.	77	4D	3 / PgDn	81	51
+	78	4E	0 / Ins	82	52
1 / End	79	4F	. / Del	83	53
2 / Down	80	50			

APPENDIX K

0 to 255 in Decimal, Hexadecimal, and Binary

0	0	00000000		48	30	00110000		96	60	01100000
1	1	00000001		49	31	00110001		97	61	01100001
2	2	00000010		50	32	00110010		98	62	01100010
3	3	00000011		51	33	00110011		99	63	01100011
4	4	00000100		52	34	00110100		100	64	01100100
5	5	00000101		53	35	00110101		101	65	01100101
6	6	00000110		54	36	00110110		102	66	01100110
7	7	00000111		55	37	00110111		103	67	01100111
8	8	00001000		56	38	00111000		104	68	01101000
9	9	00001001		57	39	00111001		105	69	01101001
10	A	00001010		58	3A	00111010		106	6A	01101010
11	B	00001011		59	3B	00111011		107	6B	01101011
12	C	00001100		60	3C	00111100		108	6C	01101100
13	D	00001101		61	3D	00111101		109	6D	01101101
14	E	00001110		62	3E	00111110		110	6E	01101110
15	F	00001111		63	3F	00111111		111	6F	01101111
16	10	00010000		64	40	01000000		112	70	01110000
17	11	00010001		65	41	01000001		113	71	01110001
18	12	00010010		66	42	01000010		114	72	01110010
19	13	00010011		67	43	01000011		115	73	01110011
20	14	00010100		68	44	01000100		116	74	01110100
21	15	00010101		69	45	01000101		117	75	01110101
22	16	00010110		70	46	01000110		118	76	01110110
23	17	00010111		71	47	01000111		119	77	01110111
24	18	00011000		72	48	01001000		120	78	01111000
25	19	00011001		73	49	01001001		121	79	01111001
26	1A	00011010		74	4A	01001010		122	7A	01111010
27	1B	00011011		75	4B	01001011		123	7B	01111011
28	1C	00011100		76	4C	01001100		124	7C	01111100
29	1D	00011101		77	4D	01001101		125	7D	01111101
30	1E	00011110		78	4E	01001110		126	7E	01111110
31	1F	00011111		79	4F	01001111		127	7F	01111111
32	20	00100000		80	50	01010000		128	80	10000000
33	21	00100001		81	51	01010001		129	81	10000001
34	22	00100010		82	52	01010010		130	82	10000010
35	23	00100011		83	53	01010011		131	83	10000011
36	24	00100100		84	54	01010100		132	84	10000100
37	25	00100101		85	55	01010101		133	85	10000101
38	26	00100110		86	56	01010110		134	86	10000110
39	27	00100111		87	57	01010111		135	87	10000111
40	28	00101000		88	58	01011000		136	88	10001000
41	29	00101001		89	59	01011001		137	89	10001001
42	2A	00101010		90	5A	01011010		138	8A	10001010
43	2B	00101011		91	5B	01011011		139	8B	10001011
44	2C	00101100		92	5C	01011100		140	8C	10001100
45	2D	00101101		93	5D	01011101		141	8D	10001101
46	2E	00101110		94	5E	01011110		142	8E	10001110
47	2F	00101111		95	5F	01011111		143	8F	10001111

144	90	10010000	192	C0	11000000	240	F0	11110000
145	91	10010001	193	C1	11000001	241	F1	11110001
146	92	10010010	194	C2	11000010	242	F2	11110010
147	93	10010011	195	C3	11000011	243	F3	11110011
148	94	10010100	196	C4	11000100	244	F4	11110100
149	95	10010101	197	C5	11000101	245	F5	11110101
150	96	10010110	198	C6	11000110	246	F6	11110110
151	97	10010111	199	C7	11000111	247	F7	11110111
152	98	10011000	200	C8	11001000	248	F8	11111000
153	99	10011001	201	C9	11001001	249	F9	11111001
154	9A	10011010	202	CA	11001010	250	FA	11111010
155	9B	10011011	203	CB	11001011	251	FB	11111011
156	9C	10011100	204	CC	11001100	252	FC	11111100
157	9D	10011101	205	CD	11001101	253	FD	11111101
158	9E	10011110	206	CE	11001110	254	FE	11111110
159	9F	10011111	207	CF	11001111	255	FF	11111111
160	A0	10100000	208	D0	11010000			
161	A1	10100001	209	D1	11010001			
162	A2	10100010	210	D2	11010010			
163	A3	10100011	211	D3	11010011			
164	A4	10100100	212	D4	11010100			
165	A5	10100101	213	D5	11010101			
166	A6	10100110	214	D6	11010110			
167	A7	10100111	215	D7	11010111			
168	A8	10101000	216	D8	11011000			
169	A9	10101001	217	D9	11011001			
170	AA	10101010	218	DA	11011010			
171	AB	10101011	219	DB	11011011			
172	AC	10101100	220	DC	11011100			
173	AD	10101101	221	DD	11011101			
174	AE	10101110	222	DE	11011110			
175	AF	10101111	223	DF	11011111			
176	B0	10110000	224	E0	11100000			
177	B1	10110001	225	E1	11100001			
178	B2	10110010	226	E2	11100010			
179	B3	10110011	227	E3	11100011			
180	B4	10110100	228	E4	11100100			
181	B5	10110101	229	E5	11100101			
182	B6	10110110	230	E6	11100110			
183	B7	10110111	231	E7	11100111			
184	B8	10111000	232	E8	11101000			
185	B9	10111001	233	E9	11101001			
186	BA	10111010	234	EA	11101010			
187	BB	10111011	235	EB	11101011			
188	BC	10111100	236	EC	11101100			
189	BD	10111101	237	ED	11101101			
190	BE	10111110	238	EE	11101110			
191	BF	10111111	239	EF	11101111			

APPENDIX L

COMMUNICATING IN BASIC

The true power of any computer would be significantly diminished without the ability to communicate. Most commercial communications programs are written in an assembly language for speed and versatility. However, IBM PC BASIC has significant communications capabilities that rival assembly language when compiled. This appendix presents an overview of the practical aspects of communicating in IBM PC Disk BASIC through the use of the statements contained in this handbook.

Where possible and appropriate, two methods for accomplishing a task, or series of tasks, will be offered in this appendix. In each case, the first method will be the simpler of the two and the preferred method for beginning to intermediate programmers. The alternate method will typically make extensive use of the INP function and the OUT statement. These BASIC features are too often avoided by BASIC programmers because they deal directly with input/output ports and status registers in memory. The explanations and examples used in this appendix should allow you greater use of these powerful features.

THE MECHANICS

Data communication is accomplished when one device successfully passes a piece of data to another device. In BASIC, the mechanics of passing that data are actually quite simple, given that the two computers are properly equipped with compatible devices, such as an asynchronous communications adapter, modem, and appropriate cables. The sending computer must deliver the piece of data to its communications port in the proper format, and the receiving computer must sense that the data has arrived at its communications port and then fetch it. A considerable amount of activity is required to transport the piece of data from the sender's communications port to the receiver's port, but that need not be of concern to the BASIC programmer. The BASIC programmer is only interested in delivering the data to the communications port and receiving data from the communications port.

The IBM PC uses two communications ports (both serial ports) under PC-DOS, designated as COM1: and COM2: in both DOS and BASIC. The absolute memory address for COM1: is &H3F8 (&H indicates a hexadecimal number) and for COM2: is &H2F8. Each port has six registers associated with it to control or record the status of various communications activities. The following table will help clarify the relative locations of the registers, and aid in understanding later discussions and examples, especially the alternate methods of task accomplishment.

APPENDIX L

Register	Abbr	Offset from COM: Port	Actual Address With COM1: &H3F8	COM2: &H2F8
Interrupt Enable Reg	IER	+1	&H3F9	&H2F9
Interrupt Identification Reg	IIR	+2	&H3FA	&H2FA
Line Control Reg	LCR	+3	&H3FB	&H2FB
Modem Control Reg	MCR	+4	&H3FC	&H2FC
Line Status Reg	LSR	+5	&H3FD	&H2FD
Modem Status Reg	MSR	+6	&H3FE	&H2FE

ESTABLISHING COMMUNICATIONS

The specific activity required within a program to establish communications is somewhat different for the originating computer than is the activity required of the answering computer. Additional differences will also be required depending on the modem used. The following discussions are independent of modem type. Assume that the answering modem is a "direct connect" modem as opposed to an "acoustical coupler" modem.

Setting the Communications Parameters In addition to matching communications hardware requirements, the two computers must also be operating with the same communications parameters. Those parameters are the baud rate, parity, number of data bits, and number of stop bits. See the discussion of OPEN COM for details. The following code will set up the operation of communications port number 1.

PRIMARY METHOD

```
10 ' * * * SETUP COMMUNICATIONS PARAMETERS * * *
15 CLS:NUM.RINGS = 2
20 OPEN"COM1:1200,N,8,1,DS,CD" AS #1
```

Line 20 opens communications port number 1 (COM1:) to operate at 1200 baud, no parity, eight data bits, and one stop bit. In addition, DS and CD are appended to the communications parameters. DS suppresses checking of the data set ready lead and CD suppresses checking of the carrier detect lead (pin #8 of the DB25 RS-232C connector). Suppressing the DS and CD leads is necessary before communication is established with the other computer to avoid unwanted error conditions. Later, when communication has been established, we'll want to enable the checking of the CD lead.

ALTERNATE METHOD

```
10 ' * * * SETUP COMMUNICATIONS PARAMETERS * * *
15 CLS:NUM.RINGS=2:PORT=&H3F8
```

```
20 HOLD = INP(PORT+3):OUT PORT+3, HOLD OR &H80
30 OUT PORT, &H60:OUT PORT+1, 0
40 OUT PORT+3, HOLD
45 OUT PORT+3, &H3
```

Lines 20 through 40 are necessary to set the baud rate. Line 20 sets bit 7 of the LCR, which allows access to the baud rate generator through the communications port and the IER. Line 40 resets bit 7 of the LCR and, therefore, returns the communications port and the IER to their normal state. Line 30 passes the necessary data to the baud rate generator to operate at 1200 baud. The values sent to PORT and PORT+1 may be changed to &H80 and &H1 to operate at 300 baud. Line 45 sets the LCR to operate with no parity, eight data bits, and one stop bit. A value of &H1A would be used for even parity, seven data bits, and one stop bit. This routine is necessary for both the originator and the answerer in order to set up the communications parameters.

Making the connection Telephonic contact must be initiated by the originator. Some modems require that a telephone set be connected to the phone line for dialing the number. Other modems are capable of dialing the number when given the command by the originator's program. Regardless of the modem and method used, the originator will cause the answerer's number to be dialed and thus generate a ring signal at the answerer's end.

Originator Once telephonic contact has been established, the originator must wait for an "answer back tone" to be generated by the answerer's modem, and a carrier signal to be established. If the modem reports to the computer when the carrier has been detected, then the primary method shown below may be used. Unfortunately, many modems do not give such indications; therefore, the alternate method must be used. Assuming that the modem reported to the computer that a carrier had been detected by sending a result word of "CONNECT", the following code would be valid.

PRIMARY METHOD

```
100 '* * * WAIT FOR CARRIER DETECT * * *
110 WHILE EOF(1):WEND
115 SOUND 32565,30:SOUND 32565,1
120 A$=INPUT$(LOC(1),#1)
130 IF INSTR(A$,"CONNECT") = 0 THEN 110
140 PRINT "CARRIER DETECTED"
```

As long as no data were sent to communications buffer #1 by the communications port, the program will loiter at line 110. As soon as any data entered the buffer, program control would be transferred to line 115. Line 120 fetches all of the data in the communications buffer (up to a maximum of 255 characters)

APPENDIX L

and assigns the data to the variable A$. If A$ contains the word "CON-NECT", indicating that a carrier has been detected, then line 130 passes control to line 140. Otherwise control returns to line 110 to wait for further input into the buffer.

ALTERNATE METHOD

When contact is established between the two modems, bit 7 of the MSR will be set to "1." Therefore, exiting the following WHILE . . . . WEND loop will indicate that a carrier has been detected and communications may begin. This method may prove better than the primary method, especially when working with different brands of modems.

```
100 '* * * WAIT FOR CARRIER DETECT * * *
110 WHILE INP(PORT+6) < &H80:WEND
120 PRINT "CARRIER DETECTED"
```

Answerer Many modems have an auto-answer capability that requires no intervention from the answerer's program, while others require a command from the program before answering the telephone line. Modems that have the auto-answer capability may not require the code listed below to detect and count the number of rings. The program may only need to respond to the carrier detect if the modem answers reliably and automatically, and then generates an answer-back tone. Some auto-answer modems report the ring signal to the computer with a code or a word such as "RING". The primary code listed below shows the alternate method for detecting the "RING" report in the same manner as the primary method above for detecting the carrier. Assume that the program had earlier initialized the variable: NUM.RINGS = 2.

PRIMARY METHOD

```
50 '* * * DETECT AND COUNT THE NUMBER OF RINGS * * *
60 WHILE EOF(1):WEND
65 SOUND 32565,20:SOUND 32565,1
70 A$=INPUT$(LOC(1),#1)
80 IF INSTR(A$,"RING") = 0 THEN 60
85 RING = RING + 1:PRINT "RING #";RING:IF RING => NUM.RINGS THEN 95
90 GOTO 60
95 'If necessary, send command for modem to answer telephone
96 PRINT #1, "ATA"
100 '* * * WAIT FOR CARRIER DETECT * * *
```

As long as no data were sent to communications buffer #1 by the communications port, the program will loiter at line 60. As soon as any data enters the buffer, program control is transferred to line 65. Line 65 delays program exe-

562

cution long enough for the modem to respond with its full result code or word. Line 70 then fetches all of the data in the communications buffer (up to a maximum of 255 characters) and assigns the data to the variable A$. If A$ contains the word "RING", indicating that a ring signal has been detected, then line 85 passes control to line 95. Otherwise, line 85 displays the number of rings on the video screen and then line 85 returns control to line 60 to wait for further input into the buffer. Lines 95 and 96 are set aside for a modem answer command if necessary, such as "AT A" with the Hayes Stack Smartmodem.

ALTERNATE METHOD

The fact that the telephone line is ringing is usually passed to the MSR in bit #6. The following code illustrates a logical operation within a WHILE ....WEND loop that will not only detect the ring but also wait for the designated number of rings to occur before exiting the loop. Assume that the program had earlier initialized the following variables: NUM.RINGS=2:PORT=&H3F8.

```
50 '* * * DETECT AND COUNT THE NUMBER OF RINGS * * *
60 WHILE NOT INP(PORT+6) AND &H40:WEND
70 RING = RING + 1:PRINT "RING #";RING
80 WHILE INP(PORT+6) AND &H40:WEND
85 IF RING => NUM.RINGS THEN 95
90 GOTO 60
95 'If necessary, send command for modem to answer telephone
96 CMD$="ATA"+CHR$(13)
97 FOR I=1 TO LEN(CMD$):OUT PORT, ASC(MID$(CMD$,I,1))
98 SOUND 32565,10:SOUND 32565,1:NEXT
100 '* * * WAIT FOR CARRIER DETECT * * *
```

In the above code, line 60 will loiter until MSR bit 6 is set to "1." Line 70 increments the ring counter and displays the number of rings on the video display. Line 80 will loiter as long as MSR bit 6 is "1" (bit 6 will reset to "0" when the ring signal from the phone line ends). Line 85 tests it to see if the desired number of rings has been reached and, if so, transfers control to line 95. Line 90 returns control to line 60. Lines 95 through 98 are the modem answer commands and delay for the Hayes Stack Smartmodem.

Once the desired number of rings have been reached and, if necessary, the answer command has been sent, the answerer must wait for a carrier to be detected in the same manner as described above for the originator.

MANAGING COMMUNICATIONS

When the answerer and originator have both detected the carrier, they must then be capable of reacting to the activity of the communications port.

APPENDIX L

When the connection between the two computers has been established, the distinction between originator and answerer is insignificant, for the most part, and the code necessary to manage the communications may be the same.

The following routines are examples of communications managers that allow keyboard input to be transmitted through the communications port while also detecting and fetching input from the communications file buffer and displaying both on the video screen.

PRIMARY METHOD

```
150 " * * *COMMUNICATIONS MANAGER * * *
160 CLOSE #1:OPEN "COM1:1200,N,8,1,CD1000" AS #1
170 WHILE EOF(1)
180     THE.KEY$ = INKEY$:IF THE.KEY$ = "" THEN 220
190     PRINT THE.KEY$;
200     PRINT #1, THE.KEY$;
210     GOTO 180
220 WEND
230 A$ = INPUT$(LOC(1),#1)
240 PRINT A$;
250 GOTO 170
```

Line 160 closed communications buffer #1 because it had been opened when the communications parameters were set up in line 20. Line 20 suppressed checking of the CD lead (pin #8), which was necessary before communications was established, but otherwise is not desirable. Therefore, line 160 enabled checking of the CD lead by reopening the communications buffer for port #1 and establishing a one second delay (CD1000) before an error interrupt is issued as a result of carrier loss. Line 170 established a WHILE . . . WEND loop through line 220. Processing will be contained within that loop as long as the communications buffer remains empty (end of file status). When data enters the buffer, processing control will be passed to line 230. Line 230 empties the communications buffer into variable A$ and line 240 displays A$ on the video screen. Line 250 returns control to line 170 to wait for more communications buffer activity. Inside the WHILE . . . WEND loop, line 180 continually tests the keyboard for input. When a key is touched, its value is placed in the string variable THE.KEY$, which is then displayed on the video screen by line 190 and then sent over the communications line by line 200. Line 210 returns control to line 180 for the keyboard scan.

ALTERNATE METHOD

```
150 ' * * * COMMUNICATIONS MANAGER * * *
160 OUT PORT+1, 1
170 WHILE INP(PORT+2) AND 1
```

```
180    THE.KEY$ = INKEY$:IF THE.KEY$ = "" THEN 220
190    PRINT THE.KEY$
200    OUT PORT, ASC(THE.KEY$)
210    GOTO 180
220 WEND
230 PRINT CHR$(INP(PORT));
240 GOTO 170
```

Line 160 enables interrupts to be issued by communications port activity. Line 170 establishes a WHILE . . . . WEND loop through line 220 as in the primary method. Processing will be contained within the loop as long as the value contained in the IIR (PORT+2) is "1," which means that no interrupts have been issued due to communications port activity. If the value of the IIR changes from "1," indicating communications port activity, processing control will be given to line 230. Line 230 will fetch the character in the communications port and print it on the video screen. Line 240 then branches back to line 170 to reactivate the loop. Inside the WHILE . . . . WEND loop, line 180 waits for keyboard activity in exactly the same manner as in the primary method. As soon as a key is touched, its value is placed in the variable THE.KEY$ displayed on the video screen by line 190, and sent to the communications port by line 200. Line 210 branches back to line 180 to wait for more keyboard input.

DUPLEX EXPLAINED

Half Duplex Communications The communications managers presented above are examples of the code required for half duplex communications. In half duplex, each computer displays the information it sends down the communications line on its own video screen and does not echo the information received from the other computer. The two computers may transmit to each other simultaneously without fear of collision of the data, but neither has the assurance that the data sent was actually received.

Full Duplex Communications The primary difference in full duplex as opposed to half duplex is that every piece of data received by one computer is transmitted or echoed back to the sender by the receiver. Full duplex affords the advantage knowing the condition of data sent by comparing it to the data echoed. Of course this method crowds the line with twice as much data as half duplex, but at the baud rates used with a BASIC program, the clutter will go unnoticed. For full duplex communications, the code listed for the communications managers above would require the following modifications:

APPENDIX L

Primary Method

```
240 PRINT A$;:PRINT #1, A$;
```

Alternate Method

```
230 PRINT CHR$(INP(PORT));:OUT PORT,INP(PORT)
```

MATHEMATICAL CONCEPTS

PART I   THE NUMBER π

The number π appears in nearly every branch of mathematics. The value of π is 3.141593 in single-precision and 3.141592653589793 in double-precision. The number π occurs in geometry as the area of the circle of radius 1. It occurs in statistics as one of the constants in the formula for the normal curve.

Whenever the number π is to be used repeatedly in a program, standard practice calls for the name PI to be assigned to 3.141593 (or 3.141592653589793) at the front of the program.

PART II   RADIAN MEASURE OF ANGLES

The ancient Babylonians introduced angle measurement in terms of degrees, minutes, and seconds, and these units are still generally used today for navigation and practical measurements. The unit of angle measurement in the metric system and in most personal computers is called the *radian*.

Consider a unit circle, that is, a circle of radius r = 1. The length of the circumference (the outer edge) of a circle is known from geometry to be 2*π*r, which in this case is 2*π*1 or 2*π. The radian system measures angles in terms of the distance around the circumference of the unit circle. Thus, for example, sweeping out 360 degrees, or one full revolution, corresponds to moving along the circumference a distance of 2*π. So 360 degrees corresponds to 2*π radians. Here are some useful comparisons between degrees and radians:

360 degrees = 2*π radians	(one full revolution)
180 degrees = π radians	(one half-revolution)
90 degrees = π/2 radians	(one quarter-revolution)
45 degrees = π/4 radians	(one eighth-revolution)

In general, the radian measure of an angle is the length of its corresponding arc on the unit circle.

One degree is π/180 radians. To convert from degrees to radians, multiply the number of degrees by π/180. The number π/180 is .01745329 in single-precision and .0174532925199433 in double-precision.

One radian is 180/π degrees. To convert from radians to degrees, multiply the number of radians by 180/π. The number 180/π is 57.29578 in single-precision and 57.29577951308232 in double-precision.

Figure 1 shows the degree and radian measures of several familiar angles.

APPENDIX M

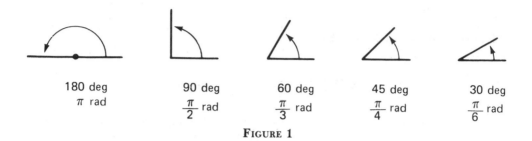

180 deg	90 deg	60 deg	45 deg	30 deg
π rad	$\frac{\pi}{2}$ rad	$\frac{\pi}{3}$ rad	$\frac{\pi}{4}$ rad	$\frac{\pi}{6}$ rad

FIGURE 1

PART III   THE TRIGONOMETRIC FUNCTIONS

Suppose that we are given an acute angle A, i.e., an angle of less than $\pi/2$ radians. We define three descriptive numbers associated to the angle A. These three numbers are called the sine, cosine, and tangent of A and are denoted SIN(A), COS(A), and TAN(A), respectively.

Consider the acute angle shown in Figure 2a. In Figure 2b we have drawn a right triangle with A as one of its angles. In Figure 2c we have labeled the other sides of the triangle by their relationship to A.

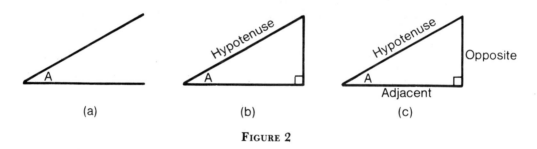

(a)   (b)   (c)

FIGURE 2

We define SIN(A) to be the length of the side opposite A divided by the length of the hypotenuse. This is abbreviated as

   SIN(A) = OPP/HYP

Similarly, we define

   COS(A) = ADJ/HYP
   TAN(A) = OPP/ADJ

EXAMPLES

1.   Consider an angle of .5235987 radians (that is, 30 degrees). Figure 3a shows a 30-60-90 right triangle with the lengths of the sides indicated. (A theorem of geometry states that in any 30-60-90 triangle, the side opposite the 30 degree angle has length one-half the length of the hypotenuse. The length of

the remaining side was determined from the Pythagorean theorem.) Referring to the triangle in Figure 3a, we have

SIN(.5235987) = OPP/HYP = 1/2 = .5
COS(.5235987) = ADJ/HYP = SQR(3)/2 = .8660254
TAN(.5235987) = OPP/ADJ = 1/SQR(3) = .5773503

SIN(A) = y   COS(A) = x   TAN(A) = y/x.

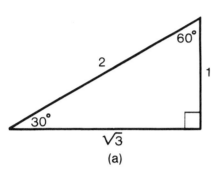

(a)   (b)

FIGURE 3

2.   Consider an angle of .7853981 radians (i.e., 45 degrees). Figure 3b shows a 45-45-90 right triangle with the lengths of the sides indicated. Referring to the triangle, we have

SIN(.7853981) = OPP/HYP = $1/\sqrt{2}$ = .7071067
COS(.7853981) = ADJ/HYP = $1/\sqrt{2}$ = .7071067
TAN(.7853981) = OPP/ADJ = 1/1 = 1.

FURTHER DISCUSSION

The definitions of the trigonometric functions sine, cosine, and tangent can be extended to angles other than acute angles. Consider an angle of A radians drawn with its vertex at the center of a unit circle and one side along the x-axis. See Figure 4. The other side of the angle intersects the unit circle at a point, call it P, with coordinates x and y. We define

SIN(A) = y   COS(A) = x   TAN(A) = y/x.

In other words, SIN(A) is the second coordinate of the point P, COS(A) is the first coordinate of P, and TAN(A) is a ratio of the coordinates of P. These three trigonometric functions are available in BASIC. There are three other common trigonometric functions which do not occur in BASIC, but can be computed in terms of the sine, cosine, and tangent functions. The cotangent of A is defined as COT(A) = x/y and is computed in BASIC as 1/TAN(A). The secant of A is defined as 1/x and is computed in BASIC as 1/COS(A). The cosecant of A is defined as 1/y and computed as 1/SIN(A).

APPENDIX M

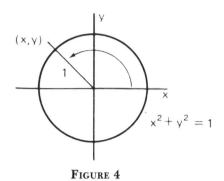

FIGURE 4

FURTHER EXAMPLES

3. The following program determines the values of several trigonometric functions at an angle specified by the user.

```
10 PI = 3.141593
20 INPUT "Give the measure of an angle in degrees. ", A
30 R = A*PI/180
40 PRINT "The sine of an angle of"; A; "degrees is"; SIN(R)
50 PRINT "The cosine of an angle of"; A; "degrees is"; COS(R)
60 PRINT "The tangent of an angle of"; A; "degrees is"; TAN(R)
70 PRINT "The cotangent of an angle of";A;"degrees is";1/TAN(R)
RUN
Give the measure of an angle in degrees. 30
The sine of an angle of 30 degrees is .5
The cosine of an angle of 30 degrees is .8660254
The tangent of an angle of 30 degrees is .5773503
The cotangent of an angle of 30 degrees is 1.732051
Ok
```

APPENDIX N

EXTENDED CODES

Key Combination	Extended Code	Key Combination	Extended Code
Ctrl-2	3	Cursor Left	75
Shift-Tab	15	Cursor Right	77
Alt-Q	16	End	79
Alt-W	17	Cursor Down	80
Alt-E	18	Pg Dn	81
Alt-R	19	Ins	82
Alt-T	20	Del	83
Alt-Y	21	Shift-F1	84
Alt-U	22	Shift-F2	85
Alt-I	23	Shift-F3	86
Alt-O	24	Shift-F4	87
Alt-P	25	Shift-F5	88
Alt-A	30	Shift-F6	89
Alt-S	31	Shift-F7	90
Alt-D	32	Shift-F8	91
Alt-F	33	Shift-F9	92
Alt-G	34	Shift-F10	93
Alt-H	35	Ctrl-F1	94
Alt-J	36	Ctrl-F2	95
Alt-K	37	Ctrl-F3	96
Alt-L	38	Ctrl-F4	97
Alt-Z	44	Ctrl-F5	98
Alt-X	45	Ctrl-F6	99
Alt-C	46	Ctrl-F7	100
Alt-V	47	Ctrl-F8	101
Alt-B	48	Ctrl-F9	102
Alt-N	49	Ctrl-F10	103
Alt-M	50	Alt-F1	104
F1	59	Alt-F2	105
F2	60	Alt-F3	106
F3	61	Alt-F4	107
F4	62	Alt-F5	108
F5	63	Alt-F6	109
F6	64	Alt-F7	110
F7	65	Alt-F8	111
F8	66	Alt-F9	112
F9	67	Alt-F10	113
F10	68	Ctrl-PrtSc	114
Home	71	Ctrl-Cursor Left	115
Cursor Up	72	Ctrl-Cursor Right	116
Pg Up	73	Ctrl-End	117

APPENDIX N

Key Combination	Extended Code	Key Combination	Extended Code
Ctrl-Pg Dn	118	Alt-6	125
Ctrl-Home	119	Alt-7	126
Alt-1	120	Alt-8	127
Alt-2	121	Alt-9	128
Alt-3	122	Alt-0	129
Alt-4	123	Alt- -	130
Alt-5	124	Alt- =	131
		Ctrl-Pg Up	132

INDEX

INDEX

INDEX

INDEX

INDEX

ABOUT THE AUTHOR

David Schneider, who holds an A.B. degree from Oberlin College and a Ph.D. from M.I.T., is currently an associate professor of mathematics at the University of Maryland. He has written five widely used mathematics textbooks and five highly acclaimed computer books.

His involvement with computers dates back to 1962 when he programmed a special purpose computer designed to correct errors in a communications system. He is currently a member of a national committee of the Mathematical Association of America concerned with the use of computers in the classroom.

Dr. Schneider bought his first IBM PC in 1981 and has spent hundreds of hours exploring the richness and subtleties of its BASIC.

RELATED RESOURCES SHELF

Advanced BASIC and Beyond for the IBM PC
Larry Joel Goldstein

An in-depth guide to the advanced skills of BASIC programming with focused coverage of files, graphics, events trapping, machine language, and subroutines. This self-study guide offers a second course on BASIC programming, with many ready-to-use programs and exercise sets throughout.

☐ 1984/368pp/paper/D3243-5/$19.95
☐ Book/Diskettes. 1983/D3251-8/$49.95

IBM PC: An Introduction to the Operating System, BASIC Programming and Applications, Revised and Enlarged
Larry Joel Goldstein, Martin Goldstein

Written in the same easy-to-read style as the classic first edition, this new edition includes two new chapters on BASIC programming. These new chapters emphasize the importance of structuring and planning programs as well as important information on debugging.

☐ 1984/448pp/paper/D5300-1/$18.95
☐ Book/Diskette/D5270-6/$43.95

Programming the IBM PC and XT: A Guide to Languages
Clarence Germain

Covers PC DOS (1.1 and 2.0) and offers start to finish instructions to the languages most commonly used with the PC. Begins with BASIC, Fortran and COBOL...and follows with Pascal and assembly language.

☐ 1984/345pp/paper/D7834-7/$19.95

TO ORDER, simply clip or photocopy this entire page, check off your selection, and complete the coupon below. Enclose a check or money order for the stated amount. (Please add $2.00 postage and handling per book plus local sales tax.)

Mail to: **Brady Computer Books, Simon&Schuster, Box 500, Englewood Cliffs, NJ 07632**

Name _____

Address _____

City/State/Zip _____

Charge my credit card instead: ☐ MasterCard   ☐ Visa

Account# _____ Expiration Date _____

Signature_____
Dept. Y   Y0510-BB(5)

Prices subject to change without notice.